Feminists Rethink the Self

FEMINIST THEORY AND POLITICS
Virginia Held and Alison Jaggar, Series Editors

Feminists Rethink the Self,
edited by Diana Tietjens Meyers

*Revisioning the Political: Feminist Reconstructions of
Traditional Concepts in Western Political Theory,*
edited by Nancy J. Hirschmann and Christine Di Stephano

Care, Autonomy, and Justice: Feminism and the Ethic of Care,
Grace Clement

*A Mind of One's Own: Feminist Essays
on Reason and Objectivity,*
edited by Louise M. Antony and Charlotte Witt

FORTHCOMING

The Feminist Standpoint Revisited and Other Essays
Nancy C.M. Hartsock

Feminists
Rethink the Self

edited by
Diana Tietjens Meyers

Westview
PRESS
A Member of the Perseus Books Group

For Virginia Held

Feminist Theory and Politics

Published in 1997 in the United States of America by Westview Press, 5500 Central Avenue, Boulder, Colorado 80301-2877, and in the United Kingdom by Westview Press, 12 Hid's Copse Road, Cumnor Hill, Oxford OX2 9JJ

Library of Congress Cataloging-in-Publication Data
Feminists rethink the self / edited by Diana Tietjens Meyers.
     p.   cm.—(Feminist theory and politics)
   Includes bibliographical references and index.
   ISBN 0-8133-2082-8 (hardcover)—ISBN 0-8133-2083-6 (paperback)
   1. Feminist theory.   2. Self.   3. Self (Philosophy)   I. Meyers,
Diana T.   II. Series.
HQ1190.F4644   1997
305.42´01—dc20   96-43121
                                                                                        CIP

PERSEUS
POD
ON DEMAND   10   9   8   7

Contents

Acknowledgments

The idea of doing a collection on feminism and the self originated with the editors of this series, Alison Jaggar and Virginia Held, and I want to thank them for inviting me to prepare this volume. Their invitation gave me an opportunity that has proved extraordinarily rewarding. The contributors to this volume share a commitment to feminist philosophy that has sparked intellectually daring, uncompromisingly rigorous writing. Working with them has been an education, and I am grateful for the insights they imparted to me. Finally, I want to thank Paula Droege for the fine index she prepared and the University of Connecticut Research Foundation for supporting the preparation of this manuscript.

Diana Tietjens Meyers

Introduction

DIANA TIETJENS MEYERS

Self-absorbed people are rarely held in high esteem. In fact, many people consider such egocentricity to be disgraceful. But this censure has never diminished the fascination that the self holds for philosophy. Self-love, self-interest, self-determination, self-fulfillment, self-sacrifice, self-respect—this small sample of topics testifies to philosophy's abiding preoccupation with the self. And no wonder, for Western culture construes the self as philosophically pivotal—a point of intersection for metaphysics, epistemology, and ethics. At this juncture, questions of ontology, knowledge, and value commingle, magnifying the urgency and potency of philosophical doctrines of the self. How the self is understood matters to one's self-image, and people care deeply about their self-image. Moreover, the implications of one's account of the self reverberate throughout one's worldview, opening up social, intellectual, and aesthetic possibilities and concomitantly limiting imagination and action.

For feminist philosophers, questions about the self are salient. Three key issues in feminist theory highlight the self:

1. How does paying attention to the experience of women—specifically, to the caregiving responsibilities traditionally assigned primarily to women as well as to the forms of victimization largely reserved for women—affect our understanding of the self?
2. If institutions of male dominance profoundly influence women's lives and minds, how can women form judgments about their own best interests and their responsibilities to others?
3. How can feminist politics survive the recognition that women's experience is diverse—that is, shaped by race, class, ethnicity, and sexual orientation as well as by gender?

Each of these questions invites a reappraisal of the concept of the self and of personal identity—an invitation to which feminist thinkers have responded by reinvigorating work on this topic.

The view of the self that has dominated contemporary Anglo-American moral and political philosophy is that of *homo economicus*—the free and rational chooser and actor whose desires are ranked in a coherent order and whose aim is to maximize desire satisfaction. This conception of the self isolates the individual from personal relationships and larger social forces. It pays little attention to how the individual's desires are formed, nor does it acknowledge the impact of the individual's emotional life. The self is identified with the instrumental rationality of the marketplace. All along, there have been prominent dissenters from this view, including Bernard Williams and Charles Taylor. Many feminists have now joined this challenge, and their wide-ranging contributions have greatly enriched the debate.

The term *homo economicus* sums up the inadequacies many feminist philosophers discern in this view. It minimizes the personal and moral import of unchosen circumstances and relationships. It eclipses interpersonal commitments, including friendship, love, and caregiving relationships. It downplays the difficulty of resolving conflicts that arise between these commitments and personal aims. It ignores the multiple, sometimes fractious sources of social identity constituted by one's gender, race, class, ethnicity, sexual orientation, and so forth. It denies the complexity of the intrapsychic world of unconscious fantasies, fears, and desires, and it overlooks the ways in which such materials intrude into conscious life. Thus, feminist philosophers have held this view to be, at best, incomplete and, at worst, fundamentally misleading.

What the individualistic, unitary conception of the self as rational chooser and actor excludes is precisely what many feminists have thought most important to emphasize. Locating the self firmly in the empirical realm, feminist theorists have conceived the self as socially and historically situated. Influenced by psychoanalysis and postmodernism, many feminist theorists have construed the self as decentered in various ways and have questioned the unity and transparency of the self. Above all, feminist philosophers have not ignored real-world concerns, especially the needs of feminist politics. Thus, they have sought to account for the tenacity of traditional gender categories and norms, to appreciate the centrality and value of traditional feminine social contributions, to provide an account of how women can recognize and overcome oppressive norms and practices without denying diversity among women, and to defend emancipatory social policies. As this collection attests, however, there is tremendous foment and variety within the field of feminist work on the self.

The first four chapters consider issues about the nature of the self, the agency of the self, and the values of autonomy and integrity. Several well-known views of the nature of the self are represented—the relational self drawn from the psychological work of Nancy Chodorow and Carol Gilligan, the narrative self drawn from postmodern theory, and the integrationist self drawn from recent analytic philosophy of mind. But the authors of these chapters place the conceptions in novel contexts—dealing, for example, with assaults on bodily and psychological integrity such as sexual trauma and with decisions about bodily integrity such as prostitution and contract motherhood—and they reject views of the self that cannot convincingly address these topics. In addition, as feminists they demand that conceptions of the self make sense of experiences of interpersonal dependency and interdependency that are central to many women's lives and that these conceptions yield an ethical view that is tenable in these intimate relationships. Finally, in thinking about the self these authors stress the need for women to preserve their autonomy and integrity in the diverse situations they confront—a requirement whose satisfaction prompts reinterpretation of these desiderata.

In Chapter 1, Susan J. Brison observes that, although philosophers have a fascination with thought experiments that slice and splice the self, they seldom consider real trauma. Her contribution, "Outliving Oneself: Trauma, Memory, and Personal Identity," rectifies that oversight. Brison defines trauma as an event in which the victim "feels utterly helpless in the face of a force that is perceived to be life-threatening." Confining her discussion to humanly inflicted trauma—including sexual assault, genocide, and war—Brison interprets the objectification of trauma and the symptoms of post-traumatic stress disorder that this objectification often causes from the standpoint of their effects on the victim's relationships to other people. She maintains that trauma victims lose their sense of self because trauma convinces them that they cannot be themselves in relation to others. On Brison's view, then, the experience of trauma victims argues for a relational account of the self.

Brison examines several key philosophical theories of the self: the embodied self, the narrative self, and the autonomous self. The "bodily nature of traumatic memory" calls into question the distinction between physical and mental criteria of the persistence of the self. Moreover, trauma deflects attention from traditional questions about whether the soul can survive the death of the body and focuses attention on the issue of whether the self can "reconstitute itself after obliteration at the hands of another." Crucial to this process of self-reconstitution is regaining the capacity to frame an autobiographical narrative. Toward this end, trauma victims need empathic listeners. But people usually resist confronting the horror of trauma and assimilating its terrifying meaning, for the testimony of trauma victims shakes the primitive sense of personal security that all of us prize. Nevertheless, some people are willing to incur the risks of empathizing with trauma victims, and their participation is indispensable to the victims' recovery. Bearing witness to the traumatic event externalizes it, and externalizing the traumatic event enables the victim to reconstruct pre-traumatic memory as well as to emotionally reconnect with the world. Through shared narrative, then, resubjectivization takes place. A final harm of trauma is its power to subvert the autonomous self—to reduce victims' control over their behavior and to neutralize many desires that were once important to them. That humanly inflicted trauma damages agency reveals the vulnerability of agency to other people's malignant actions; but, conversely, the process of recovering from such trauma shows how essential supportive relations to others are to sustaining individual autonomy. According to Brison, reflecting on trauma demonstrates the complementarity of the embodied self, the narrative self, and the autonomous self, as well as the relational structure undergirding each of these conceptions of the self.

In Chapter 2, "Autonomy and Social Relationships: Rethinking the Feminist Critique," Marilyn Friedman accents the continuity between feminist conceptions of the self and autonomy, on the one hand, and mainstream philosophical conceptions, on the other. Reviewing feminist objections that mainstream thinking on these topics neglects the social nature of the self, Friedman points out that feminists who undertake to rehabilitate autonomy insist on reconciling autonomy not only with the self's indebtedness to caregivers and to the wider cultural context that endows the self with attributes and projects but also with the value of close interpersonal bonds. This synthetic project notwithstanding, Friedman notes, feminists acknowledge that tensions between autonomy and sociality cannot be completely eliminated. Turning to prominent contemporary philosophical accounts of autonomy, Friedman contends that they recognize the importance of the social. Thus, she denies that the divergence between feminist and mainstream accounts of autonomy is as great as has sometimes been supposed.

Still, Friedman urges that feminist critiques of autonomy are not unwarranted. Some mainstream accounts are committed to excessive individualism, and the images of autonomy that prevail in popular culture represent it as a masculine virtue combining self-sufficiency and control. In addition, since mainstream conceptions of autonomy are substantively neutral, they do not rule out choosing a life dedicated to minimizing interpersonal entanglements and exercising power. Hence feminists may be justified in charging that philosophers are not doing enough to counteract popular culture and to endorse relational values. Nevertheless, Friedman herself refuses to condemn life plans that valorize independence, provided that people who pursue them are not abrogating moral responsibilities to others. Moreover, she reminds us that autonomy may require severing interpersonal ties, for some relationships are inimical to autonomy. Finally, Friedman considers the claim that social relations are not merely causally necessary for developing the desires and capacities that autonomy presupposes and that social relations are actually constitutive of autonomy. Friedman conjectures that the latter claim will become the locus of feminist controversy in the years to come.

The theme of a relational self continues in Chapter 3 with Margaret Urban Walker's "Picking Up Pieces: Lives, Stories, and Integrity." But Walker, like Brison, is concerned with the additional theme of autobiographical storytelling. Walker expresses doubts about the availability of an ordered set of universal moral principles and values and about the feasibility of working out an algorithm that will enable individuals to implement such a system of norms. Instead, Walker endorses an ethics of responsibility and a narrative-based account of moral deliberation and justification. On this view, people "are *obligated to respond* to particular others when circumstances or ongoing relationships render them especially, conspicuously, or peculiarly dependent on us." Now, it might seem that this view gives rise to exorbitant moral demands on individuals. Walker addresses this criticism by introducing three kinds of narratives—narratives of relationships, narratives of individual moral identity, and narratives of value—and by arguing that we create shared understandings of our responsibilities and renegotiate our responsibilities when necessary by telling one another these stories.

At this point, someone might object that a drawback of Walker's improvisational approach to moral responsibility is that it precludes making sense of the value of integrity. But according to Walker, it would be a mistake to construe integrity as having well-integrated principles and values, as being committed to certain principles or values unconditionally, or as consistently enacting a true self. Rather, integrity should be understood as reliable accountability—a matter of living up to one's commitments to others whenever possible and of doing one's best to make amends when honoring one's commitments is not possible. In the place of ideals of a unified identity, absolute allegiance to core principles or values, and authenticity, Walker recommends ideals of dependability and attention to the moral costs of error and change. This view of integrity is more realistic about the relational structure of people's lives and more consonant with an ethic of responsibility that expresses that structure; hence it is more attractive than views of integrity that presuppose an unrealistic, morally dubious individualism. Furthermore, in calling attention to and calling into question social disparities in the distribution of discursive resources, this view of integrity and ethics provides a basis for a broader social critique.

In Chapter 4, "Ownership and the Body," Jennifer Church approaches the issue of integrity from an altogether different angle–namely, that of bodily integrity and self-ownership. Church examines two well-known views of the relation between the self and the body—the Cartesian distinction between the self and the body and the physicalist identification of the self with the body. Whereas the Cartesian view fields a conception of self-ownership that sees the self as using the body and thereby coming to own it, the physicalist view holds that one owns things, including one's body and its attributes, when they are parts of oneself. After diagnosing serious difficulties in each of these views and suggesting that these difficulties impel us to "flip-flop" back and forth between them, Church urges us to seek a better account of selfhood.

The conception of the self that Church advocates denies that selves are separable from or identical to bodies and maintains that selves "are created and sustained by the establishment of particular sorts of interconnections between the psychological states of physical organisms." The sorts of interconnections that are constitutive of a self include those achieved through reflection, planning, and self-control—that is, through processes that integrate the body's psychological states. Church stresses that it follows from her view of the self that different people may own their bodies to different degrees and that a single individual may have stronger and weaker claims to bodily ownership at different points in time. Church then examines some practical implications of her view—how we acquire things other than our bodies, how we can have ownership rights in someone else's body, and whether prostitution and contract motherhood are permissible ways to exercise one's property rights in one's body. In each case, Church urges that her conception of the self and of self-ownership furnishes the critical leverage we need to grasp what is at stake and to address these questions fruitfully.

The theme of individual identity continues in the next two chapters, but they introduce the complications of intersecting group differences and compound stigmatization. Many feminists invoke the concept of multiplicity to capture the experience of a self whose gender is inextricable from her race, class, ethnicity, and sexual orientation. Although the term 'multiplicity' conveys the richness and vitality of women's selves, it also brings to mind the uncertainty and anxiety about how one is perceived, as well as the potential for internal conflict about where one's allegiances belong, that plague many women.

In Chapter 5, "Forgetting Yourself," Anita L. Allen inquires into an experience that is both nettlesome and all too familiar. When one forgets oneself, according to Allen, one inadvertently and temporarily deviates from community norms of decorum or decency, and these lapses place social approval and self-esteem at risk. Now, Allen stresses, to claim to have forgotten yourself is not to claim that you have literally stopped remembering who you are. Rather, it is to invoke a colloquial figure of speech. Moreover, the norms presupposed when one forgets oneself may not be norms that would survive critical scrutiny, but they are norms that, for better or worse, one has internalized. Thus, forgetting oneself can alert a person to norm-directed patterns of conformity that stand in need of critique. Yet, forgetting oneself can also be pernicious, either because it harms others or because it imperils oneself. Claiming to have forgotten oneself functions to excuse untoward or unfortunate conduct, but there are limits to the scope of this excuse. You cannot excuse serious violations of core moral duties by saying you forgot yourself, nor can you excuse frequently repeated deviations from less important norms by saying you forgot yourself.

With this account of forgetting oneself in place, Allen proceeds to examine the possibility of forgetting one's race. She describes a case in which an African American woman whom she calls Jan acts as if she were not African American. Jan rejects a white friend's suggestion to invite an African American friend to a party on the grounds that he might feel uncomfortable as the only African American at the gathering. Race-consciousness, Allen points out, is the norm among African Americans, and Jan abrogates this norm. It might be thought that forgetting one's race is desirable—the first step on the way to a color-blind, racially just society. However, Allen takes issue with this view. The United States today is a racialized society in which race categories shape social and economic relations and are used for all sorts of bureaucratic purposes. Consequently, one cannot mitigate or oppose bigotry and segregation by pretending it does not exist. Thus, forgetting one's race must be viewed as a troubling and suspect form of denial, not as an enlightened form of transcendence.

Chapter 6, Naomi Scheman's "Queering the Center by Centering the Queer: Reflections on Transsexuals and Secular Jews," is also concerned with group categories and group identity. But Scheman examines two cases in which people lack categorical homes—those of the transsexual and the secular Jew—and argues that these cases demonstrate that belonging in a group category is itself a kind of privilege. Like Walker, Scheman casts suspicion on norms of identity that require unity, transparency to oneself and others, and strict adherence to principle, and she contends that the narrative templates that suit some individuals' life stories leave other individuals without discursive resources for telling theirs. Thus, Scheman urges that it is necessary to "queer the center," which she undertakes to do by examining two systems of norms—heteronormativity, which defines lesbians and gays as alien and defective, and Christianormativity, which defines Jews as alien and defective.

Scheman uses her own experience to explore these topics. After noting that she has never found her identification as a woman problematic, she observes that this very lack of bafflement prevents her from understanding male-to-female transsexuals when they say that they are really women. In contrast, Scheman reports that she has great difficulty understanding her identification as a secular Jew. Thus, Scheman sees her experience of identity incongruity with respect to Jewishness as a point of access to the issues raised by transsexuals with respect to gender identity. Scheman rejects three accounts of group identity: (1) privileged access essentialism, (2) expert essentialism, and (3) privileged access voluntarism. This line of thought leads Scheman to conclude that the key questions are political: Who cares how one is labeled? And who has the authority to accept or reject labelings? Analogizing transsexuals to secular Jews, she explores the role of birth and that of choice in identity attributions, and she urges that, unless we learn to regard gender as an ambiguous, confusing identity category, like "Jewish-ness," transsexuals will never succeed in claiming the gender identity they desire. Since "policing" identity boundaries blocks this process of problema-tization, Scheman advocates "creatively playful, politically serious border transgressing." Whether the border police are heterosexuals guarding tradi-tional gender categories or gays and lesbians defending queer identity, exclu-sionary identity practices are repressive.

The next three chapters in the volume may be seen as addressing issues in moral social psychology. All three are concerned with moral sensitivity to suffering and with the role such sensitivity plays in enriching moral under-standing and forging political ties. Here, the theme of solidarity converges with issues in moral epistemology.

It may seem that concern with moral social psychology is a quite recent development. Before the advent of mass societies and global communica-tions, there was little reason to investigate mob psychology or ideological in-doctrination. Yet, in light of the less individualistic view of people and soci-eties that prevailed in ancient Greece, it should come as no surprise that Plato was not indifferent to problems of moral social psychology. Indeed, in Chapter 7, "Good Grief, It's Plato!," Elizabeth V. Spelman reveals an impor-tant social-psychological current in Plato's moral philosophy.

Plato's aversion to grief is famous. As Spelman explains, his brief against the tragic poets revolves around his claim that their dramas provoke exag-gerated and self-indulgent grief in their audiences—a form of grief that is morally ruinous. Yet, Spelman contends, Plato's quarrel with Thrasymachus demonstrates that he is no friend of hard-heartedness. On the contrary, soci-eties are unified and strengthened when the members rejoice and grieve to-gether, and one of Plato's objections to Thrasymachus is that the possibility of such a community of feeling escapes him. But Plato's prejudices against women seem to pose an obstacle to his endorsing shared grief, for he some-times characterizes grief as "womanish," which, in Plato's lexicon, is a term of opprobrium. Moreover, he sees men's desire for control over women as occasioning many of the predicaments and struggles that eventuate in tragedy. Still, Spelman argues that we need a nuanced view of Plato's think-ing on women and grief. Plato, she maintains, is both a critic of the conven-tional form of grief-free masculinity that Thrasymachus embodies *and* a critic of grief-prone norms of femininity. Nevertheless, he also seems to hold that so-called feminine traits, when severed from femininity, can be of value. Properly directed and kept in proportion, grief can be warranted, and war-ranted grief is compatible with manliness or virtue.

In Chapter 8, Sandra Lee Bartky takes up another moment in the history of philosophical reflection on emotion and moral social psychology—Scheler's theory of sympathy. "Sympathy and Solidarity: On a Tightrope with Scheler" begins by conceding that feminist theory has often been dedicated exclusively to theorizing the experience and subordination of relatively advantaged women and has ignored the lives and needs of women whose experience of sexist oppression is compounded by racism, poverty, ethnocentrism, and/or heterosexism. Thus, Bartky notes, many feminists call for cognitive correctives aimed at rectifying these oversights and erasures. But she urges that purely cognitive enhancements will not suffice. The new knowledge of women from diverse social groups must be transformative; and to be transformative, this knowledge must have "a particular affective taste." To explain how affectivity and knowledge might be combined in the requisite way, Bartky turns to Scheler's account of Mitgefühl—sympathy, that is, feeling-with or fellow-feeling.

Scheler delineates four forms of sympathy. In the first, one simultaneously feels exactly as the other feels. In the second form, one is infected by the other's feeling. In the third form, one identifies so completely with the other that one's identity is merged with the other's. In the fourth form, the sympathizer's identity and subjectivity remain distinct, yet the other's feeling is directly and intuitively grasped. For Scheler, this fourth form is morally valuable, both because it originates in a primordial disposition to love and consolidates love for particular individuals *and* because it involves a genuine encounter with difference that may enlarge one's moral understanding. By and large, Bartky concurs with this view and sees it as contributing to an account of solidarity. She defends Scheler's claim that sympathy stems from the immediate apprehension of the other's feeling, and she offers an interpretation of "vicarious visualization" that shields his theory from certain criticisms. Finally, reflecting on the present state of feminism, Bartky observes that Scheler's work has the salutary effect of drawing our attention to an important set of issues intermediate between pure theory and activism—namely, theoretical issues about movement building.

My contribution concludes this trio of chapters on moral social psychology. Chapter 9, "Emotion and Heterodox Moral Perception: An Essay in Moral Social Psychology," urges that, since one's moral judgments and conduct depend on how one perceives social relations, heterodox moral perception is indispensable to progressive social change. Yet—and this is the problem I address—it is far from obvious how people gain critical insight into established practices of domination and subordination or how they come to perceive social relations in ways that are conducive to emancipatory aims. Skeptical of the exalted claims some philosophers make for the power of reasoning to correct defective moral codes, I explore the role of emotion in moral perception, and I argue that several emotional attitudes that are ordinarily considered epistemic vices can be feminist epistemic virtues.

The gravity of the problem becomes evident once one recognizes that culturally entrenched gender prejudice is encoded in unconscious cognitive schemas that shape moral perception. Plainly, a feminist account of heterodox moral perception must explain how the misogyny with which these schemas imbue moral perception can be overcome. Philosophers tend to overestimate the efficacy of an outgoing, receptive emotional attitude and dispassionate critical reason with respect to counteracting distorted moral perception. I focus, instead, on four particularly vexing emotional attitudes—namely, hypersensitivity, paranoia, anger, and bitterness. Feminist philosophers have shown that conventions of interpretation authorize differential perceptions of women's and men's emotions and that these perceptions belittle women and neutralize feminist protest. However, it is important to distinguish between occurrent emotional responses and emotional attitudes that are constitutive of a person's overall moral outlook, for, I argue, this distinction enables us to grasp how these rancorous emotional attitudes can spark critical moral reflection and counteract deep-seated prejudicial schemas. Still, it is undeniable that such attitudes often have a detrimental effect on moral perception. For this reason, I suggest that understanding how hypersensitivity, paranoia, anger, and bitterness can contribute to insightful heterodox moral perception requires giving up a purely individualistic view of moral perception and inquiring into the moral economies of dissident political groups.

The concluding chapter, Eva Feder Kittay's "Human Dependency and Rawlsian Equality," focuses on dependency relationships and the implications of these relationships with regard to justice. Moral and political philosophers often take the able-bodied, healthy adult as the paradigmatic person. But, as Kittay reminds us, we are all dependent on adults in childhood; many of us will become dependent on caregivers in old age; and some of us will depend on others to some degree throughout life as a result of disability or chronic illness. It is seriously misleading, then, to conceive of moral subjects and moral patients as self-sufficient individuals. In short, moral and political philosophy must come to grips with the inescapable circumstance of depending on others and being depended upon.

Kittay pursues this point by demonstrating that it undermines the most prominent contemporary theory of justice—namely, that of John Rawls. Kittay traces her theme through five features of Rawls's theory: (1) the circumstances of justice, (2) the notion of social cooperation, (3) the defining features of a moral person and the list of primary social goods, (4) the conception of a free person as a "self-originating source of valid claims," and (5) the idealization of citizens as "fully cooperating members of society over the course of a complete life." Again and again, Rawls refuses to recognize dependency and dependency work, with the consequence that the dependent individual is denied equal moral worth and the dependency worker (usually a woman) is exploited. Whereas many feminists focus on the interdependency of the relational self, Kittay calls attention to a less tractable form of relationality—namely, one-sided dependency. Arguing that social contract theory is ill-suited to address the issues raised by dependency, Kittay sets an agenda for political theory—bringing the dependent and the dependency worker into the sphere of justice and ensuring that both receive equal justice.

one

Outliving Oneself
*Trauma, Memory,
and Personal Identity*

SUSAN J. BRISON

> I died in Auschwitz, but no one knows it.
> —Charlotte Delbo (1995)

Survivors of trauma frequently remark that they are not the same people they were before being traumatized. As a survivor of the Nazi death camps observed, "One can be alive after Sobibor without having survived Sobibor."[1] Jonathan Shay, a therapist who works with Vietnam veterans, has often heard his patients say, "I died in Vietnam."[2] Migael Scherer expresses a loss commonly experienced by rape survivors when she writes, "I will always miss myself as I was" (1992, 179). What are we to make of these cryptic comments?[3] How can one miss oneself? How can one die in Vietnam or fail to survive a death camp and still live to tell one's story? How does a life-threatening event come to be experienced as self-annihilating? And what self is it who remembers having had this experience?

How one answers these questions depends on, among other things, how one defines 'trauma' and 'the self'. In this chapter, I discuss the nature of trauma; show how it affects the self, which in turn is construed in several ultimately interconnected ways; and then use this analysis to elaborate and support a feminist account of the relational self.[4] On this view the self is both autonomous and socially dependent, vulnerable enough to be undone by violence and yet resilient enough to be reconstructed with the help of empathic others.

My methodology in this chapter differs from that used in traditional philosophizing about the self, and it yields distinctly different results. Philosophers writing about the self, at least since Locke, have puzzled over such questions as whether persons can survive the loss or exchange of their minds, brains, consciousness, memories, characters, and/or bodies.[5] In recent years, increasingly gruesome and high-tech thought experiments involving fusion, fission, freezing, dissolution, reconstitution, and/or teletransportation of an individual have been devised to test our intuitions about who, if anyone, survives which permutations.[6] Given philosophers' preoccupation with personal identity in extreme, life-threatening, and possibly self-annihilating situations, it is odd that they have neglected to consider the accounts of actual trauma victims who report that they are not the same people they were prior to their traumatic transformations.[7] This oversight may result from the fact that imaginary scenarios, however far-fetched, are at least *conceivable,* whereas the experiences of rape victims, Holocaust survivors, and war veterans are, for most of us, unthinkable. In addition, philosophers are trained to divert their gaze from the messy real world to the neater, more controllable, and more comprehensible realm of pure thought.

Recently, however, feminist theorists writing in the areas of ethics and social, political, and legal philosophy have argued for the necessity of focusing on the actual experiences of real people and have made use of first- and third-person narratives in their attempts to do this.[8] Feminist theorists have also stressed the importance of taking context into account, recognizing that we all reason from a "positioned perspective" and that some of us, with "multiple consciousness," reason from a variety of sometimes incompatible perspectives.[9] In addition, feminist theorists have adopted interdisciplinary approaches to subjects, such as personal identity, previously thought to be the exclusive domain of one discipline. I use these feminist methodologies in this chapter, incorporating survivor testimonies, situating philosophical questions of the self in the context of actual individuals' lives, acknowledging my own perspective as a survivor, and drawing on the clinical literature on trauma.

Trauma and the Undoing of the Self

There is a much clearer professional consensus among psychologists about what counts as a traumatic event than there is among philosophers concerning the nature of the self.[10] A traumatic event is one in which a person feels utterly helpless in the face of a force that is perceived to be life-threatening.[11] The immediate psychological responses to such trauma include terror, loss of control, and intense fear of annihilation. Long-term effects include the physiological responses of hypervigilance, heightened startle response, sleep disorders, and the more psychological yet still involuntary responses of depression, inability to concentrate, lack of interest in activities that used to give life meaning, and a sense of a foreshortened future (DSM III-R, 12). A commonly accepted explanation of these symptoms of post-traumatic stress disorder (PTSD) is that, in trauma, the ordinarily adaptive human responses to danger that prepare the body to fight or flee are of no avail. "When neither resistance nor escape is possible," Judith Herman explains, "the human system of self-defense becomes overwhelmed and disorganized. Each component of the ordinary response to danger, having lost its utility, tends to persist in an altered and exaggerated state long after the actual danger is over" (Herman 1992, 34). When the trauma is of human origin and is intentionally inflicted, the kind I discuss in this chapter, it not only shatters one's fundamental assumptions about the world and one's safety in it but also severs the sustaining connection between the self and the rest of humanity. Victims of human-inflicted trauma are reduced to mere objects by their tormenters: Their subjectivity is rendered useless and viewed as worthless. As Herman observes, "The traumatic event thus destroys the belief that one can *be oneself* in relation to others" (Herman 1992, 53; original emphasis). Without this belief, I shall argue, one can no longer *be oneself* even to oneself, since the self exists fundamentally in relation to others.

How one defines "self" depends in part on what explanatory work one wants the concept of a self to do. Philosophers have invoked this concept in various areas of the discipline in order to account for a wide range of phenomena. The self is, in metaphysics, whatever it is whose persistence accounts for personal identity over time. One metaphysical view of the self holds that it is bodily continuity that accounts for personal identity; another, that it is continuity of memory, character traits, or other psychological characteristics that makes someone the same person over time. There is also the view, held by post-structuralists, that the self is a narrative, which, properly construed, is a version of the view that psychological continuity constitutes personal identity.[12] In ethics the self is viewed as the locus of autonomous agency and responsibility and, hence, is the subject of praise or blame. Most traditional accounts of the self, from Descartes' to contemporary theorists', have been individualistic, based on the assumption that one can individuate selves and determine the criteria for their identity over time independent of the social context in which they are situated. In contrast, feminist accounts of the self have focused on the ways in which the self is formed in relation to others and sustained in a social context. On these accounts, persons are, in Annette Baier's words, "second persons"—that is, "essentially successors, heirs to other persons who formed and cared for them."[13] In addition, such accounts view the self as related to and constructed by others in an ongoing way, not only because others continue to shape and define us throughout our lifetimes but also because our own sense of self is couched in descriptions whose meanings are social phenomena (Scheman, 1983).

In what follows, I argue that the study of trauma reveals that the accounts of the embodied self, the self as narrative, and the autonomous self are compatible and complementary, focusing on different aspects of the self. I also argue that the study of trauma provides additional support for the view that each of these aspects of the self is fundamentally relational.

The Embodied Self

Although we recognize other persons most readily by their perceptible—that is, bodily—attributes, philosophers have been loath to identify the self with a body, for a host of reasons.[14] A dead body cannot be said to be anyone's self, nor can a living but permanently comatose one. And we do not typically use a bodily criterion of identity to determine who we ourselves are; indeed, most of us, if called upon to imagine Locke's prince, whose soul "enters and informs" the body of a cobbler, would suppose the resulting person to be the prince (Locke 1974/1694, 216). Some philosophers[15] have been concerned to show that the self can survive the death of the body, but perhaps the primary reason philosophers have not identified the self with the body is an ancient bias against our physical nature.[16] Plato praised philosophers for "despising the body and avoiding it," and urged that "[i]f we are ever to have pure knowledge of anything, we must get rid of the body and contemplate things by themselves with the soul by itself."[17] This rejection of the body has been most apparent in the denigration of the female body, historically presented as the antithesis to reason. Although, as Sara Ruddick notes, "[t]here is nothing intrinsically masculine about mind and objectivity or anything feminine about passion and physicality, . . . philosophers have tended to associate, explicitly or metaphorically, passion, affection, and the body with femininity and the mind with masculinity" (1989, 194). How some bodies came to be viewed as "more bodily" than others is a puzzle that Ruddick answers by arguing that the lack of intellectual control over menstruation, pregnancy, labor, and nursing set such female bodily functions against reason, which was viewed as detached, controlled, and impersonal—in short, as masculine.

Even Simone de Beauvoir, despite her argument that "one is not born, but rather becomes, a woman" (1953, 301), views childbirth and nursing as completely passive—and thus dehumanizing—processes, which keep women mired in immanence. She suggests that "it is not in giving life but in risking life that man is raised above the animal; that is why superiority has been accorded in humanity not to the sex that brings forth but to that which kills" (1953, 72). Although Beauvoir rejects the conclusion that this sex difference justifies male dominance, she nonetheless accepts the premise reducing childbirth to a purely "animal" function.[18]

Beauvoir was the first female philosopher I read, and, as a teenager, I shared her disdain for (socially) compulsory marriage and maternity for women in this society. I still share her concerns about constraints on women's reproductive freedom, but I reject her view of pregnancy and motherhood as necessarily passive and tedious processes, even when voluntary. The work of Ruddick and other feminists who have been redefining motherhood has led me to see the liberatory potential in *chosen* maternity, childbirth, and childrearing. Reading Ruddick's *Maternal Thinking* in 1989, I recognized the ways in which my philosophical training had exacerbated my preexisting tendency to value the cerebral over the corporeal. In pursuing the life of the mind, I had accepted unthinkingly (because unconsciously) its incompatibility with the life of the (gestating and birthing) female body. My reading of Ruddick happened to coincide with a visit to a gynecologist who told me that I might have difficulty conceiving and that if I even suspected I would want to have a child some day I should start trying now. My philosophical bias against maternity, combined with a personal (and political) reaction against what I perceived as pressure to have a baby (as in the words of one academic woman's mother who said "I'd rather be a grandmother than the mother of a Ph.D."), suddenly gave way to the startling realization that I might *want* to experience the particular kind of embodiment and connection that pregnancy and motherhood provide, and that these things were not incompatible with being a philosopher. After years of considering my body little more than an unruly nuisance, I found myself wanting to yield up control over it, to learn what it had to teach me, to experience the abandon of labor and childbirth—what Margaret Walker has called "the willing or grateful surrender of 'I' to flesh."[19]

Plato praised those "who long to beget spiritually, not physically, the progeny which it is the nature of the soul to create and bring to birth. If you ask what that progeny is, it is wisdom and virtue in general. . . . Everyone would prefer children such as these to children after the flesh."[20] It occurred to me that this preference was not, after all, universal, and that, in any case, one did not have to choose between pursuing wisdom and virtue, on the one hand, and having children, on the other. My husband (who never felt as compelled to make such a choice) and I started trying to conceive, or, rather, as a friend put it more aptly, stopped trying not to. Six months later, however, while on a solitary morning walk in the French countryside, I was jumped from behind, beaten, raped, strangled, and left for dead in a ravine. The pleasures of embodiment were replaced by the pain and terror to which being embodied makes one prey.

I have written elsewhere of the epistemological reversals of this assault (Was it possible that I was really awake during this nightmare?) and its aftermath (How could I manage to go on living in a fatally unpredictable world?).[21] I was no longer the same person I had been before the assault, and one of the ways in which I seemed changed was that I had a different relationship with my body. My body was now perceived as an enemy, having betrayed my newfound trust and interest in it, and as a site of increased vulnerability. But rejecting the body and returning to the life of the mind was not an option, since body and mind had become nearly indistinguishable. My mental state (typically, depression) felt physiological, like lead in my veins, whereas my physical state (frequently, one of incapacitation by fear and anxiety) was the incarnation of a cognitive and emotional paralysis resulting from shattered assumptions about my safety in the world. The symptoms of post-traumatic stress disorder gave the lie to a latent dualism that still informs society's most prevalent attitude toward trauma—namely, that victims should "buck up," put the past behind them, and get on with their lives. My hypervigilance, heightened startle response, insomnia, and other PTSD symptoms were no more psychological, if that is taken to mean under my conscious control, than were my heart rate and blood pressure.[22]

The intermingling of mind and body is also apparent in traumatic memories that remain in the body, in each of the senses, in the heart that races and the skin that crawls whenever something resurrects the only slightly buried terror. As Shay writes in his study of combat trauma, "Traumatic memory is not narrative. Rather, it is experience that reoccurs, either as full sensory replay of traumatic events in dreams or flashbacks, with all things seen, heard, smelled, and felt intact, or as disconnected fragments. These fragments may be inexplicable rage, terror, uncontrollable crying, or disconnected body states and sensations" (1994, 172). The main change in the modality as well as in the content of the most salient traumatic memories is that they are more tied to the body than memories are typically considered to be.

Sensory flashbacks are not, of course, merely a clinical phenomenon, nor are they peculiar to trauma. Proust describes the pleasantly vivid flashbacks brought on by the leisurely savoring of a tea-soaked madeleine (1981, Vol. 1: 48–49).[23] Trauma, however, changes the nature and frequency of sensory, emotional, and physiological flashbacks. They are reminiscent of the traumatic event itself, as Shay writes, in that "[o]nce experiencing is under way, the survivor lacks authority to stop it or put it away. The helplessness associated with the original experience is replayed in the apparent helplessness to end or modify the reexperience once it has begun" (1994, 174). Traumatic flashbacks immobilize the body by rendering the will as useless as it is in a nightmare in which one desperately tries to flee, but remains frozen.

The bodily nature of traumatic memory complicates a standard philosophical quandary concerning which of two criteria of identity—continuous body or continuous memories—should be used to determine personal identity over time. Locke's bodily-transfer puzzle, in which we are asked to decide who survives "should the soul of a prince . . . enter and inform the body of a cobbler" (1974/1694, 116), no longer presents us with an either/or choice, depending on which criterion we invoke. If memories are lodged in the body, the Lockean distinction between the memory criterion and that of bodily identity no longer applies.[24]

The study of trauma also replaces the traditional philosophical puzzle about whether the soul can survive the death of the body with the question of whether the self can reconstitute itself after obliteration at the hands of another—that is, after what Cathy Winkler (1991) has labeled "social murder." Winkler describes the way in which, during a rape, the victim is defined out of existence by the rapist's attitudes and actions, which incapacitate the victim's self. "Without our abilities to think and feel as we choose . . . our existence becomes like a body on life support," Winkler writes. "During an attack, victims have confronted social death, and grappled with it to save themselves" (1991, 14). Indeed, the victim's inability to be—and assert—her self in the context of a rape constitutes at least a temporary social death, one from which a self can be resurrected only with great difficulty and with the help of others.

In the aftermath of trauma, not only is the bodily awareness of the victim changed,[25] but she may also attempt to change her body itself in an effort to enhance her control over it. Eating disorders are a common reaction to sexual abuse, as is dressing in ways that disguise one's body. After my own assault, I wished I could add eyes to the back of my head, but I settled for cutting my hair so short that, when viewed from behind, I might be mistaken for a man.

The study of trauma does not lead to the conclusion that the self can be identified with the body, but it does show how the body and one's perception of it are nonetheless essential components of the self. It also reveals the ways in which one's ability to feel at home in the world is as much a physical as an epistemological accomplishment. Jean Améry (1995) writes of the person who is tortured that, from the moment of the first blow, he loses "trust in the world," which includes "the irrational and logically unjustifiable belief in absolute causality perhaps, or the likewise blind belief in the validity of the inductive inference." More important, according to Améry, is the loss of the certainty that other persons "will respect my physical, and with it also my metaphysical, being. The boundaries of my body are also the boundaries of my self. My skin surface shields me against the external world. If I am to have trust, I must feel on it only what I *want* to feel. At the first blow, however, this trust in the world breaks down" (1995, 126). Améry goes on to compare torture to rape—an apt comparison, not only because both objectify and traumatize the victim but also because the pain they inflict reduces the victim to flesh, to the purely physical. This reduction has a particularly anguished quality for female victims of sexual violence, for as women they are already viewed as more tied to nature than men and are sometimes treated as mere flesh.[26] It is as if the tormentor says with his blows: You are nothing but a body, a mere object for my will—here, I'll prove it!

Those who endure long periods of repeated torture often find ways of dissociating themselves from their bodies, that part of themselves which undergoes the torture. As the research of Judith Herman (1992) and Lenore Terr (1994) has shown, child victims of sexual and other physical abuse often utilize this defense against annihilation of the self and, in extreme cases, even develop multiple personalities that enable one or more "selves" to emerge unscathed from the abuse. Some adult victims of rape also report a kind of splitting from their bodies during the assault, as well as a separation from their former selves in the aftermath of the rape. Several months after the sexual assault and murder attempt I survived, I felt as though I had outlived myself, as though I had stayed on a train one stop past my destination.[27] Charlotte Delbo (1995, 240) writes of her return from Auschwitz:

> *life was returned to me*
> *and I am here in front of life*
> *as though facing a dress*
> *I cannot wear.*

A number of Holocaust survivors, whose former selves were virtually annihilated in the death camps, gave themselves new names after the war, Jean Améry (formerly Hans Maier) and Paul Celan (formerly Paul Antschel) being among the most well known. In a startling reappropriation of the name (literally) imposed on him during his incarceration at Auschwitz, one survivor retained and published under the name "Ka-Tzetnik 135633," meaning "concentration camp inmate number 135633."[28] Others were forced to assume new names and national and religious identities (or, rather, the appearance of them) in order to avoid capture, and probable death, during the war. The dislocations suffered by what Rosi Braidotti (1994) has called "nomadic subjects" can be agonizing even when the migrations are voluntary—or, as in the case of Eva Hoffman (1989), whose family moved from Poland to Canada when she was thirteen, involuntary but unmarked by violence. Given how traumatic such relocations can be, it is almost unimaginable how people can survive self-disintegrating torture and then manage to rebuild themselves in a new country, a new culture, and a new language. Nermina Zildzo, a recent refugee from the war in Bosnia, describes her new life in the United States, in which she struggles to become someone who can be herself in English, as that of "a cadaver,"[29] which is to say, not a life at all.

Some who survived the Holocaust, such as Delbo, have written about a distinct self that emerged in the camps and then, in some sense, stayed there after the liberation. "Auschwitz is so deeply etched in my memory that I cannot forget one moment of it. —So you are living with Auschwitz?—No. I live next to it," Delbo writes (1985, 2). "No doubt, I am very fortunate in not recognizing myself in the self that was in Auschwitz. To return from there was so improbable that it seems to me I was never there at all. . . . I live within a twofold being. The Auschwitz double doesn't bother me, doesn't interfere with my life. As though it weren't I at all. Without this split I would not have been able to revive" (1985, 3).

What can we conclude from these clinical studies and personal narratives of trauma concerning the relationship of one's self to one's body? Does trauma make one feel more or less tied to one's body? That may depend on one's ability to dissociate. Since I, like most victims of one-time traumatic events, did not dissociate during the assault,[30] I felt (and continue to feel) more tied to my body than before, or, at any rate, more vulnerable to self-annihilation because of my body. Those who survived ongoing trauma by dissociating from their bodies may feel that an essential part of themselves was untouched by the trauma, but even they experience, in the aftermath, the physical intrusions of visceral traumatic memories.

These responses to trauma—whether dissociation from one's body or separation from the self that one was either before or during the trauma—have in common the attempt to distance one's (real) self from the bodily self that is being degraded, and whose survival demands that one do, or at any rate be subjected to, degrading things. But such an attempt is never wholly successful, and the survivor's bodily sense of self is permanently altered by an encounter with death that leaves one feeling "marked" for life. The intense awareness of embodiment experienced by trauma survivors is not "the willing or grateful surrender of 'I' to flesh" described by Margaret Walker but, rather, is more akin to the pain of Kafka's (1948) "harrow," cutting the condemned man's "sentence" deeper and deeper into his body until it destroys him.

The Self as Narrative

Locke (1974/1694) famously identified the self with a set of continuous memories, a kind of ongoing narrative of one's past that is extended with each new experience. The study of trauma presents a fatal challenge to this view, since memory is drastically disrupted by traumatic events—unless one is prepared to accept the conclusion that survivors of such events are distinct from their former selves. The literature on trauma does, however, seem to support the view, advocated by Derek Parfit (1986), that the unitary self is an illusion and that we are all composed of a series of successive selves.[31] But how does one remake a self from the scattered shards of disrupted memory? Delbo writes of memories being stripped away from the inmates of the death camps, and of the incomprehensibly difficult task of getting them back after the war: "The survivor must undertake to regain his memory, regain what he possessed before: his knowledge, his experience, his childhood memories, his manual dexterity and his intellectual faculties, sensitivity, the capacity to dream, imagine, laugh" (1995, 255). This passage illustrates a major obstacle to the trauma survivor's reconstruction of a self in the sense of a remembered and ongoing narrative about oneself. Not only are one's memories of an earlier life lost, along with the ability to envision a future, but one's basic cognitive and emotional capacities are gone, or radically altered, as well. This epistemological crisis leaves the survivor with virtually no bearings by which to navigate. As Améry writes, "Whoever has succumbed to torture can no longer feel at home in the world" (1995, 136). Shattered assumptions about the world and one's safety in it can, to some extent, eventually be pieced back together, but this is a slow and painful process. Although the survivor recognizes, at some level, that these regained assumptions are illusory, she learns that they are necessary illusions—as unshakable, ultimately, as cognitively impenetrable perceptual illusions.[32]

In addition, though, trauma can obliterate one's former emotional repertoire, leaving one with only a kind of counterfactual, propositional knowledge of emotions. When alerted to the rumors that the camp in which he was incarcerated would be evacuated the next day, Primo Levi felt no emotion, just as for many months he had "no longer felt any pain, joy or fear" except in a conditional manner: "[I]f I still had my former sensitivity, I thought, this would be an extremely moving moment" (1993, 152–153). Indeed, the inability to feel one's former emotions, even in the aftermath of trauma, leaves the survivor not only numbed but also without the motivation to carry out the task of constructing an ongoing narrative.

Some have suggested that an additional reason why trauma survivors are frequently unable to construct narratives to make sense of themselves and to convey what they experienced is that, as Levi writes, "our language lacks words to express this offense, the demolition of a man" (1985, 9). It is debatable, however, whether that is the case, or whether the problem is simply others' refusal to hear survivors' stories, which makes it difficult for survivors to tell them even to themselves. As Paul Fussell (1975, 169ff.) observes, in his account of World War I:

> One of the cruxes of war . . . is the collision between events and the language available—or thought appropriate—to describe them. . . . Logically, there is no reason why the English language could not perfectly well render the actuality of . . . warfare: it is rich in terms like *blood, terror, agony, madness, shit, cruelty, murder, sell-out* and *hoax*, as well as phrases like *legs blown off, intestines gushing out over his hands, screaming all night, bleeding to death from the rectum,* and the like. . . . The problem was less one of "language" than of gentility and optimism. . . . What listener wants to be torn and shaken when he doesn't have to be? We have made *unspeakable* mean indescribable: it really means *nasty*.[33]

In order to construct self-narratives, then, we need not only the words with which to tell our stories but also an audience able and willing to hear us and to understand our words as we intend them. This aspect of remaking a self in the aftermath of trauma highlights the dependency of the self on others and helps to explain why it is so difficult for survivors to recover when others are unwilling to listen to what they endured.

Survivors attempting to construct narratives out of their traumatic memories also encounter the obstacle of despair, of the seeming futility of using language to change the world and the pointlessness of doing anything else. Commenting on the inability of language to convey the horror of what he witnessed in the Warsaw ghetto, Abraham Lewin wrote the following on May 25, 1942:

> Perhaps because the disaster is so great there is nothing to be gained by expressing in words everything that we feel. Only if we were capable of tearing out by the force of our pent-up anguish the greatest of all mountains, a Mount Everest, and with all our hatred and strength hurling it down on the heads of the German murderers of our young and old—this would be the only fitting reaction on our part. Words are beyond us now. Our hearts are empty and made of stone.[34]

As Langer comments, it is not "the poverty of language" Lewin rebukes in this passage but, rather, its uselessness "as a weapon against the current enemy bent on destroying him and his fellow victims" (1995b, 3). Lewin was writing this during the war, however, and one might think that this explanation would not apply to those constructing narratives out of memory from a position of relative safety and power after the war. Granted, bearing witness makes more sense, and even comes to seem imperative, once one is able to be heard by those willing to help. It can be difficult, though, for survivors to realize when this occurs, and to tell their stories when it does, due to the obliteration of their sense of time. Levi describes the disappearance of the future in the minds of the prisoners in Auschwitz: "Memory is a curious instrument: ever since I have been in the camp, two lines written by a friend of mine a long time ago have been running through my mind:

> '. . . Until one day
> *there will be no more sense in saying: tomorrow.'*

It is like that here. Do you know how one says 'never' in camp slang? '*Morgen früh*', tomorrow morning" (1993, 133).

According to John Rawls, the possession of a "rational plan of life" (1971, 561) is essential to personhood, or, at any rate, to moral personhood. Diana Meyers (1986) argues that this ability to envisage, pursue, and carry out one's rational plan of life is a prerequisite for self-respect. But the ability to form a plan of life is lost when one loses a sense of one's temporal being, as happened to Levi and other prisoners in Auschwitz: "We had not only forgotten our country and our culture, but also our family, our past, the future we had imagined for ourselves, because, like animals, we were confined to the present moment" (1989, 75). Thinking of his former life, Levi noted, "Today the only thing left of the life of those days is what one needs to suffer hunger and cold; I am not even alive enough to know how to kill myself" (1989, 143–144).

The disappearance of the past and the foreshortening of the future are common symptoms experienced by those who have survived long-lasting trauma of various kinds. As Shay observes in his study of combat trauma among Vietnam War veterans, "The destruction of time is an inner survival skill." The following passage, written by Judith Herman (1992, 89) about concentration camp prisoners, applies equally to soldiers in prolonged combat:

> Thinking of the future stirs up such intense yearning and hope that . . . it [is] unbearable; they quickly learn that these emotions . . . will make them desperate. . . . The future is reduced to a matter of hours or days. Alterations in time sense begin with the obliteration of the future but eventually progress to obliteration of the past. . . . Thus prisoners are eventually reduced to living in an endless present.[35]

The shrinking of time to the immediate present is also experienced in the aftermath of trauma, at least until the traumatic episode is integrated into the survivor's life narrative. "My former life?" Delbo wrote after being returned to Paris from the death camps. "Had I had a former life? My life afterwards? Was I alive to have an afterwards, to know what afterwards meant? I was floating in a present devoid of reality" (1995, 237). The unreality of Delbo's experience resulted not only from the absence of a past and future but also from the lack of connection with others who could understand what she had survived. Much of her writing about what she endured in the camps took the form of imagined conversations with others in her convoy (Delbo 1995, 233–354). Recreating this community of survivors who could bear witness to one another and know that they would be heard may have been a crucial part of Delbo's recovery.

By constructing and telling a narrative of the trauma endured, and with the help of understanding listeners, the survivor begins not only to integrate the traumatic episode into a life with a before and after but also to gain control over the occurrence of intrusive memories. When I was hospitalized after my assault I experienced moments of reprieve from vivid and terrifying flashbacks when giving my account of what had happened—to the police, doctors, a psychiatrist, a lawyer, and a prosecutor. Although others apologized for putting me through what seemed to them a retraumatizing ordeal, I responded that it was therapeutic, even at that early stage, to bear witness in the presence of others who heard and believed what I told them. Two and a half years later, when my assailant was brought to trial, I also found it healing to give my testimony in public and to have it confirmed by the police, prosecutor, my lawyer, and, ultimately, the jury, who found my assailant guilty of rape and attempted murder.[36]

How might we account for this process of "mastering the trauma" through repeated telling of one's story? The residue of trauma is a kind of body memory, as Roberta Culbertson notes, "full of fleeting images, the percussion of blows, sounds, and movements of the body—disconnected, cacophonous, the cells suffused with the active power of adrenalin, or coated with the anesthetizing numbness of noradrenalin" (1995, 174). Whereas traumatic memories (especially perceptual and emotional flashbacks) feel as though they are passively endured, narratives are the result of certain obvious choices (how much to tell to whom, in what order, etc.). This is not to say that the narrator is not subject to the constraints of memory or that the story will ring true however it is told. And the telling itself may be out of control, compulsively repeated. But one *can* control certain aspects of the narrative and that control, repeatedly exercised, leads to greater control over the memories themselves, making them less intrusive and giving them the kind of meaning that permits them to be integrated into the rest of life.

Not only present listeners but also one's cultural heritage can determine to a large extent the way in which an event is remembered and retold, and may even lead one to respond as though one remembered what one did not in fact experience.[37] Yael Tamir, an Israeli philosopher, told me a story illustrating cultural memory, in which she and her husband, neither of whom had been victims of the Holocaust or had close relatives who had been victims, literally jumped at the sound of a German voice shouting instructions at a train station in Switzerland. The experience triggered such vivid "memories" of the deportation that they grabbed their suitcases and fled the station. Similarly, Marianne Hirsch (1992–1993) discusses the phenomenon of "postmemory" in children of Holocaust survivors, and Tom Segev writes of the ways in which the Holocaust continues to shape Israeli identity: "Just as the Holocaust imposed a posthumous collective identity on its six million victims, so too it formed the collective identity of this new country—not just for the survivors who came after the war but for all Israelis, then and now" (1993, 11). The influence of cultural memory on all of us is additional evidence of the deeply relational nature of the narrative self.

The relational nature of the self is also revealed by a further obstacle confronting trauma survivors who are attempting to reconstruct coherent narratives—the difficulty of regaining one's voice, one's subjectivity, after one has been reduced to silence, to the status of an object, or, worse, made into someone else's speech, an instrument of another's agency. Those entering Nazi concentration camps had the speech of their captors literally inscribed on their bodies. As Levi describes it, the message conveyed by the prisoners' tattoos was "You no longer have a name; this is your new name." It was "a non-verbal message, so that the innocent would feel his sentence written on his flesh" (1989, 119).[38]

One of the most chilling accounts of a victim's body being used as another's speech is found in the biblical story of the traveling Levite, a story that also reveals the extent of our cultural complicity in the refusal to see trauma from the victim's perspective. The Levite's host had been approached at his home by members of a hostile tribe who asked him to hand over the Levite, so that they could rape him. This the host refused to do: Instead, he offered to the angry crowd the Levite's wife, Beth, who was then, with the clear complicity of the Levite, shoved out the door. She was gang-raped all night, and when the Levite found her body in the morning (whether she was alive or dead is not clarified in the text) he put her on a donkey, took her home, and cut up her body into twelve pieces, which were then sent as messages to the tribes of Israel.[39]

This biblical story is a striking example of a woman's body used as men's language. (Other instances include some forms of pornography as well as rape as the humiliation of the man whose "property" is stolen or as a nation's sign of victory in war.) Reflecting on the story reveals some parallels between the dismemberment and dispersal of Beth and the shattered self and fractured speech of the survivor of trauma. Piecing together a dismembered self seems to require a process of remembering in which speech and affect converge. This working through, or re-mastering of, the traumatic memory involves going from being the medium of someone else's (the torturer's) speech to being the subject of one's own. The results of the process of working through reveal the performative role of speech acts in recovering from trauma: *Saying* something about a traumatic memory *does* something to it. As Shay notes in the case of Vietnam veterans, "Severe trauma explodes the cohesion of consciousness. When a survivor creates fully realized narrative that brings together the shattered knowledge of what happened, the emotions that were aroused by the meanings of the events, and the bodily sensations that the physical events created, the survivor pieces back together the fragmentation of consciousness that trauma has caused" (1994, 188). But one cannot recover in isolation, since "[n]arrative heals personality changes only if the survivor finds or creates a trustworthy community of listeners for it" (1994, 188). As Levi observes, "Part of our existence lies in the feelings of those near to us. This is why the experience of someone who has lived for days during which man was merely a thing in the eyes of man is non-human" (1993, 172). Fortunately, just as one can be reduced to an object through torture, one can become a human subject again through telling one's narrative to caring others who are able to listen.

Intense psychological pressures make it difficult, however, for others to listen to trauma narratives. Cultural repression of traumatic memories (in the United States, about slavery; in Germany and Poland and elsewhere, about the Holocaust) comes not only from an absence of empathy with victims but also out of an active fear of empathizing with those whose terrifying fate forces us to acknowledge that we are not in control of our own. I recently felt my own need to distance myself from a survivor's trauma when I read the story of Ruth Elias, who was three months pregnant when she arrived in Auschwitz in December 1943. After she gave birth, Josef Mengele decided to experiment on her son to see how long a newborn could live without food. "In the beginning, the baby was crying all the time," Elias recalled. "Then only whimpering." After a week, a Jewish doctor took pity on her and gave her some morphine with which she euthanized her child. "It didn't take long before the child stopped breathing. . . . I didn't want to live anymore."[40] How she managed (and still manages) to continue living is incomprehensible to me. I realize, though, that *I* manage to bear the knowledge of such an atrocity by denying that such a thing could ever happen to my infant son. I can (now) live with the (vivid) possibility that I might be murdered. But I cannot live with even the possibility that this kind of torture could be inflicted on my child. So I employ the usual defenses: It couldn't happen here/now/to me, and so on.

As a society, we live with the unbearable by pressuring those who have been traumatized to forget and by rejecting the testimonies of those who are forced by fate to remember. As individuals and as cultures, we impose arbitrary term limits on memory and on recovery from trauma: a century, say, for slavery, fifty years, perhaps, for the Holocaust, a decade or two for Vietnam, several months for mass rape or serial murder. Even a public memorialization can be a forgetting, a way of saying to survivors what someone said after I published my first article on sexual violence: "Now you can put this behind you." But attempting to limit traumatic memories does not make them go away; the signs and symptoms of trauma remain, caused by a source more virulent for being driven underground.

In *The Book of Laughter and Forgetting*, Milan Kundera writes that "[the] struggle against power is the struggle of memory against forgetting."[41] Whether the power is a fascist state or an internalized trauma, surviving the present requires the courage to confront the past, reexamine it, retell it, and thereby remaster its traumatic aspects. An explanation is offered by Eva Hoffman, who returns repeatedly in her memoir to a past in which she was "lost in translation" after moving from Poland to Canada: "Those who don't understand the past may be condemned to repeat it, but those who never repeat it are condemned not to understand it" (1989, 278).

And so we repeat our stories, and we listen to others'. What Hoffman writes of her conversations with Miriam, her closest North American friend, could also describe the remaking of a survivor's self in relation to empathic others: "To a large extent, we're the keepers of each other's stories, and the shape of these stories has unfolded in part from our interwoven accounts.

Human beings don't only search for meanings, they are themselves units of meaning; but we can mean something only within the fabric of larger significations" (1989, 279). Trauma, however, unravels whatever meaning we've found and woven ourselves into, and so listening to survivors' stories is, as Langer describes in reading and writing about the Holocaust, "an experience in *un*learning; both parties are forced into the Dantean gesture of abandoning all safe props as they enter and, without benefit of Virgil, make their uneasy way through its vague domain" (1995b, 6–7). It is easy to understand why one would not willingly enter such a realm, but survivors' testimonies must be heard, if individual and cultural recovery is to be possible.

To recover from trauma, according to psychoanalyst Dori Laub, a survivor needs to construct a narrative and tell it to an empathic listener, in order to re-externalize the event. "Bearing witness to a trauma is, in fact, a process that includes the listener" (Laub and Felman 1992, 70). And to the extent that bearing witness reestablishes the survivor's identity, the empathic other is essential to the continuation of a self. In this connection, Laub writes of Chaim Guri's film *The Eighty-first Blow*, which "portrays the image of a man who narrates the story of his sufferings in the camps only to hear his audience say: 'All this cannot be true, it could not have happened. You must have made it up.' This denial by the listener inflicts, according to the film, the ultimately fateful blow, beyond the eighty blows that man, in Jewish tradition, can sustain and survive" (Laub and Felman 1992, 68).

The Autonomous Self

The view of the self most central to ethics, as well as to social, political, and legal philosophy (at least in the analytic tradition), is one that holds that the self is the locus of autonomous agency, that which freely makes choices and wills actions. This is a self that is considered responsible for its decisions and actions and is an appropriate subject of praise or blame. It is the transformation of the self as autonomous agent that is perhaps most apparent in survivors of trauma. First, the autonomy-undermining symptoms of PTSD reconfigure the survivor's will, rendering involuntary many responses that were once under voluntary control. Intrusive memories are triggered by things reminiscent of the traumatic event and carry a strong, sometimes overwhelming, emotional charge. Not only is one's response to items that would startle anyone heightened, but one has either an involuntary startle response to things that formerly provoked no reaction or a subtler, still voluntary one. The loss of control evidenced by these and other PTSD symptoms alters who one is, not only limiting what one can do (and can refrain from doing) but also changing what one *wants* to do.

A trauma survivor suffers a loss of control not only over herself but also over her environment—a loss that, in turn, can lead to a constriction of the boundaries of her will. If a rape victim is unable to walk outside without the fear of being assaulted again, she quickly loses the desire to go for a walk. If one's self, or one's *true* self, is considered to be identical to one's will, then a survivor cannot be considered the same as her pre-trauma self, since what she is able to will post-trauma is so drastically altered. Some reactions that once were under the will's command become involuntary, and some desires that once were motivating can no longer be felt, let alone acted upon.

Such loss of control over oneself can explain, to a large extent, what a survivor means in saying "I am no longer myself." The trauma survivor identifies with her former self not only because that self was more familiar and less damaged but also because it was more predictable. The fact that, as has been recently discovered, certain drugs, such as Prozac, give PTSD sufferers greater self-control, by making them better able to choose their reactions to things and to regulate the timing of their responses, accounts for the common response to such drugs: "[T]hey make me more myself" (Kramer, 1993). It may also be that, after taking Prozac, such a person is better able to endorse, or identify with, her new self.[42]

In order to recover, a trauma survivor needs to be able to control herself, to control her environment (within reasonable limits), and to be reconnected with humanity. Whether the latter two achievements occur depends, to a large extent, on other people. Living with the memory of trauma is living with a kind of disability, and whether one is able to function with a disability depends largely on how one's social and physical environments are set up (Minow, 1990). A trauma survivor makes accommodations, figuring out how to live with her limits, but she also realizes that at least some externally imposed limits can be changed. In the year after my assault, when I was terrified to walk alone, I was able to go to talks and other events on campus by having a friend walk with me. I became able to use the locker room in the gym after getting the university to put a lock on a door that led to a dark, isolated passageway, and I was able to park my car at night after lobbying the university to put a light in the parking lot.

These ways of enhancing my autonomy in the aftermath of my assault reinforced my view of autonomy as a function of dependency on others. Not only is autonomy compatible with socialization and with caring for and being cared for by others (Meyers 1987, 1989, 1992), but the right sort of interactions with others can be seen as essential to autonomy. In "Jurisprudence and Gender," Robin West (1988) discusses the tension within feminist theory between, on the one hand, the desire for connection and fear of alienation (in "cultural" feminism[43]) and, on the other, the desire for autonomy and fear of invasion (in "radical" or "dominance" feminism[44]). Once one acknowledges the relational nature of autonomy, however, this apparent tension can be resolved by noting that the main reason all of us, especially women, have to fear violent intrusions by others is that they severely impair our ability to be connected to humanity in ways we value. It is this loss of connection that trauma survivors mourn, a loss that in turn imperils autonomous selfhood. In order to reestablish that connection in the aftermath of trauma, one must first feel able to protect oneself against invasion. The autonomous self and the relational self are thus shown to be interdependent, even constitutive of one another.

Virginia Held (1993) defends a relational account of autonomy in which it consists not of putting walls around oneself or one's property (as in Isaiah Berlin's phrase for autonomy, "the inner citadel"[45]) but, instead, of forming essential relationships with others. Held cites Jennifer Nedelsky, who suggests that "the most promising model, symbol, or metaphor for autonomy is not property, but childrearing. There we have encapsulated the emergence of autonomy through relationship with others. . . . Interdependence [is] a constant component of autonomy" (Nedelsky 1989, 11).

Trauma survivors are dependent on empathic others who are willing to listen to their narratives. Given that the language in which such narratives are conveyed and are understood is itself a social phenomenon, this aspect of recovery from trauma also underscores the extent to which autonomy is a fundamentally relational notion.[46]

Primo Levi recalls a dream in which he is telling his sister and others about Auschwitz and they are completely indifferent, acting as though he is not present. Many others in the camp had a similar dream. "Why does it happen?" he asks. "Why is the pain of every day translated so constantly into our dreams, in the ever-repeated scene of the unlistened-to story?" (1993, 60). Why is it so horrifying for survivors to be unheard? There is a scene in the film *La famiglia,* directed by Ettore Scola in 1987, in which a little boy's uncle pretends not to see him, a game that quickly turns from a bit of fun into a kind of torture when the man persists long beyond the boy's tolerance for invisibility. For the child, not to be seen is not to exist, to be annihilated. So it is for these others: Not to be heard means that the self the survivor has become does not exist. Since the earlier self died, the surviving self needs to be known and acknowledged in order to exist.

This illuminates a connection among the views of the self as narrative, as embodied, and as autonomous. It is not sufficient for mastering the trauma to construct a narrative of it: One must (physically, publicly) say or write (or paint or film) the narrative, and others must see or hear it, in order for one's survival as an autonomous self to be complete. Hence we see the extent to which the self is created and sustained by others and, thus, able to be destroyed by them. The boundaries of the will are limited, or enlarged, not only by the stories others tell but also by the extent of their ability and willingness to listen to ours.

In the traditional philosophical literature on personal identity, one is considered to be the same person over time if one can (now) identify with that person in the past or future. One typically identifies with a person in the past if one can remember having that person's experiences, and one identifies with a person in the future if one cares in a unique way about that person's future experiences. An interesting result of group therapy with trauma survivors is that they come to have greater compassion for their earlier selves by empathizing with others who experienced similar traumas. They stop blaming themselves by realizing that others who acted or reacted similarly are not blameworthy. Rape survivors, who typically have difficulty getting angry with their assailants,[47] find that in group therapy they are able to get angry on their own behalf by first getting angry on behalf of others (Koss and Harvey, 1991).

The fact that survivors gain the ability to reconnect with their former selves by empathizing with others who have experienced similar traumas suggests that we exist only, or primarily, in connection with others. It also suggests that healing from trauma takes place through a kind of splitting off of the traumatized self, with which one then is able to empathize, just as one empathizes with others.[48] The loss of a trauma survivor's former self is typically described by analogy to the loss of a beloved other. And yet, in grieving for another, one often says, "it's as though a part of myself has died." It is not clear whether this circular comparison is a case of language failing us or, on the contrary, revealing a deep truth about selfhood and connectedness. But the essential point is that, by finding (some aspects of) one's lost self in another person, one can manage (to a greater or lesser degree) to reconnect with it and to reintegrate one's various selves into a coherent personality.

The fundamentally relational character of the self is also highlighted by the dependence of survivors on others' attitudes toward them in the aftermath of trauma. Victims of rape and other forms of torture often report drastically altered senses of self-worth, resulting from their degrading treatment. That even a single person—one's assailant—has treated one as worthless can, at least temporarily, undo an entire lifetime of self-esteem (Roberts 1989, 91). This effect is magnified by prolonged exposure to degradation, especially when the social and historical context is such that the group to which one belongs is despised. Survivors of trauma recover to a greater or lesser extent depending on others' responses to them after the trauma. And, again, these aspects of trauma and recovery reveal the deeply social nature of one's sense of self and underscore the limits of the individual's capacity to control her own self-definition.

But what can others do to help a survivor recover from trauma, apart from listening empathically? Kenneth Seeskin (1988) argues, in discussing an appropriate response to the Holocaust, that we who did not experience it cannot hope to understand it—and yet to remain silent in the aftermath of it would be immoral. And so, he suggests, we should move beyond theory, beyond an attempt to understand it, to a practice of resistance. As Emil Fackenheim (1982, 239) writes, "The truth is that to grasp the Holocaust whole-of-horror is not to comprehend or transcend it, but rather *to say no to it, or resist it.*"[49] The "no" of resistance is not the "no" of denial. It is the "no" of acknowledgment of what happened and refusal to let it happen again.

Remaking Oneself

A child gave me a flower
one morning
a flower picked
for me
he kissed the flower
before giving it to me. . . .
There is no wound that will not heal
I told myself that day
and still repeat it from time to time
but not enough to believe it.
                    —Charlotte Delbo (1995, 241)

What is the goal of the survivor? Ultimately, it is not to transcend the trauma, not to solve the dilemmas of survival, but simply to endure. This can be hard enough, when the only way to regain control over one's life seems to be to end it. A few months after my assault, I drove by myself for several hours to visit a friend. Though driving felt like a much safer mode of transportation than walking, I worried throughout the journey, not only about the trajectory of every oncoming vehicle but also about my car breaking down, leaving me at the mercy of potentially murderous passers-by. I wished I'd had a gun so that I could shoot myself rather than be forced to live through another assault.[50] Later in my recovery, as depression gave way to rage, such suicidal thoughts were quickly quelled by a stubborn refusal to finish my assailant's job for him. I also learned, after martial arts training, that I was capable, morally as well as physically, of killing in self-defense—an option that made the possibility of another life-threatening attack one I could live with. Some rape survivors have remarked on the sense of moral loss they experienced when they realized that they could kill their assailants (and even wanted to!), but I think that this thought can be seen as a salutary character change in those whom society does not encourage to value their own lives enough.[51] And far from jeopardizing their connections with a community, this newfound ability to defend themselves, and to consider themselves worth fighting for, enables rape survivors to move among others, free of debilitating fears. It was this ability that gave me the courage to bring a child into the world, in spite of the realization that doing so would, far from making me immortal, make me twice as mortal, as Barbara Kingsolver

(1989, 59) put it, by doubling my chances of having my life destroyed by a speeding truck.

But many trauma survivors who endured much worse than I did, and for much longer, found, often years later, that it was impossible to go on. It is not a moral failing to leave a world that has become morally unacceptable. I wonder how some can ask, of battered women, "Why didn't they leave?" while saying, of those driven to suicide by the brutal and inescapable aftermath of trauma, "Why didn't they stay?" Améry wrote, "Whoever was tortured, stays tortured" (1995, 131), and this may explain why he, Levi, Celan, and other Holocaust survivors took their own lives decades after their (physical) torture ended, as if such an explanation were needed.

Those who have survived trauma understand well the pull of that solution to their daily Beckettian dilemma, "I can't go on, I must go on."[52] For on some days the conclusion "I'll go on" cannot be reached by faith or reason. How does one go on with a shattered self, with no guarantee of recovery, believing that one will always "stay tortured" and never "feel at home in the world"? One hopes for a bearable future, in spite of all the inductive evidence to the contrary. After all, the loss of faith in induction following an unpredictable trauma also has a reassuring side: Since inferences from the past can no longer be relied upon to predict the future, there's no more reason to think that tomorrow will bring agony than to think that it won't. So one makes a wager, in which nothing is certain and the odds change daily, and sets about "willing to believe"[53] that life, for all its unfathomable horror, still holds some undiscovered pleasures. And one remakes oneself by finding meaning in a life of caring for and being sustained by others. While I used to have to will myself out of bed each day, I now wake gladly to feed my infant son whose birth gives me reason not to have died. He is the embodiment of my life's new narrative, and I am more autonomous by virtue of being so intermingled with him. Having him has also enabled me to rebuild my trust in the world around us. He is so trusting that he stands with outstretched arms, wobbling, until he falls, stiff-limbed, forward, backward, certain the universe will catch him. So far, it has, and when I tell myself it always will, the part of me that he's become believes it.[54]

Notes

1. Quoted in Langer (1995a, 14). The irony of calling the author of this quote a "survivor" is evident but, it seems to me, linguistically unavoidable.

2. Shay (1994, 180) writes, "When a survivor of prolonged trauma loses all sense of meaningful personal narrative, this may result in a contaminated identity. 'I died in Vietnam' may express a current identity as a corpse."

3. I do not mean to imply that the traumas suffered by these different groups of survivors are the same, or even commensurable. However, researchers such as Judith

Herman, in *Trauma and Recovery* (1992), and Ronnie Janoff-Bulman, in *Shattered Assumptions: Towards a New Psychology of Trauma* (1992), have persuasively argued that many of those who survive life-threatening traumatic events in which they are reduced to near-complete helplessness later suffer from the symptoms of post-traumatic stress disorder. I would add that they experience a similar disintegration of the self. In this chapter, I use the term 'victim' as well as the term 'survivor' to denote someone who has been victimized by, and yet survived, such a life-threatening trauma. Clearly, many civilians are more traumatized by war (and with greater injustice) than are the veterans to whom I refer here. I mention the latter simply because trauma research on survivors of war has focused on veterans, U.S. veterans in particular, whose trauma symptoms our federal government is obliged to attempt to understand and treat.

4. In defending a feminist account of the relational self, I do not mean to imply that all relational accounts of the self are feminist. Some that are not (necessarily) feminist are those advocated by Hegel, Marx, and contemporary communitarians.

5. See Locke (1974/1694), Noonan (1989), and Perry (1975) for treatments of personal identity by seventeenth- and eighteenth-century philosophers.

6. See Ungar (1990), Parfit (1986), Noonan (1989), Rorty (1976), and Perry (1975) for discussions of contemporary theories of personal identity.

7. Although most philosophers writing about personal identity have neglected to consider *any* actual transformations of real persons, there are a few notable exceptions. For example, Kathleen Wilkes argues that the "bizarre, entertaining, confusing, and inconclusive thought experiments" so common in philosophical writing about personal identity are not helpful, and, in any case, not needed, "since there are so many actual puzzle-cases which defy the *imagination*, but which we none the less have to accept as facts" (Wilkes 1988, vii). She does not discuss trauma, however, and uses third-person scientific accounts of neurological disorders rather than first-person narratives in her analysis. Although he does not discuss trauma and the self either, Thomas Nagel examines the effect of commissurotomy on the self in "Brain Bisection and the Unity of Consciousness" (1975). Three philosophers, however, have in recent writings departed from this tradition of ignoring trauma—specifically, by analyzing alleged cases of trauma-induced dissociation and subsequent recovered memories. Ian Hacking (1995) presents a deeply skeptical treatment of the alleged splitting of the self that occurs during severe child abuse. Naomi Scheman considers the multiple personalities constructed by severely abused children to be "a comprehensible, perhaps even rational, response to an intolerable situation, a way of maintaining some degree of agency in the face of profoundly soul-destroying attacks on one's ability to construct a sense of self" (1993, 164). And Diana T. Meyers, in an article in progress entitled "The Family Romance," attempts to mediate between the two former views with an account focusing, not on whether the incest trope that "figures" such recovered memories is historically accurate but, rather, on whether such a figuration is useful to the alleged victims.

8. For discussions of the usefulness of such narratives, see Brison (1995a and 1995b).

9. In this connection, see King (1988), Lugones (1987), and Matsuda (1989).

10. This is the case not (merely) because philosophers are a more disputatious lot but, rather, because psychologists need at least the appearance of clarity and agreement in order to categorize illnesses, make diagnoses, carry out research, fill out insurance claim forms, and so on.

11. Here, I paraphrase Judith Herman's (1992, 33) description of traumatic events. This description and the following discussion of trauma are distilled from Herman's book as well as from Janoff-Bulman (1992) and Shay (1994).

12. Although some post-structuralists hold that the self is a fiction, not all do; and in any case, I do not mean to equate 'narrative' with 'fiction'. On the contrary, I think the clinical studies and narrative accounts of trauma discussed below show that the self is *not* a fiction, if that is taken to mean that it is freely constructed by some narrator. No one, not even Stephen King, would voluntarily construct a self so tormented by trauma and its aftermath.

13. This quote is attributed to Baier (1985, 84). For other discussions of the relational self, see Jaggar (1983) and Meyers (1987, 1989, 1992, 1994). In addition, Virginia Held (1993, 57–64) gives an excellent survey of feminist views of the relational self insofar as they bear on moral theory.

14. An exception is Bernard Williams (1970), who presents a thought experiment that prompts the intuition that in at least some cases of so-called body transfer, we would identify with the surviving individual who has our body, and not with the one who has our memory and other psychological characteristics.

15. Most famously, Descartes (1984/1641).

16. In refreshing contrast to this disciplinary bias is the philosophical writing on embodiment by Iris Young (1990).

17. See Plato's *Phaedo*, II.65c–67d (quoted in Ruddick 1989, 188).

18. Two critiques of Beauvoir's position on maternity and childbirth are presented in Ruddick (1989, 192–193, 275n11) and Mackenzie (1996).

19. Quoted in Ruddick (1989, 212).

20. Quoted in Ruddick (1989, 192–193).

21. See Brison (1993).

22. That fear, anxiety, and so on, are psychological and, hence, controllable responses to trauma is an assumption underlying the view, held by many liberals, that victims of hate speech should simply toughen their emotional hides to avoid being affected adversely by it. This view presupposes a mind-body split more thoroughgoing than that defended by Descartes (1984/1641).

23. See also Glover's (1988, 142–145) discussion of charged memory in Proust.

24. As Ann Bumpus pointed out to me in conversation, if *all* memories were lodged in the body, this would not pose a problem for Locke. However, if memories do not reside solely in the mind or in the body but, rather, are a function of the way in which consciousness "inhabits" a body, then not only Locke's thought experiment but also those of Sydney Shoemaker (Perry 1975, 119–134) and Bernard Williams (1970) appear to be incoherent as described.

25. And, in the case of the extreme trauma endured by Holocaust survivors, their bodies themselves were drastically changed, by starvation, disease, and torture.

26. An especially striking literary illustration is the scene in *Studs Lonigan* in which the narrator says of the woman Weary Reilly is about to rape, "She was his meat" (Farrell 1935, 396). I thank Blanche Gelfant for drawing my attention to this passage.

27. What I wrote about this experience was that I felt "like Robert Lowell's newly widowed mother, described in one of his poems as mooning in a window 'as if she had stayed on a train / one stop past her destination'" (Brison 1993, 10–11, quoting

Robert Lowell, *Selected Poems* [New York: Farrar, Straus and Giroux, 1977, p. 82]). At the time, I failed to note the eerie resonance of this image with the deportation.

28. Ka-Tzetnik 135633 (1989). I thank Alexis Jetter for showing me the work of this author.

29. This quote was taken from an essay written by Nermina Zildzo for English 2 (at Dartmouth College) in Fall 1995.

30. See Terr (1994) for an account of different responses to one-time and ongoing traumas.

31. Parfit would not, however, agree with the relational account of the self I am defending here. Note, too, that in her comments on a draft of this chapter, Susan Dwyer wondered "how many people who have not suffered trauma have a clear sense of what it was like to be them at some earlier point in their lives." She guessed "not many" and suggested that this "explains a number of rituals we engage in, taking photographs of significant events, keeping a diary, marking anniversaries, valuing family (i.e., people who were there, too, who can tell you about your former self)."

32. Bruno Bettelheim specifically discusses the "personality-disintegrating" effects of being in a German concentration camp (1979, 25): "Being subjected to living in an extreme situation somehow contaminates permanently the old life and the old personality. This suggests that a personality which did not protect the individual against landing in an extreme situation seems so deficient to the person that he feels in need of widespread restructuring" (1979, 123–124). In spite of this conviction, trauma survivors are forced to reacquire at least some of their earlier illusions if their lives are to continue to be livable.

33. Quoted in Shay (1994, xx).

34. Quoted in Langer (1995b, 3).

35. Quoted in Shay (1994, 176).

36. Of course, not many rape survivors are fortunate enough to have such a experience with the criminal justice system, given the low rates of reporting, prosecuting, and conviction of rapists. I also had the advantage of having my assailant tried in a French court, in which the adversarial system is not practiced, so I was not cross-examined by the defense lawyer. In addition, since the facts of the case were not in dispute and my assailant's only defense was an (ultimately unsuccessful) insanity plea, no one in the courtroom questioned my narrative of what had happened.

37. I am not suggesting that for this reason the memories of trauma survivors are less reliable than others' memories. In the subsequent story, Yael Tamir did not have a false memory of actually having lived through the Holocaust. Rather, the cultural climate in which she was raised led her to respond instinctively to certain things (a shouting German voice at a train station) in ways characteristic of those who had actually been deported. In any case, since all narrative memory involves reconstruction, trauma survivor's narratives are no less likely to be accurate than anyone else's. (I thank Susan Dwyer for encouraging me to make this last point more explicit.)

38. Levi writes that "[a]t a distance of forty years, my tattoo has become a part of my body," no longer tainting his sense of self (1989, 119).

39. See Judg. 19:26–28, which Mieke Bal mentions in the 1988b source and discusses at length in the 1988a and 1991 sources.

40. See *Newsweek*, January 16, 1995, p. 54.

41. I thank Joan Bolker (1995, 12) for reminding me of this quote, with which she begins her review of Terr (1994). In the same article Bolker (1995, 15) also refers to "term limits on memory," which, she says, were what the U.S. electorate really voted for in November 1994.

42. For an example of an endorsement account of autonomy, see Frankfurt (1988, chs. 5 and 12).

43. Two of the most prominent proponents of what West calls "cultural" feminism (and others have called "difference" feminism) are Carol Gilligan (1982) and Sara Ruddick (1989).

44. The best-known advocate of "radical" or "dominance" feminism is Catharine MacKinnon (1987).

45. The militaristic nature of this image is brought out by an update mentioned to me by Diana Meyers: autonomy as "the inner missile silo"!

46. In addition, not simply what we are able to express, but also what we are able to feel, can be seen to be a function of one's social relations (Scheman 1983).

47. For an account of why this is so, see Brison (n.d.).

48. This is one of the positive aspects of a kind of multiple consciousness. Cf. Scheman (1993), Lugones (1987), Matsuda (1989), and King (1988).

49. Quoted in Seeskin (1988, 120).

50. When I later mentioned this to my therapist, she replied, reasonably enough, "Why not shoot the assailant instead?" But for me that thought was not yet thinkable.

51. I should make a distinction here between the ability to kill in self-defense and the desire to kill as a form of revenge. Although I think it is morally permissible to possess and to employ the former, acting on the latter is to be morally condemned.

52. See Beckett (1965, 414). What Beckett actually writes is "you must go on, I can't go on, I'll go on," translating his original ending to *L'Innommable*: "*il faut continuer, je ne peux pas continuer, je vais continuer.*" I am grateful to Thomas Trezise for pointing out this passage.

53. For a discussion of Pascal's wager, see Pascal (1958); and for a discussion of "the will to believe," see James (1896).

54. I am deeply grateful to those friends and colleagues who read and commented on earlier drafts of this paper: Joan Bolker, Susan Dwyer, Claudia Henrion, Alexis Jetter, Margot Livesey, Catriona Mackenzie, Diana Meyers, Linda Mulley, Annelise Orleck, and Ann Bumpus, with whom I also had many illuminating conversations about personal identity. I would like to thank Tonya Blackwell and Margo Conti for their superb research assistance and Shifra Levine, Martha Brison, and Mary Pearson for the loving child care that made my writing possible. My greatest debt is to Thomas Trezise, who provided all of the above, along with daily sustenance and support.

References

Améry, Jean. 1995. Torture. In *Art from the Ashes: A Holocaust Anthology*, ed. Lawrence Langer. New York: Oxford University Press.

Baier, Annette. 1985. *Postures of the Mind: Essays on Mind and Morals*. Minneapolis: University of Minnesota Press.

Bal, Mieke. 1988a. *Death and Dissymmetry: The Politics of Coherence in the Book of Judges.* Chicago: University of Chicago Press.

_____. 1988b. *Murder and Difference: Gender, Genre, and Scholarship on Sisera's Death.* Bloomington: Indiana University Press.

_____. 1991. *Reading "Rembrandt": Beyond the Word-Image Opposition.* New York: Cambridge University Press.

Beauvoir, Simone de. 1953. *The Second Sex,* trans. H. M. Parshley. New York: Vintage.

Beckett, Samuel. 1953. *L'Innommable.* Paris: Minuit.

_____. 1965. *Three Novels.* New York: Grove Press Black Cat.

Bettelheim, Bruno. 1979. *Surviving and Other Essays.* New York: Knopf.

Bolker, Joan L. 1995. Forgetting Ourselves. *Readings: A Journal of Reviews and Commentary in Mental Health* (June): 12–15.

Braidotti, Rosi. 1994. *Nomadic Subjects: Embodiment and Sexual Difference in Contemporary Feminist Theory.* New York: Columbia University Press.

Brison, Susan. 1993. Surviving Sexual Violence: A Philosophical Perspective. *Journal of Social Philosophy* 24(1): 5–22.

_____. 1995a. The Theoretical Importance of Practice. *Nomos* 37: 216–238.

_____. 1995b. On the Personal As Philosophical. *APA Newsletter* 95(1): 37–40.

_____. n.d. Victimization, Agency, and Self-Blame. Unpublished article.

Culbertson, Roberta. 1995. Embodied Memory, Transcendence, and Telling: Recounting Trauma, Re-establishing the Self. *New Literary History* 26: 169–195.

Delbo, Charlotte. 1985. *Days and Memory,* trans. Rosette Lamont. Marlboro, Vt.: Marlboro Press.

_____. 1995. *Auschwitz and After,* trans. Rosette C. Lamont. New Haven: Yale University Press.

Descartes, René. 1984/1641. *Meditations.* In *The Philosophical Writings of Descartes,* Vol. 2, trans. John Cottingham, Robert Stoothoff, and Dugald Murdoch. New York: Cambridge University Press.

DSM III-R. 1987. *Diagnostic and Statistical Manual of Mental Disorders,* 3rd ed., rev. Washington, D.C.: American Psychiatric Association.

Fackenheim, Emil. 1982. *To Mend the World.* New York: Schocken.

Farrell, James T. 1935. *Studs Lonigan,* Book 2. New York: Vanguard Press.

Frankfurt, Harry. 1988. *The Importance of What We Care About.* New York: Cambridge University Press.

Fussel, Paul. 1975. *The Great War and Modern Memory.* London: Oxford University Press.

Gilligan, Carol. 1982. *In a Different Voice.* Cambridge, Mass.: Harvard University Press.

Glover, Jonathan. 1988. *I: The Philosophy and Psychology of Personal Identity.* London: Allen Lane/Penguin Press.

Hacking, Ian. 1995. *Rewriting the Soul: Multiple Personality and the Sciences of Memory.* Princeton: Princeton University Press.

Held, Virginia. 1993. *Feminist Morality.* Chicago: University of Chicago Press.

Herman, Judith. 1992. *Trauma and Recovery.* New York: Basic Books.

Hirsch, Marianne. 1992–1993. Family Pictures: *Maus,* Mourning, and Post-Memory. *Discourse* 15(2): 3–29.

Hoffman, Eva. 1989. *Lost in Translation.* New York: Dutton.

Jaggar, Alison M. 1983. *Feminist Politics and Human Nature.* Totowa, N.J.: Rowman & Allanheld.

James, William. 1896. *The Will to Believe and Other Essays in Popular Philosophy.* New York: Longmans, Green.

Janoff-Bulman, Ronnie. 1992. *Shattered Assumptions: Towards a New Psychology of Trauma.* New York: Free Press.

Kafka, Franz. 1948. In the Penal Colony. In *The Penal Colony: Stories and Short Pieces,* trans. Willa and Edwin Muir, pp. 191–227. New York: Schocken Books.

Ka-Tzetnik 135633. 1989. *Shivitti: A Vision.* New York: Harper & Row.

King, Deborah K. 1988. Multiple Jeopardy, Multiple Consciousness: The Context of a Black Feminist Ideology. *Signs* 14(1): 42–72.

Kingsolver, Barbara. 1989. *Homeland and Other Stories.* New York: Harper & Row.

Koss, Mary P., and Mary R. Harvey. 1991. *The Rape Victim: Clinical and Community Interventions,* 2d ed. London: Sage Publications.

Kramer, Peter. 1993. *Listening to Prozac.* New York: Viking.

Kundera, Milan. 1980. *The Book of Laughter and Forgetting.* New York: Knopf.

Langer, Lawrence. 1995a. *Admitting the Holocaust.* New York: Oxford University Press.

Langer, Lawrence, ed. 1995b. *Art from the Ashes.* New York: Oxford University Press.

Laub, Dori, and Shoshana Felman. 1992. *Testimony: Crises of Witnessing in Literature, Psychoanalysis, and History.* New York: Routledge.

Levi, Primo. 1985. *If Not Now, When?* New York: Penguin Books.

_____. 1989. *The Drowned and the Saved.* New York: Random House.

_____. 1993. *Survival in Auschwitz.* New York: Macmillan.

Locke, John. 1974. (This section, on personal identity, was originally published in 1694.) *An Essay Concerning Human Understanding,* ed. A. D. Woozley. New York: New American Library, pp. 210–220.

Lugones, María. 1987. Playfulness, "World"-Travelling, and Loving Perception. *Hypatia* 2(2): 3–19.

Mackenzie, Catriona. 1996 (forthcoming). A Certain Lack of Symmetry: de Beauvoir on Autonomous Agency and Women's Embodiment. In *Texts in Culture: Simone de Beauvoir, "The Second Sex,"* ed. Ruth Evans. Manchester: Manchester University Press.

MacKinnon, Catharine. 1987. *Feminism Unmodified: Discourses on Life and Law.* Cambridge, Mass.: Harvard University Press.

Matsuda, Mari. 1989. When the First Quail Calls: Multiple Consciousness as Jurisprudential Method. *Women's Rights Law Reporter* 11(1): 7–10.

Meyers, Diana T. 1986. The Politics of Self-Respect: A Feminist Perspective. *Hypatia* 1(1): 83–100.

_____. 1987. The Socialized Individual and Individual Autonomy: An Intersection Between Philosophy and Psychology. In *Women and Moral Theory,* ed. Eva Feder Kittay and Diana T. Meyers. Savage, Md.: Rowman & Littlefield.

_____. 1989. *Self, Society, and Personal Choice.* New York: Columbia University Press.

_____. 1992. Personal Autonomy or the Deconstructed Subject? A Reply to Hekman. *Hypatia* 7(1): 124–132.

_____. 1994. *Subjection & Subjectivity: Psychoanalytic Feminism & Moral Philosophy*. New York: Routledge.

Minow, Martha. 1990. *Making All the Difference: Inclusion, Exclusion, and American Law*. Ithaca: Cornell University Press.

Nagel, Thomas. 1975. Brain Bisection and the Unity of Consciousness. In *Personal Identity*, ed. John Perry. Berkeley: University of California Press.

Nedelsky, Jennifer. 1989. Reconceiving Autonomy: Sources, Thoughts and Possibilities. *Yale Journal of Law and Feminism* 1(7): 7–36.

Noonan, Harold W. 1989. *Personal Identity*. New York: Routledge.

Parfit, Derek. 1986. *Reasons and Persons*. Oxford: Oxford University Press.

Pascal, Blaise. 1958. *Pensées*, trans. W. F. Trotter. New York: Dutton.

Perry, John. 1975. *Personal Identity*. Berkeley: University of California Press.

Proust, Marcel. 1981. *Remembrance of Things Past*, trans. C. K. Scott Moncrieff and Terence Kilmartin. New York: Vintage.

Rawls, John. 1971. *A Theory of Justice*. Cambridge, Mass.: Harvard University Press.

Roberts, Cathy. 1989. *Women and Rape*. New York: New York University Press.

Rorty, Amélie Oksenberg, ed. 1976. *The Identities of Persons*. Berkeley: University of California Press.

Ruddick, Sara. 1989. *Maternal Thinking: Toward a Politics of Peace*. Boston: Beacon Press.

Scheman, Naomi. 1983. Individualism and the Objects of Psychology. In *Discovering Reality: Feminist Perspectives on Epistemology, Metaphysics, Methodology, and Philosophy of Science*, ed. Sandra Harding and Merrill B. Hintikka. Boston: D. Reidel.

_____. 1993. Though This Be Method, Yet There Is Madness in It. In *A Mind of One's Own*, ed. Louise M. Antony and Charlotte Witt. Boulder, Colo.: Westview Press.

Scherer, Migael. 1992. *Still Loved by the Sun: A Rape Survivor's Journal*. New York: Simon & Schuster.

Seeskin, Kenneth. 1988. Coming to Terms with Failure: A Philosophical Dilemma. In *Writing and the Holocaust*, ed. Berel Lang. New York: Holmes & Meier.

Segev, Tom. 1993. *The Seventh Million*, trans. Haim Watzman. New York: Hill and Wang.

Shay, Jonathan. 1994. *Achilles in Vietnam: Combat Trauma and the Undoing of Character*. New York: Atheneum.

Terr, Lenore. 1994. *Unchained Memories*. New York: HarperCollins.

Ungar, Peter. 1990. *Identity, Consciousness and Value*. New York: Oxford University Press.

West, Robin. 1988. Jurisprudence and Gender. *University of Chicago Law Review* 55(6): 1–72.

Wilkes, Kathleen. 1988. *Real People*. New York: Oxford University Press.

Williams, Bernard. 1970. The Self and the Future. *Philosophical Review* 79(2): 161–180.

Winkler, Cathy. 1991. Rape as Social Murder. *Anthropology Today* 7(3): 12–14.

Young, Iris Marion. 1990. *Throwing Like a Girl and Other Essays in Feminist Philosophy and Social Theory*. Bloomington: Indiana University Press.

two

Autonomy and Social Relationships

Rethinking the Feminist Critique

MARILYN FRIEDMAN

Recent feminist philosophy has engaged in a love-hate relationship with autonomy. In the 1970s, feminists praised the ideal of autonomy and extolled its liberatory potential for women. They lamented only that this character trait had traditionally been idealized as a masculine achievement and unfairly repressed in females (S. B. Hill 1975; cf. Grimshaw 1988).

In the 1980s and early 1990s, this view was challenged by other feminists who rejected the ideal of autonomy as it had traditionally been conceived. This mainstream conception, so they argued, is overly individualistic. It presupposes that selves are asocial atoms, ignores the importance of social relationships, and promotes the sort of independence that involves disconnection from close interpersonal involvement with others (Keller 1985; Hoagland 1988; Nedelsky 1989; Code 1991; Benhabib 1992). The traditional concept of autonomy, feminists asserted, is biased toward male social roles and reflects male conceits and delusions.

As an alternative, some feminists in the 1980s began recommending a relational concept of autonomy, one that treats social relationships and human community as central to the realization of autonomy. The 1990s, accordingly, are witnessing a renewed feminist interest in autonomy—but as relationally conceived (Meyers 1989; Arnault 1989; Code 1991; Govier 1993; Meehan 1994; Huntington 1995).

In this chapter, I first survey prominent feminist writings that call for a relational conception of autonomy and that criticize the philosophical mainstream for lacking such an account. Second, I show that prominent mainstream accounts of autonomy do acknowledge the importance of social relationships, thus tending to converge on this point with the prevalent feminist view. Third, I raise four related feminist concerns that will, I hope, advance the discussion beyond this simple acknowledgment.

My discussion of autonomy has limited scope. Although feminists have raised a number of objections to mainstream conceptions of autonomy, I deal only with the charge that mainstream accounts do not take account of social relationships. Whether mainstream autonomy can survive the other charges against it is a topic for another occasion. It is also worth noting that the "mainstream" philosophical discussions of autonomy to which I refer belong to what is now loosely called the analytic tradition and are often explicitly linked to defenses of liberalism.

A preliminary word about terminology would be helpful. Autonomy means self-government or self-determination. The notion of autonomy can be applied to states or to persons. In regard to states, autonomy is usually called sovereignty, the supremacy of a state's rule within its own territory. In regard to persons, philosophers usually distinguish among political autonomy, moral autonomy, and personal autonomy. Briefly, the notion of *political* autonomy covers popular sovereignty, that is, government by the people, usually embodied in such political rights as voting; and also civil rights, which secure a domain of individual freedom against undue government action. The notion of *moral* autonomy is that of an individual acting according to moral principles, values, and rules that are, in some significant sense, her own. And *personal* autonomy is often defined as individual self-determination over those aspects of our lives in which we are not bound by moral requirements and may choose among a variety of morally permissible alternatives.

At the most general level, these various notions converge around the idea of self-determination, of choosing, acting, and living according to what is, in some important sense, of one's self. For the most part, I will concentrate on personal autonomy with occasional references to moral and political autonomy.

1. The Feminist Critique

Feminist philosophers have criticized mainstream conceptions of autonomy on at least four different grounds. First, those conceptions ignore the social nature of the self and the importance of social relationships to the projects and attributes of the self. Mainstream autonomy theories assume that we should each be as independent and self-sufficient as possible. This ideal, however, ignores the great importance of interpersonal relationships in sustaining everyone's life. It also promotes interpersonal distancing and adversariness by leading persons to regard one another as threats (Keller 1985; Benhabib 1992; Hoagland 1988; Nedelsky 1989; Code 1991).

A second feminist criticism of mainstream theories of autonomy is that they presume a coherent, unified subject with a stable identity who endures over time and who can "own" its choices. This presumption is challenged by postmodern notions of the subject as an unstable, fragmented, incoherent assortment of positions in discourse (Butler 1990).

Third, mainstream theories of autonomy treat the self as being transparently self-aware, as being able to grasp what it wants and to subject those wants to critical self-reflection. This view is challenged by psychoanalytic theories, which construe the self as having significant dimensions that are opaque to its own conscious self-reflection. The psychoanalytic self harbors repressed desires that are not evident to the self, and is capable of mistaking that which *is* accessible to its self-consciousness (Grimshaw, 1988).

Fourth, mainstream theories of autonomy elevate reason over emotion, desire, and embodiment as the source of autonomy, sometimes construing reason as the self's authentic or true self. Such theories make reason normatively hegemonic in the structure of the self and deprecate the moral role of emotion, desire, and embodiment (Code 1991).

My focus of concern is the first of these criticisms: the charge that mainstream conceptions of autonomy ignore the social nature of the self and the importance of social relationships to the projects and attributes of the self. Mainstream autonomy, according to this criticism, is allied with liberalism, and in particular with liberal abstract individualism. The self of abstract individualism, according to many feminist critics, is atomistic, asocial, ahistorical, emotionally detached, thoroughly and transparently self-conscious, coherent, unified, rational, and universalistic in its reasonings. This liberal grounding leads mainstream conceptions of autonomy to promote such unwelcome traits as atomistic self-definition, denial of the self's own development out of and ongoing dependence on intimate personal ties, a disregard for nonvoluntaristic relational responsibilities, detachment from others, and an impartial, universalistic mode of reasoning that ignores the self's own particularity (Jaggar 1983; Code 1991; Nedelsky 1989).

This charge derives much of its plausibility from the gender-linked manner in which mainstream conceptions of autonomy are often deployed. Popular culture as well as psychological personality studies associate autonomy with men more than with women. Popular gender stereotypes, for example, treat autonomy and independence as male but not female character ideals. By contrast, they emphasize nurturance and relationality as ideals for women. Gender stereotypes thus reinforce an autonomy/relationality split. Psychological research has supported this dichotomy by telling us that men more than women exhibit the strong ego-boundaries and relative independence from others required for autonomy (cf. Gilligan 1982, ch. 1). Since autonomy has also functioned as a general human ideal, the combined effect of popular gender stereotyping and psychological research has been to imply that women are deficient as persons when compared to men.

In the 1970s, feminist psychologists began to challenge these gender biases (Miller 1976). This research contributed importantly to the feminist philosophical critique of autonomy that emerged in the 1980s. The most prominent psychologists who contributed to the latter development are, of course, Nancy Chodorow (1978, 1985) and Carol Gilligan (1982) (cf. Benjamin 1985).

Chodorow argued famously that gendered selfhood as we know it is due to childrearing practices in which the primary caretakers of all children are women. For girls, the sense of self and of being gendered female develop from learning that they are *like* the female caretakers from whom they separate; hence their separation and differentiation are less radical, and their sense of self remains ever more enmeshed in relationality than it does for males. For boys, by contrast, a masculine core gender identity calls for a radical differentiation from the female caretaker. Their achievement of a sense of gendered selfhood is uncertain and insecure, for it is always threatened by the primordial sense of oneness with femaleness. As a result, males are more driven than females throughout their lives to shore up their ego-boundaries through separating and disconnecting from others, and through differentiation, especially from that which is female. Hence men are more likely than women to fear intimate relationships and to see other persons as threats (Chodorow 1985).

Carol Gilligan carried Chodorow's insights into the realm of cognitive moral development. In particular, Gilligan challenged Lawrence Kohlberg's influential theoretical framework for understanding the developmental of moral reasoning. This framework idealized as the highest stage of moral reasoning the autonomous moral reasoner choosing for herself according to a rational moral law that is abstract and universal, beyond mere custom and tradition. When first used to measure the cognitive moral development of real people, this scale showed women scoring on average lower than men and thus ranking as less morally autonomous or cognitively mature than men (Gilligan, 1982, 18).

Gilligan, as is now well known, argued that Kohlberg's framework was biased in favor of male moral values and ignored the different moral concerns that women were more likely to exhibit. Women's alternative moral concerns center on caring for others and maintaining interpersonal relationships. This moral orientation sets its own distinctive developmental path. Whereas men fear intimacy and attachment because it threatens their autonomy, Gilligan argues, "women portray autonomy rather than attachment as the illusory and dangerous quest" (Gilligan 1982, 48).

The impact of this work in feminist psychology has been to suggest that autonomy is a masculine but not a feminine preoccupation and that, for men, it is regrettably associated with individuation, independence, disconnection from others, and a tendency to see other persons and close relationships as threatening to the self. Some feminists philosophers have echoed that sentiment. Sarah Hoagland, for example, writes that individual autonomy seems to be "a thoroughly noxious concept," suggesting separation, independence, self-sufficiency, and isolation. She recommends replacing it with a notion of "self in community," for which she coins the term 'autokoenony', borrowing from Greek roots. The self in community has a sense of herself as a moral agent connected to others who are also self-conscious moral agents in a communal web of relationships that permits the separateness of selves without undermining mutual concern and interaction (Hoagland 1988, 144–147).

Other feminist philosophers, however, have not utterly rejected the concept of autonomy. Instead they construe the individualistic emphasis on independence and emotional detachment from others as merely one way to conceptualize autonomy: It is the traditional, mainstream, or masculine way. These feminists recommend that we develop a new and female, or feminist, conception of autonomy, one that presupposes the relational nature of human beings and emphasizes the social context required for the realization of autonomy. Although these feminists achieved the same conceptual end as Hoagland, they did so without having to introduce a neologism ('autokoenony') that many people cannot remember how to pronounce.

Thus, for example, Evelyn Fox Keller writes that the notion of autonomy admits of a range of possible meanings only one of which is "radical independence from others." Our culture's tendency to "confuse autonomy with separation and independence from others," she adds, "is itself part of what we need to explain." Labeling that view "static" autonomy, Keller offers her alternative conception of "dynamic autonomy," which, she says, acknowledges the human interrelatedness that produces autonomy, recognizes that the self is influenced by and needs others, and allows for a recognition of other selves as subjects in their own right (Keller 1985, 97–99).

Keller does admit that there is probably an unresolvable tension between "autonomy and intimacy, separation and connection, aggression and love." She argues, however, that "tension is not the same as bifurcation" and urges against thinking of autonomy and intimacy as mutually exclusive (Keller 1985, 112–113). Keller's admission is noteworthy. It exemplifies a common tension in feminist writings on autonomy throughout the 1980s. On the one hand, many feminists argue that interpersonal relationships contribute to personal autonomy and, indeed, are necessary for its realization. On the other hand, many of the same feminists also suggest that the value of autonomy should not be emphasized at the expense of the values of interpersonal relationships—as if the two were really mutually exclusive. I will return to this problem in the final section of the chapter.

Jennifer Nedelsky recommends that feminists develop a new conception of autonomy that will "combine the claim of the constitutiveness of social relations with the value of self-determination." She charges that the prevailing conception of autonomy is saturated with liberal atomistic individualism, a perspective that fails to "recognize the inherently social nature of human beings." Autonomous liberal individuals, Nedelsky writes, are "self-made . . . men." We must instead recognize, first, that social relationships and practices are necessary to foster our capacities for self-government, and, second, that the content of the laws that someone takes to be her "own" is "comprehensible only with reference to shared social norms, values, and concepts" (Nedelsky 1989, 7–11).

The contemporary liberal conception of autonomy, according to Nedelsky, is incapable of incorporating the role of the social because it presupposes a "dichotomy between autonomy and the collectivity." On the mainstream account, autonomy is to be achieved "by erecting a wall (of rights) between the individual and those around him. . . . The most perfectly autonomous man is thus the most perfectly isolated." This "pathological conception of autonomy as boundaries against others" has led us to equate personal autonomy with individual security from collective power (Nedelsky 1989, 12–15).

Interestingly, Nedelsky displays the same tension as does Keller when connecting autonomy to social relationships. Nedelsky concedes that "there is a real and enduring tension between the individual and the collective," such that the collective is both a source of and a potential obstacle to autonomy (Nedelsky 1989, 21). More particularly, Nedelsky regards democratic processes as a "necessary component of autonomy," yet autonomy "can be threatened by democratic outcomes." A "democratically organized collective" can "do violence" to its members (Nedelsky 1989, 33–34). Mindful that this concession moves her view closer to the mainstream conception of autonomy, Nedelsky takes pains to differentiate the two. The distinction, she claims, lies in her belief that individuality is inconceivable apart from the social context in which it arises. There is thus "a social component built into the meaning of autonomy" (Nedelsky 1989, 35–36).

Lorraine Code argues against what she calls the "autonomy-obsession" of mainstream philosophy. She defends instead a reconceptualization of autonomy that integrates it with the notions of interdependence and solidarity (Code 1991, 73–74). She writes that the contemporary mainstream conception of "autonomous man" is of a person who is supposed to be

> self-sufficient, independent, and self-reliant, a self-realizing individual who directs his efforts toward maximizing his personal gains. His independence is under constant threat from other (equally self-serving) individuals: hence he devises rules to protect himself from intrusion. Talk of rights, rational self-inter-

est, expediency, and efficiency permeate his moral, social, and political discourse. (Code 1991, 77–78)

Code charges that mainstream autonomy treats "self-making" and "separate self-sufficiency" as key traits, whereas relational and communal values "are frequently represented as intrusions on or threats to autonomy" (Code 1991, 78–79). "Autonomy-oriented theories" posit self-sufficiency and individuality as the *telos* of a human life, treating individuals as separate, alien, threatening, and "other" to each other. Interdependence and cooperation are seen as diminishing autonomy (Code 1991, 80).

Code further proposes that moral theory start from the recognition that persons are "essentially" what Annette Baier has called "second persons." They begin in interrelationship with and dependence on other persons from whom they "acquire the essential arts of personhood," and with whom they remain in relationships of interdependence and "reciprocal influence" throughout their lives. Writes Code: "Autonomy and self-sufficiency define themselves against a background of second personhood (Code 1991, 82–85; cf. Baier 1985, 84).

It is noteworthy that Code does not simply want to substitute a care-obsession for an autonomy-obsession; she writes that an ideal of care and connectedness has as much potential to oppress women as do autonomy-centered theories (Code 1991, 87–94). She even suggests that "autonomy-promoting values" might, in some situations, be worthier guides to practical deliberation than "traditionally female" values such as trust, kindness, responsiveness, and care (Code 1991, 108). This caution reiterates the tension in feminist thinking about autonomy that I noted in my discussion of Keller and Nedelsky, and to which I will return shortly—namely, a tension between thinking that personal relationships are necessary to the realization of autonomy, on the one hand, and thinking that they can be definite hindrances to its realization, on the other.

Seyla Benhabib censures the social contract tradition for presupposing a "disembedded and disembodied" self. The backdrop of this tradition's conception of the self is the metaphor of the state of nature, a metaphor whose profound message is that "in the beginning man was alone" (Benhabib 1992, 155–157). Benhabib cites Hobbes's recommendation that we consider men as "mushrooms, come to full maturity, without all kind of engagement to each other" (Hobbes 1962/1651, 109).

Benhabib finds this tradition of thought alive and well in John Rawls's assumption, conveyed in *A Theory of Justice*, that when establishing the social contract, individuals are to be considered mutually disinterested. In other words, they should be thought of as indifferent to each other's interests, and (to quote Rawls) as "not bound by prior moral ties to each other" (Rawls 1971, 128).[1] For Hobbes, of course, peace and social cooperation are to be found *only* according to the terms of the social contract that establishes a "common power" to keep all persons subdued. Apart from that condition, human beings are relentless mortal threats to each other and human life is not merely "poor, nasty, brutish, and short;" it is also "solitary" (Hobbes 1962/1651, 100). "The vision of men as mushrooms," writes Benhabib, "is an ultimate picture of autonomy" (Benhabib 1992, 155).

The Hobbesian social contract, Benhabib reminds us, is to be established voluntarily in light of its eminent rationality—but only by men, in whom alone reason, volition, and autonomy coalesce. Women do not engage in early modern political contracting; instead, they are invisible in the domestic realm where, among other things, they nurture the men who sally forth into the public world, some of them privileged to conduct the business of governing themselves (and everyone else). In Benhabib's view, the dichotomy between autonomy, independence, and the male governmental sphere, on the one hand, and nurturance, bonding, and the female domestic sphere, on the other, is a legacy of early modern social contractarianism that still pervades contemporary moral and political theory (Benhabib 1992, 157).

Thus, the predominant tendency for feminist philosophers writing about autonomy in the 1980s and early 1990s was both to criticize mainstream theorists of autonomy for their male-oriented neglect of interpersonal relationships and to propose the development of an alternative, relational conception.

2. The Convergence of Feminist and Mainstream Conceptions of Autonomy

Mainstream conceptions of autonomy by leading contemporary philosophers tend to display a common core notion of autonomy. They tend to regard autonomy as involving two main features: first, reflection of some sort on relevant aspect(s) of the self's own motivational structure and available choices; and, second, procedural requirements having to do with the nature and quality of that reflection (for example, it is usually required to be sufficiently rational as well as uncoerced and unmanipulated).

Mainstream discussions devote considerable attention to the conditions that hinder or obstruct autonomy. Anxieties about paternalism, governmental decrees, indoctrination, brainwashing, and a host of other social horrors crop up with surprising frequency. Feminist critiques of such literature are no doubt partly a reaction to this obsession. Nevertheless, some prominent contemporary mainstream autonomy theorists do explicitly acknowledge the importance of the social to the realization of autonomy, and have done so for some time.[2] Mainstream philosophical theorizing about autonomy is not a monolithic enterprise.

Gerald Dworkin, for example, suggests that there is a variety of traditional notions of autonomy. He himself calls explicitly for a conception of autonomy that can be endorsed from nonindividualistic perspectives (Dworkin 1988, 8). Dworkin notes that autonomy would be impossible if defined as an overly stringent sort of self-determination. The concept of autonomy should be compatible with the slow social development and maturation that human beings undergo, a development permitting the heavy influence of "parents, peers, and culture." Also, autonomy should encompass the making of reasonable choices. To make a reasonable choice, argues Dworkin, one must be governed by standards of reasoning that one could not have chosen but has probably acquired from the teachings or examples of other persons (Dworkin 1988, 12).

Dworkin is especially concerned with developing an account of autonomy that is compatible with other values that we cherish, particularly such values as "loyalty, . . . commitment, benevolence, and love." He tries to accomplish this compatibility by placing no constraints on the *content* of what someone can autonomously choose to be or do. In Dworkin's terms, autonomy does not require that people's choices be *substantively independent*; they need only be *procedurally independent.* That is, they must be arrived at in a way that is free of coercion and manipulation. On Dworkin's view, one can autonomously choose to act in a substantively independent manner (e.g., selfishly), or one can choose to act in a substantively dependent manner (e.g., benevolently), accepting "the needs of others as being reasons for altering [one's] own plans and projects" (Dworkin 1988, 21–23). Either sort of choice can be autonomous, provided that it is uncoerced and unmanipulated and that the agent is able to consider whether or not to identify with the reasons for the choice (Dworkin 1988, 15).

Most important for our purposes, Dworkin's conception of autonomy does not require disconnection from other persons. He claims that "[t]o be committed to a friend or cause is to accept the fact that one's actions, and even desires, are to some extent determined by the desires and needs of others. . . . To be devoted to a cause is to be governed by what needs to be done, or by what the group decides. It is no longer to be self-sufficient" (Dworkin 1988, 23). In addition, Dworkin notes that "[t]he self-sufficient, independent, person relying on his own resources and intellect is a familiar hero presented in novels by Ayn Rand and westerns by John Ford." Yet he makes it clear that he is not defending this notion of substantive independence. In Dworkin's view, autonomy is about giving meaning to one's life, something that one can do "in all kinds of ways: from stamp collecting to taking care of one's invalid parents" (Dworkin 1988, 30–31).

Dworkin further argues that moral autonomy in particular, contrary to the Kantian tradition lying behind this notion, could not be about creating or inventing our own moral principles. Such creation, argues Dworkin, is impossible; to think otherwise "denies our *history*" [original emphasis] and the profound influence on us of our families and other social groupings and institutions in which we participate. "It makes no more sense," he urges, "to suppose we invent the moral law for ourselves than to suppose that we invent the language we speak for ourselves." Moral principles have a "social character:" The nature of our duties to others and the precise others to which these duties are owed "are to some extent relative to the understandings of a given society" (Dworkin 1988, 36).

Thomas E. Hill, Jr., defends a modified Kantian account of moral autonomy that, he claims, "does not imply that self-sufficiency is better than dependence, or that the emotional detachment of a judge is better than the compassion of a lover." To respect someone's autonomy, argues Hill, is to grant her the right to make important decisions about her life without being controlled or manipulated by others. We can grant this right, Hill urges, without endorsing such goals as "self-sufficiency, independence, [or] separation from others." One can respect personal autonomy, on Hill's view, and still accept advice from others, sacrifice for their interests, and acknowledge one's dependence on them. Although Hill does note that "self-sufficiency, independence, [and] 'making it on one's own'" have been associated with autonomy, his argument is that these goals are not obviously morally desirable and, so, are no part of an ideal of autonomy (Hill 1991, 49–50).

Lawrence Haworth similarly stresses procedural but not substantive independence as part of his notion of autonomy. No "logical or conceptual conflict" prevents someone from aspiring to be both autonomous and communally related to other persons. A group of people might well "independently" decide on a life of deeply shared "goals, values, principles, and tastes." Haworth notes that too much procedural independence by its members might be disruptive to a community; but rather than giving up on either autonomy or community, he calls for social institutions that integrate the two, urging that "in principle the most extensive autonomy is achievable within the most intensive community" (Haworth 1986, 201–202).

Joel Feinberg's recent writings about autonomy seem at first glance to express the excessive individualism that many feminists see in the mainstream conception of autonomy. For example, the virtues that Feinberg associates with autonomy include self-possession, distinct self-identity, self-creation, self-legislation, moral independence, self-control, and self-reliance (Feinberg 1989, 31–43). In explicating these notions, however, Feinberg asserts clearly that no one can *literally* be a "self-made man," and that the habit for self-reflection must be "implanted" in a child by others if she is to play any part in directing the course of her own life (Feinberg 1989, 33).

For Feinberg, the "most significant truth about ourselves" is that "we are social animals." As he puts it, none of us select our early upbringing, country, language, community, or traditions, "yet to *be* a human being is to be a part of a community, to speak a language, to take one's place in an already functioning group way of life. We come into awareness of ourselves as part of ongoing social processes." Feinberg refers to these claims as "truisms" that "place *limits* on what the constituent virtues of autonomy can be." The literal atomistic separation of independent "sovereign" selves is impossible. Liberal autonomy, Feinberg contends, is the ideal of "an authentic individual whose self-determination is as complete as is consistent with the requirement that he is, of course, a member of a community" (Feinberg 1989, 45).

In a 1982 essay, S. I. Benn tries to modify classical liberalism so as to accommodate communitarian conceptions of the social nature of human beings and the "moral claims of 'community'." Benn makes it clear that he wants to retain "the core liberal values of individuality and autonomy" (Benn 1982, 43–44). In particular, he argues that although classical liberal individualism took little account of people's concerns for one another or of the collective enterprises in which they engage, nevertheless liberal theories can be extended to cover those practices without distorting core liberal values.

Autonomy does not, on Benn's view, preclude participation in collaborative enterprises. Indeed, individual autonomy requires the "conceptual resources" of *traditions* of rationality, inasmuch as such traditions enable a person to accomplish the sort of reasoning about rules that Benn sees as the nature of autonomous choice. Those conceptual resources are made available to an individual "by the particular cluster of sub-cultures that combined to make" her the person she is (Benn 1982, 50).

Benn does not believe that every sort of communal relationship is compatible with autonomy. Communities that demand unconditional commitment to their standards and that withdraw their concern from those persons who show "independence of judgment" actually hinder the realization of autonomy. By contrast, argues Benn, relationships of "mutuality" require autonomy of their participants. Each partner of a mutuality actively participates in creating and developing the relationship. Mutual concern for the other partners is an "ineliminable element of the mutuality enterprise." Friendships, marriages, and "sometimes families" constitute what Benn regards as the locus for mutualities. Granted, Benn thinks that mutualities are limited to small numbers of people in intimate relationships, since the partners have to know a great deal about each other and be able to monitor the relationship rather continuously (Benn 1982, 57–61). Nevertheless, Benn recognizes that autonomy is compatible with social relationships and, to some extent, requires them.

Benn makes the same acknowledgment in a 1976 paper on autonomy, even though he was not then trying to reconcile liberal individualism with communitarian critiques. In that earlier paper, Benn mentions the role relationships of father and friend as two examples of activities in the course of which agents could achieve autonomy. They would do so by identifying with the roles in question and monitoring their performance and achievements according to relevant standards (Benn 1976, 125–126). Benn also admits that the autonomous person is just as socialized as a heteronomous person, just as influenced by her society's conceptual framework for understanding the world, its traditions, and its role demands. The autonomous person, furthermore, is social in needing to derive, from the people around her, criteria for rational choice and conceptual schemes for grasping relevant issues. The notion of an autonomous person, he urges, must be made clear *within* the "conception of a socialized individual" (Benn 1976, 126).

For Benn in 1976, autonomy is a matter of "criticism internal to a tradition." More specifically, it is "an ideal available only to a plural tradition" in which there are alternative critical standpoints that can be adopted by each person for reflecting on the principles and values that she has internalized (Benn 1976, 128). Like Dworkin and Feinberg after him, Benn denies that autonomy depends on substantive independence. Pointedly noting that his account omits discussion about the content of the autonomous person's "principles and ideals," he states that he finds no reason why an autonomous person "should not be deeply concerned about social justice and community" (Benn 1976, 129–130).

In a 1973 essay, R. S. Peters explores the means by which institutions and practices of formal education can foster the development of autonomy. Along the way, he touches on the importance of relationships in home environments. In Peters's view, socialization is crucial to the development of the capacity to be a chooser, which he considers to lie at the core of autonomy. The best home environment for encouraging this capacity, recommends Peters, is one in which "there is a warm attitude of acceptance towards children, together with a firm and consistent insistence on rules of behaviour without much in the way of punishment" (Peters 1973, 129–130).

For Peters, autonomy requires authenticity, which he explicates in terms of an individual's tendency to be moved by considerations "intrinsic" to a mode of conduct rather than by extrinsic considerations such as reward and punishment; his example of an intrinsic consideration is "the sufferings of others." The school environment can contribute to the development of autonomy by providing "a general atmosphere of discussion" about rules and the reasons for them, and *not* by "an authoritarian system of control in which anything of importance is decided by the fiat of the headmaster" (Peters 1973, 134–135).

3. Advancing the Discussion

As shown in the previous section, mainstream philosophical work on autonomy has, for some time now, included prominent theorists who acknowledge the contribution that social relationships make to the realization of autonomy. Feminist philosophy and mainstream philosophy have thus been converging around this theme.[3] This is not to say, however, that feminist critiques of mainstream conceptions of autonomy are now obsolete. A number of still-relevant feminist concerns can be raised both about how philosophy contributes to a culture-wide understanding of autonomy and about the exact details of relational conceptions of autonomy. In the remainder of this chapter, I will present four such concerns.[4]

First, although *some* leading mainstream philosophers acknowledge that social relationships contribute to the realization of autonomy, it is not clear that *all* mainstream philosophers do so. In addition, philosophical understanding of autonomy seems to differ from that of mainstream *popular* culture. Indeed, the feminist critique of autonomy seems much more appropriate for the male images and role models in popular culture than for the theories of philosopher-scholars laboring over intricate explications of authenticity and procedural independence.

Popular culture has long lionized the self-made man, the ruthlessly aggressive entrepreneur who climbs over the backs of his competitors to become a "captain of industry"; the rugged individualist, the loner, the "Marlboro man" fighting cattle-rustlers out on the open range; or the he-man, the muscle-bound "superhero" avenging his way to vigilante "justice." All of these male role models are independent, self-reliant, aggressive, and overpowering. Often they defy established authorities and institutions to accomplish their goals. Usually they have no dependents or family responsibilities, but when they do, those relationships either support their aggressive efforts or become merely additional obstacles to be overcome. These male role models are always heroes or protagonists struggling against the forces set against them, whether business competitors, mob bosses, cattle ranchers, escaped criminals, or the women who want to marry them and settle down. What we see here, then, is a cultural glorification of men (but not of women) who are independent, defiant individuals. At a minimum, feminists are critical of the cultural glorification of these male role models.

If the feminist critique of autonomy is really a critique of those images of Marlboro men in culture at large, then how is it relevant to academic philosophy? One possibility is that mainstream philosophical theories of autonomy are unwittingly supporting popular masculine ideals. Perhaps the philosophical notion of autonomy actually serves to bolster the popular masculine ideal of the aggressive, independent, wholly "self-made" man.

The suggestion that philosophers have a significant impact on popular culture is, admittedly, far-fetched. Few works of serious philosophical scholarship become popular best-sellers. Nevertheless, it does seem reasonable to ask philosophers to articulate our theories in ways that ensure that, should we be read by a wider audience, our words will not be misunderstood as supporting questionable values and ideals. Feinberg, for example, warns against a literal interpretation of the common expression "self-made man" and carefully reconstrues it as entailing *extensive* participation in shaping oneself (Feinberg 1989, 33). Would an unwary audience, however, remember his careful reconstruction? In one refreshing passage, Feinberg juxtaposes the notion of someone being "her own woman" alongside the more familiar "his own man" (Feinberg 1989, 31). Yet masculine nouns and pronouns predominate throughout his discussion. "Her own woman" is eclipsed by this outmoded pronominal style.

It is important to note, however, that these concerns do not indict mainstream conceptions of autonomy for their internal particulars. Marlboro men are not necessarily autonomous according to the substantively neutral conceptions of most mainstream philosophers. Indeed, mainstream philosophical autonomy requires that men choose and live in accordance with relevant self-reflections about their motivations and values, not merely in accordance with conventional ideals of masculinity. Thus, men who each thoughtlessly strive to be independent and aggressive just for the sake of being what society considers a "real man" are not acting autonomously at all. The really autonomous man, on a *careful* reading of mainstream philosophy, is more likely to be the one at home changing his baby's diapers than the one riding off into the sunset on his Harley.

A second concern raised by the feminist critique has precisely to do with this substantive neutrality of mainstream accounts of autonomy. Many mainstream accounts of autonomy do not specify the substantive choices that someone must make in order to be autonomous (Benn 1976, 129–130; Dworkin 1988, 23–30; Feinberg 1989, 38–39). On this view, autonomy can be realized through voluntary commitments to, say, authoritarian religious orders, and through fulfillment of nonvoluntary moral role duties such as caring for one's aged parents. A substantively neutral conception of personal autonomy requires only that a self be capable of the right sort of self-reflection and sufficiently determinate so as to find within herself reference points for directing such self-reflection.[5]

A substantively neutral conception of autonomy, by itself, does not rank available alternative choices, nor does it rank the widely varied types of selves we might each become. In particular, it does not provide a critique of substantively *independent* behavior, such as isolation, narcissistic self-absorption, and indifference to the needs and desires of those to whom one is closely related. The substantively neutral concept of autonomy provides no basis for a *general analysis or critique* of such substantive independence. It neither condones nor condemns such behavior.

Many feminists are not neutral, however, about substantive independence. As Diana Meyers has carefully documented (Meyers 1989, 141–171), males in our culture, compared to females, are socialized for greater degrees of independence, aggressive self-assertion, emotional distancing from others, and the like. Thus, when men engage in self-reflection about what they "really" want, they will find, lo and behold, that they *really do want* to be independent, aggressively self-assertive, and emotionally distant from others. These attitudes, in turn, might well foster male tendencies toward evading the responsibilities of close personal relationships and exhibiting aggressive and violent self-assertion, including sexual aggression, against others.

If autonomy is indeed best conceptualized as substantively neutral, then a critique of substantively independent behavior will have to be based on something other than the ideal of autonomy. We cannot fault autonomy theories for failing to do what lies beyond their proper scope. Nevertheless, feminists may well worry that by approving procedural independence and neglecting to criticize substantive independence, mainstream autonomy theories might seem to be endorsing independence in general, thereby distracting us from the task of exploring what is wrong with overly individualistic, substantively independent behavior.

Thus, one concern implicit in the feminist critique of mainstream conceptions of autonomy is that it is the wrong ideal to emphasize for our culture. Before encouraging people simply to be more fully and coherently what they already are, we should first *think* about what it is that they already are. At this historical juncture, rather than promoting autonomy, we might be better off urging that some of us *change* what we "really" are—specifically, so as to avoid the patterns of socialization that lead males to focus obsessively on asserting themselves apart from or against others.

Notice that, like the first concern raised earlier, this line of thought is not an internal criticism of mainstream conceptions of autonomy. Rather, the argument is that substantively neutral ideals of autonomy should be *subordinated* to cultural critiques of the substantively independent selves that males are socialized and pressured to be. Mainstream (substantively neutral) autonomy is not about the *radical* reconstruction of selves. It is, more modestly, about the nonradical ownership or reconstruction of aspects of the self. Feminists who discuss autonomy are concerned instead with the need for a more thoroughgoing reconstruction of our gendered selves. A substantively neutral conception of autonomy is not useful for this task and might even tend to distract us from it.

As an aside, I myself am skeptical about the prospects of developing a feminist critique of overly individualistic, substantively independent selves or behavior as such. It is important to distinguish between individualistic behaviors and traits that *harm* other persons from those that do not. A father who abandons his dependent family for the sake of personal gratification exhibits the sort of disconnection that is morally culpable because he has harmed those who rely on him and toward whom he has special responsibilities. In general, to focus only on one's own needs and interests while ignoring our legitimate responsibilities to others, arising out of the relationships in which we find ourselves embedded and on which those others depend, is to exhibit an excessive individualism that is morally culpable.

Consider, by contrast, a person who currently lacks any special responsibilities of care, support, or companionship toward anyone else. There seems nothing morally wrong with the decision of such a person to, say, spend long periods of solitude living in the backwoods. Of course, this person may harbor delusions about just how self-reliant he really is. He might, for example, not recognize how indebted he is to those who taught him how to feed and shelter himself and otherwise survive off the land. But apart from this minor conceit, there does not seem to be anything wrong with living such an excessively individualistic life.

Thus, individualistic behaviors or styles of living do not seem intrinsically wrong. When they are wrong, I maintain, they are so in virtue of ignoring the special responsibilities we all have to care for and not harm other persons. Our culture, however, more readily tolerates or forgives men who abandon their dependents than it does women, in part precisely because individualism and substantive independence are prized in men but not in women. A critique of this cultural double standard around substantive independence is long overdue. The problem, then, is not substantive independence as such but, rather, the culture-wide glorification of *irresponsible* substantive independence on the part of men alone, to the misfortune of those who are harmed by it.

A third issue that emerges from feminist discussions of autonomy is the feminist ambivalence noted earlier between thinking that autonomy should sometimes *give way* to relational values and thinking that autonomy *is itself* relational. One of the ideas underlying the feminist call for a relational conception of autonomy is the now familiar social conception of the self. Feminists tend to share with communitarians the view that selves are inherently social. On this view, even the most independent, self-reliant, and emotionally self-contained among us are nevertheless social beings who are connected to and dependent on a great many others for material and emotional support, for the development of our capacities, for the sources of meaning in our lives, and for our very identities. This perspective on the self leads easily to the view that autonomy should also be conceptualized relationally.

At the same time, a little reflection on everyday life reveals that autonomy *sometimes* results in the *severing* of relational ties—that it does sometimes disconnect us from others, including those who are closely related to us. Adolescents often find, for example, that giving up the religious or moral views learned from their parents will lead to a deep rift in their family lives. Many people are ostracized by their peers for questioning the norms and conventions that other group members hold dear.

Can we reconcile the idea that autonomy is relational with the idea that it can also *conflict* with the maintenance and values of relationships? I think that we can. Doing so, however, will require us to give up the *unqualified* assumption that social relationships are necessary to the realization of autonomy. The conclusion has to be that relationships of certain sorts are necessary for the realization of autonomy, whereas relationships of certain other sorts can be irrelevant or positively detrimental to it. The connection between autonomy and the "social," in other words, is manifold and diverse.

Social relationships are, after all, a highly varied lot. This point should come as no surprise. Social relationships can either promote or hinder the development of autonomy competency (e.g., through the right or wrong kinds of socialization), and they can either permit or obstruct its exercise (e.g., by enlarging or constricting the range of someone's choices).[6] Not only might relationships differ from each other in their contributions to personal autonomy, but any one relationship might vary over time in terms of the bearing it has on the personal autonomy of its participants. One relationship might, furthermore, foster the personal autonomy of only *some* of its participants while at the same time hindering the personal autonomy of other participants. In relationships of domination, for example, someone asserts his or her will and someone else is subordinated to it.

In light of the variety of relationships, practices, and traditions that characterize the social sphere, it is implausible to specify one uniform sort of connection between that sphere and autonomy. Specifically, we need an account that explores how social relationships both promote and hinder the realization of autonomy. Representing these two sorts of effects with roughly accurate proportionality is, however, a formidable project. Matters of degree are notoriously difficult to resolve philosophically.

One distinctive feminist contribution to the positive side of the ledger is see how relationality contributes to autonomy in social roles that have fallen predominantly to women. As shown in Section 2 of this chapter, mainstream autonomy theorists consider roles such as those of parent and teacher to be mainly conditions of socialization that can promote or hinder the autonomy of others—children, in particular. This one-sided appraisal fails to consider how such caregiving practices affect caregivers themselves.

Feminists, by contrast, have explored the resources available to caregivers, especially female caregivers, for realizing their own autonomy. Sarah Hoagland (1982), for example, has identified subtle and covert practices of resistance to male-domination that women have exhibited as caregivers. Sara Ruddick (1989) has investigated the ideals that constitute mothering practices and the forms of thinking that are rooted in those practices. By ignoring the possibilities for women's own autonomy within their traditional relationships, mainstream autonomy theorists, who are overwhelmingly male, have unbalanced their accounts considerably.

A fourth concern raised by feminist calls for a relational account of autonomy has to do with the theoretical nature of the connection between autonomy and social relationships. As I have emphasized, mainstream autonomy theorists acknowledge that social relationships are necessary to the realization of autonomy. Marina Oshana has charged, however, that mainstream conceptions of autonomy treat social relationships merely as causal conditions that are required for autonomy but not as part of what autonomy specifically *is* (Oshana 1995, 31). Mainstream theorists admit that people must be socialized for self-reflection and the other capacities required for the achievement of autonomy (could anyone really doubt this?), but mainstream theories do not generally define autonomy as *intrinsically* social.

Are social relationships merely causal conditions that are necessary to bring autonomy about but are external to autonomy proper, rather like sunshine causing plants to grow? Or are they somehow partly "constitutive" of autonomy? Put differently, is autonomy merely the (nonsocial) result of certain other social conditions, or is it inherently social in its very nature? In Nedelsky's view, as noted earlier, there is "a social component built into the *meaning* of autonomy" (Nedelsky 1989, 36; emphasis added). This unresolved point, I suggest, is a major philosophical concern that continues to divide feminists who advocate a relational account of autonomy from mainstream theorists who acknowledge that social relationships contribute to autonomy.

The same point raises a number of questions. If autonomy is indeed intrinsically social, is this so simply because human selves and self-identity are intrinsically social? Or is autonomy *per se*, as a trait or competency of human selves, intrinsically social? In other words, is the inherent relationality of autonomy fully explained by the social nature of the selves who realize it, or is autonomy, apart from the social nature of the persons who realize it, also a social trait or process? For that matter, what could it *mean* to say that autonomy *per se* is intrinsically or constitutively social?

Charles Taylor argues that autonomy requires a certain kind of self-understanding that one cannot sustain on one's own but must always define partly in conversation with interlocutors or through the shared meanings that underlie certain sorts of cultural practices (Taylor 1985). In Jürgen Habermas's view, self-interpretation is the performative dialogical assertion and reason-based justification of one's identity to a potentially unlimited audience (Habermas 1992). Joel Anderson conceptualizes personal autonomy as the capacity to give an account to others of those commitments "that are essential to one's identity" (Anderson 1995, 23). Marina Oshana regards autonomy in part as a function of social states of affairs that are independent of someone's psychological properties—for example, security against reprisals for unconventional goals or values (Oshana 1995, 27).

Relational, or constitutively social, accounts of autonomy such as these, I believe, set the stage for the next round of feminist explorations of autonomy. A crucial goal of that study will be to determine, as queried earlier, what it could mean to say that autonomy is intrinsically or constitutively social. Another crucial goal will be to determine whether *feminism* really needs to regard autonomy as intrinsically or constitutively social. Perhaps it is enough for feminist purposes simply to recognize how relationships constitute personal identity and socialize individuals for autonomy competency. These, at any rate, are questions for another occasion.

To conclude: I have argued that mainstream philosophers of autonomy are not guilty of the feminist charge that they simply ignore social relationships in their accounts of autonomy. Indeed, they explicitly acknowledge the role of social relationships. There are, however, other concerns that feminists can raise about mainstream accounts. First, culture at large treats autonomy asocially, and mainstream philosophers might be unwittingly contributing to this culture-wide perspective. Second, the "substantive neutrality" of contemporary mainstream autonomy is itself a problem, since it fails to provide radical critiques of gendered personalities and might reinforce those personalities by distracting us from the need for such critiques. Third, social relationships both promote and hinder autonomy, and mainstream accounts have not provided an adequate account of this balance—in part because they have neglected the possibilities for autonomy available in women's traditional relational practices. And, fourth, mainstream accounts of autonomy are not *sufficiently* relational because they tend to regard social relationships merely as causal conditions promoting autonomy but do not construe autonomy as inherently social.

Notes

1. More recently, Rawls has stated his view in a different way: Those who choose principles of justice behind the veil of ignorance are indeed to regard themselves as persons who have what Rawls terms 'nonpolitical' moral commitments, including commitments and attachments to other persons. While choosing principles of justice, however, people are not to *appeal* to their nonpolitical moral commitments, since those commitments might reflect social or historical advantages that could bias their choice of principles of justice in favor of their particular social location (Rawls 1993, 22–35).

2. Some mainstream philosophers deny that the traditional notion of autonomy, even in its rigorous Kantian formulation, ever really excluded or ignored the importance of interpersonal relationships (Schneewind 1986; T. E. Hill 1991).

3. I am grateful to Claudia Card for suggesting this notion of convergence.

4. Recent feminist work concerning a relational or intersubjective conception of autonomy, in addition to the sources cited earlier, includes Meyers (1989), Meehan (1994), Christman (1995), and Huntington (1995). Recent work that is not specifically feminist (though also not antifeminist) includes Oshana (1995) and Anderson (1995). The four concerns that I present in this section are partly drawn from these sources.

5. For an argument that substantively neutral accounts of autonomy are inadequate, see Oshana (1995, 11–22). Note that Dworkin (1988, 29) does admit to believ-

ing that there are *contingent* connections between autonomy and the sort of substantive independence that involves a reluctance to accept authority, tradition, and custom uncritically. (I am grateful to Joel Anderson for bringing this point to my attention.)

6. On autonomy competency, the definitive work is Meyers (1989).

References

Anderson, Joel. 1995. Approaching personal autonomy intersubjectively: The particularity of identity, the possibility of error, and the capacity for giving an account. Unpublished manuscript.

Arnault, Lynn. 1989. The radical future of a classic moral theory. In *Gender/Body/Knowledge: Feminist Reconstructions of Being and Knowing*, ed. Alison M. Jaggar and Susan R. Bordo. New Brunswick: Rutgers University Press.

Baier, Annette. 1985. *Postures of the Mind: Essays on Mind and Morals*. Minneapolis: University of Minnesota Press.

Benhabib, Seyla. 1992. *Situating the Self: Gender, Community and Postmodernism in Contemporary Ethics*. New York: Routledge.

Benjamin, Jessica. 1985. The bonds of love: Rational violence and erotic domination. In *The Future of Difference*, ed. Hester Eisenstein and Alice Jardine. New Brunswick: Rutgers University Press.

Benn, S. I. 1976. Freedom, autonomy and the concept of a person. *Proceedings of the Aristotelian Society* 76 (January 12): 109–130.

_____. 1982. Individuality, autonomy and community. In *Community as a Social Ideal*, ed. Eugene Kamenka. New York: St. Martin's Press.

Butler, Judith. 1990. *Gender Trouble: Feminism and the Subversion of Identity*. New York: Routledge.

Chodorow, Nancy. 1978. *The Reproduction of Mothering*. Berkeley: University of California Press.

_____. 1985. Gender, relation, and difference in psychoanalytic perspective. In *The Future of Difference*, ed. Hester Eisenstein and Alice Jardine. New Brunswick: Rutgers University Press.

Christman, John. 1995. Feminism and autonomy. In *Nagging Questions: Feminist Ethics in Everyday Life*, ed. Dana Bushnell. Lanham, Md.: Rowman & Littlefield.

Christman, John, ed. 1989. *The Inner Citadel: Essays on Individual Autonomy*. New York: Oxford University Press.

Code, Lorraine. 1991. *What Can She Know? Feminist Theory and the Construction of Knowledge*. Ithaca: Cornell University Press.

Dworkin, Gerald. 1988. *The Theory and Practice of Autonomy*. Cambridge: Cambridge University Press.

Feinberg, Joel. 1989. Autonomy. In *The Inner Citadel: Essays on Individual Autonomy*, ed. John Christman. New York: Oxford University Press. [Reprinted from Joel Feinberg, *Harm to Self*. New York: Oxford University Press, 1986.]

Gilligan, Carol. 1982. *In a Different Voice: Psychological Theory and Women's Development*. Cambridge: Harvard University Press.

Govier, Trudy. 1993. Self-trust, autonomy, and self-esteem. *Hypatia* 8/1 (Winter): 99–120.

Grimshaw, Jean. 1988. Autonomy and identity in feminist thinking. In *Feminist Perspectives in Philosophy*, ed. Morwenna Griffiths and Margaret Whitford. Bloomington: Indiana University Press.

Habermas, Jürgen. 1992. Individuation through socialization: On George Herbert Mead's theory of subjectivity. In *Postmetaphysical Thinking: Philosophical Essays*, trans. William Mark Hohengarten. Cambridge, Mass.: MIT Press.

Haworth, Lawrence. 1986. *Autonomy: An Essay in Philosophical Psychology and Ethics*. New Haven: Yale University Press.

Hill, Sharon Bishop. 1975. Self-determination and autonomy. In *Today's Moral Problems*, ed. Richard Wasserstrom. New York: Macmillan, 1975.

Hill, Thomas E., Jr. 1991. The importance of autonomy. In *Autonomy and Self-Respect*. Cambridge: Cambridge University Press, 1991. [Reprinted from *Women and Moral Theory*, ed. Eva Feder Kittay and Diana T. Meyers. Totowa, N.J.: Rowman & Littlefield, 1987.]

Hoagland, Sarah. 1982. "Femininity," resistance and sabotage. In *"Femininity," "Masculinity," and "Androgyny,"* ed. Mary Vetterling-Braggin. Totowa, N.J.: Littlefield, Adams & Company.

———. 1988. *Lesbian Ethics: Toward New Value*. Palo Alto: Institute for Lesbian Studies.

Hobbes, Thomas. 1962/1651. *Leviathan*, ed. Michael Oakeshott. New York: Collier Macmillan.

———. 1966/1651. Philosophical rudiments concerning government and society. In *The English Works of Thomas Hobbes*, ed. W. Molesworth. Wissenschaftliche Buchgesellschaft, Darmstadt.

Huntington, Patricia. 1995. Toward a dialectical concept of autonomy. *Philosophy & Social Criticism* 21/1: 37–55.

Jaggar, Alison M. 1983. *Feminist Politics and Human Nature*. Totowa, N.J.: Rowman & Allanheld.

Keller, Evelyn Fox. 1985. *Reflections on Gender and Science*. New Haven: Yale University Press.

Meehan, Johanna. 1994. Autonomy, recognition and respect: Habermas, Benjamin and Honneth. *Constellations* 1/2: 270–285.

Meyers, Diana T. 1989. *Self, Society, and Personal Choice*. New York: Columbia University Press.

Miller, Jean Baker. 1976. *Toward a New Psychology of Women*. Boston: Beacon Press.

Nedelsky, Jennifer. 1989. Reconceiving autonomy: Sources, thoughts and possibilities. *Yale Journal of Law and Feminism* 1/1 (Spring 1989): 7–36.

Oshana, Marina. 1995. Personal autonomy and society. Unpublished manuscript.

Peters, R. S. 1973. Freedom and the development of the free man. In *Educational Judgments: Papers in the Philosophy of Education*, ed. James F. Doyle. London: Routledge & Kegan Paul.

Rawls, John. 1971. *A Theory of Justice*. Cambridge: Harvard University Press.

———. 1993. *Political liberalism*. New York: Columbia.

Ruddick, Sara. 1989. *Maternal Thinking: Toward a Politics of Peace*. New York: Ballantine Books.

Schneewind, J. B. 1986. The use of autonomy in ethical theory. In *Reconstructing Individualism: Autonomy, Individuality, and the Self in Western Theory*, ed. Thomas C. Heller, Morton Sosna, and David E. Wellbery. Stanford: Stanford University Press.

Taylor, Charles. 1985. Atomism. In *Philosophy and the Human Sciences: Philosophical Papers 2*. Cambridge: Cambridge University Press. [Reprinted from *Powers, Possessions and Freedoms*, ed. Alkis Kontos. Toronto: University of Toronto Press, 1979.]

three

Picking Up Pieces
Lives, Stories, and Integrity

MARGARET URBAN WALKER

> I could not understand 'I'. The Chinese 'I' has seven strokes, intri-
> cacies. How could the American 'I', assuredly wearing a hat like
> the Chinese, have only three strokes, the middle so straight? Was
> it out of politeness that this writer left off strokes the way a Chi-
> nese has to write her own name small and crooked? No, it was not
> politeness; 'I' is a capital and 'you' is lower case.
> —**Maxine Hong Kingston**, from *The Woman Warrior*

A moral philosophy can be seen as a stylized and intellectualized response to
a cluster of worries, wishes, and hopes about lives to lead, things to seek and
avoid, and people, including ourselves, to care for and to answer to. Many
contemporary moral philosophers are fond of the question "What ought I to
do?" as a frame for ethics. But questions about what I should want, what I
should try to be or become, and what I should or must take responsibility
for, both looking back and looking ahead, are at least as basic, and perhaps
more so. How could I decide what is good, best, right, or just all right to do
on any given spot without some sense of these other things? And what is the
significance of 'I'—what is particular to my own life and the fact of its being
mine—in taking stock of these other things? Is it just one more of them?

All moral philosophies have views about right or value. Not all respond
equally or in the same ways to worries about the overall shape and content
of lives, or to hopes that they might be personally worthwhile as well as interpersonally defensible. I think it is reasonable to expect moral philosophy
to shed *some* light on how to steer a morally responsible course throughout

our lives among valuable things and important commitments, while giving place to the wish that our lives might express the people we in particular are. I believe an "ethics of responsibility" of one kind is responsive to these demands. It aims to accommodate the richness and diversity of what people have reasons to care about and take responsibility for, while respecting the varieties and vagaries of the very different lives people may want to, or have to, lead.

This kind of view, however, proposes no philosophical metric for determining just what are the right responsibilities in the right order. Rather than a defect, I find this to be a virtue of the view. I do not think there is a principled way of ordering for everyone, in advance, the numbers, kinds, combinations, and weightings of things that matter morally, and with respect to which we may well be called to account. I don't think we simply haven't *yet* found an all-purpose solution for all of life, or for all lives, to the question of how far to go with which morally significant commitments, where to stop, or when to compromise or change course. The vicissitudes of projects of high moral theory in this century might well make one skeptical about the odds of achieving that.

I think the resistance of our lives to this treatment is due, in part, to the nature of things in our lives that morally matter. It is also due to the nature of these lives themselves. Morally significant things, our responses to them and responsibility for them, play very important parts in our lives, but our lives are not only about them or propelled only by them. Yet to say there's no principled way is not to say there are no ways at all. And to say there are no all-purpose solutions is not to deny that people solve these problems in their lives all the time in ways that may be found more or less morally sound for good reasons.

One thing I want to show is how a kind of responsibility ethics clarifies the structure of the moral accounts people actually tend to keep and give. It sees these accounts as individual and individuating narratives of lives that are particularly our own. But these narratives, even if individuating, cannot be private or idiosyncratic. They serve purposes of *shared* understanding, not only of self-guidance but of justification and criticism. We are neither unfortunate enough to have to go it all alone in trying to find and keep an acceptable and vital moral order in our lives nor lucky enough to have the last word on whether we have succeeded.

The other thing I want to show is how this kind of ethics does something it may be thought unable to do: to supply an intuitively recognizable understanding of integrity, and to defend the central importance of it. It is true this kind of ethics does not support a view of integrity that equates it with maximal evaluative integration, unconditional commitments, or uncorrupted fidelity to a true self. But this ethics also does not find those conceptions of integrity true to the changing, deeply relational character of human lives and the ways we make sense of them; they do not reckon with how much and how inevitably most lives are entangled with and given to others, as well as to chancy circumstance beyond our control. If we consider the several kinds of stories by means of which we keep our moral accounts, these features of our lives come to the fore.

I defend a view of integrity as a kind of *reliable accountability*. Its point is not for us to will one thing nor to be it, but to maintain—or reestablish—our reliability in matters involving important commitments and goods. This view exchanges global wholeness for more local dependability, and inexorable consistency for responsiveness to the moral costs of error and change. It trades inward solidity for flexible resiliency at those points where lives, fortune, and several kinds of histories meet. This view of integrity takes utterly seriously to what and to whom a person is true, but looks with suspicion upon true selves. It links our senses of meaning and responsibility to the stories we can tell, but notices that "we" are not all in the same discursive positions any more than we are all in the same social ones, and that these are importantly linked. There are moral problems with the social distribution of narrative resources and the credibility to use them, which this view can help us see.

1. Strains of Responsibility

Many feminists favor an "ethics of responsibility" that allows for fine-grained judgments and discretionary responses to particular persons in actual situations with distinctive histories. Perhaps the most familiar version within feminist ethics is an ethic of care, but I want to construe responsibility ethics more broadly, as an extended family of moral views that share a basic theme. I model the structure of responsibility ethics here in my own way, but I hope this way captures something important about a variety of related views. The basic theme is that specific moral claims on us arise from our contact or relationship with particular others whose interests are vulnerable to or dependent on our actions and choices. We are *obligated to respond* to particular others when circumstances or ongoing relationships render them especially, conspicuously, or peculiarly dependent on us.[1]

This kind of ethics requires a view of moral judgment with significant expressive, interpretive, and (where possible) collaborative features. If actual dependency or vulnerability (and the circumstances or histories of commitment and expectation that create it) is the basis of many moral claims, the specific nature, as well as the relative priority and stringency, of the claims cannot generally be determined in the abstract. Rather, prior abstract orderings of values ("honesty over convenience"), generic obligations ("treat persons with dignity"), or generalized conceptions of roles or interests ("friends deserve loyalty") are only rough guidelines needing to be shaped interpretively to the instance at hand. Sometimes prior conceptions or orderings will be altered or set aside when the nature of the particular case shows them to be irrelevant or unresponsive. Where available, a shared search for mutually acceptable resolutions (or for an understanding of what is irreconcilable) is preferable to unilateral decision.

Here's a problem some find with this approach. In a typical human life there will be many relationships that create varying degrees and kinds of dependence, as well as countless episodes in which unfamiliar others may be rendered dependent on us without their or our intent or control. Responsibility ethics draws together cases where developed relationships thick with commitment or expectation put demands on me; cases where incident or emergency put me in a position to provide significant aid to, or deter significant harm from, perfect or virtual strangers; and cases where I may become aware of my ability to help others who do not immediately confront me. Is there any end to the number and types of demands that, on this view, morally claim my attention? Could a life responsive along these lines exhibit the commitments and concerns distinctive of the one who lives it? How could a person make, or keep, this life her or his "own"? Responsibility ethics might seem to defeat personally meaningful life-ordering by visiting a veritable plague of commitments on each of us. It might even be claimed that such a view ignores, thwarts, or threatens a person's *integrity*.

Indeed, Carol Gilligan, explicating one version of an ethics of responsibility, called this the "the conflict between integrity and care" (1982, 157). Any human being, immersed in the complex, varied, and changing relationships and episodic contacts of real life, might be scattered, depleted, and "constantly compromised" (1982, 157) by an unlimited demand for responsiveness. This integrity problem is analogous to one raised by Bernard Williams with respect to both utilitarian and Kantian moral views.[2] Both impartial maximizing of goods (whatever they might be) and impartial respect for persons (whoever they might be) seem to demand that personally distinctive and meaningful projects, commitments, and relationships be jettisoned, and that agents view them as dispensable, whenever impartialist moral demands conflict with them, as they surely at least often (if not always) do. This seems a nightmarish scenario of a life truly not one's own, because such personally distinctive "constitutive" commitments carry a life forward, giving it meaning and making it one's own. Is responsibility ethics at least as bad, if not worse?

Some feminist critics object that Gilligan's identification of an ethic of open-ended responsiveness with women is a deeply mistaken valorization of the stereotypes of bottomless feminine nurturance and self-sacrifice that continue to haunt women while politically disempowering and personally exhausting them.[3] A care "ethic" can look like the lamentable internalization of an oppressively servile social role. Some critics of Williams, on the other hand, suggest that his plea for the agent's "integrity" is a defense of self-indulgence or a cavalier refusal to accept legitimate demands that morality makes on us (Conly 1983; Herman 1983; Flanagan 1991). And it is tempting to caricature Gilligan's and Williams's discussions as sentimental rationalizations of feminine ("What's a mother to do?") and masculine ("A man's gotta do what a man's gotta do") stereotypes.

These criticisms have merit, yet I sympathize with something both Gilligan and Williams are trying to do. They are straining against a formulaic view of selves and their others, lives and their commitments, and the role of morality in binding or shaping these. Both try to get the meanings, motives, commitments, and connections that move individuals through their distinctive lives into the right relation with morality's guiding and constraining force within those lives. Gilligan in fact argued that people's real problems of conflicting responsibilities need to be "separated from self-sacrifice" (1982, 134) and reconciled to "the truth of their own agency and needs" (1982, 138). The larger truth involves "the fact that in life you never see it all, that things unseen undergo change through time, that there is more than one path to gratification, and that the boundaries between self and other are less clear than they sometimes seem" (1982, 172). And Williams, despite deep ambiguity in his notorious discussion of a fictive "Gauguin" whose abandonment of his family may be retrospectively "justified" by artistic success (1981b), acknowledges elsewhere that commitments which constitute personally meaningful lives are normally formed within the bounds of morality (1981a, 12–13). Both use 'integrity', I think, to stand in for a demand either within or against morality for some space for a self to call its own, although it is likely that they think differently about the self who needs to stake this claim.

It is not always clear in these and other discussions exactly what integrity is supposed to be: Doing what's right? Doing what you, particularly, believe is right? Doing what's particularly and morally acceptably right for you? Doing what it takes to keep yourself or your life all in one piece? Having moral commitments so conflict-free and/or a record of performance (and prediction?) so flawless you never have to say you're sorry? There's no detaching a picture of integrity from some substantive views about morality. I suggest a way of thinking about the structure of morality—an "expressive-collaborative" model (Walker 1992, 1996)—that acknowledges a moving horizon of commitments and adjustments, allowing individual distinctiveness of commitment and situation while preserving livable flexibility in tandem with reasonable reliability.

2. Three Kinds of Narratives: Identity, Relationship, Value

Narrative understanding of the moral construction (and reconstruction) of lives is central to understanding how responsibilities are kept coherent and sustainable over substantial stretches of lives that, in important—but not imperial—ways, remain people's own. The idea is that a *story* is the basic form of representation for moral problems. Many morally problematic situations cannot be reckoned with responsibly, short of recognizing how people, relations, and even the values and obligations they recognize have gotten there. And since any morally problematic point might turn out to be part of the history of some later one, many problems are "solved" only to produce a sequel of personal and evaluative implications and remainders. Anything we do now may bear on what we are responsible for later on. These views reflect the idea of moral responsibility (in prospect or retrospect) as attaching to persons, a conception of a person as identified at least in part by a history, a history as constituted by patterns of action and response over significant periods of time, and actions themselves as conceived and reconceived in terms of their relations to what precedes and what follows them.

This last point merits underlining. It is not only for moral purposes but also for purposes of intelligibility over time that we read and reread actions and other events backward and forward, weaving them into lives that are anything more than one damned thing after another. The sense-making connections we exploit in doing so are of several kinds. Some are putative causal ones. We can describe someone's feelings as *scarred* or her replies as *defensive* only by presuming a present that results from something in the past; a decision only *restores* someone's dignity if certain kinds of things are found to issue from it. Other connections are sequential. There can be an opportunity to *regain* trust only where it has already been lost, and a man's *final* break with his youthful political convictions can only be that looking back. Sometimes sense-making connections serve to bundle up varied or repeating actions into legible configurations, such as neglecting a friendship or trying to disown a past. In such ways, features, trajectories, and whole segments of lives are given intelligible roles and even thematic meanings.

Some of these characterizations make sense of what someone has done, what someone does or doesn't care about, or who someone is. Often one of these is made sense of by means of the others. For such things we may be held, or hold ourselves or others, responsible. To know what to hold ourselves or others responsible *for* requires identifying the separate and mutual histories and understandings we bring to whatever requires our response. Three kinds of stories are central to living responsibly a life of one's own. We need to keep on keeping straight who we are, and who we have given others to understand we are, in moral terms; and we need to sustain and sometimes refurbish our understanding of moral terms themselves, of what it means to talk about kindness or respect or friendship or obligation. I call the needed stories ones of identity, relationship, and value. In taking up these stories I begin in the middle, as we all in fact do.

One required account is a *narrative of relationship*, a story of its acquired content and developed expectations, its basis and type of trust, and its possibilities for continuation. A response may be owed to others because some prior history of actual contact and understanding makes it reasonable for them to depend on me for something and reasonable for me to know of their reasonable expectation. Then it is morally important for me (and for them) to acknowledge the past character, present state, and future possibilities of *that* relationship as a way to be clearer about what is owed, why it is owed, and what latitude there may be for postponement, substitution, or release. We must also consider what this relationship, imagined in various continuations, revisions, or terminations, means for both (all) of us. In cases of purely episodic dependency (an unknown stranger in need of assistance), and where the needs and interest are entirely obvious or where the situation is urgent (a drowning child), there is no antecedent story of relationship to explore, and the imaginable interpersonal sequels are typically limited as well. These are very short stories of our moral lives, but they still may end more or less creditably, and their matter and implications may be significant parts of larger stories that reveal how well or badly we live or how easily we can make moral sense of ourselves.

So, sometimes we must do things for others because they need it, and because our ongoing relation to them makes us most likely or apt to supply it. Sometimes we do things for others as a way of creating a relationship that will become committing in that way, or as a way of honoring a history of relationship past that matters to at least one of us. And sometimes we do, and must do, things for people we did not and will not know, simply because their need is so critical or extreme, or because it is so easy for us to respond, or because there is no one else to. Things are more complex when the different demands of different persons or the different demands of the same person pose conflicting options. I must weigh different continuations against each other, deciding how much can be accommodated and what might best be sacrificed.

It is at this point, concentrating on the relationship-centered narrative, that an actor's integrity seems most strained. Integrity seems threatened because in such common situations it seems that someone is pressed to define how she goes on in terms derived from others' needs and demands, and others' unpredictable situations. But the narrative of relationship is *not* the only relevant one. Two others figure in an adequate moral construction of a situation.

One is the agent's own *narrative of moral identity*, some fairly persistent history of valuation that can be seen in a good deal of what a person cares for, responds to, and takes care of (Walker 1987; Meyers 1994). There are too many values and too many possible realizations of them, and too many people with whom these realizations might take place, for any of us to respond to all of these. In fact, most of us, whether with thought or by habit, set definite priorities among values, develop highly selective responses, and pay acute attention to particular kinds of things as well as people. Some devote primary energy and attention to friends or family, others to institutional roles, political involvement, or creative pursuits. Some care especially about honesty or loyalty, others about alleviating suffering or political change. And of course we all care especially for some particular others, whether out of our love, gratitude, or pity, or their merit, need, or right. *None* of these habitual or characteristic devotions licenses avoidable cruelty, destructiveness, or indecency to *anyone*. But the limits of minimal respect and minimally decent values are very broad ones. There are indefinitely many ways of going on *acceptably* within these moral boundary conditions, and many specific versions of moral *excellence* as well.

The significance of the ongoing narrative of moral identity is not only that we typically do have some such characteristic patterns of valuation but that we should. It shapes and controls our history of responses to others in ways we can account for. The narratives of relationship I sustain, the ways I combine and order them, the continuations I find more valuable than others, and the losses I am willing to accept or impose are controlling structures of the moral life that is specifically mine, even where its matter includes an unpredictable lot of demands that originate with others with whom I'm connected by history or occasion. This is as true of episodic or distanced relationships to strangers as of intimate, personal, or committed ones; it is as true of choices about problems on the large scale as about those of everyday and close-by. There are always too many suffering strangers and worthwhile causes on the large scale. We *will* be selective, whether in individual or collective contributions. These selections reflect and refine a moral identity that gives our deliberations greater focus and refinement. Equally important, they let others know where we stand and what we stand for.

The narratives of relationship and identity inevitably intertwine. Our identities, moral and otherwise, are produced by and in histories of specific relationship, and those connections to others that invite or bind us are themselves the expression of some things we value enough to care for. Yet there is a third kind of narrative that spans and supports both of these. It is a history of our shared understandings of what kinds of things, relationships, and commitments really *are* important, and what their relative importance is. This is the *narrative of moral values* progressively better, and sometimes differently, understood.

Throughout a person's life, moral choices confront her not only with problems of applying values and principles she acknowledges and understands to fresh cases but also with many problems of coming to understand how new situations *are* or *aren't* instances of certain previously acknowledged values or principles, and exactly what those values or principles really mean. Learning to refrain from dominating a child, condescending to a student, or depending too much on a partner may involve a new or extended understanding of what respect or self-respect can be. Terminating a lengthy friendship may involve insight into what friendship now means, or what loyalty does not.

Many moral choices reaffirm values and principles already understood and applied to new cases in familiar ways. Others bring under renewed scrutiny and reinterpretation those very standards themselves. So the narrative of "who I am" (or "who we are") and the narrative of "how we have gotten here together" is threaded through by another story, one about "what this means." The last involves a history of moral concepts acquired, refined, revised, displaced, and replaced, both by individuals and within some communities of shared moral understanding. Any moral concept has at a given time a familiar set of applications that reflects a history of choices made in light of it; think of the short, dynamic histories of modern concepts of 'equality' or 'rights'. We learn progressively from our moral resolutions and their intelligibility and acceptability to ourselves and others not only who and how we are but what our moral concepts and standards mean.

This is essential to keeping moral justification coherent within and between us. I have to make sense to myself of what reasons I have for doing things, and this means not only valuing kinds of things but recognizing when it is those kinds of things that are at stake or at issue. One might be able to acquit oneself *if* one is able to say "I was fair (kind, faithful, loyal, honest, generous, reasonable, etc.)"; yet it may be hard to decide whether one is entitled to say it. The indispensable test of both is submitting one's justification to others, sometimes (or especially) including others affected by my actions who might have wished for another outcome, always including those whose judgment one has reason to trust, and perhaps some untried bystanders for good measure. You may not get others to agree with what you have done, but you need them to recognize a possible moral justification for it in what you have to say for yourself.

Such tests are entirely fallible, and to make matters worse, the results may be mixed. That moral guidelines are not mechanical is related to the kinds of things they aim at and the purpose with which they aim at them. They aim at things important for us such as are recognizable between us, and which depend on people's care and responsibility for their maintenance. They aim at these things so that we can sustain a framework of mutual accountability that will work to preserve them. In the best case this framework can preserve our understandings of their importance even where it fails to prevent conflict over them or damage to them. They are not mechanical because things of importance are multiple, often multiply relative (in terms of importance to whom, for what, when, given what else), and (so) not obvious. This complexity is increased by the aim of shared understanding. Moral justification, then, is from the first and at the last *interpersonal*. It is with and from others we learn to do it, and learn that we must. It is to others we must bring it back to do the work it is intended for: to allow and require people to account to one another for the value and impact of what they do in matters of importance.

Just as—and because—individuals reshape their understandings of the values that ground reasons, so too do communities of people who hold each other morally accountable reconfigure over time the shared understandings that supply mutual justifications. Even the most private parts of our lives require a "public" justification, in the sense of shared intelligibility. "Private" justification in this sense is otherwise known as hypocrisy or self-deception. (And these are different again from simply acknowledging that one doesn't pretend to have anything to say on one's behalf, morally speaking. Given the alternatives of hypocrisy and self-deception, there are places where this is not the worst position one can take, even morally speaking.)

It's the coherence of each of the three narratives, and connections among them, that makes a distinctive moral life out of what could otherwise be an odd lot of disparate parts. Fabrics of life so woven may be more smooth or more knotty, some neatly and closely repetitive and some bold or even eccentric; different moral lives will have these forms of richness and regularity in varying degrees. A life's being so organized to some extent enables the person living that life to decide with good reason how and what to select, within the limits of moral acceptability, for most (or some) attention. At the same time, a life legible in these ways gives promise to others of reliable performance and accountability of specific kinds; this *nongeneric accountability* is one way the life we have is truly our own, and not interchangeable with others'.

Stories that support particular self- and mutual understandings and the distinctive responsibilities they entail are stories of distinctive and committing partiality. But they are only ever partial stories, ones limited by or dependent on other stories, and subject to change. Just how much coherence, consistency, and continuity make for integrity? I've already said I believe there is no satisfactory principled (i.e., formulaic) answer to this, but I do have a story about it. I argue that integrity is *not* the coherence, consistency, and continuity themselves but something else they make possible in varying degrees, one's *moral reliability*. More coherence, consistency, or continuity, it turns out, is *not* necessarily better, especially over the long haul of a life. We need only so much as will serve.

3. Integrity

'Integrity' is a term powerfully loaded with aesthetically attractive associations of *wholeness* and *intactness*. Magnetic images of unity and unspoiledness have exerted their pull on philosophers' discussions. It is not intuitive meanings by themselves but the sense a concept of integrity makes within a larger picture of moral life that argues for that concept. Even so, I too can invoke a familiar meaning, and images less pretty but sturdier, in supporting a view of integrity that reckons with how much of our lives are given to others, to change, and to things we cannot hope (and sometimes shouldn't wish) to control. Think of 'integrity' used to describe the sturdiness of structures people have built, the property of holding up dependably under the weights and stresses these structures are apt to encounter given the purposes to which they are put and the conditions they might encounter.

I suggest integrity as a morally admirable quality is something like that. I think of integrity as a kind of reliability: reliability in the accounts we are prepared to give, act by, and stand by, in moral terms, and dependable responsiveness to the ongoing fit among our accounts, the ways we have acted, and the consequences and costs our actions have in fact incurred. This includes keeping reasonably straight what we are doing and whether the accounts we can give of it make sense; following through short and long term on what we have given to be expected; recognizing we can't always choose our tests or control all results for which we may have to account; and being disposed to repair and restore dependability when structures we have built in our lives teeter or fail.

Cheshire Calhoun has recently argued against several kinds of wholeness and purity views of integrity. These views not only equate integrity with other things—volitional unity, psychological identity, the purity of rightness—but render integrity as essentially a self-directed and self-protective virtue rather than one "fitting us for proper social relations" (1995, 253). Calhoun proposes instead a relational view of integrity as "the virtue of having a proper regard for one's own judgment as a deliberator among deliberators" (1995, 259), of standing up for one's own best judgment under pressures and penalties from other people. A person shows integrity in taking responsibility for her part in the collective work of determining how to live. Hypocrites lack integrity, for example, because they deliberately mislead us about what is worth doing (1995, 258).

But hypocrites do not necessarily mislead us about what is worth doing; they do mislead us about what it is *they* may be relied upon by us to do. As co-deliberators they may represent worthy and admirable views. Yet even where they do so, they knowingly mislead us into reasonable expectations of performance on which we might, to our grief, rely. If we do so rely, and are deserted, the last thing a committed hypocrite will do is account for herself by acknowledging it was her moral veneer, not the trust it invited, by which she steered her (and so our) course. She will either redirect her moral display to fresh audiences or try to reengineer its credibility in our eyes. This leaves us in the original lurch; and it lays the welcome mat down for us or others on the edge of the next abyss.

I share Calhoun's view that it is a relational conception of integrity we need, a conception that makes it interpersonally, and not just intrapersonally, indispensable. Responsibly contributing to the common deliberative weal by testament of conviction and action under social pressure is a central aspect of the moral reliability I have in mind. I want to place more emphasis on the fallibility and limitations of both our deliberative efforts and our attempts to live up to their results, and how and whether we face what we are accountable for even (or especially) when things come apart. I want to get at how integrity is reliability not only *ab initio*, in the having of firm and coherent convictions and publicly expressing them, but also *post facto*, in various reparative responses, sometimes including changes of moral course. The point coming and going is our being reliably responsible in matters of our own and others goods, as well as keeping clear and vibrant the shared understanding of them.

Narratives of moral identity, relationship, and value help us determine matters we may be more or less reliable in, and so more or less securely relied upon by ourselves and others. But these are *kinds* of stories; it's a short step to noticing that within any life there may be multiple actual narratives of a given type—more than one story of identity, relationship, or value. With respect to relationships this is obvious. I am someone's daughter, sister, lover, friend; a colleague, teacher, and neighbor to more; and a friend of several kinds to many others; and so on. My self-understanding and sense of accountability might vary in these relationships (and I may not equally respect, like, approve of, or understand myself in all of them). If I do endorse some collection of these versions of me, I may not be able to cover them with any single story. My interpretations of values and the application of principles may not be uniform across different domains, relationships, or roles. My moral identities may also be plural: The structure of my commitments in certain official roles may differ from that in private encounters, for example, or my life may show stages or alternating periods during which my orderings and understandings of value may be distinct. I do not mean only that one may be inconsistent or undependable, although this is true. I mean also that one may be *differently reliable*, depending on what is at issue. Most people are.

Sometimes one has to *become* differently reliable than one has been. Circumstance can thrust upon one new responsibilities that require the reordering of others, or situations can reveal that existing responsibilities are no longer jointly sustainable. Sometimes the pressure for change or redistribution or differentiation arises out of moral concern itself. It's importantly misleading, though, to figure all the shifts and changes in the moral structure of people's lives as if morality itself were the engine of these lives. It's not. Sometimes people and possibilities just change; lives are regularly reordered by complex synergies of choice and chance. This may mean certain commitments are off, with various consequences, including moral ones. In some cases one may be culpable for injuries or losses to others. Then new reliabilities are at issue. One may be more or less reliable in repairing or compensating for damage; or one may simply be relied upon to own up, whether one can fix anything or there's anything left to fix. Whether or not there is damage to reckon, the reestablishment of reliability after changes in course—not staying in formation as before, but being *again reliably responsible* from here—may be fairly described as integrity. Sometimes, it's a matter of starting over when everything's gone to hell.

In thinking about integrity I'm trying to curb a temptation to focus exclusively on admirable performance right out of the gate—that is, on cases of sticking by principles or doing as one believes despite temptation or pressure. In fact, people are often said to have integrity when they've *already* muffed things, miscalled outcomes, left damage, and *then* taken such responsibility as ensues. Again, it's common to attribute integrity to someone who finds a way to honor commitments or act creditably in a situation compromised by someone *else's* bad behavior, recklessness, or ineptitude. Sometimes the two combine when someone shoulders burdens of setting right what he or she *alone* has not made to come undone. A central use of 'integrity', then, is to describe not only people who act well from, as it were, a standing position but also people who own up to and clean up messes, their own and others. People who don't beg off, weasel out, or deflect flack toward others as life lurches on have integrity. That some people never do this, and most people cannot always do this, makes integrity something admirable. We are lucky that many of us do this as often as we do; very much that we value for us and between us would be lost without it.[4]

I take these observations about integrity to be commonplaces. Integrity is commonly associated with forms of responsibility-taking where people might be tempted to do otherwise and things would go noticeably easier for them (and sometimes worse for others) if they did. It is especially linked with specific performances or histories of choice where opportunities to get away with or from something (such as the expectations one has invited or the comeuppance one deserves) are foregone. Often people restrict judgments of integrity to specific performances impressive in these ways ("it took integrity for her to . . . ," "he showed integrity when he . . . "). Integrity doesn't need to have a whole-life referent. It involves being reliably accountable in terms of commitments and values, and ready to respond to the results of the accounting. In short, integrity can be more or less *local*.

None of this requires a moral actor whose life is "of a piece," whose defining commitments are unconditional, or who is being faithful to a true self.[5] Lives are usually of many pieces, not always stably processing in unconflicting parallel lines. If one has more than a single significant responsibility or cherishes more than a single person, thing, or value, it is not possible to guarantee that the demands of some may not condition the fulfillment of others. And if a self is a bearer of values and responsibilities for them, and these are multiple and sometimes competitive, then the self to which one would be true is not just given. It is constructed and affirmed in intertwined histories of identity, relationship, and value. A good deal that is true *of* it consists in what it finds it can be true *to*.

A view of selves that fits with this ethics is one in which a self itself is understood in terms of a history of relationships among its various temporally distant and concurrent aspects. We are layers of various overlapping histories of traces of many encounters and relationships; these coexist in various states of stratification or alternation as we live our lives. My present self owes debts to my past one, and my future self is deeply dependent on the choices and self-understandings of my present one. I owe things to myself in these and perhaps other ways, just as I owe things to others for which they reasonably or crucially depend on me. This layered, nested, and "ensemble subjectivity"[6] might sound a little exotic; I have tried to show that it and its kind of integrity are familiar. I have suggested that we not think of this integrity as something inward and nonrelational, something buried deep inside to which one answers and may answer more or less truthfully. Instead, we should think of it as the actual display of reliable accountability and resilient dependability that we have many occasions to measure in each other and ourselves by the yardstick of shareable justification applied to narratives of varying lengths.

Morally guiding narratives are very coarse grids over the complexity of lives. If they were *not* coarse grids, we would not be able to use them, any more than we could use a map that replicated a landscape in every detail. Their point is the simplification that allows us to mark out and follow a route. First-person stories rightly enjoy a significant privilege, for although they often collect what has gone before in later edited or revised versions, their use is importantly *prospective*: We use them to determine how we might or must go on with the life only we, after all, can lead. Their privilege, however, is not that of incorrigibility. Others may call them into question, may impeach our cogency, sincerity, or integrity in trying to account for ourselves by means of them. Others may be in a position, in more ways than one, to press upon us corrections or alternatives. That this is so belongs to moral justification as essentially *between* people. But the pressures exerted on our mutually sense-making stories need themselves to be morally evaluated from more than one point of view.

4. Stories We Can Tell

Feminists have, conspicuously, explored the meaning of integrity.[7] These discussions are concerned with impediments and resistances to women's understanding what they themselves are doing, with irresolvable conflict between or division within self-interpretations available to women (and others) in both found and chosen communities, with needs for radical, life-disrupting changes that feminist consciousness may require, and with women's resisting pressures and bribes to turn against themselves or other women. Do these concerns reflect a gender-linked problem with integrity for women, or a problem with integrity for women or men who bear assigned subordinate social identities? What kind of problem is this? *Whose* problem is this?

One view is that people who are subordinated or oppressed cannot possess integrity, or are likely to be able to achieve only a hobbled or inferior version of it. This is then one more injustice done to those who are oppressed: A significant interpersonal moral good, and a source of self-respect and others' admiration, is denied to them. This view may be supported by the thought that subordinated people's lives are evidently not their own, either insufficiently under their own control for them to set their own courses more than marginally or too ridden by others' control and demands for them to follow through reliably on such courses as they might set.

I reject this view. Although I assume that very many things human beings have to or want to do are made harder, even excruciatingly costly, by deprivation or oppression, I think the belief that integrity is out of reach for people under conditions of social disadvantage represents a confusion, a mistake, or a temptation. The assumptions underlying this belief need to be confronted and resisted. If lives are distinctively our own because of the distinctive mix of circumstances thrown our ways and commitments and attachments we make under those circumstances, and if integrity is admirable reliability in response to such demands as one in fact then faces, the issue for integrity is how well one responds to that lot. There is no reason to think that many human beings under circumstances of subordination, oppression, or unfreedom of many types do not exhibit valor, perseverance, lucidity, and ingenuity in staying true to what they value within the confines of their situations. Indeed, these very confines may set the stage for exemplary achievements in just this regard.

There can be a confusion here between displaying integrity and possessing autonomy, especially in the uncontroversial sense of possessing some minimum of self-determination and socially approved or protected latitude for choice, defined either absolutely or comparatively. There is a difference between being forced to live a life very much not of one's own choosing, or being deprived of means or opportunity to live a life one most or more prefers, on the one hand, and failing to lead whatever life one happens to have with integrity, on the other. Integrity in the reliability sense and autonomy in the social-political sense may co-vary inversely. Terrible social burdens and injustices are born by many with courage, dignity, and fidelity to what and whom they love, whereas social privileges of others permit (and perhaps contain or deflect the effects of) irresponsible, craven, or dishonorable commitments and actions.

Neither will it do to identify integrity with something like autonomy in the more elusive and disputed psychological sense of one's being under control of the rational parts of one's self, or the parts of oneself one most identifies with, or the parts of oneself that best stand up to critical review, or the skills for the relevant kinds of review itself. Let's suppose one could connect integrity with these modes of psychological function and show that these modes are morally valuable, or superior to some others. Then the view that socially subordinated people lack integrity would be the claim that they (invariably? typically?) are psychologically (if not morally) stunted or damaged, that they are incapable of optimal forms of adult self-awareness and self-control. Of course, people might be so incapable, but does one want to suggest that this incapacity or childishness inveterately and especially tracks social disadvantage? If it did, which oppressions, marginalizations, or subordinations would be parts of the etiology of this particular incapacity? For oppressions, marginalizations, and subordinations are not all the same. Oppressed or subordinated people do not form a natural kind, nor are conditions of subordination uniform.

Leaving autonomy aside, might there be reason to think that subordinated people are less true, within whatever limits apply, to what they care about because they are more corruptible or less resolute? I don't think we need to assume that people under varied conditions of disadvantage are typically more likely than more privileged others to be swayed or bribed or timorous or cravenly ingratiating or self-abasing or opportunistic or duplicitous. And it would be distorting to equate conscious strategies of evasion and survival—to which people must resort under direct threat, supervision, or control—with general depravity; these strategies may be the very things that allow individuals in subordinate positions to make and be true to commitments of their own. No one should assume that lives lacking certain or many privileges are characteristically or uniformly reduced to the compliance, complicity, even slavishness, that their oppressors demand or their betters fantasize. As María Lugones reminds those with white skin privilege, "[N]ot all the selves we are make you important" (1991, 42). These hypotheses sound more like familiar rationales for subordination or disadvantage than like critical responses to it.[8]

With respect to class, bell hooks puts it flatly:

> I went to college believing there was no connection between poverty and personal integrity. . . . I was shocked by representations of the poor learned in classrooms. . . . I had been taught in a culture of poverty to be intelligent, honest, to work hard, and always to be a person of my word. I had been taught to stand up for what I believed was right, to be brave and courageous. . . . These

lessons . . . were taught to me by the poor, the disenfranchised, the underclass. (hooks 1994, 167)

These representations of the poor are familiar to me as well. I have often heard un-self-conscious comment on the lesser capacity or rectitude of those less advantaged by those more so in classrooms where the topic is ethics.

Cruelties and burdens imposed by oppressive conditions inflict miserable costs and terrible losses on people, including psychic ones. Being rendered unable to undertake certain commitments or being thwarted in one's best attempts to fulfill them, and the frustration, rage, and shame this can provoke, may be among these costs and losses. I don't deny this, and I don't suppose hooks would either. But the nature of the costs and their toll on individuals are apt to vary, given individual situations, temperaments, and resources of several kinds. There are variations in the supports supplied by oppressed communities to their members, and differences in the degrees of control and forms of enforcement that different hierarchies demand. It is the blanket assumption of diminished integrity I reject as unnecessary and implausible.

This assumption is also perilously mystifying. It deflects scrutiny of the kinds of responsibility and tests of commitment that privileged positions may allow some to duck or hand off to others.[9] It also diverts attention from the ways individuals' lives and the stories they could tell of them may be *disqualified* for some audiences as expressions of moral achievement no matter what those individuals do.

Not everyone is allowed or enabled to tell just any life (or other) story. The stuff of lives to be told, the discursive means available for telling them, and the credibility of story-tellers are apt to differ along familiar lines of class, gender, and race, and perhaps other lines, even rather local ones, as well.[10] Life stories, including moral histories, will take shape in response to specific constraints and, for some people, may be shaped as much *for* them as by them. Kathryn Addelson reminds us that "some people have the authority or power to define the terms in which their own and other people's stories are to be officially narrated" (1991, 120). And some people's standards of intelligibility may rule "informally," protected from challenge by the challengers' lack of socially recognized credibility.

This suggests another view about a special problem of integrity under conditions of subordination or oppression. The recognition of integrity (as of other esteemed qualities or achievements) may be denied to those subordinated, and the life-interpretations that support the ascription of integrity to them may be replaced or erased by others. The others who can do this are those with the power to confer such recognition authoritatively in the eyes of others like them. Some people's disqualification from giving certain accounts of themselves and being understood in the ways they intend to be can be part of the apparatus of "culturally normative prejudice" (Meyers 1994, 51–56).

One obvious way to disqualify people is to restrict recognition to certain roles or pursuits, and to preclude certain people's occupation of those roles or engagement in those pursuits. This strategy will fail, though, whenever it is noticed that integrity and other morally valuable qualities are not *in fact* coincident with or utterly dependent on the occupation of specific social roles; possession and exhibition of courage are not restricted to battlefield behavior.

What works more effectively in moral disqualification is rigging not only some aspects of lives but dominant interpretations of them, thereby invidiously biasing the interpersonal and self-understandings that the interpretations are recruited to serve. To the extent that lives themselves can't be cut to fit the approved stories of them, the socially sustained authority of some people and some stories will make offending or anomalous matter of some others' lives disappear or appear distortedly—this despite whatever self-descriptions offenders might prefer or invent (Addelson 1994). If for the official record, formal or informal, some people's self-respect is insubordination, their courage impulsiveness, their loyalty stealth, their magnanimity stupidity, their rational restraint servility, then their integrity cannot be coherently claimed, or if claimed, the claim cannot be credited.

Vivid first-order depictions of a savagely oppressive social order and the actual workings of rigged intelligibility are found in American slave narratives. These stories detail the unrelenting cruelty, the commonplace violence, the continuous humiliation of being property, and the denial of humanity visited on black slaves, as well as the bizarre strategies of tailored intelligibility needed by white Christian masters. They also present stunning counterexamples to the blanket thesis that oppression precludes integrity. Indeed, one of the strongest impressions made by stories like Harriet Jacobs's (1987) *Incidents in the Life of a Slave Girl* is of the extraordinary moral integrity shown repeatedly by their protagonists, often under conditions that seem simply unendurable.

At the same time, stories like Jacobs's exhibit strategic finesse in addressing their intended audiences. Sometimes their authors invoke familiar norms (e.g., sexual purity, scrupulous honesty) to give plausible, if contextually oversimple, justifications of themselves. At others, they circumscribe the application of these norms, either safely by appeals to readers' sympathy or more riskily by invitations to identification and empathy. They must convincingly enact the position of moral subjects even while being careful never simply to presume their entitlement to that rank. Narrative devices and conventions are used to subvert or outflank resistance to the credibility of these accounts and the moral urgency of what they tell. These are artful "counterstories" (Nelson 1995), which are as interesting conceptually as they are emotionally moving and historically important.

Of course, these stories are also political documents and rhetorical feats; I am not suggesting they are the everyday stories that most of us use to make sense of our lives, or that Jacobs used hers in this way. What they exemplify are the possibilities for cogent and powerful stories of moral achievement and integrity under unendurable conditions. Their rhetorical art shows acute awareness of how difficult it might be for these stories to be received as credible accounts at once of outrageous injustice and exemplary moral achievement under its yoke. Their ingenuity shows something about obstacles to ordinary sense-making narratives and about possibilities of overcoming them. They illuminate the complexities of unrigging and reweaving eccentric and deadly webs of interpersonal intelligibility constructed so that some people are "inexpressible" to some others as persons at all.

At times, some people are expressible to others only as a certain kind of person. Women vastly more privileged than slave women have often contested their canonical gendered scripts of motherhood, daughterhood, sexuality, or housewifery. The reason, I think, is not simply that these scripts are normative, for men's are too. They are normative stories of not merely relational but *subsumed* identities, ones that are seen in our society as functions of, or in terms of functions for, someone else (whether or not women themselves always so see them).[11] For women to whom they apply, this means being pressed toward self-descriptions that serve plot functions in someone else's tale. These self-descriptions buttress others' claims on women's dependability that are at once disadvantaging and not individually negotiable. Normative stories may be so culturally legislative for some women's lives that alternative stories are not found intelligible, or are translated into failed (or crazy) versions of the normatively preferred ones. One might still exhibit integrity within these constraints. But the costs of achieving it may be unnecessarily steep and ill-distributed, on the one hand, whereas its achievement may yet be ignored, denied, or deflatingly misdescribed, on the other.

Women and men in many situations of subordination, oppression, or marginality may find themselves targeted for normative narratives that are already given, coercive, not negotiable, and disadvantaging. Maintaining integrity is hardly the only challenge in such straits, but it is important to understand the kind of challenge it is. Feminist discussions of integrity often seem concerned with peculiar pressures on self- and mutual understanding for women, and with the predicaments and costs those pressures create. Feminist concerns with integrity look different from those nonfeminist ones that focus on wholeness or purity. Not everyone, it seems, has the same problems.

My account of the supporting narratives of identity, relationship, and value, under demands of interpersonal intelligibility, offers a framework for looking at ways we keep clear what we are to ourselves and others and what our moral values actually mean. Some challenges to doing this fall differently, or more heavily, on some people than on others. I've urged critical examination of the social definition and distribution of discursive resources, credibility, and the dominant conventions of intelligibility that determine whether and how lives can be told, to whom, and with what effects. Available means of narrative stylization and their social intelligibility and prestige for certain audiences raise questions. Who's kept quiet? What's left out?[12]

Notes

1. Care ethics has been defended and developed by Gilligan (1982), Noddings (1984), Baier (1987), Held (1987, 1993), Ruddick (1989), Manning (1992), and Tronto (1993). Whitbeck (1984) and Bishop (1987) emphasize responsiveness to particular others in specific relationships. Others who argue for a responsibility ethics, though not necessarily one so particularistic and contextual as that sketched here, include Goodin (1985) and Jonas (1984). My brief formulation of the key idea of responsibility ethics is modeled on Goodin's "vulnerability principle."

2. See Williams (1973, 1981a and 1981b) and Stocker (1976) on the dis-integration claim. Objections to consequentialist morality on the ground that it insufficiently respects, or even violates, the distinctness of persons and the importance to them of their individual lives are also found in Rawls (1971), Nozick (1974), Nagel (1979), and Scheffler (1982).

3. For some of these criticisms, especially in reference to Carol Gilligan's work, see Grimshaw (1986), Houston (1987), Card (1990), and Friedman (1993).

4. That moral responsibility is not limited by and to what a person herself controls, and that integrity has much to do with accepting this, is discussed in Card (1989) and Walker (1991).

5. Such characterizations figure in a philosophical literature on integrity. Calhoun (1995) discusses Taylor (1985), McFall (1987), and Blustein (1991), as well as Williams (1973, 1981a, 1981b). Kekes (1983) might be added to this group. Benjamin (1990) recognizes that the need for change and compromise is a realistic pursuit of integrity, but still sees the subject of integrity as a whole life. Gaita (1981) speaks instead of "due influence" of the past, not incompatible with my account here. See also Note 7 for some feminist discussions.

6. This is Lee Quinby's (1991, 136) description of the self-understanding expressed by Maxine Hong Kingston's *The Woman Warrior*.

7. See Calhoun (1995), Davion (1991), Lugones (1990), Card (1989), and Hoagland (1988). Adrienne Rich's (1979) beautiful essay on women and honor might also be seen in this context.

8. Morgan (1987) is one powerful original discussion of the double binding, invisibility, and "moral madness" of women. I urge more reserve in assuming that rigged terms of intelligibility for women and others actually commonly corrupt or disintegrate agency. I emphasize instead the first two problems. There is also something in between: See Mann (1994, 54–61) on "surd" behavior, an inability to make both complete and coherent sense of what one is doing at a given time under mutations and misalignments of social practices and assumptions.

9. See Tronto (1993) on "privileged irresponsibility."

10. Neisser and Fivush (1994) offer varied discussions of the nature and production of story-telling constraints. And Addelson (1994) strikingly illustrates narrative pressure from authorities and authoritative discourses.

11. Mann (1994) analyzes the female counterpart of the male liberal citizen-peer as a "subsumed nurturer" and explicitly connects this position to being unable to act "in one's own name."

12. I thank the following people whose reactions to or comments on earlier or other versions of this chapter helped me see what I was trying to do or hadn't done: Simon Blackburn, Judith Bradford, Paul Lauritzen, Diana Tietjens Meyers, Hilde Nelson. I especially thank Cheshire Calhoun for private communication about the strong similarity as well as the difference in emphasis between our views; I can't say she would agree with how I have represented that here.

References

Addelson, Kathryn. 1991. *Impure Thoughts*. Philadelphia: Temple University Press.
_____. 1994. *Moral Passages*. New York: Routledge.
Baier, Annette. 1987. The Need for More Than Justice. In *Science, Morality & Feminist Theory*. Marsha Hanen and Kai Nielsen, eds. Calgary, Canada: University of Calgary Press.
Benjamin, Martin. 1990. *Splitting the Difference*. Lawrence: University Press of Kansas.
Bishop, Sharon. 1987. Connections and Guilt. *Hypatia* 2: 7–23.
Blustein, Jeffrey. 1991. *Care and Commitment: Taking the Personal Point of View*. New York: Oxford University Press.
Calhoun, Cheshire. 1995. Standing for Something. *Journal of Philosophy* 92: 235–260.
Card, Claudia. 1989. Responsibility and Moral Luck: Resisting Oppression and Abuse. Paper presented to the annual meeting of the Eastern Division of the American Philosophical Association.
_____. 1990. Gender and Moral Luck. In *Identity, Character, and Morality*. Owen Flanagan and Amelie Rorty, eds. Cambridge, Mass.: MIT Press.
Conly, Sarah. 1983. Utilitarianism and Integrity. *The Monist* 66: 298–311.
Davion, Victoria. 1991. Integrity and Radical Change. In *Feminist Ethics*. Claudia Card, ed. Lawrence: University Press of Kansas.
Flanagan, Owen. 1991. *Varieties of Moral Personality*. Cambridge, Mass.: Harvard University Press.
Friedman, Marilyn. 1993. *What Are Friends For?* Ithaca: Cornell University Press.
Gaita, Raimond. 1981. Integrity. *Proceedings of the Aristotelian Society*, Supplementary Volume 55: 161–176.
Gilligan, Carol. 1982. *In a Different Voice*. Cambridge, Mass.: Harvard University Press.
Goodin, Robert. 1985. *Protecting the Vulnerable*. Chicago: University of Chicago Press.

Grimshaw, Jean. 1986. *Philosophy and Feminist Thinking.* Minneapolis: University of Minnesota Press.

Held, Virginia. 1987. Feminism and Moral Theory. In *Women and Moral Theory.* Eva Kittay and Diana Meyers, eds. Totowa, N.J.: Rowman and Littlefield.

_____. 1993. *Feminist Morality.* Chicago: University of Chicago Press.

Herman, Barbara. 1983. Integrity and Impartiality. *The Monist* 66: 233–50.

Hoagland, Sarah Lucia. 1988. *Lesbian Ethics: Toward New Value.* Palo Alto, Calif.: Institute of Lesbian Studies.

hooks, bell. 1994. *Outlaw Culture.* New York: Routledge.

Houston, Barbara. 1987. Rescuing Womanly Virtues: Some Dangers of Moral Reclamation. In *Science, Morality & Feminist Theory.* Marsha Hanen and Kai Nielsen, eds. Calgary, Canada: University of Calgary Press.

Jacobs, Harriet. 1987. *Incidents in the Life of a Slave Girl.* In *The Classic Slave Narratives.* Henry Louis Gates, Jr., ed. New York: Penguin Books.

Jonas, Hans. 1984. *The Imperative of Responsibility.* Chicago: University of Chicago Press.

Kekes, John. 1983. Constancy and Purity. *Mind* 92: 499–519.

Kingston, Maxine Hong. 1989. *The Woman Warrior.* New York: Vantage Books.

Lugones, María. 1990. Hispaneando y Lesbiando: On Sarah Hoagland's *Lesbian Ethics. Hypatia* 5: 138–146.

_____. 1991. On the Logic of Feminist Pluralism. In *Feminist Ethics.* Claudia Card, ed. Lawrence: University Press of Kansas.

Mann, Patricia S. 1994. *Micro-Politics.* Minneapolis: University of Minnesota Press.

Manning, Rita. 1992. *Speaking from the Heart.* Lanham, Md.: Rowman and Littlefield.

McFall, Lynn. 1987. Integrity. *Ethics* 98: 5–20.

Meyers, Diana. 1994. *Subjection and Subjectivity.* New York: Routledge.

Morgan, Kathryn Pauly. 1987. Women and Moral Madness. In *Science, Morality, & Feminist Theory.* Marsha Hanen and Kai Nielsen, eds. Calgary, Canada: University of Calgary Press.

Nagel, Thomas. 1979. *Mortal Questions.* New York: Cambridge University Press.

Neisser, Ulrich, and Robyn Fivush. 1994. *The Remembering Self.* Cambridge: Cambridge University Press.

Nelson, Hilde Lindemann. 1995. Resistance and Insubordination. *Hypatia* 10: 23–40.

Noddings, Nel. 1984. *Caring.* Berkeley and Los Angeles: University of California Press.

Nozick, Robert. 1974. *Anarchy, State, and Utopia.* New York: Basic Books.

Quinby, Lee. 1991. *Freedom, Foucault, and the Subject of America.* Boston: Northeastern University Press.

Rawls, John. 1971. *A Theory of Justice.* Cambridge, Mass.: Harvard University Press.

Rich, Adrienne. 1979. Women and Honor: Some Notes on Lying. In *Lies, Secrets, and Silence.* New York: W. W. Norton.

Ruddick, Sara. 1989. *Maternal Thinking.* Boston: Beacon Press.

Scheffler, Samuel. *The Rejection of Consequentialism.* New York: Oxford University Press.

Stocker, Michael. 1976. The Schizophrenia of Modern Ethical Theories. *Journal of Philosophy* 73:453–466.

Taylor, Gabriele. 1985. *Pride, Shame, and Guilt: Emotions of Self-Assessment*. New York: Oxford University Press.

Tronto, Joan. 1993. *Moral Boundaries*. New York: Routledge.

Walker, Margaret Urban. 1987. Moral Particularity. *Metaphilosophy* 18: 171–185.

———. 1991. Moral Luck and the Virtues of Impure Agency. *Metaphilosophy* 22: 14–27. (Reprinted in *Moral Luck*. Daniel Statman, ed. Albany: State University of New York Press, 1993.)

———. 1992. Feminism, Ethics, and the Question of Theory. *Hypatia* 7: 23–38.

———. 1996. Feminist Skepticism, Authority, and Transparency. In *Moral Knowledge? New Readings in Moral Epistemology*. Walter Sinnott-Armstrong and Mark Timmons, eds. New York: Oxford University Press.

Whitbeck, Caroline. 1984. A Different Reality. In *Beyond Domination*. Carol C. Gould, ed. Totowa, N.J.: Rowman and Allanheld.

Williams, Bernard. 1973. A Critique of Utilitarianism. In *Utilitarianism, For and Against*, with J.J.C. Smart. Cambridge: Cambridge University Press.

———. 1981a. Persons, Character and Morality. In *Moral Luck*. Daniel Statman, ed. Cambridge: Cambridge University Press.

———. 1981b. Moral Luck. In *Moral Luck*. Daniel Statman, ed. Cambridge: Cambridge University Press.

four

Ownership and the Body

JENNIFER CHURCH

The conviction that I own my body—that my body *belongs* to me, and that I have certain rights over it in virtue of the fact that it is *mine*—is as central to traditional theories of property rights as it is to contemporary disputes over abortion rights or the legalization of prostitution.[1] We may question the line of reasoning that leads Locke from ownership of one's body to ownership of the land that one cultivates, to ownership of the products of that cultivation, and so on, but we rarely question his starting point—namely, that we own our own bodies.[2] Likewise, we may question whether a woman's rights over her own body should be limited by a fetus's rights, or a father's rights, or even a state's rights, but we rarely doubt that she does have some rights over her own body in virtue of the fundamental fact that it is *hers*.[3]

In the face of such widespread agreement, any attempt to analyze or justify ownership of one's body may seem pointless. Why not accept bodily ownership as one of the few points upon which we can all agree, and focus our energies instead on disputes about the ownership of various other things, or disputes about the relative importance of rights to one's body versus various other rights? There are, I think, at least two good replies to this question. First, the most controversial cases in which competing rights are said to override one's right to one's own body are cases in which these competing rights concern the rights of other people to their bodies—the rights of women over their pregnancy versus the rights of the unborn to their bodies, for example, or the rights of biological fathers to their sperm and its products versus the rights of biological mothers to their ovum and its products. Resolving these controversies seems to require some better understanding of just what bodily ownership *is*—who owns what and on what basis. Second, because our ownership of things other than our bodies is often treated as an *extension* of our ownership of our bodies (as in Locke's line of reasoning, cited above), disagreements about what constitutes bodily ownership tend to spill over into disagreements about what constitutes ownership of land, factories, ideas, and so on. Without insisting that *all* disputes about ownership are due to underlying disagreements about the nature of bodily ownership, I do want to suggest that greater clarity about the nature of bodily ownership is an important step toward the resolution of various disputes about ownership, bodily and otherwise.

Is it possible, though, to give an analysis of bodily ownership that is not merely a reflection of where one's sympathies lie in the various controversies surrounding ownership? If not, it is hard to see how an *analysis* of bodily ownership could help to resolve rather than reinforce disagreement. One might recognize the importance of clarifying and even strengthening points of disagreement in the process of working toward eventual agreement, but it is hard to see how a partisan analysis of bodily ownership could convert the opposition. Fortunately, I do not think this is our predicament. If we can agree that persons are embodied, and that persons have ownership rights over their *own* bodies (*my* body is *mine*)—in other words, that here as elsewhere the possessive pronoun implies some sort of ownership relation—then we can expect more or less plausible accounts of the person/body relation to coincide with more or less plausible accounts of the relation of bodily ownership. In short, we can look to the metaphysics of personhood or selfhood (I shall be using these two concepts interchangeably) for guidance on the norms of ownership. Indeed, I suggest, it is at least partly because contemporary discussions of ownership have not kept up with contemporary discussions of personhood and selfhood that conflicts over ownership rights seem so entrenched.[4]

1

In our ordinary thought and talk about our bodies, we tend to fluctuate between two equally problematic alternatives—a conception of ourselves as something wholly distinct from our bodies that causally interacts with our bodies, and a conception of ourselves as identical to our bodies. (These contrasting conceptions of selfhood mirror the traditional contrast between God conceived as transcendent and God conceived as immanent.) The first, Cartesian, conception faces the problem of explaining what sort of thing a self is, if it is not a body, and how it is supposed to interact with a body. The second, physicalist, conception faces the problem of explaining why some bodies and not others constitute selves, and how it is possible for people to be at odds with their bodies. These are familiar problems, often rehearsed and refined within literary theory and feminist theory as well as within more narrowly philosophical discussions. As Terry Eagleton (1993) has recently stated, "[I]t is not quite true that I have a body, and not quite true that I am one either."

As long as we hold that one must be either independent from or identical to one's body, while finding neither of these options acceptable, we are caught in a dilemma. There have been numerous attempts at resolving this dilemma, of course. Descartes (1980/1641) asserts that "nature also teaches that I am present to my body not merely in the way a seaman is present to his ship, but that I am tightly joined and, so to speak, mingled together with it, so much so that I make up one single thing with it" (*Meditation* 6, para. 81). And Eagleton writes: "What is special about the human body, then, is just its capacity to transform itself in the process of transforming the material bodies which surround it. . . . [I]f the body is a self-transformative practice, then it is not identical with itself in the manner of corpses and dustbins" (1993, 7). Before turning to the resolution that I favor, however, I want to highlight the effect this dilemma has on discussions of ownership; for, I contend, our ordinary thinking about bodily ownership, and about ownership in general, has also tended to fluctuate between these two alternatives, creating problems of its own.

Correlated with the conception of a self as something independent of the body is a conception of ownership as the imposition of the self on the body: We own things because we apply our will to them, we *use* them. If I am a thing independent from my body, it seems natural to suppose that a body becomes mine only if I *make* it mine—by subduing it, as it were, and causing it to work for me (as opposed to cases in which my body may control, or "own" me). Kant (1991/1797), for example, who conceived of persons as autonomous wills, defined 'possession' as "the subjective condition of the use of anything" and maintained that Nature gives us possession—that is, use—of our bodies (ch. 1, sec. 1). Hegel (1952/1821), too, conceived of ownership in terms of the imposition of an autonomous will when he wrote, "The person has for its substantive end the right of placing its will in any and every thing, which thing is thereby mine" (sec. 44). And in the same vein, Marx insists that it is the workers who express their wills through the products of their labor who are the rightful owners of those products.

The claim that the user of a thing is its owner is usually supplemented with a "first use" clause to the effect that once a person uses and thus owns something, it cannot be used and thus owned by another without the consent of the original owner. In short, anything I use is mine as long as no one else is already using it, and once it is mine I have complete say over its use.[5] Among other things, this clause seems to secure my ownership of the body I now "inhabit" since I am bound to have been the first user of it (but see discussion below). Furthermore, if ownership is thought of as deriving from use, it is common to suppose that ownership ends when use, or the imposi-

tion of one's will, ends. Locke (1924/1690), for example, maintains that we
come to own land by cultivating it and that we cease to own land when we
cease to cultivate it; if one fails to use what one owns, one forfeits ownership.
My ownership of my body, however, is probably not something I can forfeit
through disuse without also forfeiting the capacity to will anything at all—
and, hence, forfeiting my status as a self (on a Cartesian or Kantian conception of selfhood). Thus, again, if I exist at all, my ownership of my body
seems pretty much guaranteed on this conception of ownership.

However, in order to determine who first uses a thing, and whether that
thing continues to be used by that person, it is necessary to be more precise
about what it means to use something. Suppose that a person counts as using
a thing just in case she causally interacts with the thing for the purpose of fulfilling her aims or desires. I use a telephone, for example, when I causally interact with it for the purpose of speaking with someone I wish to speak with.
If this is what is meant by 'use', and if use secures ownership, then ownership
appears to be both too easy to acquire (for most any unused thing can be
owned merely by using it) and too easy to lose (for the only way to retain
ownership of a thing is through more or less continual use). So, for instance,
climbing a tree in the wilderness to get a view would suffice to make the tree
mine (for a time), whereas letting the plants in my yard grow wild would
(after a time) result in a loss of ownership over them. Likewise, with regard to
this body, if my mother is the first purposefully to interact with it (at a time
before I even have desires, perhaps), then she is the first owner; and if I cease
to have the use of this body (e.g., because I become paralyzed) then I cease to
be its owner. A defender of this conception of ownership might simply accept
such consequences, of course, or might avoid them by appeal to various other
factors. For example, the difficulty of monitoring use or the inefficiency of
frequent transfers of ownership might recommend a simplified conception of
ownership for legal purposes; other rights such as welfare rights or wilderness
rights might sometimes override ownership rights; or some more nuanced
analysis of the relevant notion of use might be offered. It is not my intention
to pursue these refinements here. Noting the key points of difficulty for the
ownership-as-use view is enough for my purposes.

The alternative conception of ownership, which is correlated with the
conception of selves as identical to bodies, maintains that we own things (at
least in the first instance) because of who we are, where we are, or what we
happen to be—regardless of any effort on our parts.[6] Whatever is a part of
me (head, hand, or fingernail), or a property of me (a smile, a gesture, a particular coloring), automatically belongs to me. Bodily ownership, on this
view, is not acquired through an effort of the will so much as it is a state of
being bestowed on us by the fact of our very existence. Whatever body parts
and properties I was born with or developed over time count as *mine*,
whether or not I "do" anything with them. (Strictly speaking, on this view, it
makes sense to speak only of parts or properties of my body—rather than of

the body in entirety—as mine, given that they are parts or properties of the whole that *is* me.)

It is possible to think of ownership of things apart from my body, in accordance with this identity-based conception of ownership, if one thinks that who I am—what is part of my identity—includes more than this body. The fact that I have grown up in a certain place may make that place a part of me such that I have certain ownership rights over it (i.e., ownership through occupancy). The fact that I am my parents' daughter may make them a part of who I am, regardless of my will, thus securing me automatic ownership rights over what is theirs (i.e., inheritance rights). Or the fact that I am the subject of a series of much-publicized photographs, through no effort of my own, might make them a part of my identity and give me certain ownership rights over them.[7] But if the previous ownership-as-use conception made ownership too easy to gain and too easy to lose, this ownership-as-identity conception appears to pose the opposite problem: It is too hard to gain or lose ownership if we own just that with which we are physically identified, because it is too hard to alter our physical identities. Furthermore, the farther one strays from the boundaries of one's body proper, the vaguer the relevant notion of physical identity becomes—and the stronger the temptation to at least supplement identity-based ownership with something like use-based ownership.

In our thinking about bodily ownership and about ownership more generally, then, there is a tendency to vacillate between the two conceptions outlined above. On the first conception, ownership is earned through the competitive exercise of one's powers and is deserved; on the second, ownership depends simply on what and where one happens to be and is as arbitrary as existence itself. On the former view, ownership is essentially active; on the latter, it is essentially passive.

The contrast between these two, fundamentally opposed conceptions of selfhood and ownership is closely aligned with the contrast between feminists (generally liberal, American feminists) who insist that what we are and what we have should be the result of the free exercise of independent wills, regardless of the bodies we happen to inhabit, and feminists (generally "radical," French feminists) who emphasize the unchosen, bodily basis of our identity and who view with suspicion the affinity between liberal conceptions of the self and capitalist conceptions of ownership.

The inadequacies of each view repeatedly toss us from one to the other. In order to move beyond this incessant flip-flop, then, a more subtle account of selfhood is necessary. Ownership of a body by a self is not possible without a distinction between self and body, for simply being a (human) body does not suffice for being a person or a self. But neither is a person or a self an independent entity that merely uses the body. Instead, I suggest, we must understand the self as constituted by certain interrelations between the psychological states of a body—interrelations that simultaneously create a self and create a relationship of ownership between the body and the self. Properly understood, ownership, like selfhood, is neither autocratic nor automatic; it depends, rather, on achieving particular sorts of integration and coordination among the aims and desires of our bodies.

2

The alternative I shall outline accords with much recent work on the nature of personal identity or selfhood—including work in such fields as the philosophy of mind, literary theory, and feminist theory.[8] It maintains that persons, or selves, are neither separable from nor identical to bodies but, rather, are created and sustained by the establishment of particular sorts of interconnections between the psychological states of physical organisms. The relation between a body and a self is, on this account, the relation between a physical thing and an interconnected set of its psychological states. On such a view, it is not correct to say that the self *interacts* with the body, since the self is constituted out of psychological states that are themselves states of a body; nor is it correct to say that the self *is* the body, since the interactions between states that are necessary for selfhood are not necessary to the body as such.

Just what sorts of interconnections between psychological states are necessary for the emergence of a self? First, in order for an organism to have psychological states at all, its states must form an interlocking *system* of attitudes. The idea of an organism with beliefs and desires that are so isolated one from another that there is no modification of one belief by another belief, no modification of one desire by another desire, and no coordination of beliefs and desires to produce action, is, I take it, an incoherent idea. The existence of inclinations that mirror implication relations between the contents of one's beliefs and desires—that is, the existence of a certain degree of *reasonableness* in one's mental life—is, at least in part, what makes it the case that one has the beliefs and desires that one does.[9] Some interactions between the psychological states of an organism are, therefore, necessary to the very existence of psychological states. But being an organism with psychological states does not suffice for being a person or a self. Rats and bats seem to act on the basis of fairly well-coordinated and sustained beliefs and desires (beliefs about the objects before them and their relative locations, desires for food and warmth, etc.), yet they do not have selves. Why not? For one thing, they are incapable of taking a larger, or longer, view of their lives; they are incapable of reflection, planning, and self-control. Rats do not, for example, deliberately delay gratification for the sake of long-term rewards (not because those long-term rewards are more vivid at the moment but, rather, because they are expected to give more satisfaction in the long run); nor are they capable of recognizing that their past behavior was premised on faulty assumptions and must be rejected (a recognition that goes beyond the mere replacement of past beliefs to the registration of their falsity); nor are they capable of reflecting on and seeking to change harmful habits (not merely in reaction to pain but in anticipation of an imagined alternative); and so on.[10] Exercising these abilities, I suggest, is essential to being a self, and it involves a much deeper, more layered sort of integration between mental states than that required merely in order to have mental states.[11]

The contrast I have in mind, between being a body with psychological states and being a body with a self, is much like the contrast that Freud draws between the id and the ego. According to Freud, the id comprises an assortment of unreflective beliefs and desires (assumptions and impulses) that more or less automatically generate unconscious actions, whereas the ego is constructed out of these beliefs and desires insofar as they are integrated into an overall self-conception and plan of action that governs what we do consciously. At their most basic, our desires are directed toward objects or ends whose attainment causes pleasure, and when the desired object or end is not attainable, the desire will be deflected onto substitute objects (with almost any object capable of serving as an unconscious substitute for another as long as some associative connection between the two has been established).[12] These processes of the id—the unconscious playing out of bodily desires—may be reasonable in the short term but distinctly counterproductive in the longer term; short-term pleasure can cause long-term grief. In contrast, the processes of the ego—the workings of consciousness–serve to coordinate one's various desires into a rational plan of action that seeks long-term satisfaction in the face of the many constraints presented by reality. It is the job of the ego, or of consciousness, to separate memories of the past from perceptions of the present, to contemplate hypothetical possibilities, and to recognize and correct for its own biases.

The self, or the ego, is not a separate entity with independent desires. It is, rather, a certain way of coordinating unreflective beliefs and desires—a way that depends on the emergence of certain rational capacities (e.g., the capacity to understand objective time, causation, and negation), which themselves emerge with the capacity for reflection (i.e., the capacity to view oneself as a self). The reflective integration of a body's desires is precisely that process which transforms mere *motivations* into full-blown *intentions*, or the psychological states of a body into the psychological states of a person or self.

The desirability of creating and sustaining a self, given this account of selfhood, has been contested, of course. It is no accident that neo-Lacanian feminists, such as Luce Irigaray and Julia Kristeva, who align the feminine with the Unconscious, tend also to align the feminine with the bodily and to deny the intelligibility, let alone the desirability, of a feminine self (versus a feminine plurality of polymorphous desires[13]). I agree with Nancy Hartsock (1987) and others who view such discrediting of selfhood, especially for women, with some alarm, for, it seems, with a loss of selfhood goes a loss of agency and a loss of individual rights. (The loss of agency and of individual rights may be a welcome result for others.) I can't pursue this important and complex debate here, however. I mean only to clarify the conceptual underpinnings of ownership, and of bodily ownership in particular.

What I am proposing, then, is this: A body belongs to a person when and if the psychological states of that body are integrated through reflection in such a way as to constitute a person or a self. When and if the mental states of a body are not so integrated, no ownership (of this fundamental kind) is possible because there is simply no person or self to be the owner; nothing can be *your* body if there is no *you*. Thus, coming to be a person or a self and coming to own one's body are not two different processes (first the creation of a will and then its application) but, rather, two faces of the same process—a process whereby the psychological states of a body are simultaneously integrated *by* and integrated *into* an overall conception of the self.

Why, we might ask, ought we to call this relationship between self and body one of ownership? It was relatively easy to understand, on the previously outlined conceptions of ownership, why the *use* of something by someone might be thought of as constituting that person's possession or ownership of that thing, or why something that is a *part* of something else might be said to belong to and, hence, be owned by the whole. But why should a self that is constructed through the reflective integration of bodily desires be thought of as *owning* the body whose desires it integrates? Well, to some extent, both of the above rationales apply here as well: The self, through reflection, combines psychological states of the body into a whole, of which individual states belong as a part (thus: ownership of parts by the whole), and this self-conception, arising from reflection, has a significant role in directing the body's actions (thus: ownership of the used by the user). There is, however, another important sense of ownership that additionally obtains on our proposed alternative—namely, ownership in the sense of "owning up to" or taking responsibility for something; for in the shaping of bodily desires into the relevant sort of whole, one must consciously *acknowledge* one's various desires—owning them insofar as one accepts them as part of who one is.

Although, on this account, being a self depends on having a conception of oneself (for it is only through the conceptualization of oneself that the disparate desires of a body can be integrated so as to constitute a self), it is not the case that one is whatever one conceives oneself to be. Some self-conceptions, or some aspects of one's self-conception, do not reflect the integration of a body's psychological states so much as they simply reproduce other people's conceptions of oneself. If others' conceptions can be realized in one's body—can generate real, though acquired desires—they will indeed form a part of oneself; to the extent that they are not so realized, however, one's self-conception will remain at odds with oneself. This is not always a bad thing (indeed, it may be a necessary stage in moral development[14]), but it does highlight the fact that an integrated *conception* of oneself, though necessary for a self (for there is no self without self-consciousness), is not the same thing as an integrated self (for there is such a thing as self-deception).

Note that if a person is a set of integrated psychological states, then one can *be a person* or a self to a greater or lesser degree depending on the extent to which one integrates the body's psychological states. And if this is right, then one will *own a body* to a greater or lesser degree depending on the degree to which its psychological states are integrated into a self.[15] Strange as this may sound at first, I think it is exactly right. In particular, if the psychological states of a body are integrated in very partial or erratic ways (either because one's self-conception disregards most of the body's beliefs and desires or because one continually fluctuates between conflicting self-conceptions), then the person will have a relatively weak claim to ownership of her body.[16]

Consider, in this regard, what one might call the phenomenology of bodily ownership. One experiences a body (or a body part) as no longer one's own when it either becomes lifeless or takes on a life of its own—that is, when it resists integration into one's life, or acts independently on the basis of beliefs and desires that are not a part of one's self-conception. This can result from a loss of bodily sensation and/or a loss of control over one's body (which occurs in an extreme form in patients who lose proprioception) or from a dissociation between one's self-conception and one's bodily acts (which occurs in an extreme form in patients who have no memory of acts they have committed). In such cases, people tend to speak of a body (or a body part) that is no longer their *own*, that no longer *belongs* to them.[17]

3

With an improved account of bodily ownership in hand—an account that seeks to apply some relatively recent and subtle descriptions of the self/body relation to the question of bodily ownership—we are now in a better position to evaluate appropriate versus inappropriate extensions of and limitations on bodily ownership.

For ownership of things other than one's body to be an extension of ownership of one's body, it seems that one would need to integrate the states of these other things into one's self in much the same way that one integrates the states of one's body into one's self. How is this possible? Samuel Wheeler III (1980) has argued that the natural parts of one's body, the artificial (and possibly removable) parts of one's body, one's personal car, and the oil refineries that one controls are all, equally, extensions of one's self, for all are instruments that enable us to act, and thus to be agents; and because there is no clear line to be drawn between a limb and an oil refinery with respect to the self, he maintains that our rights to oil refineries (appropriately acquired) should be just as inviolable as our rights to our own bodies. In light of the above discussion, however, this argument can be seen to rest on two importantly mistaken assumptions: first, the assumption that our identity as persons or selves depends on our identity as users of our bodies and other things—so it assumes that the loss of such use constitutes the loss of our very identity as selves; and, second, the assumption that the lack of any clear line between ownership of limbs and of oil refineries prevents us from making distinctions of degree—in particular, by disregarding the possibility that our ownership rights over our bodies may be *stronger* than those over our oil refineries in virtue of the fact that the former is *more* essential to our identity as persons.[18] I have urged that it is not so much our use of our bodies that makes them ours as it is the integration of our bodily states into a whole, and that such integration comes in degrees. With respect to things other than one's body, integration into our selves is bound to be more partial and fragmentary (objects such as cars are not always with us, after all, and they do not have beliefs and desires that we may integrate with our own) and thus our ownership of them is bound to be weaker.

Once the idea of *degrees* of ownership, or stronger and weaker ownership rights, is accepted, it should be possible to decide that although I have ownership rights over an oil field (in virtue of the psychological integration of that oil field into my very self), those who work the oil fields have still stronger ownership rights. Likewise, it should be possible to decide that my ownership rights, or those of the workers, are too weak (given the limited extent of its integration into our selves) to override, for example, certain welfare rights.[19] Despite Marx, it does not seem a foregone conclusion that workers are more closely identified with the products of their labor than are managers or investors. Different people exhibit different degrees of attentiveness, responsiveness, coordination of needs, and long-term planning with respect to the objects they encounter; and, as in the case of one's relation to one's own body, these different degrees of involvement make for different degrees of ownership. And as we've seen in the case of one's body, ownership is a relation that involves something more than mere interaction with, or use of, a thing, but also something more than mere identification with a thing. Neither causal interaction, nor self-conscious identification, nor a combination of the two, suffices for ownership, for interactions may be mindless and self-conceptions may be deluded. What is needed, rather, is some degree of integration of the thing into the fabric of one's life; and different degrees of integration will exist for different people in different circumstances.[20]

Once we accept degrees of ownership, it also becomes possible to think of different people owning a single human body to a greater or lesser extent. It is easy to construct science-fiction examples of this possibility, or to view the dilemma of single bodies with multiple personalities in this light, but there are also many ordinary cases involving multiple owners of a single body. For whenever we integrate the beliefs and desires of other people into our very selves, we will, on the conception I am proposing, own their bodies to some degree (i.e., their bodies will, to some extent, be ours). A mother's ownership of her ten-year-old child's body will not usually be such as to override the child's ownership of her body, but (given sufficient integration) it will be ownership nonetheless. When we assume that close friends and relatives should have a say in decisions concerning the treatment of a comatose patient's body, we are not simply turning to those most likely to know what that patient herself would want but are also registering the fact that the patient (and hence her body) has to some extent become a part of the relatives' selves, and for this reason they ought to have some rights over the body. Furthermore, since people may own their bodies to different degrees, and since sometimes human bodies (e.g., fetuses or brain-dead patients) lack selves entirely, it is sometimes possible for a person to have overriding ownership rights to more than one body.[21]

Let us consider next just what (primary) ownership of one's body allows one to do—what rights it confers. So far we have been speaking rather loosely of rights to control or rights to determine what is done with one's body. Does this include rights to sell one's body—that is, to exchange it on the market? Margaret Jane Radin (1987) suggests that my body, unlike my hat or my car, is *inalienable* property—literally, something that I cannot alienate or separate from myself in the way that exchange requires. I agree that it is not possible for us to transfer ownership of our bodies in their entirety; for in order to *transfer* ownership of something, the owner must *relinquish* ownership, and in the case of our bodies owner and owned are inseparable. More precisely, to exist as a self at all, I must continue to own my body; relinquishing ownership of my body amounts to suicide of the self, not exchange.[22] It is, however, perfectly possible for us to relinquish ownership of *parts* of our bodies—organs, parts of organs, skin, hair, and so on—without endangering our very existence. Indeed, their loss or exchange may help to strengthen the self by restoring health, by saving someone else of importance to oneself, or simply by providing the money necessary to meet other important needs. Although there may be many reasons, of a utilitarian sort, to put legal restrictions on the exchange of bodily parts, there is, I think, nothing incoherent about such exchange.

Between the evident incoherence of selling one's entire body and the evident coherence of selling certain bodily parts lie a number of more difficult cases. I shall briefly consider just two, of current interest—prostitution and paid pregnancy—in order to indicate how the proposed account of bodily ownership might usefully reorient disputes over these issues.

As is the case with many other politicized disputes in this country, popular disputes over both prostitution and paid pregnancy tend to revolve around the notion of freedom of choice and contractual agreement. On the one hand: Shouldn't the prostitute or the surrogate mother be free to do what she chooses to do with her body? And shouldn't both be held to their contractual agreements? On the other hand: Can the prostitute or the surrogate mother really choose freely? And can either be said to really understand the terms and consequences of the contracts to which they agree? Orienting discussion of prostitution and paid pregnancy around the requirements of free choice and genuine contracts, however, overlooks what is most distinctive about these cases. After all, the choices surrounding prostitution and paid pregnancy are not less free than many other choices we make about work and family, and the contracts (whether implicit or explicit) are not less understood. What is distinctive about prostitution and paid pregnancy concerns, rather, the particular challenges it poses for the notion of *bodily* ownership. The fundamental challenge of prostitution is, I suggest, the challenge of selling an isolatable part of one's body rather than one's entire body in the context of sexual exchange; and the fundamental challenge of paid pregnancy is the challenge of determining whether, and to what extent, the body of a newborn belongs to the selves of the various adults involved.

Several authors have suggested that prostitution involves selling more of oneself, so is closer to selling one's whole self, than do other forms of paid labor. Then, on the assumption (endorsed above) that selling oneself as a whole is not a right we have—because the selling that presupposes legitimate ownership simultaneously undermines the very possibility of ownership—it is argued that we do not have the right to prostitute ourselves. Carole Pateman (1983), for example, maintains that one's sexual identity is more central to one's self than one's identity as a farmer, a teacher, a technician, an artist, or any other aspect of one's identity that is commonly sold for wages, and thus that selling one's sexual services threatens one's identity in ways that selling other services does not. David Archard (1989) develops a somewhat different line, arguing that prostitution, unlike other common forms of paid labor, requires not only certain actions but certain role-playing, and that such role-playing requires the relinquishing of one's very identity in ways that most jobs do not.

I think these writers are on the right track in supposing that prostitution involves selling more of oneself than do most other forms of work, and hence is more suspect, but I find the details of their arguments unconvincing. I'm not at all sure, for instance, that my identity as a woman is more central to my self than my identity as a writer or a teacher; and there is certainly more extensive role-playing involved in being an actor (which, I assume, is a career I have a right to pursue) than in being a prostitute. What *is* true, I think, is that erotic satisfaction involves some kind of merger of selves (however temporarily), and that in the context of prostitution this is standardly achieved through the total submission—even obliteration—of the prostitute as a person.[23] Prostitutes may, of course, restrict their submission in some clearly defined ways; but, quite apart from the problems surrounding the enforcement of these restrictions, there remains a certain tension between the aim of providing erotic satisfaction and the aim of keeping one's self intact. It is also possible, of course, to want to submit oneself to another's wishes, but in these cases one tends to identify with another person, and hence to make that person a part of oneself, so that submitting oneself to another is simultaneously a way of recreating and repositioning oneself. I would not insist that nothing like this can be a part of the experience of prostitution, but it is certainly not the norm. In general, then, prostitution by its very nature—as the selling of erotic services—involves something like the temporary selling of oneself.

Temporary selling of oneself, or the selling of a temporal phase of oneself, is, of course, quite different from the permanent selling of oneself—into slavery, for example. Nevertheless, I think, just as the state should not allow people to sell themselves into permanent slavery (and should ensure that this is not the only way for individuals to survive), so too the state should not allow people to sell themselves as temporary slaves. The only way to ensure this end, though, is to regulate and oversee commerce in bodily services in such a way that limitations and restrictions on one person's use of another's body are enforceable—that is, to legalize prostitution in order to strengthen the prostitute's control over the situation by enforcing her restrictions on the *scope* of the sale. I dare say that, for many, this measure would also restrict the potential eroticism, but eroticism bought at the price of a person is not an acceptable exchange.

Let us look, even more briefly, at the issue of surrogate mothering, or paid pregnancy. Here, the assumption underlying much of the discussion is that a baby—as a human being—cannot rightfully be *owned* by anyone, including its natural parents, and thus cannot rightfully be *sold*. On this assumption, it is often argued (and often legislated) that a surrogate mother must be paid not for the child but only for the labor of pregnancy. This is not what typical payment arrangements indicate, of course (the bulk of the payment comes only after delivery of a healthy baby); so critics of surrogacy argue that it really does amount to selling a child, and that such an act is wrong.[24] (The fact that this criticism can so easily be met, by a change in payment arrangements, is one sign that it misses its mark.)

On my view of what bodily ownership amounts to, though, worries about the selling of newborns should not be construed as analogous to the selling of one person by another. The latter is illegitimate given that each person is the (primary) owner of his or her own body; but the newborn is not yet a person on the analysis of persons here offered. Becoming a person is a gradual process, of course, and it is better for the law to recognize personhood too soon rather than too late; but personhood does not begin at birth.

The legitimate worry about ownership and paid pregnancy is, rather, a worry about competing ownership rights to a newborn. If ownership of bodies comes in degrees, and degrees of ownership depend on the degree to which the psychological states of a body have been integrated into a self, then there can be no *general* answer to the question: Who has primary ownership of a newborn—the woman who has delivered it or the person who has contracted for its delivery? The right answer will always depend on the particulars of the situation. Hence, as long as the involved parties are agreed as to whose baby the baby is, there should be no objection to surrogacy on the grounds of ownership violation. (Other sorts of objection to the practice of paid pregnancy may be quite valid, of course. I have no quarrel with laws prohibiting the selling of newborns, only with a rationale that rules out the possibilities of ownership rights over children.) When there is disagreement, however, the relative strengths of competing ownership rights ought to be weighed—based not on prior contracts or genetic ties but on the degree to which the baby has become a part of the respective selves of the involved parties (as well as on some concern for the well-being of the person the baby will become). King Solomon's test for the "real" mother of a contested baby, however impractical, was exactly the right one, as it was a test of who was most attached to, and most identified with, the psychological states of the baby. This observation is also in line with standard policy regarding older children, whereby the desires of children—presumably reflective of the degree to which their identities are integrated with that of the parent—help to determine custody arrangements.[25]

Practical and detailed legal recommendations on these topics must answer to a number of considerations other than those addressed here, but it has not been my aim to formulate such recommendations. Instead, I have sought to explicate the nature of bodily ownership (which I take to be the fundamental sort of ownership) in such a way that it makes good sense in its own right, thereby clarifying just what the appropriate extensions and limitations of bodily ownership might be.[26]

Notes

1. For a good discussion of just how deep-seated and uncontested this assumption is, within classical Marxism as well as classical liberalism, see G. A. Cohen (1986). There are, of course, many cultures—both past and present—that deny that a wife or a slave or a subordinate of any kind owns his or her own body; also, more radically, there are cultures that seem to do without (individual) ownership rights altogether. My starting point, though widely shared, is certainly not universally shared.

2. Locke (1924/1690) suggests that God is actually the original owner of everything, including us. This story, of course, just shifts the question back a step: In virtue of what does God own all? Does he own everything because he owns himself, and it is out of himself that he creates everything?

3. I shall, rather blithely, call these rights *ownership* rights since they concern rights to control what is *mine*. Stephen R. Munzer (1990, ch. 3) wishes to distinguish ownership rights from property rights, and he argues that we have limited property rights rather than ownership rights over our bodies—because of restrictions on the legitimate *transfer* of our bodies. I agree that there are legitimate restrictions on the transfer of bodies, for reasons that will become clear later, but I do not therefore deny that the rights involved are ownership rights. Munzer also suggests that those who argue from the claim that this is *my* body to the claim that I *own* my body are confusing self-identity with self-ownership (1990, 41n). I, in contrast, think that the claim that this is my body is not a claim about identity but, as the possessive pronoun suggests, a claim about ownership (of a particularly fundamental and intimate sort).

4. As should be evident, the approach of this chapter runs counter to that of legal positivism, whereby the analysis and justification of rights amount to no more and no less than a systematization of the laws that concern rights. I think that legal systems should be answerable not only to precedent but to various prelegal conceptions of rights—conceptions of rights bound up with our prelegal conceptions of personhood or humanity, for example.

5. A more unwieldy alternative to the "first use" constraint would be a "most use" constraint. The latter is in fact closer to the position I shall defend, although it is not use so much as involvement that matters on my view.

6. Defenders of the view that I *am* my body sometimes reject the idea that I *own* my body on the grounds that ownership requires a distinction between owner and owned that doesn't exist in the case of one's body. Eliot Deutsch (1993), for example, maintains that bodily ownership is, at best, a metaphorical notion. But it is seldom denied that my body is *mine* and that *therefore* I have certain *rights* over its destiny; it is not clear to me what else literal ownership requires.

7. One could even argue, along lines suggested by Spinoza (1982/1677), for example, that my body is constituted by much more than this human organism since my body is identical with the object of my thoughts—that those I love and all the objects of my thoughts, for example, actually become a part of my physical self. But this argument would amount to a revisionary proposal regarding the criteria of bodily identity—a rejection of the usual criterion of spatial-temporal continuity.

8. Texts I have in mind include Williams (1973), Corngold (1986), Smith (1988), White (1991), Scheman (1993), and Flax (1993). The assumptions I make, however, are broad enough to gain the acceptance of many other theorists currently working on the mind/body relation and on the nature of personal identity. I am not, for example, committed to the view that psychological states can be *reduced* to physical states, or even to the view that a self can be *reduced* to an interconnected set of psychological states, insofar as that would require all relevant states to be specifiable without reference to the person to whom the states belong—something that seems impossible if, as I argue, second-order intentional states are necessary to personhood. (For an effective argument against the latter type of reduction, see Campbell [1992].)

9. This assumption is central to functionalist accounts of psychological states, of course, but it is also widely accepted by anti-reductionists as a constraint on the attribution of intentional states. (See, for example, Donald Davidson [1974].) Note that in order to accept this, one need not be a complete holist, insisting that every causal

connection between mental states contributes to their content; molecularism of some sort will do.

10. Just which animals are or are not capable of reflection, and hence of selfhood, is not my concern; and I certainly don't mean to suggest that when animals lack selves we have no obligations regarding their bodies. But I do hold that, because they lack selves, these obligations are not obligations we have on account of their ownership rights over their bodies.

11. I say more about this in Church (1987, 1990).

12. Freud (1915a) tends to assume that a desire carries a certain cathexis, or a certain amount of energy, that can be deflected but cannot simply disappear. Central as this assumption is to much of Freud's theorizing, it is not essential to the theory I am here putting forth.

13. One of the clearest (and most contentious) statements of this position occurs in the title essay of Irigaray (1977).

14. See Church (1991).

15. Or one might speak of stronger and weaker property rights, as does Margaret Jane Radin. She maintains that "the more closely connected with personhood, the stronger the entitlement" (1982, 986), and she discusses some actual legal decisions in light of this criterion.

16. Jerome Segal (1991, ch. 3) distinguishes between the strong degree of integration necessary to selves and the rather weaker degree of integration necessary to persons, although it is not clear whether he thinks that selves have any rights over and above those of persons. Some may even prefer to foster weak selves and weak ownership rights rather than the more traditional strong selves and strong ownership rights. See for example, Vattimo and Rovatti (1983).

17. For vivid presentations of two representative cases, see Freud's (1915b) account of the woman who insists that her eyes are not her own and Sacks's (1970) account of a woman who disowned her body.

18. This latter assumption is effectively exposed and criticized in Braybrooke (1980). See also Radin (1982) and Waldron (1990) for somewhat different, Hegelian defenses of the inextricability of private property from personhood; both versions are effectively criticized in Becker (1992).

19. I do not want to commit myself to the view that ownership rights usually override welfare rights, or even that conceptualizing such conflicts in terms of rights is appropriate. My point is only that, given these standard assumptions, distinguishing between weaker and stronger ownership of a thing may help us to see how to balance such claims.

20. Clearly, there are many practical reasons for insisting on sharper and simpler determinations of ownership within the law. But, as I said earlier, I am concerned here not so much with prescribing legal distinctions as with clarifying the metaphysical distinctions that, I take it, do and should underlie the determination of laws concerning ownership.

21. There are various practical reasons for respecting and enforcing a person's wishes regarding her property, including her body, after she has ceased to exist as a person. But, on the assumption that there can be no ownership rights in the absence of an owner, these sorts of cases must rely on the assignment of a new owner (per-

haps on the basis of some prior, contractual agreement) who will want to carry out the wishes of the prior owner.

22. I do not mean to suggest that we have no right to commit suicide. Suicide, or euthanasia, may sometimes serve to preserve the self in the sense of making the whole of one's life more integrated, and more of a whole, than the alternatives can bring about. This is an argument advanced by Ronald Dworkin (1991, 1993).

23. For a useful explication of this assertion, see Hartsock's (1983) discussion of the erotic in chapters 7 and 8 of her book.

24. The difficulty of maintaining the distinction between payment for services and payment for child is brought out nicely in Shanley (1993).

25. The rights of "nannies" versus those of biological parents present another interesting, difficult, and underdiscussed case. I see no reason to preclude (at least in principle) the possibility of a "nanny" becoming so invested in the children she cares for, and they in her, that she could have stronger ownership rights over the children—and thus a stronger say in what happens to them—than the biological parents.

26. I am grateful to Mary Shanley, Uma Narayan, and Diana Meyers for their comments on an earlier draft of this chapter, and I would like to thank participants in a seminar at Vassar College, devoted to issues of property and personhood, for their stimulating discussions of these and related issues.

References

Archard, David. 1989. Sex for Sale: The Morality of Prostitution. *Cogito* 3.

Becker, L. 1992. Too Much Property. *Philosophy and Public Affairs* 21(2).

Braybrooke, David. 1980. Our Natural Bodies, Our Social Rights: Comments on Wheeler. *Nous* 14(2): 195–202.

Campbell, John. 1992. The First Person: The Reductionist View of the Self. In *Reduction, Explanation, and Realism.* David Charles and Kathleen Lennon, eds. Oxford: Oxford University Press.

Church, Jennifer. 1987. Reasonable Irrationality. *Mind* 96(3): 354–366.

_____. 1990. Judgment, Self-Consciousness, and Object Independence. *American Philosophical Quarterly* 27(1): 51–60.

_____. 1991. Morality and the Internalized Other. In *The Cambridge Companion to Freud.* Jerome Neu, ed. Cambridge: Cambridge University Press.

Cohen, G. A. 1986. Self-Ownership, World-Ownership, and Equality. In *Justice and Equality Here and Now.* Rank S. Lucash. ed. Ithaca, N.Y.: Cornell University Press.

Corngold, Stanley. 1986. *The Fate of the Self.* New York: Columbia University Press.

Davidson, Donald. 1974. Psychology as Philosophy. In *Essays on Actions and Events.* Oxford: Oxford University Press. (Reprinted in 1980.)

Descartes, René. 1980/1641. *Meditations on First Philosophy.* Donald A. Cress, trans. Indianapolis: Hackett Publishing Co.

Deutsch, Eliot. 1993. The Concept of the Body. In *Self as Body in Asian Theory and Practice.* Thomas Kasulis et al., eds. Binghamton: SUNY Press.

Dworkin, Ronald. 1991 (January 31). Your Right to Death. *New York Review of Books.*

_____. 1993. *Life's Dominion: An Argument About Abortion, Euthanasia, and Individual Freedom.* New York: Knopf.

Eagleton, Terry. 1993. Review of Peter Brooks's *Body Work. London Review of Books* 15(10): 7–8.

Flax, Jane. 1993. *Disputed Subjects: Essays on Psychoanalysis, Politics and Philosophy.* London: Routledge.

Freud, Sigmund. 1915a. Instincts and Their Vicissitudes. *The Standard Edition of the Complete Psychological Works of Sigmund Freud,* vol. 14. London: Hogarth Press.

_____. 1915b. The Unconscious. *The Standard Edition of the Complete Psychological Works of Sigmund Freud,* vol. 14. London: Hogarth Press.

Hartsock, Nancy. 1983. *Money, Sex, and Power: Toward a Feminist Historical Materialism.* New York: Longman.

_____. 1987. Foucault on Power: A Theory for Women? In *Feminism/Postmodernism.* Linda J. Nicholson, ed. London: Routledge. (Reprinted in 1990.)

Hegel, Georg W. F. 1952/1821. *Philosophy of Right.* T. M. Knox, trans. Oxford: Oxford University Press. (Reprinted in 1967.)

Irigaray, Luce. 1977. *This Sex Which Is Not One.* Catherine Porter, trans. Ithaca, N.Y.: Cornell University Press. (Reprinted in 1985.)

Kant, Immanuel. 1991/1797. *The Metaphysics of Morals.* Mary Gregor, trans. Cambridge: Cambridge University Press.

Locke, John. 1924/1690. *Two Treatises of Government.* London: J. M. Dent & Sons Ltd. (Reprinted in 1973.)

Munzer, Stephen R. 1990. *A Theory of Property.* Cambridge: Cambridge University Press.

Pateman, Carole. 1983. Defending Prostitution: Charges against Ericson. *Ethics* 93(3).

Radin, Margaret Jane. 1982. Property and Personhood. *Stanford Law Review* 34(5): 957–1015.

_____. 1987. Market-Inalienability. *Harvard Law Review* 100(8): 849–937.

Sacks, Oliver. 1970. The Disembodied Lady. In *The Man Who Mistook His Wife for a Hat.* New York: Harper and Row.

Scheman, Naomi. 1993. *Engenderings: Constructions of Knowledge, Authority, and Privilege.* London: Routledge.

Segal, Jerome. 1991. *Agency and Alienation: A Theory of Human Presence.* Savage, Md.: Rowman and Littlefield.

Shanley, Mary L. 1993. Contract Motherhood: Social Practice in Social Context. *Signs* 18(31).

Smith, Paul. 1988. *Discerning the Subject.* Minneapolis: University of Minnesota.

Spinoza, Baruch. 1982/1677. *The Ethics.* Samuel Shirley, trans. Indianapolis: Hackett Publishing Co.

Vattimo, Gianni, and Rovatti, Pier Aldo, eds. 1983. *Il pensiero debole.* Milan: Feltrinelli.

Waldron, Jeremy. 1990. *The Right to Private Property.* Cambridge: Cambridge University Press.

Wheeler III, Samuel. 1980. Natural Property Rights As Body Rights. *Nous* 14(2): 171–193.

White, Stephen. 1991. *The Unity of the Self*. Boston: MIT Press.

Williams, Bernard. 1973. *Problems of the Self*. Cambridge: Cambridge University Press.

five

Forgetting Yourself

ANITA L. ALLEN

The self is the basic unit of personality and personal identity. It is who and what we are. Philosophers debate competing theories of the self. These theories portray the self as, for example, a "bundle of perceptions" (Chisholm 1994, 97); a rational agent structured and motivated by internalized general norms (Piper 1985); a homuncular system of effective agents and subagents (Johnston 1988); and a duality of conscious and unconscious motives accessible through psychoanalysis (Erwin, 1988). Philosophers also debate the seeming capacities of the self, such as self-knowledge and self-deception. Self-knowledge—what it means to "know thyself"—has been a frequent subject for explorations of mind, language, and epistemology (Cassam 1994), whereas self-deception has been a favorite topic of contemporary moral psychology (McLaughlin and Rorty 1988).

We humans may be able to *know* ourselves and *deceive* ourselves, but, according to an idiomatic English-language expression, we also are able to *forget* ourselves. Though fundamental to persons, selves can be forgotten. Consider this hypothetical instance of forgetting oneself.

> **Case 1:** Jo takes care of her elderly mother, who is in poor health. Jo normally behaves lovingly toward her mother, as she believes she ought. But one day Jo is especially tired and feeling sorry for herself. When her mother makes a request that Jo would ordinarily fill without hesitation or protest, Jo curses, denies the request, and storms away. Afterward, Jo is ashamed and feels fortunate that others did not witness her discourteous behavior.

Jo has "lost her cool." Her outburst is an example of forgetting oneself.

As I shall explain it, to forget yourself is, inadvertently and temporarily, to abandon the manners or morals—the communal norms of decorum or decency—that generally sustain both social approval and self-esteem. Forgetting yourself typically stems from lapses of self-awareness or, as in Case 1, self-control. Often, forgetting yourself is to be in what Gilbert Ryle described as one of those "situations in which a person admits that he did not know at the time what he was doing, although what he was doing was not an automatism but an intelligent operation" (1994, 25). A person who forgets himself or herself is not "alive to what he is doing all the time he is doing it" (1994, 27).

Self-deception also involves failing to be wholly alive to what one is up to. When taken literally, forgetting yourself, like deceiving yourself, is a puzzling phenomenon. Self-deception, literally construed, is a matter of fooling the self; it paradoxically entails believing and disbelieving the same propositions at the same time. Forgetting yourself, literally construed, paradoxically entails simultaneously remembering and not remembering your own identity as a person who accepts and adheres to particular norms. If we accept as valid the appealing but controversial conception of the self characterized by Amelie Rorty (McLaughlin and Rorty 1988, 13) as "strongly integrated, capable of critical, truth-oriented reflection, with its various functions in principle accessible to, and corrigible by, one another," both forgetting and deceiving yourself should be impossible. Anyone but one's own self should be forgettable. Anyone but one's own self should be deceivable.

Nevertheless, in hypothetical Case 1, Jo manages to forget herself. A person with Jo's responsibilities might also deceive herself. Imagine the self-deception of sons and daughters like Jo who resent obligations of elder-care but cannot acknowledge resentment concerning the care of their own mothers. Imagine, too, that paradoxes of self-deception and forgetting yourself operate in tandem in such instances: You deceive yourself about the burdens of caring for your mother, refuse to hire a private-duty nurse, allow your frustrations to grow, and eventually forget yourself in a regrettable outburst.

Forgetting yourself has affinities to *akrasia*, also known as "moral backsliding" or "weakness of the will"—a phenomenon Georges Rey (1988) has discussed in connection with self-deception. Like self-deception and forgetting yourself, *akrasia* has a paradoxical quality. Assuming a certain contested conception of the self as rationally motivated and free, how is it possible for a person to know what is right, good, best, or virtuous, but fail to do it? *Akrasia* occurs, if it occurs at all, when a rational person deliberately breaches what he or she knows to be a morally binding behavioral norm. According to my analysis, forgetting yourself also consists of breaching what you know (or at least believe) to be a binding behavioral requirement. But the chief differences between forgetting yourself and *akrasia* are these: First, instances of forgetting yourself can involve nonmoral as well as moral norms; and second, forgetting yourself involves lapses of self-awareness or self-control rather than intentional, deliberate behavior. By contrast, paradigmatic instances of *akrasia* involve strictly moral norms and self-aware,

deliberate acts of noncompliance. A moral backslider with the responsibilities of Jo in Case 1 might slip away for an hour each week to satisfy her crav-
ing for a certain television program, thereby deliberately violating her admit-
ted obligation to continuously monitor her elderly mother's needs. By
definition, then, *akrasia* is a moral breach. (Morality certainly cannot recommend the negligent abandonment of one's helpless charges.) Yet *akrasia* may
function to relieve pent-up resentment of the sort that can lead frustrated
people to forget themselves.

Philosophers have written volumes about the phenomena of self-knowledge, self-deception, and *akrasia*. The same cannot be said of forgetting
yourself. A comprehensive philosophy of the self would include an account
of this interesting phenomenon. My purpose is to frame such an account and
then to link it to current concerns about awareness of group membership
and racial identity. Achieving the liberal ideal of a "color-blind society" may
be a practical impossibility. In order for a color-blind society to emerge, people need to be able to put race out of their own minds and keep it out of the
minds of succeeding generations of youth. I want to suggest that although it
is doubtless possible to put race out of one's mind, many Americans are too
racially self-aware and/or race-conscious to do so. Among many African
Americans, race-consciousness has become a matter of group pride. For
them, forgetting race is "acting white" and acting white is something for
which a black should be condemned. To the extent that it breaches an
African American subgroup norm against acting white, forgetting race
would seem to be explicable as an instance of forgetting yourself.

I do not defend a particular conception of the self, although my analysis
may entail some conceptions or rule out others. My account of "forgetting
yourself" is consistent with at least one important conception of the self—
namely, the conception of the self as governed by rule-like norms. There is
considerable appeal to the notion that we are "Kantian" selves "defined by
. . . general prescriptive principles [internalized in the normal process of so-
cialization] to which we are usually disposed to conform our emotions, action and habits" (Piper 1985, 182–183). Forgetting ourselves can be seen,
from within a "Kantian" framework, as failing to do as we are generally motivated to do—that is, as failing to conform "our emotions, action and
habits" to certain socially instilled general prescriptive principles.

1

Forgetting Decorum and Decency

According to another old-fashioned, idiomatic English-language expression,
selves can be forgotten. I can forget myself. You can forget yourself. We can

forget ourselves. Even the awkward people described as "self-conscious" and the commanding ones described as "self-possessed" are capable, on occasion, of forgetting themselves.

"Forgetting yourself" is a figure of speech. It is not a literal act. When we "forget ourselves," we have not literally ceased to remember who we are. We know who we are. More precisely, we know as much about ourselves as we ever did. We retain memories of our unique and individual personal identities. We can recall facts about ourselves, such as our names, occupations, ethnicities, and tastes. But when we "forget ourselves," we breach applicable rules, standards, virtues, or other behavioral norms. We fail to comply with norms of social decorum or moral decency applicable to persons with our traits, capacities, roles, and good characters. Fine actors, for example, occasionally forget their lines, and fine citizens occasionally forget to be decent and decorous.

We are social creatures, products of communal forms of life. Communal relationships and values are sometimes said to be constitutive of personal identity, shaping who we are and what we value (Benhabib 1992, 73–74). The social character of the self as dependent upon the material and normative resources of communities does not entail the assumption that people are more automaton than autonomous. To varying degrees, people can and do reflect on the point of conformity to communal conceptions of appropriate and inappropriate affects, attitudes, and conduct.

In many instances, conformity to communal norms of decorum and decency strikes us as something about which we have a choice. And in most instances we choose to go along. Indeed, our decision to conform to well-established or pervasively accepted patterns of behavior often helps to sustain our self-concepts as responsible, cooperative members of society. Thus, the same "good" behavior that wins social approval also earns self-esteem. Capable of what Gilbert Ryle called "higher-order self-dealings" (quoted in Cassam 1994, 39), we adults take on the aspect of "prefect[s] regulating [our] own conduct." We are responsible people who deserve self-esteem and the esteem of others, not because we have blindly adhered to communal norms but, rather, because we have chosen to regulate our conduct in accordance with reasonable social expectations.

Most people behave as they are supposed to, according to social rule and role. Yet whereas many social expectations are hardy enough to survive wintry critique, others wilt under cool scrutiny (Benhabib 1992, 74). In recent decades, the latter has been the fate of the distinctly oppressive social expectations that once confined women and people of color to subservient roles in the national economy of the United States. So, when we say in earnest that someone has forgotten himself or herself, the norms we presuppose may be widely accepted, entrenched communal norms of the sort that the best political, moral, or legal theories would not endorse.

Why We Forget Ourselves

People typically forget themselves either because they are inattentive (to what they are doing or where they are doing it) or because they are overcome or excited by emotion. Jealousy, anger, lust, and fear can lead individuals to forget themselves. Sometimes it is a drug or alcohol that makes a person less attentive or more subject to their emotions. In fact, people commonly drink to lower their inhibitions. And for the most part, they do so in what mainstream American cultural norms deem appropriate settings and contexts. They drink at home, in bars, and at parties. But I would stress that deliberately ingesting drugs or alcohol so that one can "let down one's hair" is not the same thing as forgetting oneself. Normally, when we are hoping to let down our hair, we are not hoping to forget ourselves. It is one thing to take a drink, hoping it will embolden us to ask a friend to bed; and something else to make a pass, unexpectedly, at our friend's spouse. Only the latter counts as forgetting ourselves. I would also stress, in connection with altered states of consciousness, that although we may joke that a stand-offish, somber person made giddy and gregarious by a drink has forgotten himself, we do not mean it. We are making light of that person's disposition to take the virtue of sobriety to an extreme.

People try not to forget themselves even when they are tired, angry, and intoxicated. For although the consequences of forgetting ourselves can be trivial and amusing, sometimes they are highly shameful and harmful to ourselves and others. The following hypothetical case illustrates an inconsequential, trivial instance of forgetting oneself. In this instance the breach stems from inattention, a lapse of attention brought on by exhaustion and ennui.

> **Case 2:** Pam is a vice president at a major corporation. She is sitting at a table in a windowless conference room filled with staid colleagues who are politely debating proposed strategies for marketing a new product. It is very late in the evening and her mind begins to wander. She begins to think about a pleasant musical she attended the night before. She starts to hum one of its tunes. A close friend sitting nearby gently nudges Pam to restore her attention. Pam then realizes that she had forgotten herself.

Here, forgetting oneself has resulted in a minor breach of social etiquette and professional decorum.

In the United States, people hum aloud in public, but typically in churches or at music lessons, parties, rock concerts, and such. It is not the rule (though also not rare) to hear someone humming while applying for a bank loan or observing the cross-examination of a star witness in court. Sophisticated professionals avoid humming at business meetings. They consider it inappropriate. They know that humming in the midst of a meeting suggests absentmindedness or indifference. Absentminded inattention undermines the confidence of clients, customers, and colleagues. Of course, some successful businesspeople are tolerated as eccentric individualists who are either prone to absentmindedness or consciously unwilling to "play the role." For the latter group, humming during lulls in meetings might be ordinary, self-aware behavior.

A significant feature of Case 2 is that Pam's close friend, rather than another person sitting nearby, nudges her to attention. Forgetting oneself is an asocial moment: The forgetting subject goes private, slipping away from the constraining norms of the public, communal realm. Friends want us to keep our jobs, our "faces," our standing in the community. Good-hearted strangers may want the same thing for us. But there is a limit on acceptable and comfortable paternalistic intrusion by non-intimates. In the realm of mere etiquette and decorum (as in Case 2), perhaps the most polite thing a stranger, mere acquaintance, or co-worker can do when someone forgets himself or herself is to pretend it did not happen. If others convincingly pretend not to have noticed, they spare the forgetting subject the embarrassment of knowing for certain that others witnessed his or her deviance. By contrast, our friends have duties as friends that go beyond polite evasion. They ought not allow us to make fools of ourselves by, for example, violating workplace or other norms. Friends have special permission to reach into our privacy and, with a nudge, a telling glance, or a reprimand, to draw us back into the public arena.

Rebellion and Critique

Forgetting oneself is an act of nonconformity, though not an intentional act of rebellion or critique. But, clearly, failing to conform to established norms is sometimes a good thing. Pam (from Case 2) is no rebel against corporate culture, and she is embarrassed by her lapse of decorum. Yet her lapse possibly has a beneficial consequence. It may usefully signal to others that their meeting has gone on too long and should be ended. Similarly, in a society where women are not supposed to talk back to men, beneficial consequences may flow when a normally subservient woman "forgets herself" by telling off her husband or father. Stubbornly conventional cultural insiders would view the woman's behavior as "misbehavior." But letting off steam in response to oppression may have psychological and political advantages that incline outsider or insider culture critics to view inadvertent misbehavior with favor.

A third hypothetical case illustrates a consequential instance of forgetting oneself. In Case 2 the "forgetting" was a matter of inattention; in the following case, as in Case 1, it is a matter of unbridled emotion.

Case 3: Min is a high school teacher. For the third day in a row she is trying to teach history to a group of unruly students who have come to class unprepared. She is angry. In response to a simple question, a volatile student she knows to be suffering from poor self-esteem gives her an especially ill-informed answer. Min blurts out: "Idiot! That's the stupidest thing I've heard all year, and I've heard plenty of stupid things in this class!" The student hurls a pile of textbooks in Min's direction and sobs. Min immediately realizes that her testy words to the vulnerable student were imprudent and wrong.

Min has forgotten herself. And forgetting herself has resulted in a breach of what many might regard as a role-related ethical responsibility. In contemporary American education, name-calling is considered intemperate behavior for teachers. Most teachers do not engage in it at all; but almost anyone can forget himself or herself when sufficiently provoked.

If forgetting ourselves involves innocuous behavior such as humming show tunes at work, it can win us approval as "spontaneous" and "original." But if forgetting ourselves involves injurious behavior such as demoralizing children or the elderly, it can damage our reputations, relationships, and self-esteem. The social realm is constituted such that we forget ourselves only at our peril.

For some, the peril is mortal. In the Jim Crow era, southern blacks who forgot themselves in spontaneous displays of passion in their dealings with whites risked being jailed or lynched. The film version of Alice Walker's *The Color Purple* included a fictional account of a feisty young woman named Sophia who was beaten and jailed for swearing at the white mayor's wife. When dealing with whites, Sophia normally remembered her place, her communal role as a social inferior. But that day, the mayor's scatter-brained wife innocently insulted Sophia in the presence of Sophia's children—and Sophia lost her temper. She forgot herself, and then nearly lost her life.

Social norms of the Old South appear to have made it possible for one and the same behavior to count as moral misdemeanor or serious offense depending upon the race of the offender and victim. My impression is that a white man discovered to have made a spontaneous pass at a white or black woman rarely had cause to fear serious retribution in the hands of black or white society; but a black man discovered to have made a spontaneous pass at a white woman risked death in the hands of an angry white mob. In short, a racist society may construct a particular action as either "forgetting yourself" or "heinous crime" depending upon the race of the offender.

An Internal Conception

As social beings, our personal identities are intimately linked with our communities of origin and influence, and thus with the behavioral norms they prescribe for us. Individuals internalize (i.e., accept as binding) many of the behavioral norms that they learn from social interactions with others. When individuals conceive of themselves or others as having forgotten themselves, these internalized values are their points of reference. Forgetting oneself, then, entails failing to conform to behavioral norms of the sort we know to be constitutive of individuals situated in communal forms of life.

On what I shall call the "internal" conception of forgetting oneself, to forget oneself is to deviate briefly from an internalized behavioral norm. We can imagine that Pam and her friend from Case 2 have internalized the positive norms of the corporate world as their own. They do not regard humming show tunes as appropriate behavior during business meetings. If in a rare moment of distraction Pam audibly hums, she has acted inappropriately, against the norm. Pam's short-lived deviation from the internally endorsed no-humming norm is an instance of forgetting herself. But now compare Pam to Peter.

> **Case 4:** On his first day with the company as a management trainee, Peter hums to himself during a lull in an important meeting with Pam and others. As it happens, Peter thinks nothing of public humming. He does it anywhere, everywhere, all the time. Peter is unaware that Pam and others regard such behavior as unprofessional. Pam, who is embarrassed for Peter, thinks "That man has forgotten himself."

From an internal perspective, Peter has not forgotten himself at all. He has not internalized the norms of the corporate world. The self that he is values public humming as an appropriate or neutral distraction.

Pam's attribution of "forgetfulness" registers her own values. Indeed, her value judgment has social determinants and is shared by most others in her corporate professional milieu. Her assessment of Peter tells us something about Pam and the social groups to which Pam belongs. Pam is not unlike the adults who say of mannerless children that they have "forgotten themselves," when the children have simply not (yet) grown to accept the norms of the adult world as their own internal social norms. Parents say "Behave yourselves!" and "Don't forget yourselves!" to children to exhort them to use good manners and adhere to social rules. They say these things despite the "truisms of the playroom and schoolroom" (Ryle 1994, 38) that adhering to norms of self-restraint is higher-order behavior and that "[h]igher-order actions are not instinctive" (Ryle 1994, 38). Learning to be a certain sort of disciplined self and learning not to forget that self are components of early childhood education. Sometimes when an adult says "You're forgetting yourself!" to a child displaying socially inappropriate behavior, the truth of the matter is that the child has not yet become a fully socially groomed self. The child cannot forget a self that he or she has not yet become. And like

Peter from Case 4, the child cannot breach a norm he or she does not yet recognize as binding. The admonitions of the parent are *ex cathedra:* "Do not forget yourself!" really means "Do not violate communal norms; do as you are supposed to do!"

2

Euphemism, Metaphor, and Excuse

Aggregated in this section are the key features of my analysis of forgetting yourself, as suggested by the foregoing hypothetical cases. First, the expression "forgetting yourself" functions as a metaphor. It does so because when we say people have forgotten themselves, we fully realize that no such thing has literally occurred. There is no amnesia. It is only *as if* their memories of the socially or morally compliant people—the proper selves—we know they are have slipped away.

Forgetting oneself is a *deviation* from a person's ordinary patterns of behavior, which include a tendency to obey social rules of etiquette, morality, and law. People can forget themselves in the internalist sense and violate rules they accept but think are silly; or forget themselves and violate rules they accept and judge to be sound. Whether forgetting oneself will be a source of regret or remorse depends upon the significance one attaches to the patterns or standards of conduct one has breached and their possibly adverse consequences. One might not regret having forgotten oneself and told an amusing off-color joke at a dull family gathering. But one might well regret having forgotten oneself and flown into a violent jealous rage.

Second, "forgetting yourself" functions as euphemism. "She forgot herself" or "He forgot himself" is a distinctly polite way of saying, for example, that a sophisticated person has been vulgar; a sensitive person, insensitive; a kind person, malicious; a calm person, passionate. Speakers normally reserve the "forgetting yourself" expression for situations in which an adult whose behavior, though generally in line, gets out of line, failing to be socially decorous or morally decent.

Third, forgetting oneself is a *brief* and *infrequent* deviation from practice. It is a temporary lapse. Forgetting oneself is not a persistent habit or pattern of ill-mannered or immoral behavior. Forgetting oneself involves short-lived inattention, absentmindedness, and similar lapses of self-awareness; it also entails "losing one's head" to passionate emotion and similar lapses of self-control. The expression "losing oneself" can refer to longer-term lapses of self-awareness. An artist may "lose himself" or "lose herself" in work for hours or even days. Forgetting oneself is not unlike "acting out of character." However, as the phrase is generally understood, people can "act out of character" for a period of time, but they cannot "forget themselves" for more than a few seconds or several minutes. If I join a week-long criminal conspiracy hoping to get money to pay off debts, I act of out character; I do not forget myself.

It seems basic to the concept of forgetting yourself that episodes of inattention (as in Case 2) or unbridled emotion (as in Cases 1 and 3) are infrequent and brief. A typically decorous teacher who experiences several outbursts of anger in one day could aptly report that she repeatedly forgot herself that day. Better yet, she could aptly report that she was not herself that day. But a typically decorous teacher who routinely began breaching rules of decorum and decency day after day would seem to have undergone a change of personality or moral character. Of such a person one might say "He is not himself." Teachers who habitually lash out in anger at their students do not qualify as people who have forgotten themselves. Rather, they are insensitive people with poor self-control. Similarly, it would violate standard conceptual usage to say that people who always swear at the elderly, chew their nails in public, or hum the scores of musicals in meetings have "forgotten themselves."

Fourth, forgetting oneself can be *morally culpable* behavior. Case 3 provides an example. The teacher's behavior in that case is wrong, though perhaps forgivable and excusable, assuming certain familiar facts about the working conditions of the teaching profession. One reason for ascribing moral fault is the recognition that many human beings have the power to cultivate habits and virtues that make forgetting oneself (in the form of, say, absentmindedness and emotionality) less likely. Conversely, inadequate sleep, alcohol consumption, and the use of narcotics—all of which may be quite deliberate and intentional—can lead to lapses of self-control and self-awareness. But the essential point here is that it makes sense for us to hold one another responsible for bad conduct that results from predictable lapses to which we substantially contribute.

Forgetting oneself can have adverse consequences that are either trivial or serious, but *not too serious*. If, for example, the consequences of a person's immoral behavior include very serious physical or emotional injury to others, the expression "forgot himself or herself" no longer comfortably applies. The reason is that saying someone "forgot himself" carries with it the sense that the person has made a mistake of the sort people are entitled to make occasionally. Of course, there is no set list of the kinds of mistakes people are entitled to make. But brutal murder surely should not appear on such a list. Indeed, to describe a vicious murderer as someone who "forgot himself" (as opposed to someone who was temporarily reckless, insane, or enraged) would be to trivialize the infraction in a way that would seem appropriate only in the context of sarcasm or satire.

Finally, the expression "forgetting yourself" serves to excuse or forgive apparently rare or inappropriate conduct. It conveys the message that people who generally do as they are supposed to do are entitled to make a mistake. Every dog is entitled to one bite and every human being is entitled to an occasional social breach. People who forget themselves, then, are not ill-mannered or immoral people, vulgar or bad in essence. If they were, we would describe their misfeasance differently. "Forgetting yourself" presupposes a conception of the self as mannerly or moral. The people who forget themselves are thus understood to fall into the category of corrigible people whom one fully expects to behave well in the future because they have generally done so in the past. We categorize their nonconforming conduct as forgivable, excusable, and rare by attributing it to metaphorical lapses of memory (of their rule-, standard-, or other norm-governed, mannerly, or moral selves) rather than to lapses of virtue. It follows that when a person sincerely declares, "I forgot myself," he or she is imploring others to forgive or excuse what that person regards as atypical, episodic misbehavior.

3

Forgetting Race

I want to set aside, for a moment, the concept of "forgetting yourself" and focus briefly on simple, literal forgetting. Forgetting is a kind of cognitive disassociation that occurs all the time. Most of the individual acts and events that constitute our lives are forgotten. Most of the things we happen to remember or try to remember, we eventually forget. And some of the things we forget are subject to later recall. Consider Marcel Proust's *Remembrance of Things Past,* in which the author narrates lush, subtle depictions of the sensory stimuli—tastes, smells, sounds—that lead one to recover pleasant and unpleasant memories of the forgotten past from seeming oblivion.

The capacity to forget is remarkable, as are the range and significance of what we humans are capable of forgetting. We have all heard of people who have forgotten to eat, to pick up their children from school, or to pay for merchandise before leaving a store. Lately, I seem to forget the names of my students once a semester has passed. I frequently forget where I have placed my car keys until I "retrace my steps." I once forgot that I had purchased a bag of ginger-candy of a sort I am wont to crave, until I discovered it in my pantry a week later. I even forgot that I had had a bitter argument with an old friend, until I telephoned him after fifteen years without contact and he (still miffed) reminded me.

Once, I momentarily forgot my race. I forgot that I am an African American in a situation quite like this one.

> **Case 5:** Jan is a university student. She is planning a party. She is discussing possible guests with her close friend, Peg. Peg suggests inviting Bob, who is an African American. Jan likes the idea, but suggests that Bob might feel out of

place as the only African American at the party. Puzzled, Peg reminds Jan that *she*, Jan, is also an African American and, therefore, that Bob would not be the only African American at the party. Bemused, Jan realizes that, at least for a moment, she had forgotten her race.

This case, and my own experience, would seem to indicate that race is a forgettable attribute. Yet I would conjecture that forgetting race is an unusual occurrence among African Americans living in the United States. African Americans who escape acute forms of what I call "racial self-consciousness" are still prone to "race-consciousness." These two modes of self-awareness ensure that forgetting race is rare. I would conjecture that even American blacks who are well assimilated into white or multiracial communities are subject to episodes of acute racial self-consciousness and/or race-consciousness.

Racial self-consciousness is awareness of belonging to a putatively inferior racial group, aggravated by feelings of shame and inferiority. I first fell victim to racial self-consciousness back in the 1960s when, at the age of six, I learned that I was a "Negro," called "out of my name" as "nigro," "black," and "nigger."

Race-consciousness, by contrast, is the tendency to select one's race as a subject matter of thought and conversation, but without feelings of personal inferiority. African Americans dwell on race because our dwelling-place is a society with a history of heinous forms of legally enforced racial discrimination and residual racism. Although I seldom talked about race during my childhood and teenage years in mostly racially integrated schools and neighborhoods, I thought about it all the time. Race looms large in black thought, even when it is not a topic of conversation. Conversations among blacks of every social and economic class routinely focus on the causes and consequences of racial disparities in the economic, social, or legal spheres touched by their lives. Indeed, many African Americans develop race-consciousness when they are still very young; and many African American intellectuals possess a highly developed, theoretically sophisticated race-consciousness.

Racialized Selves

Not everyone has a significantly racialized identity. But I believe most Americans do. 'Race', for present purposes, is a generic name for the familiar categories that we in the United States pervasively employ when identifying individuals and groups for varied public and private purposes. We use racial categories for everything from choosing friends and lovers to allocating employment opportunities.

Our conceptions of race are remarkably functional. They establish social boundaries and set behavioral norms, even though they are complex admixtures of color concepts (White, Black, Red, Yellow, and Brown); quasi-scientific divisions (Caucasian, Negroid, and Mongoloid); and bureaucratic groupings for data collection and census-taking (White, Negro or Black, Asian or Pacific Islander, American Indian, Aleut, and Eskimo). Further complicating matters is the fact that conceptions of race blend a miscellany of popular distinctions, some derogatory, reflecting beliefs about national, continental, or linguistic origins (Irish, German, African American, Korean, Hispanic, Chicano, Haitian, Cuban, Puerto Rican, Multiracial, Eurasian); physical characteristics (cracker, chink); and social or citizenship status (WASP, wetback, dago, nigger). Although our conceptions of race are ambiguous, inconsistent, and, as noted, often derogatory, racial identity becomes an element of personal identity over the course of our lives.

Racial self-consciousness (self-awareness of supposed racial inferiority) is a social pathology. Race-consciousness (awareness of the societal significance of one's race) is not. Indeed, some people regard the *absence* of race-consciousness as pathological, contending that for an African American to lose or fail to acquire race-consciousness is to lose or fail to acquire an appropriate identity. Without such an identity, they argue, the ability to flourish in contemporary American society is seriously impaired. A commonly lodged objection to the adoption of black children by whites is that black children reared mainly among whites will fail to acquire race-consciousness and racial identity. Similar concerns about the loss of racial awareness and identity are voiced about suburban and affluent black teenagers who associate with white rather than black peers; and about black adults who marry whites or members of other racial groups. Out-marriage by black women seems especially likely to raise these concerns, owing, perhaps, to the assumption that husbands dominate their wives. A white husband, it is assumed, will culturally dominate his black wife and mixed-race children, to the detriment of their identities and to the ultimate detriment of black culture.

It has been many years since the time I forgot my race. But against the background of pervasive concerns about the loss of race-consciousness, identity, and culture, it has been hard to forget that I once forgot.

Forgetting Race as Forgetting Yourself

I presented Case 5, involving the black student who forgets that she is black, as illustrative of ordinary literal forgetting. I suggested that a person can forget that she purchased ginger-candy until reminded and, likewise, that she can forget her race until reminded. But I now want to consider the possibility that forgetting race, as in Case 5, is forgetting yourself.

In some respects, Case 5 is like Case 2, the case of the humming vice president who, in the metaphorical sense elaborated above, "forgot herself." In both cases, a friend brings to another's attention a fact of which the latter was not mindful. In Case 2, a vice president is told that she is humming; in

Case 5, a university student is told that she is a member of a certain racial group.

To distinguish the cases, one might begin by pointing out that in Case 2 someone is *informed* for the first time of a fact she did not know, whereas in Case 5 someone is *reminded* of a fact she knew but was not alive to at that moment. Yet the vice president is also, in a sense, reminded of something. She is reminded that she and others believe humming in a business meeting is inappropriate.

Another effort to distinguish the cases might center on the argument that Case 2 involves inadvertent violation of a prescriptive norm (i.e., the no-humming rule), whereas Case 5 involves a mistake of fact and no such violation. For this reason, perhaps Case 5 is best characterized as illustrating an ordinary lapse of memory rather than the phenomenon of "forgetting yourself."

Does speaking to another as if you do not believe you are a member of the race of which you are in fact a member violate a normative prescription? To clarify that the university student in Case 5 was violating a behavioral norm, I want now to look at her behavior, not from the standpoint of general morals and mores but from that of the morals and mores of her African American subgroup. From this perspective Jan is potentially culpable of breaching norms against "acting white." Upon first consideration, it might appear that a black person's ability to forget his or her race is a good thing. Isn't the capacity to forget race, after all, a step toward the color-blind society that the United States Supreme Court has pronounced as our collective, constitutional ideal? If forgetting race is "acting white" and many blacks consider "acting white" bad, so much the worse for blacks' values. They are an impediment to the color-blind society!

I want to suggest that Case 5 is no unambiguously hopeful sign that the color-blind society is on its way or even possible. The norm against "acting white" is indeed problematic for its tendency to stereotype African Americans. But by far the larger problem than that of blacks' expectation that other blacks will not "act white" is the pervasive context of racism and inequality that makes continued segregation attractive.

Community Norms

Large communities—nations, states, and cities—generate complex behavioral norms applicable to members of the community. These communal norms generally include "universal" norms that prescribe behavioral standards for everyone in the community and "group-specific" norms that prescribe behavioral standards only for individuals belonging to certain groups within the community. Thus some communal norms may apply only to adults, women, the aristocracy, a religious minority, a race, or a segment of a race. Group-specific communal norms commonly privilege some groups (e.g., Christians in the Third Reich; white males in the Antebellum South) and subordinate others (e.g., Jews in the Third Reich; white women, Indians, and blacks in the Antebellum South).

Some of a community's universal and group-specific norms are fundamental. They structure the relationships on which depend the survival of the community and its various social units—groups, subgroups, families, individuals. People seldom neglect the many norms associated with attributes of personal identity that structure paramount social relations, whether or not they accept those norm as valid. The costs of inattention to the norms that structure and sustain social hierarchies of gender and race can be especially high. For this reason, women and people of color tend to be alive to group-specific norms that safeguard their welfare and peace of mind. Before federal civil rights laws were enacted in the 1960s, prudent southern blacks made a point of being very much alive to their manners and morals when dealing with whites.

Yet periodic inattention to social norms relating to race, gender, and other socially key traits does occur. Recall Alice Walker's Sophia, the black woman who swore at the white mayor's wife, breaching the dominant community's social norms. She was cursed, beaten, and thrown into jail. The story of Sophia makes for powerfully dramatic fiction precisely because it depicts an understandable but atypical hot-headed response to oppressive social subordination.

By contrast, the cost of inattention to the nonfundamental group-specific behavioral norms of a community is generally trivial. No one really cares if a woman spits on the sidewalk, even though public spitting, especially by a woman, is socially disapproved behavior. I have heard the words "She thinks she's a boy!" spoken, with more humor than sanction, in reference to a physically active girl old enough to begin to understand society's behavioral expectations for women. In days past, when gentlewomen and girls failed on occasion to follow the rules of behavior expected of "ladies," such as sitting with the knees pressed together and ankles crossed, they were politely described (without further sanction) as having forgotten themselves. Initiating sexual intimacy could also count as "forgetting yourself" when undertaken by a member of the appropriately modest female sex. Frequent breaches of gender-specific sexual norms were once considered exceedingly risky. Reputedly "promiscuous" women hoping to find "respectable" husbands and providers could easily fail.

Group and Subgroup Norms

A large community imposes behavioral norms on its members, as do groups within such communities. In fact, groups often generate prescriptive norms applicable to their members. Some of these group-generated norms apply universally to all group members, whereas others apply only to specific subgroups. For example, the African American community has generated norms that apply to all African Americans as well as norms that apply only to African Americans of one sex or the other. Indeed, black women were once expected to assume caretaking roles with respect to orphan grandchildren, nieces, and nephews that black men were not expected to assume.

In addition, as a matter of courtesy, African Americans in traditional neighborhoods in the South were expected to "speak" to other African Americans they met in passing (i.e., to acknowledge them with a polite greeting or nod of the head). Yet they were not expected to behave in this way toward members of other groups, nor did they expect members of other groups to behave in that way toward them. A black person preoccupied in thought, who on that occasion failed to speak, might be viewed as having forgotten herself or himself (although "forgetting" oneself is not, to my knowledge, an expression with much currency in black English or among blacks). The indignant query "Don't you speak?" might also be posed to a person who forgot herself, to shame her into conformity. To cite another example of group-specific norms and their breach, a moral standard still applicable in some segments of the African American community discourages black women from having sex with white men. But a black woman can "forget herself" when passion unexpectedly presents itself.

Americans of all hues share core moral values relating, for example, family responsibility, theism, and other important matters. I do not assume that people of different races have altogether different behavioral standards. The African American custom of greeting others, known as "speaking," doubtless applies with minor variations within other groups and in other regions of the country. Yet members of racial groups have (and are held to) at least some culturally specific standards of decorum and decency that are not shared with members of other groups. In this connection, a grave concern of the 1990s is that young blacks warped by the culture of crack are developing uniquely self-destructive, deviant subgroup norms that could undermine the well-being of vast segments of the African American communities.

Acting White

Inattention can lead one to "forget" that one is a professional in a business meeting. Emotion can lead one to "forget" that one is a caregiver for an elderly relation, or a teacher with responsibility for vulnerable teenagers. There is no limit to the kind of norms that can fall prey to inattention and emotion. However, some classes of norms may be especially resistant to breach when compared to others. Any class of well-internalized norms will be resistant to breach. Yet, quite possibly, well-internalized norms seen as binding but trivial (like some rules of etiquette) are breached more readily than those seen as vital (like rules of law).

We are not so much born with race as born into race as a feature of our social worlds. Yet our racialized social worlds exert such an influence that we
seldom entirely escape the pull of constitutive norms. Whether generated by
the larger community or by racial subgroups, race-related behavioral norms
command such a degree of attention and self-control that noncompliance
stemming from brief inattention is especially unusual. In the American context, which has been shaped by a history of colonialism, slavery, legal segregation, and prejudice, we may be particularly unlikely to "forget" the subset
of manners and morals that shape the expectations and identities of people of
our races. Members of minority groups are highly self-conscious about
racial identity and the implications of racial identity for routine transactions
with others. Indeed, minority-group members feel they are "different," and
that difference colors social experience so pervasively that being inattentive
to the racial norms that apply to specific individuals is, for some, barely conceivable.

Jan, the university student in Case 5, forgot her race. Do we fault her, as
someone who has wrongfully allowed her African American race to slip out
of her mind? Has she forgotten herself—specifically, by failing to be attentive to the norms of her racial group? Jan discussed a party with a white
friend. Participating in such a discussion was a form of behavior governed
both by community norms and by a set of African American group norms
applicable to Jan (like it or not) by virtue of her race.

Among many African Americans, communicating with whites is governed
by a whole set of race-specific rules of engagement. Certain affects, topics,
and aspects of vocabulary and body language are taboo. One rule dictates
against "airing dirty linen"—that is, publicly criticizing other blacks. Another rule dictates against allowing frequent association with white people to
cause one to "act white." Jan's behavior—namely, the fact that she thinks and
speaks like a white liberal—violates African American social norms against
acting white. And behind the norm against thinking and speaking "white" is
the notion that to be as psychologically healthy, authentic, and useful as one
ought to be, one is obligated to be race-conscious. One is obligated to be
alive to being black.

The people condemned most severely for "acting white" are the blacks
who are race-conscious but deliberately choose to act white. Acting white
means dressing in certain clothes, attending certain events, living in certain
neighborhoods, befriending certain people, and so on. Arm-chair psychology suggests that these individuals might act white because they are victims
of racial self-awareness searching for self-esteem. Some blacks voice contempt both for light-skinned blacks who "pass" for white and for highly
successful blacks who adopt conservative "white" ideologies, such as
Supreme Court Justice Clarence Thomas. But fears about losing blacks who
"act white" to white society are by no means solely connected either with

passing as white or with political conservatism. On the contrary. Parents who value race-consciousness worry about sending their black children to white-dominated public and private schools. Teenagers who value race-consciousness worry about "interracial" dating. And policymakers who value race-consciousness in high culture and politics worry about the survival of historically black colleges, art forms, and civil rights organizations.

Moreover, some people who "act white" are viewed with empathy and concern rather than with contempt. The phenomenon of acting white is a by-product of the civil rights movement. In the present era of integration and affirmative action, which began in the mid-1960s, many blacks have existed in isolation from other blacks, in white-dominated neighborhoods, schools, and workplaces. Many middle-class and affluent young blacks are not thoroughly socialized as blacks. Marked isolation from majority-black communities has permitted some blacks to shed, or even fail to develop, a black identity, racial self-awareness, or race-consciousness. These young blacks act white because they are, in a sense, culturally white.

To know whether Jan's episode of acting white in Case 5 merits contempt or compassion relative to the values and concerns of African Americans, we would have to know more about her. If she is full of self-hate and deliberately acts white to win white approval, she might deserve some of the contempt that would inevitably be heaped upon her by many of her black peers around the nation. But if Jan does not normally "act white" and her doing so on this occasion was inadvertent, her breach of the African American moral rule against acting white could be interpreted with compassion as an excusable instance of "forgetting yourself." Rather than participating in the discussion with her white friend in a way that was mindful of the black person she knows she is, Jan participated (at least for a moment) as if she were white—as if she were a white person of the sort who befriends blacks and cares about their comfort.

Whether Jan forgot her racial identity in the literal or metaphorical sense, her example is troubling. An educated adult black should be race-conscious and, hence, incapable of making an assertion that logically entails that she is white. A lapse like Jan's—and mine—is probably the result of having so closely and frequently associated with whites that one begins unwittingly to imitate the habits of mind and speech of white society, many of which entail that the thinking and speaking subject is white. For six years—all of my four years of college and two of the four years I spent as a graduate student in philosophy—I had little intimate contact with blacks and a great deal of intimate contact with whites. After all, it was the decade of the 1970s, the heyday of affirmative action, and I was bestowed with educational opportunity by elite white institutions. Given the liberal ideal of a color-blind society, it might have been a good thing that I forgot my race, had I not *remembered everyone else's*. Whatever vision of race relations one holds dear—segregationism, nationalism, integrationism, or multiculturalism—one cannot be sanguine about cultural forms that lead people to maintain a racial perspective, yet mistake their own race and its significance.

Alive to Our Selves

The expression "forgetting yourself" is decidedly old-fashioned. However, the polite concept for which it stands is far from irrelevant to contemporary concerns. As I have shown, the idea of "forgetting oneself" bears an interesting relationship to concerns about group alienation and racial identity.

Overall, the United States is remarkably segregated by race. This is the context in which the group norms against acting white and forgetting race have emerged. Despite a constitutional jurisprudence that nominally promotes a "color-blind" society, most people seem to prefer single-race neighborhoods, schools, churches, and workplaces. At the same time, a special peril of displacement and disapproval flows to members of certain minority racial groups guilty of being dead to their own races.

Yet blacks and other minorities fearing political, economic, and cultural exclusion are not the only ones motivated to remain alive to race. Just about everyone is. Whites are motivated by the fear that inattention could threaten not only their personal safety but also their educational and cultural institutions. I am very drawn to the ideal of a society in which people of differing races enjoy cultural pride but have moved beyond racism, xenophobia, and turf wars (Allen, 1996). Yet it is by no means clear as to how this move is to be made, particularly at a time when racial self-consciousness and race-consciousness are so deeply embedded in our behavior and values. The choice facing African Americans today, then, is whether to think about race as black persons or as white persons, rather than not to think about race at all.

African Americans rigidly adhere to race-specific norms (even trivial formalities) *internal* to their racial communities as a means of sustaining communal bases of self-esteem in a seemingly hostile nation. And they rigidly adhere to race-specific norms *external* to their racial communities to avoid conflicts with members of other groups. These behaviors, along with continued racism, xenophobia, and discrimination, have proven to be powerful barriers to meaningful racial integration in the United States.

So many of the public policies debated today—everything from family values, to women's rights, to gay rights, to rights for the disabled, to welfare, to racial justice, to religious and political expression—ultimately relate to the matter of defining selves in opposition to and in light of community and group values. No one wants to be forced out of communion with who and what they believe they really are. Yet with all the current focus on community, social ethics, and personal responsibility, people are more concerned than ever about the downside risks of failing to conform to reasonable social expectations. It seems that everyone wants to be themselves, but no one wants to be without some group basis for sustaining identity and moral self-esteem. Successful navigation of the world thus requires all the attentiveness and emotional control one can muster.

References

Allen, Anita L. 1996. "The Half-Life of Integration." In Stephen Macedo, ed., *Re-Assessing the Sixties*. New York: W. W. Norton.

Benhabib, Seyla. 1992. *Situating the Self: Gender, Community and Postmodernism in Contemporary Ethics* (New York: Routledge).

Cassam, Quassim, ed. 1994. *Self-Knowledge* (Oxford: Oxford University Press).

Chisholm, Roderick. 1994. "On the Observability of the Self." In Quassim Cassam, ed., *Self-Knowledge* (Oxford: Oxford University Press), pp. 94–108.

Erwin, Edward. 1988. "Psychoanalysis and Self-Deception." In Brian McLaughlin and Amelie Okenberg Rorty, eds., *Perspectives on Self-Deception* (Berkeley: University of California Press).

Johnston, Mark. 1988. "Self-Deception and the Nature of Mind." In Brian McLaughlin and Amelie Okenberg Rorty, eds., *Perspectives on Self-Deception* (Berkeley: University of California Press).

McLaughlin, Brian, and Rorty, Amelie Okenberg, eds. 1988. *Perspectives on Self-Deception* (Berkeley: University of California Press).

Piper, Adrian. "Pseudorationality." In Brian McLaughlin and Amelie Okenberg Rorty, eds., *Perspectives on Self-Deception* (Berkeley: University of California Press).

_____. 1985. "Two Conceptions of the Self," *Philosophical Studies* 48: 173–197.

Proust, Marcel. 1961. *Remembrance of Things Past*, trans. C. K. Scott Moncrieff (New York: Random House).

Rey, Georges. 1988. "Toward a Computational Account of *Akrasia* and Self-Deception." In Brian McLaughlin and Amelie Okenberg Rorty, eds., *Perspectives on Self-Deception* (Berkeley: University of California Press).

Rorty, Amelie. 1988. "The Deceptive Self: Liars, Layers, and Lairs." In Brian McLaughlin and Amelie Okenberg Rorty, eds., *Perspectives on Self Deception* (Berkeley: University of California Press).

Ryle, Gilbert. 1994. "Self-Knowledge." In Quassim Cassim, ed., *Self-Knowledge* (Oxford: Oxford University Press), pp. 19–42.

six

≈

Queering the Center by Centering the Queer

Reflections on Transsexuals and Secular Jews

NAOMI SCHEMAN

Confusing yourself is a way to stay honest.
—Jenny Holzer

Twentieth-century liberatory activism and theorizing have lived with and on the tension between two visions: For one the goal is to secure for the marginalized and oppressed the relief from burdens and the access to benefits reserved for the privileged, including the benefits of being thought by others and oneself to be at the center of one's society's views of what it is to be fully human. For the other the goal is to disrupt those views and the models of privileged selfhood they underwrite—to claim not the right to be, in those terms, fully human but, rather, the right to be free of a stigmatizing, normalizing apparatus to which one would not choose to conform even were one allowed and encouraged to do so. Struggles in the arenas of race, colonialism and imperialism, gender, class, and sexuality have all, in varying ways and to differing degrees, in different times and places, been pushed and pulled, shaped and molded, formed and deformed by the tensions between these two visions.

Among the perquisites of modern Eurocentric privilege are socially supported expectations that one can and will conform to certain norms of selfhood: One will be a person of integrity—whole and of a piece, someone to be counted on, stable and steady; one's beliefs, attitudes, and feelings will be explicable and coherent; one's actions will follow straightforwardly from one's intentions; one will be simultaneously solid and transparent—a block of unclouded substance.[1] (That the very wealthy and powerful are often allowed, or even expected, to be creatures of unpredictable caprice and inexplicable temperament is the exception that proves the rule: The acquisition and in most cases the maintenance of privilege are matters of discipline, so that flamboyant flouting can be a sign that, by one's own efforts or by the inheritance of the efforts of one's ancestors, one is so securely privileged as to be able to let the discipline go. In short, part of how one flaunts one's privilege is by acting as though one need do nothing to continue to earn it.)

As María Lugones has argued (in a talk at the University of Minnesota), such an ideal of integrity is not as straightforward as it may seem. The direct, unmediated route from intention to action that is one of its hallmarks is typically more apparent than real: We are taught not to see the elaborate collaboration provided to the privileged by a compliant social structure. By contrast, the necessary survival strategies of the oppressed make these marks of full, moral humanity unobtainable: Manipulation, deviousness, fickleness, and other stigmata of less than fully straightforward, solidly transparent subjectivity can be the signs not of defects of character but of the only available ways of getting by in a hostile world. If the straight roads are ones that require tolls one cannot afford to pay, and if they are laid out not to go where one needs to, then one has no choice but to find alternative routes, routes that snake around the roadblocks thrown up by those who have no interest in your getting anywhere you want to go.[2]

Among the coherencies that philosophers from John Locke to Derek Parfit have put at the criterial heart of personal identity is the continuity of memory. Such continuity marks what it is to be the same person throughout time, thus to be the bearer of responsibility, the maker and receiver of promises, the recipient of trust. From a wide range of causes—notably including childhood abuse—memory is subject to distortion and even erasure, making it difficult for those who have suffered such a loss to fashion a sufficiently coherent narrative of themselves to be credible. (At the extreme, such abuse can lead to the literal fracturing of the self: One of the distinguishing features of multiple personality disorder is the failure of memory across at least some of the different personalities—A has no recollection of doing what B did.)

Insufficiently noted by philosophical theorists of personal identity is the role of the memory of others in constituting selfhood. It is not just that we are the persons we remember ourselves as being: We are equally, for better or worse, the persons others remember us as being. The others around us may be loving or arrogant,[3] thoughtful or careless, with their memories of us; and we can be grateful or resentful or both for being held in their memories, for being continuous with the persons they remember us as being. Persons who are forgotten or not well remembered—if those in whose memories they might have been held are dead or gone, absentminded, or uncaring—are seen and often see themselves as diminished. And some, in order to be the persons they are becoming, or believe themselves always to have been, need to detach themselves from the memories of those who would hold them too firmly in mind, trapping them in selves that no longer, if they ever did, fit. They need to reinvent themselves, to live without the coherence of a shared, remembered past.

One could argue at this point (especially with regard to the role of memory), as adherents of the first vision would, that the picture of privileged subjectivity is not in itself a problematic one: The problem is in its exclusivity. Nor are wily survival strategies inherently admirable, as much as we may admire those who manage by means of them to survive: Surely people often have to do things to survive that they would far rather not have to do. We need, on this view, to be careful not to romanticize oppression by celebrating the character traits it breeds.

Adherents of the second vision would counter that we equally ought not to celebrate ideals of humanity that have been realized literally on the bodies of others to whom those ideals have been denied. Privileged subjectivity is not some neutral good that just so happens to have been scarfed up by an unscrupulous few. Rather, it is a form of subjectivity well suited to unscrupulous scarfing up, that is, to a view of oneself as naturally meriting a far larger than average share of the world's benefits and a far smaller than average share of its burdens—as having, in Marilyn Frye's (1983) terms, the right to graft onto oneself another's substance. The privileged self, on this view, is not only engorged but also diminished: It has split off and projected onto those same others the parts of itself deemed too messy or embarrassing to acknowledge. Its seamless integrity is achieved by throwing out all the parts that don't quite fit, secure in the knowledge that one can count on commandeering sufficient social resources not to need a fully stocked, even if incongruously jumbled, internal tool kit.[4] Even memory works in some ways like this: The coherent remembered narrative, shared with others who hold us in mind, is an artifact of privilege in terms of both what it contains and what it omits. People do not remember everything that happens to them, and culturally available story lines help give shape to the stuff of some lives (make them "memorable") while leaving others gappy and jerky. Narrativity *per se* may be humanly important, but we have no access to narrativity *per se:* What we have are culturally specific narratives, which facilitate the smooth telling of some lives and straitjacket, distort, or fracture others.

Resistance to the disciplining apparatus that defines privilege (even the "privilege" of full humanity) can take a romantic outlaw form, lived on what are taken explicitly, defiantly, to be the margins, shunning, insofar as possible, what is acknowledged as the center. Alternatively, in ways that will be the focus of this chapter, resistance can take the form of challenge to the stable cartographies of center and margin. Such resistance aims to cloud the transparency of privileged subjectivity, making it visible, and visibly "queer," by revealing the apparatus that goes into normalizing it. The status of the "normal" can, that is, be problematized, rather than either aspired to or rejected—or replaced by some competing normalizing picture.[5] I want to explore the possibilities for what I call "queering the center" by looking at two specific normalizing apparatuses: heteronormativity and what I call "Christianormativity."

1

As David Halperin (1995) argues in a discussion of Foucault,[6] heteronormativity is productively slippery: A large part of its power comes from its deployment of two mutually incompatible discourses—that of (biological) normality and that of virtue. Heterosexuality, as both unremarkedly normal and markedly virtuous, is privileged indirectly: Not itself a site of inquiry, it is constructed by implicit contrast with the equally mutually incompatible characterizations of homosexuality—as sickness and as crime or sin. Arguments against one mode of stigmatization tend notoriously, in the maze of heterosexist (il)logic, to buttress the other: So, for example, arguing that gay men and lesbians don't choose their sexuality reinforces the view of that sexuality as sick, whereas arguing that gay men and lesbians show no more signs of psychopathology than do straight people reinforces the view of their sexuality as chosen and culpable.

Heteronormativity constructs not only sexual identity but gender identity: In order properly to regulate desire it must divide the human world unambiguously into males and females. The discourses of queerness are marked by specifically gender transgressiveness, by a refusal to allow gender to remain unproblematized in a struggle for the rights of same-gendered sexual partners. Such transgressiveness can also be found in some feminist, especially lesbian feminist, attempts to redefine women (or "wimmin" or "womyn"), as something other than not-men. That is, such feminist attempts recognize both that the gender divide is predicated on the sexuality of heterosexual men ("women" = sexual objects for heterosexual male subjects) and that the male/female gender dichotomy is actually a male/not-male dichotomy (see Frye, forthcoming).

There is a striking similarity between the heteronormative representation of the homosexual and the representation of the Jew in what I call "Christianormative" discourse. Analogously to the androcentrism of heteronormative gender, Christianormativity purports to divide the world into religions (all presumed to be like Christianity except for being mistaken) while really having only two categories: Christian and not (yet) Christian. The Christian model of religion misrepresents many of the indigenous cultures that Christians have evangelized, just as heteronormativity misrepresents what it is to be a woman. Like homosexuals, Jews are not only misrepresented but abjected by the normative scheme, not properly caught in its classifications. Since the start of the Christian era Jews have been defined by their closeness to and knowledge of Christianity, just as homosexuals are defined by their closeness to and knowledge of gender difference: In both cases there is a perverse refusal/inability to act on the knowledge they all too clearly have.

On the one hand, the Jew is the quintessential (potential) Christian: Christianity is a matter not of birth but of choice; the paradigmatic Christian is a convert—originally, and most naturally, from Judaism.[7] On the other hand, the Jew is indelibly marked on her or his body: An extraordinary range of body parts have been taken in anti-Semitic discourse to mark Jews (Gilman 1991). Jews are both profoundly culpable for continuing to deny the divinity of Jesus and unable, no matter what we do, to shed the racial heritage of Jewishness.[8] This contradictoriness, as in the case of heteronormative discourse, is productive: It grants to Christians the simultaneous statuses of natural (the way humans are meant to be, the default state for humanity) and especially virtuous.[9] Literally, of course, Christianity is not supposed to be biologically natural, as heterosexuality is, but it is part of most Christian orthodoxy to believe that everyone is loved by Jesus in the way he loves Christians: What is called for is acknowledgment of that love, not the earning of it. Heterosexuality can be seen similarly, as part of essential human nature, so that homosexuality counts as the willful denial of one's true self, just as Jewishness counts as the willful denial of God's love.

Heteronormativity and Christianormativity both have, in addition to their dichotomizing aspect, a universalizing aspect: They both imagine a world of sameness, even as they continue to require not only objects of desire (proselytizing or sexual) but also abjected others. The emphases, on maintaining difference or striving toward sameness, may differ, but the tensions between the two animate both discourses. Although Christianity is officially universally proselytizing, there is reason to believe that Jews play a sufficiently important role in the Christian imaginary that if we didn't exist, they'd have to invent us; and certainly assimilating Jews have met with less than full cultural acceptance, often being stigmatized precisely for conforming to the norms of Christian society (see Prell 1992). Heteronormativity officially envisions a world of only heterosexuals, while similarly requiring the homosexual as a negative definition of normality; and, as Daniel Boyarin and Natalie Kampen have persuaded me, even the gender dichotomy itself contains a universalizing moment alongside the more obvious, official emphasis on ineluctable difference. Although men don't typically proselytize women into sex change (that women are important to the male imaginary seems clear), there is a strong current of mono(male)-gender utopianism, both in Pauline Christianity (see D. Boyarin 1994) and in Enlightenment thought. (Notably, in both cases, the body is meant to be transcended: It is in our minds, or our souls, that we are all really men.)

2

The inconsistent conjunction of sin and sickness, nature and virtue, that characterizes heteronormativity and Christianormativity strikingly (but unsurprisingly) characterizes modern Western conceptions of subjectivity. The clearest statement is perhaps Kant's (1969/1785, Sec. 2). The rationale for the categorical imperative—the answer to the question of why it ought to motivate us—is that only by seeing ourselves as bound by it can we see ourselves as free. Our noumenal identities, if expressible at all, are expressed through duty; the alternative is being determined by inclination—that is, by natural forces no more expressive of our freedom than are any other causal determinations. Virtue may be impossibly difficult to realize, but it is in an important sense natural, not imposed from outside. Kant is left with the problem of accounting for culpable wrongdoing: If acting freely is always acting morally, how can we hold someone responsible for acting badly? The problem is at the heart of Kant's account of the nature of morality and agency: If he allowed the possibility of acting freely in a way that didn't accord with the categorical imperative, he would have to answer the moral skeptic, who challenges the motivational charge behind the categorical imperative. The question of why we should do what duty commands would be a real one and, in Kant's terms, unanswerable, if freely, rationally, we could do otherwise. So the person who heeds not duty but inclination (who might be all of us, all of the time) is not only immoral but (contradictorily) unfree.

Epistemologically, as well, the emphasis has been less on the positive difficulty of obtaining knowledge than on the negative challenge of avoiding error—from Descartes' emphasis on resisting assent when ideas are less than fully clear and distinct, to the positivists' emphasis on the error-producing dangers of subjectivity. Both morally and epistemically the knowing subject is characterized as both generic (normal, universal) and as especially virtuous. The connection is in a sense unpuzzling: As a matter of fact most people most of the time won't be thinking in the manner argued to be the correct one, thus inescapably raising the question of what makes such thinking correct. What is it about those who do think in the privileged ways that makes their thought right for all the rest of us? The distinctively modern (i.e., liberal) answer to that question cannot be that those people are in some way special, with the authority to do the important thinking for the rest of us.

Rather, they have to be seen as us—all of us—at our best, where "best" means simultaneously most natural (uncorrupted, healthy) and normatively most excellent. The two have to go together in the absence of anything other than "natural" for normative excellence to refer to.

One can, therefore, see the naturalizing moves of much of twentieth-century analytic philosophy, with its characteristic problems of theoretically justifying normativity claims, as rooted in the fundamental project of liberalism—what I have elsewhere referred to as "democratizing privilege" (Scheman 1993, 77). That oxymoron reflects the tension between the universalistic theories and the inegalitarian practices of modernity, with the attendant need to explain the inequalities that theoretically ought not to exist, especially those that are uncomfortably correlated with the supposed irrelevancies of race and gender or the supposed anachronism of class. In the absence of anything to account for inequality other than what people actually do—and can properly be held responsible for doing—the accounting has to be in terms of the wrong—or at least the less than optimally right—behavior of those who fail to prosper, without there being any independent, non-question-begging way of characterizing "wrong" or "right." The coupling of the apparently contradictory discourses of nature and virtue (or sickness and sin) are the inevitable result of the need to maintain a normativity that cannot speak its name.[10]

In the work of many philosophers, notably Descartes, there is nothing to mark those who exemplify the norms—in his case, by thinking properly—from those who don't: We are all equally capable of careful and of sloppy thought. Other philosophers, notoriously Kant (1960/1771, 81)—who thought duty and obligation meant nothing to women—have been less egalitarian: It is only some among us who actually have the capacity to reason in the ways supposed to be generically human. The rest of us have been marked by the odd conjunction of moral turpitude and natural incapacity that are taken to characterize the homosexual and the Jew. We have, that is, been characterized as constitutionally incapable of instantiating what is nonetheless supposed to be the essence we share with more privileged humans. Their generic status and the privileges that go with it require that we be essentially like them, whereas the terms of our exclusion, resting as it does on what we are, not on anything we may do, requires that we be essentially different from them.

Those of us so marked have variously struggled against such stigmatization, most often using the tools of liberalism: We have denied our alleged natural incapacity and claimed an equal share in humanity's essential attributes. Thus, for example, Jews have sought civil emancipation, gays and lesbians have sought civil rights, and women have sought equal rights: In all cases the argument has been made that howsoever members of these groups differed from the already-fully-enfranchised, such differences were of no importance when it came to the status in question, typically that of citizen. Given the distressing hardiness of racism, anti-Semitism, sexism, and homophobia, it has been easy for liberals to argue that doing otherwise—asserting the relevance of difference, however socially constructed; resisting offers, however genuinely goodwilled, of acceptance into the ranks of the same—is political suicide.

I do not want to minimize the truth in this argument, nor to dispute the goodwill of those who make it, but it does have the logic of a protection racket, as noted (by Peterson 1977) in relation to the discourse around male violence toward women: There are afoot very bad people who will do you grave harm, and your safety lies in availing yourselves of the protection we offer. What makes the offer suspicious, no matter how sincere and empirically grounded, are the connections between the protectors and those who pose the danger. Protection is problematic when one's protectors benefit from one's acceptance of the terms on which that protection is offered— feminine docility in the case of protection from male violence, and acceptance of the paradigmatic status of the privileged in the case of protection from racism, anti-Semitism, sexism, and homophobia. As women are supposed to acknowledge needing men, those who are "different" are supposed to acknowledge the "honor" of being regarded as essentially the same as straight white middle-class Christian men.

The disputes currently roiling college campuses concerning "multiculturalism" illustrate the normativity of the paradigmatic. The deepest challenge of multiculturalism is to the paradigmatic centrality of the privileged: From whose vantage point is the world most accurately seen? Whose art and literature set the standards of aesthetic excellence? Whose experiences represent generically human encounters with life, death, the natural and social worlds? Shifting the center with respect to questions such as these—shifting which work is taken as most interesting, innovative, significant, worth supporting and encouraging (i.e., taken by those who set curricula, give grants, make decisions about hiring and tenure and promotion)—has nothing to do with freedom of speech or academic freedom; but it is so profoundly threatening to those whose placement at the center has seemed to them a fact of nature that, faced with such shifts (which are, to date, minuscule), they are convinced, I suspect in some cases sincerely, that their rights *must* be being violated. Similarly, one finds the conviction, probably also in some cases sincere, that the shifting of norms means the abandonment of the true ones, those that can seem to come from nowhere only so long as they come from an unchallenged center, at once privileged and universal.

The liberal strategy is to leave unchallenged the paradigmatic status of the privileged, but to argue that it does not in theory, and ought not in practice, entail the exclusion or even the marginalization of others: The others are, in all the respects that ought to matter, essentially the same as the privileged. If this argument were a good one, then shifting in the other direction ought not to matter: It ought to be unproblematic to put at the center some groups previously relegated to the margins, to say not that black people are just like white people except that their skin is darker, but that white people are just like black people except that their skin is lighter.[11] But, as the near hysteria around "political correctness" indicates, such shifts are hardly unproblematic: Being the standard of comparison is a very big deal, no matter how liberally others are deemed to measure up to it.[12]

For the remainder of this chapter I want to work at "queering the centers" of heteronormativity and Christianormativity by juxtaposing two subject positions, neither of which makes sense in the respective normative terms: the transsexual and the secular Jew. The juxtaposition is in part fortuitous: I am a secular Jew, and I have for some time been trying to figure out what that means; and, as a born-female feminist, I have been pressed to understand the experiences and perspectives of those whose attempts to deconstruct gender have an embodied literalness absent in my own life. Furthermore, living outside the norms exacts disruptions of memory and integrity for transsexuals and secular Jews significantly more than for homosexuals and religious Jews. With such experiences at the center, I want to ask what it is to live an intelligible and admirable life—what the structures of subjectivity look like from perspectives other than those of normalizing privilege. The question is an explicitly transcendental one: It starts from what I take as the fact that such lives are lived, hence livable, and asks after the conditions of that possibility.[13]

My hope is that starting from the intelligibility of the normatively unintelligible can serve to uncover the problematic assumptions that make secular Jews and transsexuals incoherent, assumptions that sustain both the status of the normatively coherent (including, in the case of gender, me) *and* the larger hierarchies in which those identities are embedded. I want to argue that placement at the intelligible center is always a matter of history, of the playing out of privilege and power, and is always contestable. One reason for the contestation is to lead us beyond the impasse between the two visions with which I began—both of which, as usually understood, tacitly accept the structures of normalization, whether by claiming one's rightful, central place in them or by defining oneself as outside of or marginal to them. Relocating the gaze to a place of normative incoherence can help to destabilize the center, upsetting the claims of those who reside there to that combination of naturalness and virtue that characterizes normativity.

3

As our (modern Western) world is now, failure to conform to the norms of gender is socially stigmatizing to an unbearable extent: To be human just *is* to be male or female, a girl or a boy or a man or a woman. Those who cannot readily be classified by everyone they encounter are not only subject to physically violent assaults but, perhaps even more wounding, are taken to be impossible to relate to humanly, as though one cannot use the pronoun 'you' with anyone to whom one cannot with total assurance apply either 'she' or 'he'. Those who are not stably, unambiguously one or the other are, as Susan Stryker puts it (1994, 240), "monsters."[14] In such a world, boundary blurring carries psychic costs no one can be asked to pay, and the apparently conservative gender-boundary–preserving choices (surgical, hormonal, and behavioral) of many transsexuals have to be read in full appreciation of what the real options are.

One need not downplay the oppression of women to acknowledge that a certain sort of privilege, one essential for social validation as human, attaches to being located squarely on one side or the other of the gender divide.[15] Those of us who, as stably female-gendered feminists, would choose to see that boundary blurred to oblivion need to learn how to see and be seen as allies by those whose lives it slices through. The work of blurring that boundary is being taken on by a growing number of theorists and activists who are variously resisting the imperatives of gender conformity, including the imperative that transsexuals move decisively from one side to the other. (See, for example, Bornstein 1994, Feinberg 1993, Gabriel 1995, Stone 1991, and Stryker 1994.) To the extent that the social construction of gender is against the interests of all feminists, it ought to fall to those of us who occupy positions of relative safety and privilege to complicate our own locations, to explore the costs of our comfort, and to help imagine a world in which it would be safe to be non-, ambiguously, or multiply gendered.[16]

My own gender identity has never been a source of confusion, nor have I puzzled over what it means to say that I am a woman, and this certainty has been untouched by my increasing inability to define gender.[17] My certainty has its original grounding in my relatively easy conformity with heteronormativity: As theorists as diverse as Catharine MacKinnon (1990) and Judith Butler (1990) have argued, sexual identity, particularly as it is shaped within the structures of compulsory heterosexuality, grounds, rather than depends upon, gender difference. My questioning of heterosexuality (including my own), along with the other norms of gender, came rather late in my life (after adolescence) and in communities that tended toward an empirical stability (if not essentialism) concerning who women were: Lesbians, for example, were woman-identified and woman-loving, not "not-women."[18]

I was, therefore, initially puzzled by how to understand the claim of (most) male-to-female (MTF) transsexuals to be women—how, that is, to make their claims (their lives and experiences) intelligible.[19] My inability to understand seemed to come from the fact that, despite my own unshakeable sense of being a woman, there was nothing I could point to as constituting my gender identity when I abstracted from a lifetime of unambiguous gender ascription on the part of others and an unambiguously female body. Surely, it seemed to me, if there was something independent of social role and body that male-to-female transsexuals could recognize as their gender identity, I should be able to find whatever it was in my own sense of identity—but there simply didn't seem to be anything like that there. (I was reminded of Hume's inability to find in himself a substantial Cartesian self.) Whatever they meant when they said they were women, it didn't seem to be what I meant. What, then, did they mean? And how, to put a Wittgensteinian spin on the question, were they able to mean it?

For various reasons, reinforced by Leslie Feinberg's (1993) eloquent politics of solidarity, I found myself moving away from the feminist suspicion that lay behind that puzzlement, a suspicion that tended to see male-to-female transsexuals as men, with typical male arrogance, claiming female identity; and female-to-male (FTM) transsexuals as self-hating, male-identified women. Those analyses singularly failed to fit the people whose voices I was hearing and reading, especially those who were seriously concerned about being allies in feminist struggles. Nor did those analyses fit with a commitment I thought I had to the deconstruction of gender (in reality, not just in theory).

Even with the motivation of solidarity, I still just did not understand. But that motivation—and the political thinking it engendered—did lead me to what it ought not have taken me so long to see: I was keeping to myself the position of unproblematized, paradigmatic subject, puzzling over how to understand some especially recalcitrant object. To put it in Wittgensteinian terms, I was finding one sort of phenomenon to be maddeningly opaque because I was taking another sort of phenomenon to be transparent. I couldn't understand the gender identity of transsexuals in part because I thought I understood my own—or, more accurately, could take it for granted, as not in need of understanding. (Wittgenstein suggested that part of the reason we were hopelessly puzzled about how it was possible to figure out what other people were thinking and feeling was that we thought there was nothing to figure out in our own case.)

The very overdetermination of my gender identity, the congruence of body, socialization, desire, and sense of self—the fact that everything pointed the same way—was what made it hard to see what was going on, hard, in fact, to see that anything was "going on" at all.[20] I am (unlike very many diverse nontranssexual women, who for all sorts of reasons do not conform in so many particulars to the norms of femaleness) so close to the paradigmatic center that I am in a very bad position to see how the apparatus works, to get a feel for how diverse forces could push and pull one in different directions. I may not like the forces that construct gender identity, but their tugs on my body and psyche tend more to hold me in place than to unbalance me: I don't know them, as others do, by the strains they exact in the attempt to stand erect. Clearly what I needed to do was to problematize my own gender identity.

Easier said than done.

4

By contrast, I don't have to work at finding my Jewish identity problematic. Unlike my gender identity, my Jewishness, though a central and unquestionable part of who I am, is a puzzle to me. Not only, as with gender, can't I define it, but I can't figure out what it means to say of me that I am a Jew, nor what I might be conforming to in order to count as one. Although I have no doubt about it, or about its centrality to who I am, I am genuinely puzzled about how to understand it—and, unlike my gender, it does seem to need to be understood. That is, although the ways I live gender make its operations unproblematically transparent to me, as invisible as the air, the ways I live Jewishness are maddeningly opaque. But opacity, of course, is also visibility: Again, in Wittgensteinian terms, what seems to get in the way of seeing clearly is what we need to be looking at, and recognizing as what we need to know. In my case there is a rich set of mostly familial experiences that inform my sense of Jewishness, in ways that link it with my rationalism, my respect for science, my judgmentalism, my sense of humor and irony, and (most centrally) my passionately internationalist, socialist sense of justice. But my awareness of how less-than-fully shared these commitments are among Jews, along with the absence in my life of a community that takes these as constitutive even of one way of being Jewish, makes such experiences, and the identity they ground, seem not to be an answer to the question of what I know about myself when I know myself to be, specifically, Jewish.[21]

Nowadays in the United States, the questions to which "Jewish" is the correct answer are almost always questions about religion. Being Jewish here and now is one identity in a contrastive set that includes Christian (with all the subsets thereof), Buddhist, Muslim, and so on. Forms of Christianity, most centrally forms of mainstream Protestantism, are the paradigm cases of religions in the United States, so Judaism is distinguished by its most noteworthy distinguishing features from a Christian perspective: Its adherents go not to church but to synagogue or temple, and they go not on Sunday but on Saturday or on Friday night. If you're in the hospital (one place you're likely to be asked your religion) and take a turn for the worse, they'll send for a rabbi, not for a priest, minister, or pastor. For some Jews this religious way of thinking about what sort of identity Jewish identity is may work reasonably well (though I think even for observant Jews there has been a problematic "Christianizing" of identity in, for example, the moving of religious observance for all family members from the home to the synagogue). But it makes no sense at all to secular Jews like me (as, for different reasons, I suspect it makes no sense to Buddhists, among others).

I don't have a religion: I'm a life-long atheist on increasingly principled moral grounds; I know very little about Jewish religious observance and feel comfortable with less; and though I know I had religious ancestors, among them my paternal grandparents, what I share with them, as with other Jews, does not feel to me to be a religion. Religion is rather what estranges me from many other Jews, for much the same reason as it estranges me from Christians and others: I am nonreligious, even antireligious, about as deeply as I am Jewish.

But I am Jewish. No one, actually, would dispute this, even though many people would insist on misrepresenting it. So far as anyone knows (albeit, as is the case for most European Jews, this is not very far), I have only Jewish ancestors, and that settles it. Were I to deny that I was Jewish, I would be accused (rightly, I think) of self-hatred, of internalized anti-Semitism. As I was growing up I was told (apocryphally, perhaps—my mother's source was the film *Gentleman's Agreement*) that Einstein said he would consider himself Jewish as long as there was anti-Semitism in the world, and certainly by the definitions of anti-Semites I am Jewish. That is surely part of it: Disaffiliation is dishonorable.

But that isn't—or shouldn't be—all there is to Jewish identity, even for the most secular. Surely, it seems, the Nazis and their ilk ought not to be the arbiters of our identity. What is it I know about myself when I know that I am a Jew?

As with questions about gender identity, part of my questioning comes from trying to understand someone who claims to share this identity with me but who seems clearly not to have it in the same way that I do. In the case of Jewish identity my questions have concerned converts—in particular, converts to Judaism.[22] In Christianormative terms, individual faith and knowledge are at the heart of identity, and conversion to Judaism is a religious process, governed by rabbis and requiring large amounts of religious instruction. The consequence is that converts to Judaism are intelligible as Jews in a way that I am not. Christianity is quintessentially a religion for converts: Being born a Christian may make you one in the sense that you are part of a Christian community, but to be a "real" Christian you have to acknowledge for yourself the place of Christ in your life, and being born to a Christian family merely makes that more likely. Similarly, converts to Judaism know a lot more about Judaism as a religion than I do, which also makes them more intelligible on Christian terms: One can't be a real Christian if one is ignorant of creedally appropriate interpretations of scripture, for example. If it is hard for me to understand how one can be a woman other than by being born female, it is all too easy to understand how one can be a Jew having been born something else. But that's not how I am a Jew.

Problematically, the Jewishness of converts is intelligible, even to me, in a way that my own is not, since theirs, unlike mine, fits the conceptual framework of Christianormativity. Part of that framework is that there be a definite "there" there, typically involving confirmation (as it is called) by a designated authority. And part of my problem is that, were I required to submit to such confirmation, I would surely fail. The rabbinical authorities charged with deciding who will get to become a Jew decide on grounds that have no connection to my own Jewishness. I am not, of course, required to be so confirmed: Those same authorities, specifically as they interpret the Israeli Law of Return, would unquestionably include me (having a Jewish mother is sufficient). But even so, their authority feels irrelevant to me. Rabbis are religious authorities, and my Jewishness is not a religious identity.

Contemporary Jewish thinking is deeply concerned with what it is to be an authentic Jew: In particular, there are those who deny the possibilities of authentic nonreligious identity after the Holocaust, or of authentic diasporic Jewish identity after the founding of the state of Israel[23] (Goldberg and Krausz 1993). And though no one would deny that I am a Jew, there are many who would question the authenticity of my Jewish identity, who would claim that as a Jew I have obligations I am turning my back on. I, too, am tempted to make similar claims on others: It seems to me profoundly un-Jewish to be a Republican or to oppose affirmative action or, for that matter, to oppose the rights of Palestinians to self-determination. Unlike the rabbis, I have no power to enforce my claims, but what is it that grounds my making them: What do I mean by them? What am I doing in attempting to police the boundaries of an identity I find unintelligible? And how might figuring that out help me to understand my temptations to police the boundaries of an identity I find all too intelligible?[24]

5

When I bring the murkiness of my Jewish identity together with the suspicious transparency of my gender identity, one question that suggests itself is: Who cares? To whom does it matter, and why, that I have the identities that I do, and that I do or do not share them with certain others? Another, related question is: Who gets to decide, and on what grounds? How are some people counted in and others out? These are, I think, better—more useful, more practically pressing—questions than the ones I started with, namely: What can a transsexual mean when she says she is a woman, and what can I mean when I say I am a Jew?

One way of framing the shift from the earlier questions to the later ones is by way of a Wittgensteinian account of why the earlier ones seem so intractable. The focus on what we mean (rather than on what we do and why, as though we can answer the one without the other) usually leads to one of three possibilities, or to an oscillation among them. The first is some form of privileged access essentialism: Femaleness or Jewishness is just there, an abstractable part of one's overall identity, a definite, discernible something. Aside from the well-known problems both with privileged access and with essentialism, a serious problem with this approach, from my perspective, is that it leaves me out: If being a woman or a Jew consists in a particular inner state, knowable independently of the body or the history one happens to have or of how one is regarded by others, then I fail to be one. And though I am willing to consider forgoing paradigmatic status, I do think any definition of either women or Jews that simply leaves me out is quite likely to be wrong.

The second possibility is expert essentialism. On this view, such identities are complex and not necessarily introspectively accessible, but, by exercising some combination of scientific and legislative authority, experts can make determinations. This view does in fact capture much about current practice. There are in both cases experts who are in the business of making such determinations, though, as I've argued above about Jewishness, they do so in ways that I and many others find troubling. The situation is even clearer when we look at the experts who determine gender, especially as this is done in the case of transsexuals.[25] The physicians and psychiatrists who have had the authority to decide who is "really" gendered differently than they are biologically sexed have tended (though this is changing, as transsexual activists are gaining some influence with the medical establishment) to reinforce precisely the gender stereotypes feminists have attempted to undermine: To be a woman in their terms has meant to be feminine. There has also been (though this too is changing) a conflation of gender and sexual identity: A real woman is supposed to be heterosexual.

Also, curiously, in the case of gender, though not in the case of Jewishness, the experts insist on the inbornness of gender identity, even when it is discordant with biological sex. Those who would convert to Judaism do not have to demonstrate to the rabbis that they have "really" been Jewish all along—one can quite openly be a convert. But, as Kate Bornstein (1994, 62) sardonically notes, the only way to be a "certified" transsexual is to deny that you are one—that is, to convince the doctors (and agree to try to convince the rest of the world) that you are and always have been what you clearly are not, namely, simply and straightforwardly a woman (or a man). Since you cannot have had a history that is congruent with such an identity, you are left without a past (Feinberg 1993). As I argued above, it is not only in our own memories but in the memories of others that our selves take shape, and the institutionalization of transsexuality functions as a theft of selfhood, in making a transsexual life not only closeted but literally untellable, incoherent.

The theft is premeditated, carried out with malice aforethought. The illusion of the naturalness of sex and gender requires that we not see what the magician is up to before the impossible being—a newly born adult man or woman—emerges from beneath the surgical drape. Our (nontranssexual) comfort requires that we fail to acknowledge transsexuals as such, seeing what the surgery and the hormones and the scripted behavior intend for us to see: a "natural" man or woman. If the illusion fails—perhaps because those who "rise up from the operating tables of [their] rebirth . . . are something more, and something other, than the creatures [their] makers intended [them] to be" (Stryker 1994, 242)—we respond to the affront to that comfort by seeing the transsexual as, to quote the term Stryker uses and appropriates, a "monster."

"The transsexual body," as Stryker points out, "is an unnatural body. It is the product of medical science. It is a technological construction. It is flesh torn apart and sewn together again in a shape other than that in which it was born" (1993, 238). But so are the bodies of women who attempt to stave off aging by multiple plastic surgeries. So, especially since my hysterectomy, is my body. And none of us, for reasons as natural and unnatural as the full complexities of our lives, is the shape we were when we were born. We are all creatures, as Stryker (1994, 240) reminds us, in the face of our unwillingness to remember, not just in our mortal corporeality but in the constructedness of our psyches and our bodies. The illusion of the naturalness of bodies and psyches that conform to the dictates of heteronormativity is maintained when identity boundaries are policed by experts committed to keeping their work under wraps. Even when the experts are facilitating the crossing of sex and gender boundaries, they do so in ways that attempt to do as little damage as possible to the clarity of the lines: They may be crossed, but they are not to be blurred.

A third possibility for how it is that an identity can be claimed—privileged access voluntarism—has, in the face of the inadequacies of the other two, seemed very attractive, especially to some transgendered people. On a privileged access voluntarist account, one is a woman if one says one is, and the claim means whatever one takes it to mean: It is not up to anyone else to tell me whether or not I am a woman, nor is there some particular essential property I have to have in order to be one; being a woman might in fact mean something quite different to me from what it means to you. The problem with this picture is that, in appearing to give the individual everything, it in fact gives nothing at all. As Wittgenstein has argued, meaning cannot be a private matter: A word means what it does not because I have joined it in my mind to an idea or an image (as Locke would have it) but because there exists a set of social practices in which I participate, in terms of which I can get the meaning right or wrong. Allowing that 'woman' means whatever anyone who applies it to herself takes it to mean gives the freedom of self-naming at the cost of there being any point to the activity, any content to the chosen name, any reason for saying that one is a woman, rather than a man—or, for that matter, a car or a chrysanthemum.[26]

In practice, of course, naming oneself a woman is neither capricious nor unconnected to cultural meaning, even if, for some people—as Kate Bornstein suggested in a radio interview—what is really intended is that one is not a man, in a world in which there are simply no other conceptually allowable alternatives. On this view at least some MTFs are—or would be if conceptual space allowed—not women but something else altogether. It will also be true that for those transsexuals who do think of themselves as women, the associations with womanhood that seem especially resonant may well be idiosyncratic, and there is no reason why they cannot pick and choose among them—why, that is, transsexuals should not have the same freedom as born women to embrace some aspects of womanhood and vehemently reject others. But once we drop the idea that there is a specific something (knowable either internally or to experts) in which being a woman consists, while holding onto the idea that there has to be some substantive, shareable content to the assertion, we have moved toward my second set of questions, those concerning who cares and who gets to decide.

The shift to this latter set of questions hinges on seeing meaning as something that we do, not something that we discover, as the introspective essentialist would have it. Both the expert essentialist and the privileged access voluntarist seem to recognize this fact, but in different ways they obscure the practices involved—the latter by making those practices empty, and the former by granting to experts a problematically unquestionable authority. To take seriously the idea that meaning is something we do is to raise questions about who "we" are and why and how we do what we do; it holds us accountable for how we mean what we say.[27]

I know myself to be a woman and a Jew because of how I was named at birth: Neither of them seems to come from anything that I have done. But what do I now do when I take these identities to be in this way given, and what is my role in maintaining systems that identify people at birth? Such a role can seem quite troubling. Susan Stryker experiences rage at the moment of "nonconsensual gendering" (in which she sees herself as complicit) at the birth of her lover's daughter: "A gendering violence is the founding condition of human subjectivity; having a gender is the tribal tattoo that makes one's personhood cognizable. I stood for a moment between the pains of two violations, the mark of gender and the unlivability of its absence" (1994, 250). The complexity of her rage is in that dilemma: It is not as though, in the world we know, one would better treat a child by withholding gender, since, in the world we know, one would be withholding personhood.

Recognition of the oppressive nonconsensuality of natal gendering need not obviate the significance of the feminist insistence on the specific oppressiveness of female, in contrast to male, gendering, although emphasizing one rather than the other has led to political and conceptual conflict. Such conflict has emerged in the political antagonism between (some) transsexual women and men and (some) feminists, especially lesbian separatists, conflict that emerges in differing understandings of the meaning of "women-only" spaces. As Sarah Hoagland has reminded me, separatists were concerned with the creation of new meaning within self-defined spaces, not with the boundaries that marked off those spaces: Attention circulated within lesbian space, rather than being focused on those on the outside, following Marilyn Frye's (1983) definition of lesbians as women whose attention was drawn to other women. Furthermore, as Anne Leighton pointed out to me, many lesbians, especially separatists, were more than ready to acknowledge transsexuals as such, as (another species of) "impossible beings."[28] Nor, of course, is "woman" a category lesbian separatists have had any particular fondness for, let alone any desire to maintain the clarity and distinctness of. Self-identified women, I am told, have never been asked to submit to tests aimed at "proving" their womanhood as a condition of entry to "women-only" spaces such as the Michigan Women's Music Festival. Why, then, the battles over the inclusion in such spaces of (those who identify as) MTF transsexuals?

The interpersonal politics of such encounters are complex and surely not to be resolved by an armchair observer. But, aside from echoing Kate Bornstein's (1994) admonition that lesbian separatists are hardly the most politically savvy choice of adversary for transsexuals (and vice versa), I would like to introduce a possibly helpful piece of terminology to get at what I think separatists have in mind when they use such problematic terms as 'womyn-born-womyn' to exclude MTF transsexuals. A major reason for the existence of separatist space is to engage in the activity of self-naming and self-creation, and it is clearly inconsistent with such an aim to allow the definitions of the heteropatriarchy to determine who is to be allowed in. (The use of 'womyn' indicates that the identity in question is specifically not the one with which one was labeled at birth, whereas the people to whom it is intended to apply are precisely those who were so labeled.) But separatism exists against the recognition of the Adamistic assumption that men have a natural right to name anything they deem worth naming, and of the fact that wresting that supposed right from them requires vigilance. It also starts from the recognition of the specific harms that flow from the natal ascription of femaleness in a misogynist world. To get at the importance of these concerns, I suggest the term 'perinatally pinked', which refers to the condition of having been named female around the time of birth: by chromosome-testing or ultrasound visualization beforehand, by visual inspection at birth, or by surgical "correction" shortly after birth (see Kessler 1990).[29] Separatist space (and other feminist practices that recognize the separatist impulses that inform even non-separatist-identified female self-assertion; see Frye 1983) can be seen as a space of healing from having been perinatally pinked, and from living in a world in which being so marked makes one a target for subordination and abuse. Being in the company of others who, like one, were perinatally pinked, and creating collectively with them the affirmative identity of "womyn," is for many separatists of the utmost importance to their survival in such a world. That MTF transsexuals were not perinatally pinked is a simple statement of fact, and it in no way diminishes the oppressiveness of their experiences of gendering—nor, importantly, does it preclude separatists' support of their claim to inclusion in the category of women. That category is one that operates in heteropatriarchal space—the space that requires unambiguous gender-ascription for intelligibility—and in such space many lesbians are natural allies in the struggle to fight the harassment (or worse) that targets those who visibly fail to conform to gender norms.[30]

If heteronormativity requires natally ascribed gender as the sign of intelligibility, Christianormativity tends to make the natal ascription of identity unintelligible. Abstract individualism, a distinctively Christian view of persons, views group identity as properly a matter of choice, and as subordinate to one's unmarked humanity in constituting identity.[31] In practice, of course, individuals are hardly unmarked at birth, and not only by gender: The obvious additional natal mark is race, and, as argued above, all sorts of deviations from normality get labeled inborn. But identities thought of as inborn are seen not as a matter of group membership but as traits inhering in individuals. Group membership is meant to come later, and to be chosen. So the only intelligible way to be born a Jew is if Jewishness can be seen as a "trait," or a cluster of traits—a ground of intelligibility that anti-Semitic discourse has been only too happy to provide.

But what if we resist the dictates of Christianormativity on this point, and insist on the intelligibility of being born a member of the Jewish people? Can we find in such an exercise a way of thinking that makes better sense of what it is to be born a male or a female (see Boyarin 1994), where one criterion for "better sense" is the greater intelligibility of those who come later to dispute the gender membership into which they were born?

One thing to note is that Jewishness would not be the sort of identity it is if some people were not born into it: It is in this way not (or not just) a religious identity. Being born Jewish is not the only way to be Jewish, nor is it necessary for born Jews to be thought of as more authentic or "real" Jews than converts (though often they are). What is true is that born Jews have certain histories that converts do not, though it is important to keep in mind just how diverse those histories are, including not only the wide range of different experiences of Jewishness but also the possibility of not knowing for most of one's life that one is Jewish: Discovering that one is means discovering something about one's own history. (You may, for example, have been born to Jewish parents and adopted by Christians and discover your Jewishness when discovering your birth parents. Note that in the reverse situation, it would be wrong to say that you would discover you were Christian.)

Part of the difficulty involved in thinking about Jewishness is acknowledging the importance of history, along with group identity. Ignoring or theoretically deconstructing the role of history—of the given, the unchosen— leads to the sort of arrogating voluntarism I discussed above. The denial of the relevance of the body and of history (often, confusedly, in the name of anti-essentialism) also seems to me to be both masculinist and Christian, insofar as both those discourses privilege the mind over the body, the chosen over the given.[32] That some of us confront some of our identities as ineluctable, as constitutive of who we are, as something about ourselves we cannot change, is to say something about how certain experiences are socially constructed; it is not to be committed to essentialism.

To speak of Jewishness as paradigmatically unchosen has, of course, an additional resonance, since to be Jewish is to be "chosen." That is, it is God who gets to do the choosing; one is chosen whether one chooses to be or not. Jewish atheists are in general a peculiar breed: We are given to having deeply disputatious relationships with the God we don't believe in, often centered on just what He had it in mind to choose us for. My own sense is that we were chosen to be canaries. Just as one sends canaries down mines to see if the air is safe to breathe—if it will kill anything, it will kill a canary—so Jews are, over the long run, a good test of the oppressiveness of a social environment (at least in those parts of the world where Jews have historically lived). Sooner or later those who are committed to ideologies of domination and subordination will reveal themselves as anti-Semites.

Thus, the quintessentially Jewish injunction that "none is free so long as any are oppressed" is for Jews a literal truth, no matter how hard individuals or groups may work at denying it, whether by assimilating within a Christian culture or by militarizing the state of Israel: A canary on steroids is ultimately still a canary. Affluent conservative American Jews may think that their interests lie in opposing affirmative action and other efforts to undo anti-black racism, but they are mistaken. The black-Jewish alliance of the civil rights era may have been romanticized, but it had its roots in a deep truth: Racists are also anti-Semites, and Jews have no business consorting with them, even if they allow us into their subdivisions, universities, and country clubs. Our mortgages, degrees, and membership cards will not make us safe: The world will not be truly safe for the Jews until it is safe for everyone, and we forget that at our peril.

A consequence of this notion of chosenness is that power is a misguided and ultimately ineffective response to danger.[33] Precisely because one cares about an imperiled identity, one has to resist the temptation to protect it with fortified barricades. Thus, one can think of conversion to Judaism not in the context of Rabbinic law (although for those for whom religious faith is at the heart of their Jewishness, chosen or otherwise, Rabbinic law will be something to engage, perhaps, as it has always been engaged, disputatiously, or of the intricacies of the Israeli Law of Return) but in the terms Ruth used in following Naomi: "Thy people shall be my people."

Conversion to Judaism is more like marrying into a family than it is like conversion to Christianity, including analogous problems around the policing of families by, for example, the social and legal restrictions of marriage. A notion of family that broke free of such restrictions would function like the notion of "my people" that Daniel and Jonathan Boyarin (1993) call "diasporic"—nonpoliced, not shored up by apparatuses of institutionalized power. Belonging to such a family or a people would mean being related in some complex amalgam of chosen and unchosen bonds to a group, some of whom are born members, others of whom are, we might say, "naturalized."[34]

The term is both precisely right and deeply wrong. It is deeply wrong in its association with citizenship, that most quintessentially state-regulated of identities.[35] Its very suggestive rightness lies in its making evident the fact that "natural" is something one can become (there is a process that produces it), and in its marking a contrast that distinguishes collectivities that at least some members are born into from those that are wholly chosen. Being a born member of such a collectivity is, importantly, a matter of genealogy—that is, of history, not of essential traits: There is no suggestion that the whole shebang (the *ganze megillah*) is anything other than a social construction. A further important feature of such collectivities is that one shares one's membership in them with others with whom one would not choose to be associated and whom one cannot expel.

What happens when we bring these reflections on Jewish identity to the questions about sex and gender identity as raised by, specifically, MTF transsexuals? If we push the analogy, the fact that there are born women is constitutive of the category "woman," just as the fact that there are born Jews is constitutive of the category "Jew." What counts, of course, is not who one's parents (or mother) are but how one is enrolled into the sex/gender system at birth. The category "woman," however, can also include variously "naturalized" members, where naturalization has to do with a deeply felt identification with at least some (and almost certainly only some) earlier members, a feeling that one is in some sense "like them." (When identity is officially regulated, those who are not officially naturalized have the status, as it were, of undocumented aliens—an apt description of not-officially-certified transsexuals, caught in a position in which they are unable to acquire usable driver's licenses or other forms of identification [Feinberg 1993].) Such identification has to be acknowledged by at least some earlier members, as one cannot become a Jew without the acknowledgment of at least some already-Jews, though not necessarily by all of them, and not necessarily by born members.³⁶ Those who are "naturalized" women are no less women than those who are born female, though the category would not be what it is were no one born into it.

An important disanalogy is that conversion to Judaism tends to be much more a matter of choice than does sex or gender change, and conversion may well have been preceded by a long period of quite comfortable identification as, say, Christian. The disanalogy marks a deep difference in how different identities work: One need not be recognized as Jewish or non-Jewish in order to be intelligible, and we have the conceptual space to narrate a history that goes between them.³⁷ But the disanalogy reflects aspects of gender practice that we might want to think about changing: That is, thinking about sex/gender identity as more analogous in these ways to Jewish identity might help us to imagine a less oppressive way of "doing gender." The experiences of transsexual people tend to be quite different from the experiences of converts to Judaism—but that may be due to aspects of our sex/gender system that could be imagined otherwise.

There are, I think, other advantages to pushing this analogy. It is less constraining of identity than are the operations of those who expertly police the gender divide: The significance of natal assignment is not to pick out the "real" women from the others but, rather, to note that there would be no categories of the sort that genders are if some people were not assigned to them at birth. There would, that is, be no such thing as a woman to believe that one was if there were not people who were assigned female at birth, just as there would be no such thing as Jewishness to convert to if there were not people who were Jewish from birth. (Again, the same is not true of Christianity.) To deny this conceptual role to natal assignment—to think of gender as more like Christianity, as a system of categories that people sort themselves into based on their own self-identifications—is to ignore the ways in which, as a matter of historical fact, no less real for being contingent and alterable, gender is socially constructed and, hence, the ways in which it functions in people's lives. (Part of the quarrel of lesbian separatists with transsexuals is a disagreement about how gender works. For many separatists, gender is a social imposition that places them in a threatened category: Women are created as the objects of misogyny, whereas for many transsexuals gender is an inner identity that needs to be asserted in the face of social mislabeling. I want to suggest that both these conceptualizations are too restrictive to get at all the complex ways in which gender works, though each captures an aspect of gender that is, for some purposes, especially salient.)

Whether or not, or to what extent, the sex/gender system is disrupted by the gender experiences of transsexuals depends on the extent to which those experiences are thought of as paradigmatic. The irony is that in order to support transsexual claims to clear, stable, and unambiguous gender identities, those identities must themselves remain marginal. Only a system that takes natally gendered persons as paradigmatic—that maintains the illusion of the normality of "natural" gendering—can have the solidity to ground *anyone's* unambiguous gender claims. The more important it is for transsexuals to claim a stable and unproblematic gender, the more conceptually dependent they are on their own marginality, as rare exceptions to a fundamentally natural dichotomy. The extent of this importance varies enormously from person to person—as it does for nontranssexuals. But it is a feature, surely alterable, of present-day Western cultures that stable and unproblematic gender identities are expected of everyone—so that those who resist claiming and enacting one such identity live the perilous lives of "outlaws." A sex/gender system in which, by contrast, not only natal members are paradigmatic, in which paradigm status can be shared with transsexuals, would be much more like the system that underwrites Jewish identity: full of ambiguity, unclarity, and vagueness. (In the *Philosophical Investigations* Wittgenstein tried to disabuse us of the Fregean conviction that ambiguous, unclear, vague concepts were not concepts at all: Having been so disabused, we can contemplate the possibility that we have reason in some cases not just to tolerate but to prefer ambiguity, unclarity, and vagueness.)

It is also, I would argue, an advantage to the analogy that it highlights the differences between the relationships of MTF and FTM transsexuals to the born members of their respective genders. Analogizing specifically womanness with Jewishness (an exercise that has, of course, a long and exceedingly complicated history) draws attention to anti-Semitism and misogyny as parts of the social world in which those categories have meaning and in the light of which they are lived. It helps us make sense of the particular anxieties felt by some Jews and some women about the possibility that core definitions of those identities will shift if the boundaries are not policed; and it can help, if not to allay those anxieties, at least to suggest that they are counterproductive. So long as I have no say (and given what sort of category "woman" is, I can have no say) about whether Margaret Thatcher is a woman, it avails me nothing politically to try to keep Kate Bornstein or Sandy Stone or Susan Stryker from being one. Ironically, it is the fact that some people are born women that provides one of the strongest arguments against attempts to police the boundaries of womanhood.

The analogy also shifts the question What is it to be a woman (or a Jew)?—as though there were something there, in me, to be discovered—to, instead, How did I get to be one? How was I claimed or assigned? How was I chosen—by whom and for what? And, having been chosen, to whom do I have what responsibilities, with whom is my fate tied and how? Conversion to Judaism is not, like conversion to Christianity, a matter between an individual and God or an individual and an institutionalized church. It is a matter of joining a "people," of coming to share their history, and their fate. An MTF transsexual may be no more a feminist than Phyllis Schlafly, but she is no more immune to sexism and no less accountable for her failure to identify with the struggle against it.

Such accountability will mean different things to different ones of us and different things to each of us at different times. But one thing it always means is a recognition of and active resistance to the misogyny and anti-Semitism that are part of the inherited histories and contemporary realities of women and Jews. (And a failure of accountability is a moral failure, not an identity test: One has failed to be, in this instance a good person, not a "good Jew" or a "good woman," still less a "real" woman or Jew.) Resistance entails not just fighting the attacks but, equally, refusing the benefits that are advertised as coming with closeting, silence, collaboration, or disaffiliation. I would regard it as profoundly dishonorable to pass—as there is frequent occasion to do—as an "honorary" man or Christian. The emphasis is on the "honorary": It is no dishonor to be taken to be a man or a Christian; what is dishonorable is to let stand the implication that one is therefore more worth respecting than if one were a woman or a Jew. (As a woman currently monogamously involved with a man, I regard it as dishonorable to pass, in this sense, as a heterosexual, which is rather different from identifying as a bisexual.)[38]

Resistance is connected to solidarity, which is a matter of identifying *with*, rather than *as*.[39] As such, it can bind different groups rather than divide them, but typically it does primarily bind groups–and individuals, insofar as they are members of groups. Daniel Boyarin (1994, 257), in his deeply suggestive articulation of what he calls "diasporic identity," makes this point: Such identity is particularist but not isolationist. As nonhegemonic others (he has in mind primarily, of course, diasporic Jews), we live in larger, diverse communities to which we are deeply bound and to which we are responsible in part as a condition of our group identity. Solidarity, identifying with, is at the heart of the Passover seder, and in some traditions, such as the socialist ones of my family, the celebration of the liberation of "our people" is inseparable from a rededication to solidarity with all the continuing liberation struggles in the world. Similarly, I think, AIDS has come to play a role in lesbian identity, not because lesbians are at particular risk of HIV infection—which, course, they are not—but as an expression of solidarity with gay men who are, a solidarity that is at once "natural" (grounded in shared resistance to homophobia) and conscientiously chosen: My sense is that AIDS-related politics has greatly increased the numbers of lesbians who identify with gay men, and that lesbian identity has, as a consequence, been reshaped. Whom one identifies with is inseparable from what one identifies as.

6

I have (despite my recurrent temptations) no real interest in policing the boundaries of either womanhood or Jewishness, nor is it a job I want anyone

else to do: Both identities are better left undefined—or, more strongly, incoherent and confused. If the meaning of identity, like the meaning of anything
else, is a matter of the practices that shape it, then it would be both intellectually mistaken and politically unwise to give either of these identities more
clarity and coherence than are warranted by their structuring practices. And
those practices are a mess—a jumble of oppression and resistance, history
and imagination, drudgery and heroism: If meaning is use, 'woman' and
'Jew' have been and continue to be put to such a dizzying variety of contradictory uses that any coherent account of either would have to be untrue.
Furthermore, and importantly, it may well be incoherent identities, those
that do not fit into the available taxonomies, that bear particularly liberatory
potential. María Lugones (1990) has been articulating this vision in, for example, arguing for the embracing of "multiplicitous" identities lived across
worlds and in what, following Victor Turner, she refers to as "anti-struc-
ture—places of creative liminality" (see also Lugones 1994).

     What does that leave us with as a way of finding identity intelligible?
Family resemblance, for one: Male-to-female transsexuals or Jewish converts
see in my identity—or the identity of some other women or Jews, born or
not, perhaps very different from me—a variation of what they feel or want
themselves to be; they look at some of us and see kin. (Talk of family is notoriously dangerous, as white feminists are reminded about the talk of "sisterhood," and as Jacob Hale has reminded me again. But, aside from its
Wittgensteinian implications, I think it's worth engaging with—carefully. It
helps to remember that family resemblance, like any other form of resemblance, is only very weakly transitive; and one thing we know about relatives
is that they can cause us to be related to people we cannot imagine having as
kin. But, imagine it or not, we do.) What I see when I look back is not a simple matter. I may look at a MTF transsexual and see not a woman but a man
who, with stereotypically masculine arrogance, claims both the right to define what it is to be a woman and the right to take anything he wants, even if
it's my identity. Increasingly, this is not what I see, and the change has to do
both with my looking more carefully—seeing, for example, the ways in
which the oppressiveness of gender affects those who inhabit its unnameable
borders at least as much as it affects those who live near the center of the female side—and with a growing feminist consciousness among transsexuals.

     Part of being careful about the use of familial imagery involves displacing
its role as a primary site of heteronormativity. Using the family in counter-
normative ways is one sort of response to the reactionary deployment of
family rhetoric: Rather than rejecting the family (as image or social arrangement), we can "queer" it. David Halperin (1995) proposes 'queer' as a term
not for a particular identity, constructed, as all identities are, by complex
amalgams of normalizing and stigmatizing practices, but for positionality: as
a flexible strategy of resistance to the practices of heteronormativity.[40] Such

flexibility is suggested, he argues, by the flexible illogic of heteronormativity: It is strategically better suited than any affirmation of, say, positive gay identity to slipping over, under, around, or through the stigmatizing net. Queer identity, so conceived, is a slap in the face to the illusory "straightness" of heterosexuality, an illusion maintained by diverting attention away from those who are supposed to be the unmarked "normals" and toward the crafty maneuvering of those who try to live lives they can respect in the face of contradictory imputations of sickness and sin.

The question of who is queer (along with the related question of whether queer is a useful and appropriate identity for gay men and, even more controversially, lesbians) has taken on some of the controversy that surrounds questions about who is a woman or who is a Jew. With the ascendancy of queer theory in some parts of the academic and cultural worlds it has become chic to be queer, and many gay men and (perhaps) more lesbians have felt that their identities—and, more important, their histories and struggles—were being ripped off.[41] As Halperin puts it, in a caveat: "Lesbians and gay men can now look forward to a new round of condescension and dismissal at the hands of the trendy and glamorously unspecified sexual outlaws who call themselves 'queer' and who can claim the radical chic attached to a sexually transgressive identity without, of course, having to do anything icky with their bodies in order to earn it" (1995, 65).

I want to argue for the claiming of queer identity as an important liberatory strategy—in part because of the challenge it poses to the paradigmatic status of privileged subjectivity—while maintaining the tension between the boundary-shiftiness of queerness and respect for the historically and personally specific experiences of those who have "found themselves" (with the mix of activity and passivity that term implies) in identities whose boundaries they encountered as given and fixed, whether as a matter of internal certainty or of unyielding social decree.[42]

The symbolic appropriation of marginalized, oppressed, or stigmatized identities is the flip side of the expert policing of identity boundaries. The policing of boundaries requires definitive statements of who is or is not a "real" Jew or woman or homosexual, whether in the name of valorizing and defending the category or of keeping those in it from getting out. Symbolic appropriation often displaces those who have been thus defined—who may, in part because of such policing, regard those identities as central to their senses of self—in favor of others whose nonliteral (i.e., nonbodily) identifications become what it is to be a "real" Jew or woman or queer. Some male Jungians talk this way about their anima, and it is the suspicion (no doubt in at least some, though I suspect not many, cases well founded) that this attitude characterizes MTF transsexuals that is behind much of the feminist resistance to acknowledging MTFs as women. Daniel and Jonathan Boyarin (1993) have explored the phenomenon of the (lowercase) "jew": the outsider and nonconformist in the European imagination—the *real* Jew, realer for not being confined by a limited and limiting history.[43] There are good reasons to resist this symbolic appropriation of identity, even as it seems to be made possible by—and positively to further—the breaking down of confining definitions.

But there are equally good reasons for encouraging creatively playful, politically serious border transgressing on the part of those who could, given what seem to be the facts about them, safely reside on the more privileged side.[44] Adrienne Rich, writing in the 1970s, articulated a conception of lesbian identity that has affinities with queerness, and it met with similar resistance (see Zita 1991 and the discussion in Rich 1986). Rather than focusing on the specificities of the experiences of some women, Rich wrote about—and to—the lesbian in every woman: "It is the lesbian in us who is creative, for the dutiful daughter of the fathers in us is only a hack" (1979, 201). The "lesbian continuum" encouraged any woman to find and identify with her own rebelliousness against heteropatriarchy (Rich 1986). The concern of Rich's critics was that such expansiveness drew attention away from the radical core of lesbian identity—an embodied erotic connection to other women. Rich wasn't advocating the position I referred to above as privileged access voluntarism, so the problem isn't that 'lesbian' becomes contentless; rather it's that the specific transgressiveness of lesbianism is lost if the sexual is downplayed. The dispute is over which practices will be taken as constituting the language game, and, consequently, which family resemblances will emerge as salient.

It was Rich's strategy—as it is the strategy of queer theorists—to be expansive about the practices that constitute lesbian identity, in part as a means of destabilizing those that constitute heterosexual identity. Such destabilization is not just conceptual: Heteronormativity (akin to Rich's notion of compulsory heterosexuality) functions in part through the quotidian complicity of those who cannot imagine—or desire—an alternative. Similarly, in poems such as "Transcendental Etude" and "Sibling Mysteries," Rich (1978) reminds women of mother/child eroticism and of the unnaturalness of abandoning a woman's body for a man's: She is "queering" (women's) heterosexuality, in a way similar to Michael Warner's (1993) discussion in the introduction to *Fear of a Queer Planet*. Queerness is not meant to contrast with straightness so much as to displace it, to reveal its inherent contradictions and instabilities. Thus, queer readings of canonical texts are not attempts to demonstrate that some hitherto believed-to-be-straight author was really gay but, rather, are subversions of our reading practices, disruptions of our imputations to authors of the sort of straightforward, transparent integrity that characterizes privileged subjectivity.

Other theorists have urged the privileged to find in themselves the shreds and patches of transgressive identities. María Lugones (1987) suggests that "world"-travel—the movement into a social world in which one is marked as other, something the oppressed and marginalized have to do for survival—can be embarked on "playfully" by those among the privileged who have the courage and the loving commitment to learn how they are seen by those in whose eyes their privilege marks them as other. Sandra Harding (1991, 288) urges those who are privileged to learn to think out of "traitorous" identities, conscientiously disloyal to their privilege. Daniel and Jonathan Boyarin (1993) suggest diasporic identity as an alternative to nationalist identity: a history- and body-laden sense of identity (a sense that these particular others are "my people")—is viable (nonracist) only when it is uncoupled from state power.

Strategies of "queering the center" will vary as the identities in question are variously constructed, policed, and transgressively lived—in particular, as one or the other side of the oxymoronic natural incapacity/willful refusal construction is dominant. Womanhood and Jewishness are illustrative of these differences. Part of heteronormativity is the assumption that gender is not chosen but "natural": given and immutable, either inscribed on the body or, even if in some "deviant" cases at odds with it, set one way or the other at a very early age. As I noted above, the medical control of transsexual experience has served to reinforce, rather than to undermine, the fixity of gender. In the face of this rigidity, it can be liberatory to blur the boundary (both by straddling and by crossing it), to argue for the ways in which gender is neither definite nor fixed. Doing so need not, as many feminists have worried, undermine the intelligibility and efficacy of feminist politics, for which the undeniable reality and oppressiveness of sex/gender systems, however historically mutable or even arbitrary, are grounds enough. It can also be important to claim the power of self-naming, including the power of boundary setting. But the "selves" that do the naming need not be confined to those who in the dominant view of things count as women: A politics of solidarity can underwrite transgressive boundary *marking*, as well as blurring or straddling.

Jewishness, on the other hand, is aberrant in a Christianormative culture in being paradigmatically a matter not of choice but, as Daniel Boyarin puts it, of "genealogy" (1994, 236–246). From a Jewish perspective, postmodern anti-essentialist arguments can sound suspiciously Protestant, resting, as they often do, on the idea that any identity at all is "nothing but" a social construction, and that taking oneself to be anything as a matter of birth is bad faith. Furthermore, the conflation of givenness (i.e., the denial of voluntarism) and essentialism is a mistake, as is the opposition between givenness and social construction: Jewishness is no less socially constructed for being heritable.[45]

It is important, I think, to assert Jewishness specifically as an identity that is paradigmatically not a matter of choice—that is, to resist not only the assimilation of individual Jews into Christian culture but the assimilation of

Jewish identity itself. (The term 'Judeo-Christian' is an example of such as-similation: Not only does it amalgamate Jewishness with Christianity, but it makes Jewishness out to be the larval form, important not in its own right but as a precursor to Christianity.) Concerning gender and sexual identity, I would argue that, although a case can be made for more body-based, less voluntaristic conceptions than are currently popular in gender studies, given the fit between such a view and that of heteropatriarchy, the dangers proba-bly outweigh the benefits. But, tentatively, I have suggested that some ways of thinking about Jewish identity can provide a helpful model for breaking the hold on us of the rigidities of gender identity, by providing a middle way between the supposed dichotomy of either unproblematically natural or un-grounded and arbitrary.[46]

There is no single answer to the question of whether an explicitly, flexibly constructionist or a historically given, body-based view of identity is more politically progressive. (I am assuming, of course, that in some sense there is no "fact of the matter," that questions concerning categorization do not admit of nonstrategic answers: That is, on the metaphysical level, I am as-suming some version of social constructionism.) It depends on who is assert-ing what sort of identity when and where and why, in the face of what other sorts of assertions, especially those that have authoritative standing. My sug-gestion is that here and now there are good reasons to queer the centers of both heteronormative and Christianormative discursive practices and that such queering can proceed by way of exploring the ways in which some of us live as impossible beings, emphasizing those aspects of our lives that ren-der us impossible: the shape-shifting of the transsexual and the unchosen givenness of the secular Jew. Against the normative backgrounds of essen-tialized gender and chosen religion, such emphases move the two identities onto a shared middle ground of complex—and normatively unintelligible—mixtures of givenness and choice.

In these ways and others—in articulations of *mestizaje* (see Anzaldúa 1987) or exhortations to become "world"-travelers (Lugones 1987), and in diverse invocations of trickster subjectivities (see Haraway 1991, 199; Gates 1988)—the experiences of variously marginalized people provide alternative models of subjectivity, less seamless and transparent, less coherent and solid, than those of privilege. Each of them is grounded in the specificities of the experiences of historically particular groups, but all suggest that taking such experiences as paradigmatic of the human can both shatter the illusions of the naturalness of privilege and offer ways out of the constraints of its nor-mativities. The point is not to generate legions of chic lesbian or mestiza or black or American Indian or Jewish wannabes, but to offer alternative, vari-ously queer, provisional paradigms in relation to which each of us tells our own, shifting stories. The issue, then, is not who is or is not really whatever, but who can be counted on when they come for any one of us: The solid ground is not identity but loyalty and solidarity.[47]

Notes

1. I am deeply indebted in my thinking about issues of identity, subjectivity, and integrity by reading, listening to, and talking with María Lugones for fifteen years.

2. See also Hoagland (1988 and forthcoming) for the related argument that what is read as incompetence or unreliability on the part of subordinated people is often, in fact, sabotage.

3. Frye (1983) discusses the distinction between loving and arrogant perception.

4. In this connection, see Anzaldúa (1987), Sherover-Marcuse (1986), and Miller (1984).

5. (a) The norm-flouting I have in mind here has a political meaning at odds with that of privileged eccentricity, but the two are not always easy to distinguish, especially when class privilege accompanies, for example, a stigmatized sexual identity. The risks and costs of being "out" vary enormously, and some forms of politically progressive transgression can be more easily available to those who are otherwise comfortable and safe. Alliances between those who do not have the choice to pass, for whom strategic inventiveness is required for bare survival, and those whose transgressions are more a matter of choice are precarious—at risk on one side from the need for protective coloration that can be read as overconformity, and on the other from the possibility of playfulness that can be read as unseriousness. The responsibility for establishing trusting alliances is not, however, equally shared: Nancy Potter (1994) has argued that the burdens of creating trust properly fall disproportionately on the relatively privileged. (b) 'Problematize' is a word that has gotten something of a reputation as a piece of theory-jargon. I think the reputation is undeserved, as I know of no other noncumbersome way of referring to just this activity, which is a crucial one for any liberatory theorizing: the rendering problematic (questionable, in need of explanation) of some phenomenon taken to be transparent, natural, in need of neither explanation nor justification.

6. Halperin also draws on Eve Sedgwick's (1990) discussion of the productive incoherence of heteronormative and homophobic discourses.

7. In a liberal Christian society, such as the present-day United States, there is a presumption of Christian identity that works much like the presumption of heterosexuality: People are given the "benefit" of the doubt and assigned, in the absence of positive counterevidence, to the privileged category. Nor, as Jacob Hale has pointed out, is the privilege that comes of being born to Christian parents easily shed, especially since the alternatives to it that most occupy the American imaginary are racialized: Even if the question "Are you a Christian?" is typically about faith, the presumption of Christian identity is usually not.

8. As Lisa Heldke has reminded me, there is a common way of resolving this tension, by dividing Jewish identity in two—the religious component and the racial or cultural component. The resolution doesn't work, in part because it simply pushes the problem back one step: What is the relationship between the two "components,"

and how are we to characterize the second—since on any plausible notions of race or culture, Jews belong not to one but to several or many. (The problem was literally "pushed back" by the Nuremberg Laws, by which the Nazis sought to racially classify the Jews: Jewishness was defined in terms of religious observance in the grandparental generation [Pascale Bos, personal communication].)

9. Putting the matter this way highlights the fact that Christianormativity and Christianity are no more the same thing than are heteronormativity and heterosexuality: In both cases there are particular histories of ascendancy to centrality, which histories need to be told in tandem with the complementary histories of the corresponding stigmatized identities.

10. For reasons much like these, David Halperin (1995) has called heterosexuality "the love that dare not speak its name" (i.e., that dare not name itself as one sexuality among others, needing, like them, to explain itself). Thanks to Diana Tietjens Meyers for pointing out that the discourses of normality and of virtue are not contradictory if normality is read in a normative way. The contradictoriness comes in when that normativity is occluded, camouflaging undefended, possibly indefensible, claims about excellence—when, that is, we are not supposed to be able to ask: "Says who?" or if we do, the answer is: "Nature."

11. The specific example is Elizabeth V. Spelman's (1988, 12), and she makes the general point especially well. See also Sarah Hoagland's (1988 and forthcoming) refusal to take up the question of whether or not women ought to have equal rights, since it presupposes the rights of men as the unquestionable norm against which women need to stake a claim.

12. For an excellent discussion of paradigm case reasoning and its role in the maintenance of privilege (as well as its difference from "essentialism"), see Marilyn Frye (forthcoming).

13. Marcia Hagen (during a conversation) drew my attention to the historical specificity of the unintelligibility of secular Jewish identity, by pointing out the persistence in Canada, for one generation more than in the United States, of a vibrant secular Yiddish culture. My discussion is grounded in post–World War II U.S. culture, where the terms that governed assimilationist possibilities joined with the memory of the Holocaust to make impossible the thinking of Jewishness in anything like racial terms. And, in the American imaginary, religion was the only remaining possibility. (I wonder if the centrality of distinct Québecois identity, however problematic, to Canadian thinking helps to provide conceptual space lacking in the United States)

14. Thanks to Jacob Hale for stressing the importance of this point. The monster Stryker (1994) has most particularly in mind is Frankenstein's, but the figure of the monster—as "unnatural" because created, a "creature"—is central to her discussion of what she calls "transgender rage." See also Feinberg (1993) for a harrowing and moving portrayal of the experiences of a "he-she," and Frye (1983) for a discussion of the extent to which gender ascription shapes our responses to each other.

15. Analogous work is being done around race and the experiences of those who are not readily racially classifiable–in particular, those of mixed race (see, for example, Camper 1994 and Zack 1995). There are, of course, enormous differences: Miscegenation provides an all too easily imagined answer to the question of how someone "came to look like that," and looking and otherwise seeming more white is more a

matter of privilege for people of color than looking and otherwise seeming more male is for women (though in some circumstances the former can be more problematic and the latter more privileging than is usually acknowledged).

16. Being "stably female-gendered" is not an all-or-nothing thing: The dividing line of gender slices through at least the edges of many lives. In our culture's terms, as a feminist and a philosopher I may not be a best paradigm case, and certainly many others are even less so—notably lesbians, who are routinely told, and often, especially as children believe, that they are not "real women." And certainly not all feminists share the desire to end gender as we know it—one may, for example, be more concerned to fight for the recognition of one's identity as a woman despite one's gender-role nonconformity or one's less than stereotypical appearance. My appeal here is to those feminists who do share the desire to radically transform the meaning of gender, if not to eliminate it altogether, and who have the privilege of at least sufficient gender conformity to, for example, use a women's restroom without being hassled. Obviously, the challenge will be different depending on one's circumstances: I'm addressing most directly those who, like me, have lived close enough to the center never to have directly experienced the knife-edge of the gender divide.

17. I share this confusion with many if not most feminist theorists. Kessler and McKenna's (1978) book played an important role in moving us away from the premature sense of intelligibility expressed in the sex/gender distinction of most 1970s feminist theory. As I will argue, this confusion is entirely appropriate at this point in history: We have good reason to distrust *any* conceptually coherent account of gender.

18. (a) Jacob Hale (1996), in a discussion of Monique Wittig's claim that lesbians are not women, provides a subtle and complex (Austinian) analysis of the diverse meanings of 'real woman', along with a persuasive argument that any understanding of gender or sexuality has to proceed by way of an understanding of the margins: It is in the experiences and perspectives of those who inhabit the boundaries that the contours of a contested conceptual space are articulated. I have, of course, been surrounded by sophisticated discussions about the ways in which women are not born but made, and made specifically by patriarchy for its ends—but underlying those discussions has been a virtually untouched dualism dividing those who were slated to be made into women from those who were not, along with a sense of the centrality of that constructed identity even for those who in many ways rejected it. (b) The impetus to explore these issues came largely from an invitation to a conference on "Sissies and Tomboys," held on February 10, 1995, at the Center for Gay and Lesbian Studies, City University of New York Graduate Center. I was invited by the organizer, Matt Rottnek, whose confidence that I did, despite my skepticism, have something to say about these questions, led to my beginning to pull these thoughts together. I was enormously helped, in preparing for the conference, by several of the programs (including Leslie Feinberg's plenary address) in "Differently Gendered Lives: A Week of Programs About Transgender and Transsexual Experiences," sponsored by the University of Minnesota Office of Lesbian, Gay, Bisexual, and Transsexual Programs, and held from January 28 to February 3, 1995.

19. Sarah Hoagland (1988) and Jan Binder (personal communication) have helped me to see the political implications lurking in questions of intelligibility: Who has to make themselves intelligible to whom, in what terms, for what reasons, against what

forms of resistance, with what resources? Heteronormativity requires for intelligibility that one be one gender or the other: But some transsexuals are beginning to resist this requirement, in particular as enforced by "medical, psychotherapeutic, and juridical institutions" that police the gender boundary (Stryker 1994, 252), and hence no longer to identify as women (or men), plain and simple (Bornstein 1994; Stone, in Gabriel 1995; Stryker 1994; Jacob Hale, correspondence; Susan Kimberley in discussion at the University of Minnesota conference).

20. Aside from being a feminist, a philosopher, and an adult-onset bisexual (and having loved math and logic), my only major failure to conform to the norms of femaleness is that I have never been pregnant and I am not a mother. But I managed to leave those options at least hypothetically open until this summer, so never confronted the implications for my inclusion as a "real woman." I am writing the final draft of this chapter while recuperating from a total hysterectomy, surgery that removed not only the possibility of pregnancy but the internal organs most definitive of my femaleness. The timing is coincidental, but suggestive.

21. Irena Klepfisz's (1990) account of her experience of a vanishing Yiddish culture in New York helped give me a sense of what it would be like to have a community-based sense of secular Jewish identity.

22. As in the case of gender, I respond differently to people who "go the other way," who give up the identity they share with me for another: female-to-male transsexuals and Jewish converts, especially to Christianity. I feel abandoned, as though someone I thought was "on my side" had gone over, if not exactly to the enemy, then to the class of others who historically have oppressed us. I'm learning, largely through listening to and reading Leslie Feinberg and, more recently, reading and corresponding with Jacob Hale, to think and feel differently about FTM transsexuals, but it is harder to accept Jews who convert to Christianity. The difference, I think, is that although it is no part of sexism to get women to defect and become men (not, at least, in this world and in bodily form; see Boyarin [1994] for an argument that Pauline Christianity does envision women's becoming spiritually men), it is at the heart of orthodox Christianity to get others, most especially Jews, to defect and become Christians. If there is anything I think is essential to Jewish identity in Christian cultures, it is the resistance to Christian proselytizing. At the very least, a convert can be held accountable by Jews, as an FTM transsexual can be held accountable by women, for conscientiously dealing with newly acquired Christian—or male—privilege.

23. Natalie Kampen has pointed out to me the importance of the idea of authenticity to Jewish identity, and the relation to similar discussions concerning, for example, black or Chicano identity. The concern revolves around a subordinated community's fears in relation to the dominant community: for example, that those members most acceptable to the white or Christian world will be assimilated, while the others are increasingly stigmatized. It is an understandable response to such (realistic) fears to accuse the more "acceptable" of being inauthentic; but, as María Lugones argued in a talk at a Philosophy, Interpretation, and Culture (PIC) conference at Binghamton University (in April 1994), it's misguided and self-defeating, reinforcing the oppressor's logic.

24. Thanks to Diana Tietjens Meyers, Lisa Heldke, and Jacob Hale for pointing out to me that, in earlier versions of this chapter, I had (repeatedly, even after being

warned) succumbed to these temptations. Rather than claim finally to have overcome them, I would note here that such lapsing into the perquisites of privileged subjectivity is not only a demographic but an occupational hazard, and the effort to give up identity policing needs to be an ongoing one. (This chapter may be finished, but its author is a work in progress.)

25. For a discussion of sex-assignment at birth in cases of genital ambiguity, see Kessler (1990): Feminist suspicions about the phallocentrism of the sex/gender system are reinforced by her argument that the determining factor for sex-assignment is the presence or absence of a "good-enough" penis.

26. See Nelson (forthcoming). Also, Leon J. Goldstein's chapter, "Thoughts on Jewish identity" (especially p. 81), in Goldberg and Krausz (1993), similarly rejects the coherence of the idea of Jews as simply self-identifying.

27. The metaphysical underpinnings of the idea that social classifications (such as race and gender) are the real products of social actions—in other words, that constructivism is compatible with realism—are being developed in detail by Michael Root.

28. One of the best articulations of what it is to be an "impossible being" is, in fact, Marilyn Frye's, in her *tour de force* essay "To Be and Be Seen" (in *The Politics of Reality*, 1983): In the logic of patriarchy, it must, she demonstrates, be impossible to see women as lesbians see them. That she starts this essay by quoting Sarah Hoagland on the conceptual impossibility of lesbians further reinforces the point that lesbian separatist suspicion of MTF transsexuals need not rest on an essentialist or biologistic account of who women are. Both Frye (1988) and Hoagland (1988) are clear on the constructedness of female identity and on the inextricability of that construction from the subordinating projects of male domination. They are also both insistent that the focus of lesbian attention is in other lesbians, not on the borders that might be taken to define either 'lesbian' or 'woman'. (See, especially, Hoagland's [1988, 70] refusal to define 'lesbian' in part because of her refusal to engage in what she takes to be the diversionary activity of boundary making.)

29. 'Perinatally pinked' has, of course, another meaning, one that in this context demands at least acknowledgment: as a description of the circumcised penis of the Jewish male. For discussion of the ramifications of this way of inscribing Jewishness on the male body—that is, in a way that can be read (cannot but be read?) as feminizing—see D. Boyarin (1995), who in turn quotes Geller (1993) quoting Spinoza to this effect.

30. (a) Many thanks to separatists at the Fall 1995 meeting of the Midwest Society for Women in Philosophy—especially Marilyn Frye, Sarah Hoagland, and Anne Leighton—for helping me to understand a separatist point of view on the dispute between MTF transsexuals and separatists, particularly focusing on admission to the Michigan Women's Music Festival. They are not responsible for 'perinatally pinked', nor am I certain of whether they would agree on its usefulness. I've been helped in understanding transsexual womyn's arguments against their exclusion from the Michigan festival by reading letters and articles in several issues of *TransSisters*, especially Issue No. 7 (1995), and of *Transsexual News Telegraph*. (b) It was also helpful to read in both publications about the controversy over the exclusion from the New Woman's Conference of pre- or nonoperative MTF transsexuals. The argument is made that it is a conference for those who share a very specific experience: that of having "lived so-

cially as a man at some time, . . . currently living socially as a woman, and [having] had genital surgery that resulted in making her genitals appear more female than they originally were" (*TransSisters* 7: 11). In that same issue, both a letter writer, Riawa Smith, and the editor, Davina Anne Gabriel, suggest, what was apparently decided on, that the conference should change its name to reflect better just whom it is intended for, rather than using a name ("New Woman") that others feel an equal need and right to claim. (c) As with my suggestion about "perinatally pinked," the idea here is that different people will find that different parts of their complex identities and histories are especially salient and, in particular, define a space of safety and refuge—of home, in one of the senses of that loaded word; and that such identities and spaces are vitally important but, as Riawa Smith echoes Bernice Johnson Reagon (1983), not to be confused with the space of activist politics, even as they make such politics possible, by providing a space both of refuge and of wild imagining.

31. See Gordon Lafer's chapter, "Universalism and particularism in Jewish law: Making sense of political loyalties," in Goldberg and Krausz (1993).

32. Having had these thoughts rather inchoately for a long time, I was excited to find them developed in scholarly detail in Boyarin (1994), where he discusses the implications of Paul's proclaiming in Galatians that "[t]here is neither Jew nor Greek; there is neither slave nor freeman; there is no male and female. For you are all one in Christ Jesus."

33. See Boyarin and Boyarin (1993), to which, along with conversations with Daniel Boyarin, I am deeply indebted for pulling together these ideas.

34. Thanks go to Michael Root for suggesting the use of 'naturalized citizen' in the context of thinking about transsexual identity change. Judith Shapiro (1991, 259–260) makes similar use of the term.

35. See Boyarin and Boyarin (1993) for an argument that the particularism of Jewish identity is morally defensible only if *not* coupled with state power.

36. See Asa Kasher's chapter, "Jewish collective identity," in Goldberg and Krausz (1993).

37. Again, see Gordon Lafer's chapter, "Universalism and particularism in Jewish law: Making sense of political loyalties," in Goldberg and Krausz (1993)–this time, for the suggestion that traditionally Jewishness was much "deeper" and more connected to what made one socially intelligible. Also, as Diana Tietjens Meyers has reminded me, it is Judaism, the religion, to which converts convert, leaving that murky identity—"Jewishness"—still murky. It is both unclear and, in some communities and families, a matter of real dispute as to whether or not one can "become Jewish," and, if so, just what that means.

38. Thanks to Jacob Hale for pressing me on the need to think about passing as a man from the perspective of an FTM transsexual. What is important, as he pointed out, is grappling seriously with the male privilege that one acquires. What counts as the avoidance of "honorary" status is not always clear. For example, if I teach my classes and attend meetings on the high holy days, I am in effect setting myself apart from those "other" Jews who won't conform to the "normal" (i.e., Christian) calendar; but it feels dishonest to stay home, since neither synagogue attendance nor any other way of specifically marking the new year has any place in my life. Is it a matter of solidarity not to treat those days like any others in support of those faculty, staff, and students who—in the face of lack of cooperation or understanding—do observe the holidays?

39. See Cora Diamond's chapter, "Sahibs and Jews," in Goldberg and Krausz (1993).

40. For a related discussion of positionality as a way of thinking about identity that escapes essentialism without becoming empty, see Alcoff (1988).

41. For discussions of related phenomena, see Zita (1992) on "male lesbians," Boyarin and Boyarin (1993) on "the jew" [*sic*], and Kaminsky (1993) on exile.

42. The arguments here are related to those concerning how to think about racial identity: There are both scientific and political reasons to argue that race is unreal, but doing so obscures the histories and in many cases the antiracist politics of those whose lived experience of race is very real indeed. See, for example, DuBois (1966), Appiah (1986), and Outlaw (1992).

43. Daniel Boyarin (1994, 224ff.) is explicit about the parallels between this erasure of the specificity of Jews and "the post-structuralist deconstruction of the sign 'woman'."

44. In a video performance piece entitled "Cornered," Adrian Piper confronts presumptively white viewers with the challenge to acknowledge that, at least by the terms of the "one drop rule," many of them are actually black, and to consider claiming that identity.

45. These are among the clarifications being developed by Michael Root.

46. After completing this chapter I encountered a paper of Jonathan Boyarin's (1995) in which he makes a similar argument, by way of a specifically Jewish intervention into a dispute he stages between Charles Taylor and Judith Butler concerning identity. I have also just begun to learn, from Laura Levitt among others, about the emerging conversation among Jewish feminists concerning the nature of Jewish identity: As with other identities, it is helpfully articulated from its own, in this case gendered, margins.

47. Many thanks to the challenging audiences for earlier drafts at the University of Minnesota and at meetings of the Canadian and Midwest Societies for Women in Philosophy and of the American Academy of Religion, and, especially, to Lisa Heldke, Diana Tietjens Meyers, and Michael Root for their extensive comments. Unfortunately, those comments were interesting and provocative, and the result is a denser, more complex chapter and not, as they intended, a clearer one. The largest portion of the blame for the density and complexity, however, lies with Daniel Boyarin and Jacob Hale, who have between them done a wonderful job of confusing me.

References

Alcoff, Linda. 1988. Cultural feminism versus post-structuralism: The identity crisis in feminist theory. *Signs* 13(3): 405–436.

Anzaldúa, Gloria. 1987. *Borderlands/la frontera: The new mestiza.* San Francisco: Spinsters/Aunt Lute.

Appiah, Anthony. 1986. The uncompleted argument: DuBois and the illusion of race. In *Race, writing, and difference*, ed. Henry Louis Gates, Jr. Chicago: University of Chicago Press.

Bornstein, Kate. 1994. *Gender outlaw: On men, women and the rest of us.* New York: Routledge.

Boyarin, Daniel. 1994. *A radical Jew: Paul and the politics of identity*. Berkeley: University of California Press.

————. 1995. Freud's baby, Fliess's maybe: Homophobia, anti-Semitism, and the invention of Oedipus. *GLO: A Journal of Lesbian and Gay Studies* 2(1–2): 115–147.

————. forthcoming. Judaism as a gender: An autobiography of the Jewish man.

Boyarin, Daniel, and Jonathan Boyarin. 1993. Diaspora: Generation and the ground of Jewish identity. *Critical Inquiry* 19(4): 693–725.

Boyarin, Jonathan. 1995. Before the law there stands a woman: *In re Taylor v. Butler* (with court-appointed Yiddish translator). *Cardozo Law Review* 16(3–4): 1303–1323.

Butler, Judith. 1990. *Gender trouble: Feminism and the subversion of identity*. New York: Routledge.

Camper, Carol, ed. 1994. *Miscegenation blues: Voices of mixed-race women*. Toronto: Sister Vision.

DuBois, W.E.B. 1966. The conservation of races. In *Negro social and political thought 1850–1920*, ed. Howard Brotz. New York: Basic Books.

Epstein, Julia, and Kristina Straub, eds. 1991. *Body guards: The cultural politics of gender ambiguity*. New York: Routledge.

Feinberg, Leslie. 1993. *Stone butch blues*. Ithaca, N.Y.: Firebrand Books.

Frye, Marilyn. 1983. *The politics of reality*. Trumansburg, N.Y.: Crossing Press.

————. forthcoming. Ethnocentrism/essentialism: The failure of the ontological cure. In *Social justice and the future of feminisms* (working title), ed. Center for Advanced Feminist Studies collective, University of Minnesota.

Gabriel, Davina Anne. 1995. Interview with the transsexual vampire: Sandy Stone's dark gift. *TransSisters: The Journal of Transsexual Feminism* 8: 14–27.

Gates, Henry Louis, Jr. 1988. *The signifying monkey: A theory of African-American literary criticism*. New York: Oxford University Press.

Geller, Jay. 1993. A paleontological view of Freud's study of religion: Unearthing the *Leitfossil* circumcision. *Modern Judaism* 13: 49–70.

Gilman, Sander. 1991. *The Jew's body*. New York: Routledge.

Goldberg, David Theo, and Michael Krausz, eds. 1993. *Jewish identity*. Philadelphia: Temple University Press.

Hale, Jacob. 1966. Are lesbians women? *Hypatia* 11(2): 94–121.

Halperin, David. 1995. The queer politics of Michel Foucault. In *Saint Foucault: Two essays in gay hagiography*. New York: Oxford University Press.

Haraway, Donna. 1991. Situated knowledges: The science question in feminism and the privilege of partial perspective. In *Simians, cyborgs, and women: The reinvention of nature*, ed. Donna Haraway. New York: Routledge.

Harding, Sandra. 1991. *Whose science? Whose knowledge?: Thinking from women's lives*. Ithaca, N.Y.: Cornell University Press.

Hoagland, Sarah Lucia. 1988. *Lesbian ethics: Toward new value*. Palo Alto, Calif.: Institute of Lesbian Studies.

————. forthcoming. Moving toward uncertainty. In *Re-reading the canon: Feminist interpretations of Wittgenstein*, ed. Naomi Scheman. University Park: University of Pennsylvania Press.

Kaminsky, Amy Katz. 1993. Issues for an international literary criticism. *Signs* 19(1): 213–227.

Kant, Immanuel. 1969/1785. *Foundations of the metaphysics of morals*, trans. Lewis White Beck; ed. Robert Paul Wolff. Indianapolis: Bobbs-Merrill.

_____. 1960/1771. *Observations on the beautiful and sublime*, trans. John T. Goldthwait. Berkeley: University of California Press.

Kessler, Suzanne J. 1990. The medical construction of gender: Case management of intersexed infants. *Signs* 16(1): 3–26.

Kessler, Suzanne J., and Wendy McKenna. 1978. *Gender: An ethnomethodological approach*. Chicago: University of Chicago Press.

Klepfisz, Irena. 1990. *Dreams of an insomniac: Jewish feminist essays, speeches and diatribes*. Portland, Oreg.: Eighth Mountain Press.

Lugones, María. 1987. Playfulness, "world"-travel, and loving perception. *Hypatia* 2(2): 3–19.

_____. 1990. Structure/antistructure and agency under oppression. *Journal of Philosophy* 87(10): 500–507.

_____. 1994. Purity, impurity, and separation. *Signs* 19(2): 458–479.

MacKinnon, Catharine A. 1990. Sexuality, pornography, and method: Pleasure under patriarchy. In *Feminism and political theory*, ed. Cass R. Sunstein. Chicago: University of Chicago Press.

Miller, Alice. 1984. *For your own good: Hidden cruelty in child-rearing and the roots of violence*, trans. Hildegarde Hannum and Hunter Hannum. New York: Farrar, Straus, and Giroux.

Nelson, Hilde Lindemann. forthcoming. Wittgenstein meets "woman" in the language-game of theorizing feminism. In *Re-reading the canon: Feminist interpretations of Wittgenstein*, ed. Naomi Scheman. University Park: University of Pennsylvania Press.

Outlaw, Lucius. 1992. Against the grain of modernity: The politics of difference and the conservation of "race." *Man and World* 25(4): 443–468.

Peterson, Susan Rae. 1977. Coercion and rape: The state as a male protection racket. In *Feminism and philosophy*, ed. Mary Vetterling-Braggin, Frederick A. Elliston, and Jane English. Totowa, N.J.: Littlefield, Adams, & Co.

Potter, Nancy. 1994. Trustworthiness: An Aristotelian analysis of a virtue. Ph.D. dissertation, University of Minnesota.

Prell, Riv-Ellen. 1992. Why Jewish princesses don't sweat: Desire and consumption in postwar American Jewish culture. In *People of the body: Jews and Judaism from an embodied perspective*, ed. Howard Eilberg-Schwartz. Albany: SUNY Press.

Reagon, Bernice Johnson. 1983. Coalition politics: Turning the century. In *Home girls: A Black feminist anthology*, ed. Barbara Smith. New York: Kitchen Table Women of Color Press.

Rich, Adrienne. 1978. *The dream of a common language: Poems 1974–1977*. New York: W. W. Norton.

_____. 1979. "It is the lesbian in us. . . . " In *On lies, secrets, and silence: Selected prose 1966–1978*. New York: W. W. Norton.

_____. 1986. Compulsory heterosexuality and lesbian existence. In *Blood, bread, and poetry: Selected prose 1979–1985*. New York: W. W. Norton.

Scheman, Naomi. 1993. Though this be method, yet there is madness in it: Paranoia and liberal epistemology. In *Engenderings: Constructions of knowledge, authority, and privilege*. New York: Routledge.

Sedgwick, Eve Kosofsky. 1990. *Epistemology of the closet.* Berkeley: University of California Press.

Shapiro, Judith. 1991. Transsexualism: Reflections on the persistence of gender and the mutability of sex. In *Body guards: The cultural politics of gender ambiguity,* ed. Julia Epstein and Kristina Straub. New York: Routledge.

Sherover-Marcuse, Erica. 1986. *Emancipation and consciousness: Dogmatic and dialectical perspectives in the early Marx.* Oxford: Basil Blackwell.

Spelman, Elizabeth V. 1988. *Inessential woman: Problems of exclusion in feminist thought.* Boston: Beacon Press.

Stone, Sandy. 1991. The *Empire* strikes back: A posttranssexual manifesto. In *Body guards: The cultural politics of gender ambiguity,* ed. Julia Epstein and Kristina Straub. New York: Routledge.

Stryker, Susan. 1994. My words to Victor Frankenstein above the village of Chamounix: Performing transgender rage. *GLQ: A Journal of Lesbian and Gay Studies* 1(3): 237–254.

Zack, Naomi, ed. 1995. *American mixed race: The culture of microdiversity.* Lanham, Md.: Rowman and Littlefield.

Zita, Jacquelyn. 1981. Lesbian continuum and historical amnesia. *Signs* 7(1): 172–181.

_____. 1992. The male lesbian and the post-modern body. *Hypatia* 7(4): 106–127.

seven

Good Grief, It's Plato!

ELIZABETH V. SPELMAN

It is difficult to read parts of Plato's *Republic*—especially those decrying the damaging effects of tragic poetry—without concluding that in the well-ordered state and the well-ordered soul there is little place for grief. Moreover, given the central role that women in classical Athens played in funeral rites as mourners, and vivid Socratic castigations of weeping and lamenting as womanish behavior, attempts in the *Republic* to mute grief appear to be aimed at minimizing powerful forms of typically "feminine" behavior.[1]

But it would be hasty to infer simply that Plato wanted to diminish the force of grief because it was "feminine." First of all, as we shall see, it is not at all clear that Plato really wanted to get rid of grief entirely. Moreover, part of Socrates' arguments with his various protagonists in the *Republic* concerned what ought to count as "womanish" or as "manly" behavior. Merely reminding ourselves that Plato regarded grief as quintessentially "feminine" doesn't invite us to look closely at just what it is about grief that bothered him so much. It may distract us from seeing that despite his worries about members of tragic audiences being overly attracted to the grief of heroes and heroines, he certainly did not want people to think they could not and should not in an important sense grieve with others.

These complications in the *Republic*'s treatment of grief begin to come clear when we juxtapose the attack on the poets with the attack on Thrasymachus. Audiences bewitched by the powers of tragic poets are all too liable to have their own capacity for debilitating grief kindled by beholding the grief of others. But young men bewitched by the rhetorical powers of a Thrasymachus are equally liable to think that other people's grief and suffering have no hold on them at all. We are to learn from the criticism of the poets that giving in to grief is conduct unbecoming those whose capacity for reason qualifies, indeed obliges, them to rule and thus to do their part in maintaining unity and order in the state. But at the same time we are to learn from the attack on the moral and psychological blindness of Thrasymachus that another great principle of unity in the state is the capacity of all to rejoice and grieve over the same events. And, as will become clear, the prospects for a community of people grieving over the same events are said to depend in part on women not being the private property of men.

So, as we shall soon see in more detail, Plato's views about grief and related forms of suffering command our attention for a number of reasons. First of all, whatever differences there are between us as contemporary readers of Plato and the Greek audiences Plato had in mind (including differences in styles of and occasions for grieving), clearly we no less than they are capable of grief—where grief is, paradigmatically, intensely felt anguish over the death of loved ones, and, at its outer edges, is suffering suffused with the sense of irreparable loss. We might well ask how central figures in western philosophy such as Plato contribute to our understanding of such basic human experiences.[2]

Second, as is well known, and is particularly clear in the *Republic*, Plato was greatly troubled by the power and authority of Homer and the tragic poets in matters of grief and other responses to common human affliction. In his view philosophy has something much better to say about such matters and ought to displace poetry as the major source of moral guidance.

Finally, and central to the concerns animating this anthology: Although Plato's views about grief are not reducible to his views about gender traits and gender relations, neither are they fully understandable without them. And no examination of Plato's views about women is complete without an exploration of his views about grief.[3]

A word about terminology: Plato, as we shall see, wants us to understand the proper place of grief in individual and collective life, but he also wants us to come to correct beliefs about the nature and meaning of pain, pleasure, and happiness; and in the *Republic*, of course, all this happens in the context of a lengthy exploration of justice. Plato did not, and we should not, treat 'grief' and 'suffering' and 'pain' and 'unhappiness' as synonymous.[4] In what follows it should be clear from the context whether the topic under discussion is grief in particular, other forms of physical and psychological suffering more broadly, or, most generally of all, a sense of unhappiness.

1. Tragedy and the Misunderstanding of Grief

According to Plato, when you get grief wrong you get very much else wrong too. Homer and the tragedians were dangerously wrong about grief and about how to assess the events to which it is a response. They come under Socratic scrutiny as creators (among other things) of mimetic poetry.[5] Such poetry is defined in Book 10 of the *Republic* as that which "imitates human beings acting under compulsion or voluntarily, and as a result of their actions supposing themselves to have fared well or ill and in all this feeling either grief or joy" (603c). Whether or not Plato had Oedipus in mind when proffering this definition, he can be invoked by way of illustrating what appears to be Plato's point: *Oedipus Rex* enacts the story of a man, apparently acting voluntarily, who unwittingly kills his father and marries his mother; though for some time he assumes he has fared well, he comes to see what in fact he has done, and, realizing the great ills that have befallen him and his family and his city, he becomes sorely grieved. Tragic heroes typically are presented as being driven in their grief to lamentation and breast-beating (605d). Oedipus, of course, goes a bit further and gouges out his own eyes.

Plato is worried about the powerful effects such portrayals of grief have on their audiences. These effects are complicated. On the one hand, Plato says, audiences tend to react with pleasure: We "feel pleasure, and abandon ourselves and accompany the representation [of suffering and grief] with sympathy and eagerness, and we praise as an excellent poet the one who most strongly affects us in this way" (605d). The pleasure presumably is due to the audience's delight not in what the hero finds grievous but in the feeling of sympathy for the aggrieved hero and in the ability of the poet to affect the audience so powerfully.[6]

This pleasure seems to presuppose a kind of distance between the hero and the audience member: The hero is suffering greatly, the audience is in full delight. But at the same time—and this is why the effects of mimetic poetry are so complicated—what Plato finds disturbing about the power of such poetry is that, as he sees it, the pleasure produced in the audience members strengthens their willingness to give in to their own grief. The pleasure they take in the representation of the pain of another strengthens the part of them that would grieve for themselves. This "plaintive part" of the soul by its very nature hungers for "tears and a good cry and satisfaction" (606a); it shamelessly praises and pities "another who, claiming to be a good man, abandons himself to excess in his grief" (606b). If we take pleasure in seeing another grieve, then we will not restrain our own grief, for we will take pleasure also in our own grieving: "For after feeding fat the emotion of pity there, it is not easy to restrain it in our own sufferings" (606b). Such pleasure in our own grief is dangerous, Plato insists, because the heaving grieving we praise in the theater is "that of a woman"; it is unbecoming for noble men to allow themselves to give in to such grief. It undermines their capacity to "remain calm and endure" when "affliction comes" in their real lives (605 d–e; cf. 395e).

In short, the great tragic scenes make grief seductive—even for those who know better—by highlighting and underscoring the pleasures of grief. Members of the audience presumably are not pleased by the sufferings of the hero, but they are pleased by the chance to satisfy their desire to wail and shed tears. Mimetic poets know all too well how to appeal to the part of us that grieves, "the part of us that leads us to dwell in memory on our suffering and impels us to lamentation, and cannot get enough of that sort of thing . . . the irrational and idle part of us, the associate of cowardice" (604d).

Mimetic poets are dangerous because they strengthen the power of this irrational part of the soul over the rational part. The part of us with which we grieve is at odds with the "nobly serious part" (603c), in virtue of which one follows "reason and law" (604a–b). (In terms of the *Republic*'s tripartite division of the soul into reason, spirit, and appetite [439a(ff.)], the emotion of grief seems to be located in the spirit—the part that is capable of serving the rational part by reining in the unruly forces belonging to the third, appetitive part. But Socrates' references to the voraciousness and insatiability of grief also implicitly liken it to a kind of appetite that knows no limits.)[7]

A "good and reasonable man" can't help but feel pain when in his own actual life something horrible happens, such as the death of a son. But he will be "moderate in his grief" (603e). This is because reason tells him that "it is best to keep quiet as far as possible in calamity and not to chafe and repine, because we cannot know what is really good and evil in such things and it advantages us nothing to take them hard, and nothing in mortal life is worthy of great concern, and our grieving checks the very thing we need to come to our aid as quickly as possible in such case" (604c).[8] One needs to think through what has happened and what one ought to do, rather than "clapping one's hands to the stricken spot and wasting the time in wailing" (604d); in addition, one should "accustom the soul to devote itself at once to the curing of the hurt and the raising up of what has fallen" (604d). Grieving simply makes the condition that has made us grieve even worse, because it distracts us from attending thoughtfully to the situation that is so grievous.

Homer and the tragedians are masterful in rendering the pleasures and pains of their characters, and they know how to create pleasure and bittersweet pain in their audiences. But they know next to nothing about the proper role of pleasure and pain in human life. More specifically, they don't know how to take the proper measure of grief.

Moreover, in their explanations of the role of the gods, the poets put forth dangerously misleading ideas about the cause of human misery more generally. They say that "the gods themselves assign to many good men misfortunes and an evil life, but to their opposites a contrary lot" (364b); and that the gods can be bought off by evil men, who then will not have to pay for their wrongdoing (364d–e). In short, "if we are to believe [the poets], the thing to do is to commit injustice and offer sacrifice from the fruits of our wrongdoing. For if we are just, we shall, it is true, be unscathed by the gods, but we shall be putting away from us the profits of injustice, but if we are unjust, we shall win those profits, and, by the importunity of our prayers, when we transgress and sin we shall persuade them and escape scot free" (365e–366a).

Such views, Plato insists, are deeply and insidiously wrong. Although the gods are responsible for what is good, they are not responsible for what is evil (379c). It is imperative for humans not to think the gods are the cause of evil: "[E]very man will be very lenient with his own misdeeds if he is convinced" that gods do dreadful things to other gods or to humans (391e, 619c).

In sum, there are many reasons why, according to Plato, we should be careful not to be taken in by the scenes of grief so poignantly rendered by Homer and the tragedians. The poets seriously mislead us about the source of human misery. Their powerful representations of suffering and anguish stir up our insatiable appetite-like desire for experiencing grief. Grief subverts reason, making otherwise noble men act irrationally and behave in an unmanly fashion. Once we get caught up in the pleasure of satisfying our appetite for grief, we wallow in it and fail to pay proper attention to what we ought to do about the grievous situation. Our sense that grief is an appropriate response to misery and death presupposes that we clearly understand what is good and what is evil. Or in more contemporary terms: The poets' treatment of grief misleads us theologically, ethically, and epistemologically.

2. Thrasymachus and the Individuation of Grief

Mimetic poets know how to appeal to an audience's capacity to tune in to the grief of a character. But however skilled they are at presenting scenes of human suffering, and at involving the audience in the grief of the characters, they don't understand the relationship between such wretchedness and justice. Part of what Plato sees as so dangerous about them is that they provide powerful dramatic "examples of men who, though unjust, are happy, and of just men who are wretched" (392b). In so doing they join forces with Thrasymachus, the blustery *provocateur* of Book 1 of the *Republic*, to whose views about justice the rest of the dialogue is a response.

According to Thrasymachus, "the most consummate form of injustice . . . makes the man who has done the wrong most happy," whereas "those who are wronged and who would not themselves willingly do wrong [are] most miserable" (344a). Socrates appears to get him to change his mind. But as Book 2 opens, Socrates' young friends Glaucon and Adimantus desperately appeal to him to respond at greater length to Thrasymachus because, they insist, much of the culture around them affirms Thrasymachus' view that any fool knows it is better to be unjust than to be just. From Thrasymachus and "innumerable others" (358d) young men hear that although the reputation for justice brings one rewards, justice itself is an "affliction" (358a).

The Thrasymachus-inspired case for the wretchedness of the just man, and the happiness of the unjust, is this: The desires about which justice has something to say are desires having to do with the possessions of others. When one worries about what justice requires of him, he is worrying about how far justice allows others to satisfy their desires at the expense of his own. The just man does not satisfy his natural desires to take as much as he can from everyone else around him. Given that these desires are natural for others to have about your possessions, it not only cannot benefit you to be just, but your being just will benefit those who act unjustly. By the very nature of their desires, other men will "do wrong" to you. They will take your possessions, steal your wife (note that women do not appear in Thrasymachus' discussion except as the objects of male desire), kill you if they please, enslave you if they can get away with it, and so on (360b–c). Justice, on this view, arises in order to mitigate the starkness of these options: It is a "compromise between the best, which is to do wrong with impunity, and the worst, which is to be wronged and be impotent to get one's revenge" (359a). So you might agree to be just, but only because you figure that even if this means your desires for the possessions of others cannot be satisfied, at least other people's desires for your house and wife and life cannot be satisfied either.

Thrasymachus seems to be assuming that the desires it is so natural to want to satisfy are desires for things the possession of which necessarily will involve frustrating the desires of others. More simply, the view is that your happiness requires the misery of others, and their happiness requires that you be wretched. Satisfying your desires means leaving other people's desires thwarted. You either do harm to others or have it done to you.

Socrates thinks Thrasymachus' view is mistaken from head to foot: It is mistaken about human nature, about the nature of justice, and about the meaning of happiness and misery. For our particular purposes, a crucial difference between Thrasymachus and Socrates turns on the possibility of seeing one's own happiness as compatible with the happiness of others, and of seeing other people's misery as affecting the possibility of one's own.

Thrasymachus seems to see happiness as a zero-sum game: If I am happy, I must be doing something that is making someone else unhappy, since the desires I need to satisfy in order to be happy are desires for what belongs to someone else and would make them unhappy to be without. But according to Socrates, the happiest person is the just person, and the just person is one in whom each part of the soul is playing its appropriate role. Reason is master of the appetites (if not your own reason, then someone else's). So the happiness of one person is fully compatible with the happiness of another. (Indeed, the justice of the state depends upon the justice, and the happiness, of each of its members: The state cannot be just unless all members perform the kind of task that is appropriate for each of them, by reason of their natural capacities. And they will not be able to perform those tasks well unless there is the appropriate harmony and unity of reason, spirit, and appetite in them.)

Implied in Thrasymachus' views about happiness and misery is the assumption that the misery of other people doesn't touch us. Yet, although other people's misery is not itself the object of your desires, it is the necessary by-product of the satisfaction of them. The misery of other people is the necessary consequence of my being happy, but it is of no direct concern to me—except insofar as their own unsatisfied desires make them prey upon me. I am interested in what brings pleasure to me, not what brings pleasure or pain to anyone else.

For Socrates, how people think about the relation between their own and other people's suffering is directly connected to how well run a state is and how its citizens fare. The greatest evil for a state is whatever "makes it many instead of one" (Book 5, 462b). But citizens cannot be bound together and be as if one when "some grieve exceedingly and others rejoice at the same happenings" (462b–c). Crucial to the existence of a unitary, unfragmented community, then, is a "community of pleasure and pain," which we can observe when "all the citizens rejoice and grieve alike" at the same things (462b); when, "as far as practicable," there is "one experience of pleasure and pain" (464d).

Whether a community has shared or individual experiences of grief and joy is said to depend on the extent to which it allows individual ownership of property. Some of the most famous, or infamous, passages from Book 5 of the *Republic* are those in which Plato presents arguments against the private ownership of property, be it in the form of material objects or human beings. One sure source of fragmentation and dissension among people is said to be the possibility of men referring to things as "mine" rather than "ours," "one man dragging off to his own house anything he is able to acquire apart from the rest, and another doing the same to his own separate house, and having women and children apart" (464d). On the other hand, if they "have nothing in private possession but their bodies, but all else in common . . . we can count on their being free from the dissensions that arise among men from the possession of property, children, and kin" (464e). In short, on this view it is individual ownership that "introduc[es] into the state the pleasures and pains of individuals" (464d). Individualization of pleasure and pain, a grave threat to the unity of the state, is due to individualization of property.

Thrasymachus assumed that, as a matter of course, men (again, women are objects and not subjects of desire for him) distinguish their own pleasures and pains from the pleasures and pains of others, and seek to pursue what brings them pleasure at the expense of bringing pain to others. But Socrates insists that it is not a given, as Thrasymachus assumes, that we will take pleasure in performing actions that we know to cause great misery in others. We can learn to take pleasure in what pleases other people; we can learn to grieve at what gives them pain; indeed, we can come to be pained by and take pleasure in the very same things they do. People will grieve over misfortunes they count as theirs, and rejoice in good things they do or that happen to them. But what they count as "theirs" or "not theirs" depends on the kind of polity in which they live.

So, among the complaints Socrates makes against Thrasymachus is that he gets grief wrong no less than the poets did. He badly misunderstands its place in human life. He imagines that you can't help but grieve if your desires are not satisfied—not only because it is natural to want to satisfy your desires, and thus presumably natural to feel miserable when they are thwarted, but also because the only conceivable cause of your not satisfying your desires is that another person is satisfying his, necessarily at your expense. He believes that no one can gain unless another person loses, that his loss has to be somebody else's gain. Indeed, Thrasymachus doesn't understand the plasticity of our desire, so he can't imagine the possibility that, rather than one person's happiness necessarily being paired with another's misery, people can come to be grieved by and rejoice in the same thing.

3. The Poets, Thrasymachus, and Socrates

In Section 1 we saw that Socrates' insistence, in Book 10, on eliminating mimetic poetry was based in part on the poets' misrepresentation of the proper role of grief in human experience. Grief has appetite-like characteristics: Readily whetted, it also is insatiable. So it is easy to want more, and difficult to get enough. The seductive pleasure of grieving with characters in a theater, Socrates insists, makes it very difficult for us not to give in to our own grief in real life. But if we do, we put off or sabotage what we really should be doing when faced with the loss of loved ones, the injustice of others, the difficult infirmities of life, the bony certainty of death: Try to cure what can be cured, try to put together what has been rent asunder, try to be brave, fearless, resolute.

The mimetic poets also misrepresent the connection between justice and misery. Tragedy seems not only to allow but to require that those who are most just are also the most wretched. This view about the inverse relation between justice and misery is heartily endorsed by Thrasymachus. But notice how differently, at least as we see them through the eyes of Plato, the poets and Thrasymachus portray grief and other forms of misery.

The tragedians are said to make getting caught up in the grief of another a pleasurable experience; in any event it makes getting caught up in our own grief allowable, even seductive. But Thrasymachus never talks about grief or other forms of suffering in a way that makes experiencing them, even vicariously, seem at all attractive. On the contrary, Thrasymachus implies that people in a position to grieve about their lot are at best pitiable weaklings who have bought a bill of goods about the importance of being just and end up being the most wretched of humans. There is nothing great about their suffering. It has nothing to teach them, or those who observe them, except the lesson that the happiest people are those who are unjust.

So, from the perspective of the *Republic*, we have from the tragedians the idea that justice is perhaps worth striving for but often leaves one miserable or dead; from Thrasymachus, the idea that justice is not worth striving for precisely because it will lead to misery; and from Socrates, the idea that justice is worth striving for and not only will not leave one miserable but will in fact bring one happiness properly understood. Dead-set as he in on countering Thrasymachus' views, Socrates is closer to him than he is to the tragedians (as Socrates sees them) in deflecting the gravitational pull of grief.

Nevertheless, reflection on the complaints against both the mimetic poets and Thrasymachus suggests some puzzles about the *Republic*'s view of grief. The poets are to be criticized for appealing to our easily triggered desire to grieve (whether for ourselves or for others), whereas Thrasymachus comes under severe scrutiny for assuming that any man worth his salt will avoid situations that cause him grief—that is, will do his best not to give in to the demands of "justice," which will stand in the way of the satisfaction of his natural desires. If Socrates thinks we shouldn't give in to grief, oughtn't he to at least welcome Thrasymachus' strong exhortations to avoid situations that we know will bring us grief and other kinds of pain? And if we recall that one of the reasons Socrates offers for not giving in to grief is that it diverts one's attention from responding appropriately to the situation that brings such grief, we may note with interest that according to Thrasymachus the smart and happy man will vigilantly avoid relationships with other people that are likely to bring misery of any sort to him—for according to Thrasymachus the smart and happy man will not subscribe to "justice" precisely because that would require him to lose, or never even to gain, at least some of what is most desirable to him.

Although there is a Platonic response to Thrasymachus' insistence on seeing justice as a zero-sum game, it leads us to another puzzle suggested by a comparison between the Platonic treatment of the poets and of Thrasymachus. This one centers on the possibility and desirability of grief being shared rather than individualized. As we have seen, part of Socrates' reply to a Thrasymachus-inspired view is that occasions for grief not only can but should be shared, if a community is to have any hopes of unity. But how is this "community of pleasure and pain" (Book 5, 462b) different from what Socrates himself says happens at the theater? Isn't what is problematic about the mimetic poets precisely that they are so adept at creating communities of pleasure and pain in the audience? How can tragedy be so bad, if it affects large groups of people in such a way that they jointly rejoice in the success of the hero, jointly wail at his demise?

The Platonic response would seem to go something like this: Yes, the unity of a community depends on all the members of the community grieving and rejoicing over the same things. In that sense there appears to be some place for grief in the best city. However, the community must grieve and rejoice in the *right* way over the *right* things. In this connection, as we saw earlier, according to Socrates any grieving we do should not be premised on false views about the gods nor ignorant assumptions about the significance of affliction or death.

Here we may see a strong connection between what Plato says is distracting about grief and his radical proposals for political restructuring in the *Republic*. First, when we grieve over what happens to great heroes and their families and cities, and are tempted to conclude that great suffering is endemic to human life, we fail to ask whether the kinds of social and political conditions under which they lived nourished the very conditions that ultimately led to such suffering and grief.[9] Second, if no man owns any particular woman, his own wife cannot be taken away from him. This proposal considerably reduces the kind of occasions for mad jealousy such as those that led to the Trojan War; at the very least, Menelaus could not have complained that Paris took his wife. And, third, if any child from a given generation is to be considered any woman's own child, potential Jocastas can hardly use as an excuse that they had no reason to think their betrothed is their own flesh and blood.

Worries about women thus are central to Plato's views about grief: Women are presented as the paradigmatic grievers, and battles among men over the ownership of women are implicated in the grave tragic situations that the mimetic poets present in such dangerously powerful ways.

4. Women and Grief

It might be tempting to conclude that in finding no good use for grief, Plato was finding no good use for what he appears to regard as a characteristically feminine trait: the capacity to grieve.

This is not an implausible suggestion. As we have seen, in his brief against grief, Socrates tries to underscore the shamefulness of giving in to grief by describing such weakness as the behavior of a woman. And although Plato appears to argue in Book 5 of the *Republic* that women as well as men are rightfully included among the philosopher-rulers, both groups would have to be considerably de-griefed beforehand. So, to the extent to which giving in to grief is a feminine trait, neither the male nor the female philosopher-rulers would be feminine in this way.

But Plato also appears to be concerned about the conceptions of manliness embraced by Thrasymachus.[10] As reprised by Socrates' friend Glaucon, the position of Thrasymachus and "innumerable others" (358d) about the desirability of acting justly is that "anyone who had the power to do [injustice] and was in reality 'a man' would never make a compact with anybody neither to wrong nor be wronged" (359b). "Real men," on such a view, don't care about the harm they do others and have no doubt about the pleasures associated with satisfying their desires for other people's property. In countering this view Plato does his best to suggest that a far more attractive picture of manhood centers on a man's being the master of his appetites; indeed, a man who is a slave to his appetites should feel as much shame as a man who finds himself the slave of another man. Insofar as one gives in to the various beasts of appetite within, one can be charged with "softness" or "effeminacy" (590b).[11]

In short, the debates that Plato stages between Socrates and the poets, and between Socrates and Thrasymachus, include, not surprisingly, taunts about who is more manly than whom, and who is more effeminate than whom. To the extent that grieving is considered a feminine trait by Plato, it is fair to say that in hoping to check grieving he was hoping to mute the feminine. This does not mean that he wished to get rid of the female: After all, females are to be found among the philosopher-rulers. But they are to be cleansed of "feminine" traits such as readiness to grieve.

And yet at the same time there is the suggestion that "feminine" traits need not be unacceptable, if they cease to carry with them the implication that they are feminine. A clear example occurs in the *Phaedo*, when one of the officers who condemned Socrates to death weeps at the impending death of a man he has come to admire (116d). Earlier, Socrates had implored his friends to take his wife Xanthippe home because she "cried out and said the sort of thing that women usually say" (60b; also 117d). But the officer's tears were not unwelcome and were not taken in any way to be a sign of effeminacy—perhaps not simply because they were being shed by a man but also because he shed them in a becoming way, and there was no threat of their being unlimited, boundless, uncontrollable.

The foregoing suggests that the significant correlation here is not between certain kinds of behavior and "manliness" or "womanliness" but, rather, between the use of "feminine" to indicate disapproval of a form of behavior and the use of "manly" to signal one's approval. Socrates' and Thrasymachus' disagreement is in part a disagreement about what constitutes manly behavior—that is, right or appropriate behavior—but not about whether "manliness" is a term of praise. Similarly, his complaints about the mimetic poets are in part about what constitutes effeminate behavior, but he never doubts that the lovers of tragedy take "womanly" to be a derogatory term; otherwise, it would make no sense for him to try to convince them of the ill-effects of tragedy by associating grieving with what women do.

So thinking about whether the virtual de-griefing of the polis is in part a de-feminizing of it does not lead to the conclusion that Plato wished to get rid of women. Nor does it lead to the conclusion that he simply wanted them to be like men. An expression of grief is not necessarily "womanly" when expressed by a woman, nor necessarily "manly" when expressed by a man. Although the description of behavior as "manly" never seems to have a negative valence, this does not mean that Plato was not involved in debates over what ought to count as "manly" behavior. And although the description of behavior as "womanly" never seems to have a positive valence, this does not mean that the behavior itself can't come to be seen as acceptable, even desirable—it means only that, should this happen, the behavior will not be describable as "womanly." (Thus, as Martha Nussbaum [1986, 18] has pointed out, the Plato of the *Phaedrus* includes grief over the death of a loved one within the repertoire of acceptable emotions. Though no explicit attempt is made to rehabilitate the emotion as "manly," there certainly is not a celebration of it as "feminine.")

Finally, it is not entirely clear just how free of grief Plato expects the polis to be. One confounding factor is the tension in his depiction of the grounds of unity among polis members. When discussing what makes justice possible in the polis, and in individual members of it, Plato, as is well known, focuses on the division of labor among constituents of the state and of the soul. Rulers, auxiliaries, and artisans all have their specific functions in the state. When they acknowledge the necessity of that and recognize their shared interests in not trying to do work other than that appropriate for their group, there will be no sources of disharmony and disunity within the polis.[12] The same is said to hold for the three constituent parts of the soul—reason, spirit, appetite.

But, as we have also seen, at times the ground of unity in the polis is said to be the shared grieving and rejoicing of everyone in the community. This implies a more positive and robust role for grief than that allowed for in the tripartite state and tripartite soul, in which contexts grief is portrayed as one of the capacities that threatens the control of the rational over the irrational.

Nevertheless, everything else in the *Republic* suggests that such grief should be contained and controlled. There are other, much more rational ways of organizing human life than those leading to the tragic events explored by the mimetic poets, or those that a Thrasymachus assumes would ensure individual human happiness. As long as there is grief, everyone should feel it on the same occasion for the same reason. But more generally, tempted as students of Homer and the tragedians may be to believe otherwise, suffering need not be the human condition. Such, at any rate, appears to be the lesson of the *Republic*.[13]

Notes

1. Both kinswomen and hired female mourners (severely curtailed in the sixth century by Solon's laws) played prominent roles in ritual lamentation. See, for example,

Alexiou (1974, 5, 6, 10, 21); Humphreys (1983, 86, 150); and Fantham et al. (1995, 76–78. The characterization of grieving as feminine is discussed here and there throughout the chapter.

2. That such experiences are basic is attested to, not undermined by, the variety of cultural responses to them.

3. This observation is a staple of feminist (and, not infrequently, nonfeminist) commentary. See, for example, Saxenhouse, in Tuana (1994, 68); Spelman, in Tuana (1994, 98); and Nussbaum (1986, 131, 230). The analysis presented here differs from Nussbaum's in locating the *Republic's* treatment of grief not only in the context of its attack on tragedy but also in relation to Socrates' response to Thrasymachus.

4. Though the Greek 'lupe' can mean pain either of body or of mind, Plato uses it frequently in the *Republic* to refer to a psychological capacity.

5. In Book 10 of the *Republic*, the analysis of poetry in terms of *mimesis* and its effects on the soul differs rather wildly from that given in Books 2 and 3—particularly with respect to how much poetry is mimetic, what *mimesis* is, and just how it appeals to the "baser" parts of the soul. For a helpful summary of these differences, see Julia Annas (1981, 336–344).

6. Plato often has been criticized for failing to appreciate audiences' abilities to distinguish between what is represented on a stage and what occurs in real life. For a particularly helpful examination of this criticism, see Nehamas (1988, 214–234).

7. If, along with Irwin (1995, 212), we take it to be characteristic of the "spirited" part of the soul (*thumoeides*) that it "has evaluative attitudes, resting on some belief about the goodness or badness of its object," grief would appear to belong to the spirited part, since it is constituted in part by a belief that someone or something valuable has been lost. On the other hand, if, following Gould (1990, 33), we focus on passages such as 606a (about the part of the soul that has "hungered to lament and to get enough grieving and to be satiated, it being its nature to yearn for these things" [Gould's translation]), we are reminded that sometimes Plato explicitly locates grief in the appetitive part of the soul (*epithymetikon*). Indeed, Gould seems to have no doubt that the correct way to describe Plato's central concern about the poets is that they "have nothing to say to the rational element in our souls, or to its angry ally, the middle part. They appeal only to the lowest element in our beings"—that is, to our appetites (1990, 31).

8. Socrates appears to contradict himself here: If we can't really know what is good and evil, how can we know that nothing in our mortal life is worthy of concern? Perhaps his point is that to grieve is to assume without question that the loss is not good and that it keeps one from thinking about what would be best to do in light of the loss. (Of course, to exculpate Socrates from self-contradiction is not necessarily to agree with him about the substantive claims.)

9. Martha Nussbaum remarks, on the engagement of Plato with many of the issues central to the tragedies, that "[f]ar from having forgotten about what tragedy describes, he sees the problems of exposure so clearly that only a radical solution seems adequate to their depth" (1986, 18).

10. Sabina Lovibond insists that we can read the *Republic* as Plato's "statement of position on a question with which a good deal of Greek ethical theory is preoccupied: that of true masculinity, or manliness, and how to achieve it" (Lovibond 1994, 95).

11. Concerns about manliness surface in the *Gorgias* as well. For example, at 485c–d Callicles accuses Socrates of being "unmanly" (*anandreia*) and "less than a man" for taking philosophy so seriously into his adult life. The issue arises again at 500c–d.

12. For a helpful discussion of the place of the division of labor in Plato's notion of justice, see Annas (1981, 109–152).

13. For their close readings and very helpful suggestions, many thanks go to Susan Levin, Helen Longino, Diana Tietjens Meyers, Martha Minow, and a wonderfully doubt-filled audience at Miami University.

References

Alexiou, Margaret. 1974. *The Ritual Lament in Greek Tradition.* Cambridge: Cambridge University Press.

Annas, Julia. 1981. *An Introduction to Plato's Republic.* New York: Oxford University Press.

Archer, Leonie J., Susan Fischler, and Maria Wyke. 1994. *Women in Ancient Societies: An Illusion of the Night.* New York: Routledge.

Fantham, Elaine, Helene Peet Foley, Natalie Boymel Kampen, Sarah B. Pomeroy, and H. Alan Shapiro. 1995. *Women in the Classical World.* Oxford: Oxford University Press.

Gould, Thomas. 1990. *The Ancient Quarrel Between Poetry and Philosophy.* Princeton: Princeton University Press.

Humphreys, S. C. 1983. *The Family, Women and Death: Comparative Studies.* London: Routledge & Kegan Paul.

Irwin, T. H. 1995. *Plato's Ethics.* New York: Oxford University Press.

Lovibond, Sabina. 1994. An Ancient Theory of Gender: Plato and the Pythagorean Table. In *Women in Ancient Societies: An Illusion of the Night,* ed. Leonie J. Archer, Susan Fischler, and Maria Wyke. New York: Routledge.

Nehamas, Alexander. 1988. Plato and the Mass Media. *Monist* 71: 214–234.

Nussbaum, Martha C. 1986. *The Fragility of Goodness: Luck and Ethics in Greek Tragedy and Philosophy.* Cambridge: Cambridge University Press.

Plato. 1961. *Gorgias* (Woodhead, W. D., trans.), *Phaedo* (Tredenick, H., trans.), and *Republic* (Shorey, P., trans.). In *The Collected Dialogues,* eds. Edith Hamilton and Huntington Cairns. New York: Bollingen Foundation.

Price, A. W. 1995. *Mental Conflict.* New York: Routledge.

Saxenhouse, Arlene W. 1994. The Philosopher and the Female in the Political Thought of Plato. In *Feminist Interpretations of Plato,* ed. Nancy Tuana. University Park: Pennsylvania State University Press. [Also reprinted from *Political Theory* 4(2) (1976): 195–212.]

Spelman, Elizabeth V. 1994. Hairy Cobblers and Philosopher-Queens. In *Feminist Interpretations of Plato,* ed. Nancy Tuana. [Also reprinted from Elizabeth V. Spelman, *Inessential Woman: Problems of Exclusion in Feminist Thought.* Boston: Beacon Press, 1988.]

Tuana, Nancy, ed. 1994. *Feminist Interpretations of Plato.* University Park: Pennsylvania State University Press.

eight

Sympathy and Solidarity
On a Tightrope with Scheler

SANDRA LEE BARTKY

It is by now widely conceded that feminist theories of the Second Wave (not to mention the First Wave), whatever their other virtues, have been race and class biased, heterosexist and ethnocentric, that they have often construed as the experience of women generally what was merely the experience of those women who, by virtue of relative race or class privilege, were in a position to theorize their experience in the first place. Disadvantaged feminists have charged relatively advantaged feminist theorists with having visited upon many of the world's women what androcentric political theory has visited upon women generally—enforced invisibility or else the distortion and falsification of the substance and texture of their lives.[1]

1

These charges are serious indeed in a movement that seeks to unite women across ethnic, racial, and, whenever possible, class divisions. The feminist community has tended to react to these charges in two different ways. On the one hand, activists have organized workshops where, for example, white women could "work on" their racism: This "work" involves first, an unearthing of internalized racism and, second, the development of greater understanding of and increased sensitivity to the lived experience of women of color. What is aimed at in such political practice is, clearly, a transformation of self—a transformation in the direction of expanded knowledge, wider sympathies, and the acquisition of greater skill in the exposure, and extirpation from one's psyche, of submerged attitudes of superiority or condescension.

On the other hand, feminist political theorists, especially those influenced by post-structuralism, have tended to regard the failure to do justice to the experience of the Other (i.e., to what is commonly called "the problem of difference") as largely a cognitive error. For feminists influenced by Derrida, the "occlusion" of difference is due to logocentrism, the mistaken belief that there is some ultimate word, presence, essence, reality, or truth that can provide a foundation for theory, experience, and expression. Such founding concepts—*logoi*—are supposed to stand outside systems of signification and guarantee truth. But for Derrida and his followers, there are only signifying systems, systems of "difference" in which meaning is not a function of correspondence to something ultimate that stands outside the system but, rather, something that inheres in the differences between and among signs themselves. Further, the founding concepts of metaphysics are implicated in binary oppositions (God/world; mind/matter) in which the superior term depends covertly for its intelligibility on the inferior term, which it typically denies or tries to ignore. The binary oppositions that ground racism, imperialism, and sexism function in just the same way and are typically linked to more familiar philosophical binaries: Masculinity, for example, in a philosophical tradition that values rationality, is associated with a superior ability to reason, femininity with a denigrated intuition or emotion. As I read many postmodern texts, the critique of logocentrism and of hierarchical opposition in general construes them as cognitive: untenable metaphysical assumptions that rest on a flawed theory of meaning.[2]

Other, more empirically oriented theorists have called for more inclusive research programs: In particular, relatively advantaged women need to learn more about the disadvantaged; they need to study the lives of others, to look and see, to ask and be instructed. Thinkers influenced by Habermas have called for the establishment of an "ideal speech situation" that would entail access for everyone to the means of interpretation and communication. Although this state of affairs could come about only after prolonged political struggle, were such a struggle to succeed, moral and political consensus, which is now manipulated by the privileged and powerful, could be built on the force of the better argument alone. Once more, the resolution of the problem of difference is conceived in largely cognitive terms.

Theorists, whatever their orientation, know that self-interest, not failure of understanding alone, often lies at the heart of the misrecognition of the Other: The solution to this disturbing insight, however, is typically posed in terms of more and better cognition. Here and there one encounters the suggestion that cognitive deficits—regardless of whether they're grounded in self-interest—are not the only things locking in the flawed texts of contemporary feminist theory. Our capacity to enter imaginatively into the lives of others—their joys and sorrows, the peculiar texture of their suffering—is also limited. Elizabeth V. Spelman, in her splendid and essential *Inessential Woman*, has this to say about imagination as a corrective to bias:

> I must try to enter imaginatively into the worlds of others. Imagination isn't enough, but it is necessary. Indeed, it is a crucial starting point: because I have not experienced what the other has, so unless I can imagine her having pain or her having pleasure I can't be moved to try to help put an end to her pain or to understand what her pleasures are. Against the odds I must try to think and feel my way into her world. (Spelman 1989, 179)

Having said this, however, Spelman does an immediate about-face, whereby imagination becomes an enticement, a snare. Imagining who the other is, she says, is much easier than "apprenticing" oneself to the other. Apprenticeship is demanding:

> While I am perceiving someone, I must be prepared to receive new information all the time, to adapt my actions accordingly, and to have my feelings develop in response to what the person is doing, whether I like what she is doing or not. When simply imagining her, I can escape from the demands her reality puts on me and instead construct her in my mind in such a way that I can possess her, make her into someone or something who never talks back. (Spelman 1989, 181)

In feminist theory, then, a measure of consensus has developed around the idea that the proper means to overcome bias is cognitive in nature: We must learn to identify false beliefs—for example, the belief that gender oppression can be fully understood in isolation from the oppressions of race and class (Spelman 1989, 176). We are to avoid overgeneralization, develop adequate research programs, and abandon assumptions flawed by ethnocentrism, logocentrism, binary thinking, or plain self-interest.

Now all of this is important indeed, but it cannot be the whole story. When, after the Clarence Thomas hearings, women went around saying to each other, "Men just don't get it," we were demanding more from men than the mere acquisition of knowledge. Similarly, when feminists of color take white feminists to task for racial bias, I understand them to mean more than that white feminists acquire additional information or that they abandon assumptions that once seemed self-evident. What they are demanding from white women and what women, particularly feminists, demand from many men, I venture, is a knowing that transforms the self who knows, a knowing that brings into being new sympathies, new affects as well as new cognitions and new forms of intersubjectivity. The demand, in a word, is for a knowing that has a particular affective taste. But what taste is this?

Few feminist theorists assume that knowledge and feeling are as distinct as my discussion to this point has suggested. Indeed, many philosophers have argued, quite correctly, that knowledge and feeling cannot, in all cases, be construed as conceptually distinct.[3] Certainly, particular feelings-outrage, indignation, sympathy, perhaps "empathy"—fuel the search for a more adequate knowledge of the Other; moreover, they give shape and form to this knowledge. But in my view, few theorists have examined closely enough the emotional dimension that is part of the search for better cognitions or the affective taste of the kinds of intersubjectivity that can build political solidarities.

What does it mean, exactly, to become more "sensitive" to the Other—in addition, that is, to my learning more about her circumstances? Does it require that I feel what she feels? Is this possible? Is it desirable? Does it require that I somehow "share" her emotion without feeling precisely what she feels? What does it mean to share an emotion with someone, anyhow? Does an understanding of someone else's feelings require that I "identify" with her? If yes, what exactly is "identification"? Does a heightened sensitivity require an imaginative entry into the affective life of the Other? Again, what would such an entry be like? Is such an entry really possible? Might it have the dire consequences Spelman predicts? Does greater sensitivity require perhaps a merging of self and Other? But what would merger mean in such a context and again, is such merger possible? If it were possible, would it be desirable?

These questions call other, related questions to mind, questions that for reasons of space I shall mostly merely pose; a few I consider only briefly in the body of this chapter. Is a special affective repertoire necessary for the building of solidarities across lines of race and class that is not necessary when these lines are not crossed? We assume that the advantaged have a special obligation not only to know—in a narrow sense of "know"—but to cultivate in themselves certain affective states vis à vis the disadvantaged. Is it in the interest of the disadvantaged that they do likewise? Or, as some have maintained, do the disadvantaged know already all they need to know about those whose "moral luck" has cast them into more privileged social locations? Do I decide first on some purely theoretical basis who my coalition partners are to be and then somehow generate toward them the appropriate emotions? Or, since the kind of politics I am considering—feminist politics—bears an important relationship to human suffering in some if not all ways, does my emotional response to the suffering of others first select those others with whom I wish to be in solidarity? If I am right about the relationship between politics and suffering, and if, as is likely, everyone suffers, on what basis can I offer myself to some sufferings and deny myself to others? And given the persuasiveness of suffering and the multitude of forms such suffering may take, how can I keep myself from getting so spent emotionally that I burn out and so turn out to be useless as a political agent? In what follows, I shall not dismiss the call, current in much feminist theory, for a better, even a radically other, cognitive stance toward the Other. But instead of pursuing lines of inquiry laid out by theorists, I shall follow the lead of activists whose activism has been directed to the project of self-transformation, hence to the growth and refinement of our affective repertoire.[4]

2

Phenomenologists have made the terms 'Mitwelt' (shared world) and 'Mitsein' (being-with) familiar to students of continental philosophy; less well known is the concept of 'Mitgefühl'—literally, feeling-with. The only canonical figure in European phenomenology to have offered an extended analysis of 'Mitgefühl' is Max Scheler, in *Zur Phänomenologie und Theorie der Sympathiegefühle und vom Liebe und Hass*, translated as *The Nature of Sympathy*. In frustration at what I take to be the excessive intellectualism of much contemporary feminist theory, I have turned back to the grand tradition of European phenomenology. Are there resources for feminist theory in this tradition?

The English term 'sympathy' and the German 'Sympathie' are not synonymous. The former has undergone crass commercialization, as in the saccharine Hallmark "sympathy" card; moreover, there are echoes of condescension in the English term that Scheler hears not so much in 'Sympathie' as in the German 'Mitleid' (pity or compassion), referring as it does to a heightened commiseration bestowed from above and from a standpoint of superior power and dignity (Scheler 1970, 40). Since it is precisely the superior power that the more advantaged feminist wishes to suspend in her intersubjective encounter with the Other, she is well advised to avoid terms like 'pity', 'sympathy', or 'compassion'—though the last seems less objectionable. Scheler is more likely to use the term 'Mitgefühl' than 'Sympathie'; but here again, there is no precise English equivalent. Scheler's translator renders 'Mitgefühl' as 'fellow-feeling'—a good enough term, though slightly ludicrous in a discourse that seeks to interrogate relationships among women. In lieu of anything better, and considering that I was once myself a Bunting Institute "fellow," in what follows I shall use this term, also the very literal 'feeling-with', and sometimes the German 'Sympathie'.

For Scheler, there are four kinds of fellow-feeling: one "true," two relatively base and lacking in moral worth, and one "genuine." Scheler's conditions for "true" fellow-feeling are extremely narrow: "Two parents stand beside the dead body of a beloved child. They feel in common the 'same' sorrow, the same anguish . . . they feel it together, in the sense that they feel and experience in common" (Scheler 1970, 12). A friend who enters the room may commiserate with the parents' grief, but her feeling will not—indeed, cannot—be identical to their feeling because her relationship to the child is not the same. Hence, "true" fellow-feeling is feeling identically and at the same moment what the Other is feeling, this by virtue of the fact that both feelings have the same cause. The eminent Scheler scholar, Manfred Frings, has this to say of "true" fellow-feeling: "This experience is ultimate and immediate in that the other's feeling or sorrow *is* one's own and vice-versa, so that there is no object relation to the other's feeling. Both parents are a unified subject of irreducible, unifying sorrow" (Frings 1965, 60). Scheler is not much interested in the epistemology of the situation, whether, for example, one parent can ever know for certain if the other is feeling precisely what she is feeling; he might, after all, be pretending. Scheler's aim is to describe immediate affective givens in situations of intersubjectivity, not to ponder abstract skeptical doubts that might later arise. For our purposes, there is little to be learned from Scheler's "highest" form of feeling-with. The gulf between the advantaged and the disadvantaged is due in part to the fact that the causes of the misery of the one are often absent from the lives of the other. There are, of course, those who renounce their privilege by trying to produce in their own lives the conditions that cause the suffering of others. Simone Weil, for example, is said to have starved herself to death during World War II in order to share the sufferings of its victims. Weil is for this reason a moral heroine to many, but her self-inflicted sufferings seem to me to have been futile, if not masochistic. To stand in solidarity with others is to work actively to eliminate their misery, not to arrange one's life so as to share it.[5]

A second form of fellow-feeling, one without moral value for Scheler, he calls Gefühlsansteckung ("emotional infection"). This occurs, for example, when I am infected by gaiety (even though I may have been depressed beforehand) upon attending a party at which others are lively and laughing. I can also be infected with the grief of others at the funeral of someone I knew only very slightly. Characteristic of such "infection is the absence either of a conscious directing of one's feeling upon the Other as well as the absence of any effective knowledge of the causes of the Other's feeling" (Scheler 1970, 15). Through a process of reciprocal effect, then, emotional infection may gather momentum "like an avalanche," issuing in mass excitement or even in a mob hysteria that is "so easily carried beyond the intentions of every one of its members and does things for which no one acknowledges either the will or the responsibility" (Scheler 1970, 16). According to Frings (1965, 62), what Scheler has in mind are panics, revolutions, revolts, demonstrations, strikes, and so on. The case against mass emotion rests on an alleged domination of more primitive drives (survival, perhaps of the herd-excitement in animals), a decrease in the level of collective intelligence, readiness for submission to a charismatic leader, and, as mentioned above, an eclipse of personal responsibility. In short, "[m]an becomes more of an animal by associating himself with the crowd and more of a man by cultivating his spiritual independence" (Scheler 1970, 35).

Although this text was written well before the rise of Nazism, we are hard-pressed not to read into it a premonition of the fate that was to befall Scheler's Germany. Nevertheless, this is a deeply conservative position and, finally, an indefensible one. Both the value ascriptions and the ontological assumptions that ground Scheler's critique are questionable. Scheler places the highest value on the uniqueness and irreplaceability of the single individual; hence, the highest forms of intersubjectivity involve the sharing of emotion by two individuals or, as we shall see shortly, the intuitive apprehension of the feeling-state of one such individual by another. In emotional infection, the uniqueness of the Other never comes into play.

Scheler is one of a long line of European philosophers, stretching from Kierkegaard at least to Heidegger, who see in many social forms called for by industrialization and urbanization nothing but a threat to the survival of individuality. A powerful countercase has been made, however, to the effect that certain of these forms—for example, the lesbian and gay communities that first sprang up in large urban centers—both shielded and encouraged the emergence of new forms of individuality. At any rate, one can value the uniqueness and value of individuality without insisting that we must persist in retaining our sense of ourselves as discrete individuals at all times and in all places.[6] This subsumption of ourselves into a collective experience may free us temporarily from the prison-house of personality—from excessive self-absorption or stagnant self-obsession. Moreover, the assimilation of certain forms of collective action—revolts, demonstrations, and strikes—to the worst excesses of mob rule seems entirely unwarranted. Allowing for the fact that we are often unable to foresee the consequences of what we do, and all other things being equal, the moral worth of collective action is a function of its specific ends and of the means employed to realize these ends. So the immersion of the self in collective life, renewed periodically by an emotional "infection" that sustains such immersion, may give us the courage to develop or to express aspects of ourselves that were heretofore submerged; in this way, emotional infection may encourage not the extinction but the development of individuality.

Scheler's charges against emotional infection are misdirected inasmuch as he both overestimates the dangers of mass excitement to individual integrity and seriously misdescribes the problem in question. Consider the political demonstration as a paradigm case of reciprocal action "mass-excitement." We go to demonstrations not only to get a point across to those against whom we demonstrate but precisely to allow ourselves to be "emotionally infected" by one another. What infects us with the joy we feel at a good demonstration is a heightened sense of the sanity and rightness of our cause, this against the seductive "common sense" of those who stayed at home. Common sense, the sense of the "herd" that Scheler so fears, rarely needs to demonstrate. Even if we demonstrators are in the minority nationally, we, who usually feel so powerless, are infected by a sense of power emanating from the human mass we make together; moreover, the physical presence of each pledges silently to the others our continued support—and in this way, we reduce our fear of isolation and defeat. We may infect each other with utopian dreams as well, with dreams of "a new heaven and a new earth." Though the political aims of our demonstration may, in this conservative period, be quite modest, the visionary dimension that is so much a part of the women's movement greatly exceeds such modesty; perhaps the only way a utopian vision can be kept alive and made palpable now is precisely through periodic emotional infection. When we chant or sing together the emotional infection Scheler condemns threatens to turn into the immediate community of feeling—the "true" fellow-feeling—he lauds. Indeed, emotional infection as a builder of solidarity is promiscuous: Its utility rests precisely in its capacity to unite in feeling persons from a very wide spectrum of social locations.

"Emotional identification" is a third form of fellow-feeling. There are two ways in which such identification can come about: I can feel-with the Other to such an extent that my self disappears entirely into her self, or else I can take her ego wholly into my own (Frings 1965, 62–64). Both forms are thus extreme limiting cases of psychic infection or contagion in that individual consciousness remains intact in neither. "Primitive" peoples, says Scheler, are prone to such loss of self when they identify themselves with animals or ancestors. Identification can occur in dreams, in hypnosis, in episodes of schizophrenia, in the bond between a mother and her child, in the process of "playing mother" to a doll when, for all intents and purposes, a child becomes the mother, in states of mystic frenzy, and in unvarnished sexual intercourse. Like emotional infection, emotional identification lacks moral worth, because it works directly against the development and affirmation of "deep" subjectivity—that is, against the unique individuality Scheler so values. Nell Noddings' description of care in *Caring: A Feminine Approach to Ethics and Moral Education* would flunk Scheler's test. As Noddings puts it: "I set aside my temptation to analyze and to plan. I do not project; I receive the other into myself and I see and feel with the other" (1984, 14, 30).

We come at last to the fourth and last category: "genuine" fellow-feeling. The feelings associated with this form of *Sympathie* are intentional; that is, they have objects, indeed, objects of understanding. As is not the case with "community of feeling," the feeling states of others are here given directly and immediately as intentional objects in the outward manifestations of emotion. The otherness of the Other is maintained throughout the act of genuine feeling-with; in this way, the genuine article is distinguished from contagion or identification. "For sympathy [i.e., "genuine" sympathy] presupposes that awareness of distance between selves which is eliminated by identification" (Scheler 1970, 23).[7] Further, fellow-feeling proper "presents itself in the very phenomenon as a *re-action* to the state and value of the other's feelings—as these are 'visualized' in vicarious feeling. . . . [T]he two functions of *vicariously visualized* feeling and participation in feeling are separately given and must be sharply distinguished" (Scheler 1970, 13). I shall return later to the somewhat problematic notion of "vicarious visualization": Suffice it to say that in this passage, Scheler is trying to underscore the distinction in feeling between the one who feels and the one who feels-with.

Scheler takes violent issue with those thinkers who claim that Sympathie is grounded in some kind of comparison of my feelings or feeling-memories with the Other's feelings, which feelings of mine I then project into or onto the Other. On this view, I can understand and participate in your feelings only insofar as they correspond with feelings, bits of feeling, or starts of feeling I have had myself. Here, Scheler takes on Theodor Lipps, whose name for this process of identification, comparison, and projection is 'empathy'.[8] As Scheler reads Lipps, genuine fellow-feeling begins from a question I ask myself: "How would it be if this had happened to *me*?" (1970, 39) Scheler attacks Lipps with great ferocity: He offers a number of arguments in an attempt to rebut the empathy or what he (Scheler) sometimes calls the genetic theory.

First, the genetic theory is said to be ontologically unsound, holding dogmatically to a theory of human nature such that the person is a natural egoist; on such a view, fellow-feeling is indeed and can be nothing but a *"consequence or counterpart of some kind to the self—regarding sentiments and attitudes"* (Scheler 1970, 40). Second, the theory is said to be phenomenologically unsound. We will remember from Scheler's discussion of "emotional infection" that knowledge of the Other's circumstances forms a necessary background for a genuine Mitgefühl. When this condition is satisfied (together with certain other conditions that will be examined below), the Other's feeling is just *given* to me as an intentional object; I do not find in the immediacy of this "givenness" any of the psychic processes (e.g., the sorting through of my experiences, the selection of appropriate emotion-memories, the projection into another of these memories) that are supposed to ground the fellow-feeling that allows me to commiserate with the Other's misery or take joy in her joy:

> In true fellow-feeling there is no reference to the state of one's own feelings. . . . In commiserating with B, the latter's state of mind is given as located entirely in B himself; it does not filter across into A, the commiserator, nor does it produce a corresponding or similar condition in A. It is merely "commiserated with," not undergone by A as a real experience. (Scheler 1970, 41)

The genetic theory, so Scheler claims, is morally unsound as well: "If in commiseration or rejoicing, we could do so only under the momentary impression, or illusion even, of undergoing the process ourselves, our attitudes would indeed appear, phenomenologically speaking, to be directed merely upon our own sorrow or joy and would therefore be an *egoistic* one" (Scheler 1970, 42).

If all I felt in apprehending your suffering was in some important way merely a rehearsal of my own suffering, I would direct my attention away from you entirely and toward the amelioration of my own misery; but this isn't what happens in genuine fellow-feeling, nor is it what should happen. The moral worth of feeling-with, for Scheler, lies in its value for love. Love, in the broadest sense, is one primordial disposition of the person toward experience *per se*—more specifically, toward the appearance of higher values in what is experienced and in the possibility of their realization. Egoistic rediscovery of myself in the Other gives me no appreciation of the Other's uniqueness as a personality, hence, of the Other's value-possibilities—this being, for Scheler, a necessary condition for the emergence of human love. A loving orientation toward the Other is at the basis of my desire to feel-with her; without this orientation, I would apprehend the intentional object that is the Other's emotion in a spirit of detachment or, what is worse, in a spirit of cruelty; in such a spirit, I might even take pleasure in my vicarious visualization of the Other's misery. There is circularity here, but it is not, I think, vicious: The search for value-possibility, the loving orientation, fuels my desire for a beneficent Mitgefühl: Mitgefühl, in turn, can become the occasion for a centered and specific love for just this specific individual.

Finally, Lipps' "genetic" account is flawed in that it is unable to explain how we can grow morally and spiritually in the act of encountering the Other. This theory "does nothing to account for positive unalloyed fellow-feeling which is a genuine *out-reaching* and entry into the other person and his individual situation, a true and authentic *transcendence* of one's self" (Scheler 1970, 46) Empathy theories, for Scheler, turn intersubjectivity into something akin to intrasubjectivity; they "entail that our fellow-feeling must necessarily be confined to processes and incidents in other people's experience such *as we have already met with in ourselves*" (Scheler 1970, 47). We would be incapable of any enlargement of self in its explorations of intersubjectivity if fellow-feeling were a mere epiphenomenon, hovering over the Other but having its actual grounding in us.

Scheler insists that we can have a vivid experience of someone else's joys and sorrows—even when these are merely narrated by a third party—without our having had such experiences ourselves. "*My* commiseration and *his* suffering are phenomenologically *two different facts,* not *one* fact. . . . [A] person who has never felt mortal terror can still understand and envisage it just as he can also share in it" (Scheler 1970, 13, 47). Again, speaking of Jesus' despair in the Garden of Gethsemane, Scheler insists that "for every candid heart which steeps itself in that desolation, it operates not as a reminder or revival of personal sufferings, great or small, but as the revelation of a new and greater suffering hitherto undreamed of" (Scheler 1970, 21).

3

"Genuine" fellow-feeling: How adequate an account has Scheler given us of what we can and cannot achieve in the domain of "genuine" shared emotion? There is much in Scheler's account of Sympathie that will interest feminists struggling with the problem of difference. I find attractive Scheler's idea that what motivates the effort to establish a positive affective bond with the Other is love. 'Love' is not precisely the term we need: Perhaps 'solidarity' or even 'sisterhood' or a strong disposition toward sisterhood or solidarity would serve our purposes better. Feminist theory is mistaken in having elevated cognition over this affective dimension that, whatever it is, is somehow akin to love. Second Wave feminists were wrong or even arrogant in believing that we had already achieved sisterhood, but we were surely wrong, too, in allowing ourselves to be shamed for having committed ourselves to it at all. Finally, then, it is an affect—something akin to love or to the yearning for a more solidary world in which one might love others and be loved by them in return—that sounds consistently, like an organ-point, under the multifarious attempts to reduce the cognitive deficits in our understanding of the Other.

Theories of normative intersubjectivity that rely too heavily on cognition are unbalanced, but theories that give it too little weight are flawed as well. Scheler's emphasis on knowledge of the Other's circumstances as a necessary precondition for genuine fellow-feeling echoes nicely Spelman's idea of an "apprenticeship" of the more advantaged to the less advantaged. It is precisely the lack—or putative lack—of an adequate knowledge of the Other that motivates Scheler's attack both on emotional infection and emotional identification. Valuable too, in Scheler's account, is his emphasis on the ineradicable otherness of the Other, as well as his uncompromising insistence that "genuine" fellow-feeling must provide an occasion for moral and, I would add, political development.

The otherness of the Other: What does this mean? Some feminists might describe as excessively masculinist Scheler's insistence on the maintenance of ego-boundaries in cases of genuine fellow-feeling. Furthermore, as I argued earlier, the loss of a sense of oneself as a distinct self in the experience of merger with a collective subject as happens, for example, in political demonstrations, can be a powerful impetus to the building of solidarities. Now, although such experiences can be a source of political bonding, they are fleeting. When the parade is over, the disadvantaged stands before the one advantaged in her stigmatized and despised social identity; the one advantaged faces the Other secure in, say, her enjoyment of heterosexual privilege or in her "shameful livery of white incomprehension" (Bulhan 1985, 122). To maintain a sense of separateness even within a profound experience of feeling-with can be a powerful deterrent to the dangers inherent in such a situation. The ineradicable distance between persons can act against the temptation on the part of the one disadvantaged—if she finds profound commiseration and understanding in the one advantaged—to try to overleap and deny her oppressed condition in an act of emotional merger. It can discourage the temptation on the part of the advantaged one to believe that her oppressor's guilt can be overcome through heroic acts of ego-identification. The emphasis on the nonidentity of the feeling of the one who feels and on the feeling of the one who feels-with works against the tendency on the part of the advantaged, through *a priori* constructions of all kinds, to rob the disadvantaged of her specificity and uniqueness: In short, the preservation of the otherness of the Other works against her re-colonization.

Finally, Scheler's emphasis on the necessity of some emotional distance in acts of Sympathie may shed light on a problem posed earlier, which I shall call the "wretchedness" problem: Insofar as political activists are fully cognizant of and emotionally attuned to the wretchedness of the wretched of the earth, how can we save ourselves from despair, or from a psychological paralysis that could rob us of political effect? The relatively advantaged in the developed world are for the most part culpably indifferent to the miseries of most of the rest of the world as well as of the less fortunate in their own societies. Many blame victims for their victimization. Most lead excessively privatized lives that lack any effective or persistent sense of political outrage: The retreat into private life is quite consonant with the highly convenient belief that "you can't change the system." But for those sufficiently advantaged to have a choice, it is difficult to steer a course between privatization on the one hand and despair at the vastness of human misery on the other. Perhaps Scheler's distinction between feeling and feeling-with hints at a solution. We do not share the sufferings of those with whom we want to stand in solidarity. Their suffering is the intentional object to which our commiseration, a "vicarious visualization," is directed. Although there are points of similarity between a feeling and that feeling commiserated-with (as my discussion below will indicate), nonetheless, *the two are not identical.* I commiserate with your sufferings and take joy in your joys (how odd that we have no verb for this in English!), but I experience neither your suffering nor your joy; they are *yours.* Perhaps the wretchedness problem arises because we fear that were we to open ourselves fully to the miseries of others, we would be plunged headlong into the very depths of this misery. Scheler's cautionary phenomenology of "genuine" feeling-with assures us that this need not happen.

4

Though I find Scheler's account of authentic Sympathie highly suggestive for the construction of a political phenomenology of solidarity, as I shall argue below, I find it exceedingly impressionistic and, in important ways, incomplete. Sympathie, for Scheler, consists in this: The immediate, intuitive apprehension of the Other's feeling given to me *as* "vicariously visualized" by myself. Now, the first part of this, the idea of "immediate apprehension," seems plausible to me. Understood, of course, is the existence of a complex set of background circumstances that surround this givenness: for example, the linguistic competence sufficient to know what to call what is given, or knowledge of the sorts of circumstances that produce the given as well as its behavioral manifestations in my culture or, as the case may be, in other cultures. "Vicarious visualization" is far more problematic; I shall return to it later.

The idea of "immediate apprehension" is Scheler's way of insisting that I need not experience an emotion first myself in order to recognize what it is. Like the American pragmatist, George Herbert Mead, Scheler maintains that knowledge of self does not precede the knowledge of others: Originally, "[t]he child feels the feelings and thinks the thoughts of those who form his social environment, and there is one broad roaring stream of living in which he is totally immersed. It takes a long time before vortices form within this stream, which draw together what later on will clearly be recognized as 'mine' and 'other'" (Stark 1970, xxxix). There is of course some question whether the emotional capacities of children are still present, at least incipiently, in adults. But to deny that they are is to maintain the depressing view that our emotional repertoire is established in childhood and never again subject to significant expansion. Moreover, the idea that I cannot understand what you are feeling unless I have felt something similar myself recalls the odd notion of *anamnesis*—that is, the idea that I can never learn anything new, only remember what it was I already knew. We would not want to claim that it is *anamnesis* that makes possible our knowledge of physical objects or of mathematical signs; why, then, do we make this claim for our understanding of other people's emotions?

Scheler's phenomenology addresses the following sort of question: How can I understand, on some level at least, the horror of the Holocaust without having been a Holocaust victim myself? As I read Scheler, he maintains that this sense of horror appears, phenomenologically speaking, not to have been put together out of bits and pieces of my own experience but to arise from my capacity to intuit the feeling states and experiences of others. I do not construct the phenomenon out of my own affective materials: I grasp it, not inferentially but intuitively, "immediately." Nor is there anything incorrigible about immediate apprehension: Such apprehension does not guarantee that I always get things right. We must remember that Scheler's primary concern is to offer a descriptive phenomenology of Mitgefühl, not to resolve questions concerning its veracity. At any rate, the skeptical doubts that we might raise about the reliability of my fellow-feelings can be brought against Lipps' genetic theory as well.

The idea of comparison as the primary structure of Mitgefühl is one that Scheler associates with an essentially self-regarding view of the person, just as he associates the idea of intuition with the notion that we have important other-regarding capacities. I do not ascribe to Scheler the denial that we ever infer what others are feeling, only the claim that inference is not the paradigmatic core of Mitgefühl. Nor does the "immediacy" of Sympathie mean that no mediation is required to narrow the distance between myself and the Other: As noted earlier, substantial background information is often needed, as well as linguistic competence, ordinary emotional capacities, and so on. What is "immediate" here, I venture, is the idea that once the proper background conditions are satisfied, I can "leap" out of my own experience into an intuitive understanding of the Other's emotional life. This leap from the 'I' to the 'Thou' is not a merger with the 'Thou', nor is it a comparison between an 'I' and a 'Thou' that would be little more than a reconstructed 'I'. Lipps' genetic theory, then, also does not account for the transformative character of Scheler's Mitgefühl: The barriers that ordinarily separate selves fall and I behold something *new*, something that may well transform my self, even the self whose state I "intuit."

Scheler never sets out clearly what he means by 'vicarious visualization'. 'Vicarious' is defined in my dictionary as "performed or suffered in place of another," as "taking the place of another," or as "felt or enjoyed by imagining oneself to participate in the experience of others" (*Random House Dictionary* 1980, 969). Given Scheler's extended polemic against Lipps, the choice of the term 'vicarious' seems singularly inapt, if not inconsistent. In spite of this, and in the absence of any textual direction from Scheler, I shall now simply stipulate a meaning for the idea of 'vicarious visualization' that will, I hope, flesh out Scheler's rather thin theory of Sympathie while preserving the core of his critique of Lipps.

I suggest that we take 'vicarious visualization' to refer to imagination. No account of Mitgefühl, in my view, can omit imagination as a core factor in its phenomenology; nor does imagination need to be reduced to a function that is fundamentally self-regarding. Imagination must share triple billing with cognition and "love" in any phenomenology of Sympathie.

5

Earlier I cited Spelman, who rejects imagination on behalf of cognitive apprenticeship. But there are in fact two senses of imagination at work in Spelman's text: One kind of imagining is inattentive to the Other, merely constructing her "in my mind in such a way that I can possess her" (1989, 178). Spelman's rejection of imagination of this sort echoes Scheler's claim that both "emotional identification" and empathy theory can find in fellow-feeling merely a form of egoism in disguise. But Spelman notes that there is another way to imagine, one that involves the capacity "to enter imaginatively into the worlds of others," without stretching these others on the Procrustean bed of my own experience.

Consider in this connection the words of the Haggadah, the service for the Jewish Passover. According to this text, it is incumbent upon every Israelite in every generation to imagine if *he* [sic] has actually gone out from Egypt (*Passover Haggadah with Music* n.d., 29). I must imagine that I myself was oppressed with great rigor as a slave in Egypt, that with signs and portents I myself was led out of Egypt by Jehovah with a mighty hand and an outstretched arm, and so on. The question, then, is this: Am I an egoist if I obey the instruction of the Haggadah? If I imagine myself part of that multitude, have I thereby put myself at center stage? Have I usurped a place that belongs to others, or have I achieved, in Scheler's words, a "genuine *out-reaching* and entry into the other person and his individual situation . . . ?" (1970, 22).

I might of course make myself the star of the show, but I need not; I can imagine the scene from Exodus any way I like. Imagination, says Edward Casey (1976), is the least constrained of all our faculties. So I can, if I wish, see myself merely as one of a terrified multitude, with the Pharaoh's army at our backs and the still unparted sea before us. Or I can imagine what it would be like to be someone, indeed anyone, on that distant shore: That someone need not be myself. Such imagining, if sufficiently vivid, is surely in harmony with the spirit of the Haggadah, if not with its letter. Now, there is a trivial sense in which *my* imagining as *mine* always bears some reference to myself, but it does not follow from this either that my imagining of another's feeling is invariably a sign of egoism or that in such imagining I must always put myself in the picture.

Indeed, there are situations in which I can imagine the suffering of others without putting myself in the picture at all. Nawal El Saadawi (1980), the noted Egyptian feminist, describes in *The Hidden Face of Eve* how, as a small child, she was awakened in the middle of the night by her mother and some other of her female relatives, dragged from her bed, and then, without anesthesia, forced to undergo a clitoridectomy. She had not been told about the practice of clitoridectomy and was utterly unprepared for what was done to her. I can imagine this scene without in any way substituting myself, who never endured such treatment, for the small child who did.

What, one might ask, is the difference between just knowing the facts of this case—a knowledge virtually certain, at least among Western knowers, to produce a powerful emotional response—and an imaginative projection into it? Although I will not try to define 'imagination' *tout court*, inasmuch as the term names a wide variety of mental acts, the kind of imagining to which I refer would involve specific forms of ideation, including "visualization." In this case, it seems plausible to claim that the better I can visualize the sets of circumstances that give rise to the Other's emotion, as well as the behavioral aspects of the emotion ("She screamed in terror," "She begged for mercy"), the better I can feel-with the victim. Clearly, there is a difference between a mere knowing-that (even a knowing that can list concretely and in detail the circumstances of the case) and a "vicarious visualization" that causes these circumstances to come alive in the theater of my mind.

This discussion is plagued by the overreliance in Western philosophy on metaphors of seeing: visualization, 'intuition' (from the Latin 'to look upon'), my own earlier 'beholding', now 'theater of the mind', an image that reinforces the idea of spectatorship. Although the idea of an internal seeing has an important role in the conception of imagination and is certainly appropriate in the case we are considering, we ought not forget its limitations. Thus, in reading El Saadawi's text, I must, to be sure, produce an active and vivid picturing to myself of the details of the scene, a more active and vivid picturing than is necessary to grasp the bare facts of the case. I must conjure up in my "mind's eye" the dark bedroom, the shadowy figures of the adults. But here the idea of seeing must give way to something else: I may "see" the utter terror of the child, her bewilderment and sense of betrayal, but I must imagine as well what it was for her to have *felt* this terror, this absolute incomprehension in the face of the cruelty of those she trusted. I must imagine not only the sight of the knife but what she *feels* as it cuts her flesh. (How unfortunate that even our term 'imagination' contains within it the idea of an 'image'—of something seen—when much of what we must learn to imagine is not something seen at all.)

With Scheler and against Lipps, I can do this—can I not?—without putting myself in place of the child; I do not think of myself at all. Nor is my imagining really mine in any but the most trivial sense: El Saadawi's description of the scene is so vivid that to read it is to be haunted by it for perhaps the rest of one's life. She, as author of her text and authority on her memories, is stage manager and director; I am not. Nor, when I imagine myself in the Exodus, do I direct that scene. It seems to me that I am seeing either the strange medieval woodcuts in my parents' ancient Haggadah or else some film.[9]

Furthermore, far from putting myself in El Saadawi's picture, I can imagine a sadly indefinite number of small girls, past, present, and future, subjected to similar ordeals. Thus my intentional objects have proliferated; differently put, a collective intentional object has emerged for which I have Mitgefühl. This observation points up another feature of Scheler's phenomenology that stands in need of elaboration. His model of fellow-feeling takes as paradigmatic a one-on-one relationship between, say, the one who is assaulted and the one who commiserates with the one assaulted. He has nothing to say about the experience of fellow-feeling for an entire class of persons rather than for a single individual, or about that of one human collective for another.

Scheler's phenomenology of Mitgefühl raises a host of questions it cannot answer. How can one learn to feel-with the many, not just the one? Whence comes that "love"—that deep need for solidarity—that makes us want to know the Other in all her complexity? Indeed, why are most peoples' sympathies so narrow? Why can they feel-with, at most, an individual stranger, a friend or two, family members, or the occasional beached whale? Why are so many of us unable to feel-with—"the wretched of the earth"? Do contemporary modes of the transmission of information deprive us systematically of the kind of context that is integral to feeling-with? Or does the fault lie perhaps within ourselves, in an underdeveloped imagination, in a willed withholding of feeling for the unfortunate, in culpable ignorance of the state and condition of millions of our fellow creatures? Is it the case, as Diana Tietjens Meyers (1994) has argued, that culturally entrenched figurations of despised, different others block feeling-with? Or are we afraid that such widespread suffering demands sacrifices of us that we are unwilling to make? Does the refusal or inability to feel-with lie perhaps in the very vastness of human suffering, in the frustration we encounter in trying to represent to ourselves what is unrepresentable? Does it lie perhaps in the anxious fear that we ourselves may fall into the abyss that has claimed so many others? How can the rush of normally temporary compassion brought on by reports of some current injustice be mined for progressive political ends? One thing is clear: The effort to construct a phenomenology of feeling-with cannot go forward without the parallel construction of its opposites: feeling too little for others or feeling nothing at all. And so we walk a tightrope with Scheler: To fall to one side is to land in a state of despondency, excessive privatization, or indifference; to fall the other way is to plunge into the manifold deformations of fellow-feeling, into constructions of the other that are self-serving, phantasmatic, or condescending.

6

Having framed this chapter in terms of feminist theory, I shall conclude it with a few remarks that bear on the relationship of the foregoing discussion to political feminism. Few of the mass-based movements that took shape in the 1960s and 1970s have survived the long shift to the right that followed; of these movements, the contemporary women's movement, it seems to me, has demonstrated the most consistent commitment to the building of solidarities across lines of class, race, ethnicity, and sexual orientation. The results of this commitment have been, not surprisingly, mixed.

Postmodern feminism seems today to enjoy hegemony, at least among academic feminists. Its defenders claim that postmodernism is superior to other feminisms: first, because it alone properly valorizes "difference," so often submerged and denigrated within the conventional conceptual hierarchies of totalizing Western theory, and, second, because it calls in radical fashion for the "deconstruction" not only of gender—the cultural meanings inscribed in biological sex—but of "sex" itself. Our ideas of "the biological" with its division into "natural kinds" is said to be no less socially constructed than other, more obvious markers of sexual difference (Butler 1990, 1993).

Postmodern feminism is, in some respects, a theoretical advance over some of the feminisms that preceded it. But, to paraphrase Marx on Hegel, it is not enough to valorize difference in thought when our movement has yet to develop a practice adequate to the real diversity among women, nor is it sufficient to "deconstruct" gender in thought when it continues to inhabit our consciousness and to structure much of our everyday life. Questions of practice—indeed, *theoretical* questions about appropriate practice—have latterly been neglected in favor of "pure" theory. But between the purest of theory and the most concrete practice there lies an intermediate sphere, a sphere concerned chiefly with problems of movement building. This sphere is quite vast; in writing this chapter I took up residence in one corner of it, asking more questions than I answer. More attention should be paid to the theorizing of a more fruitful practice; otherwise, feminist theory may well become a theory without a practice. If feminism is primarily addressed to the suffering of women, what could be more urgent?[10]

Notes

1. See, for example, hooks (1981, 1984), Spelman (1989), and Lugones and Spelman (1993).

2. For an excellent sample of Derridean and other post-structuralist approaches to feminist theory, see Butler and Scott (1992).

3. See, for example, Kenny (1963), Wilson (1972), Gordon (1974), Solomon (1976, 1977), Thalberg (1964), Davidson (1976), and Taylor (1985).

4. Since I write from the perspective of a relatively advantaged woman, the "Other" in this chapter is relatively disadvantaged. But questions about the affects and intersubjective postures that are appropriate to the building of cross-class and cross-racial solidarities are important for the disadvantaged as well. In certain respects, then, the roles of self and Other here can be reversed.

5. Sometimes, of course, the nature of one's political work requires the sharing of hardships of the poor, the oppressed, and so on; but sometimes it does not.

6. Scheler assumes here and in other writings a stable, core self, an assumption that has come under attack from postmodernists and others (i.e., some psychoanalytic theorists). An in-depth examination of this issue would take me far afield. But for the

purposes of this chapter I shall assume, with Scheler, a self sufficiently stable to participate in the forms of intersubjectivity he describes.

7. I have added the material in brackets.

8. The modern use of the term 'empathy' dates from 1897, when Lipps introduced the term 'Einfühlung' in a treatise on aesthetics. There the latter term refers to the tendency of the viewer to lose self-awareness and fuse with the object of aesthetic consciousness. It was Edward B. Titchener of Cornell who first introduced the term 'empathy' as an equivalent for Lipps' 'Einfühlung'. We now use 'empathy' very broadly to characterize even the kinds of Sympathie that inhabit Scheler's phenomenology. What is important to remember is that Scheler is offering a specific critique of Lipps' account of the origin and nature of Mitgefühl, sympathy, fellow-feeling, or—if we slip into current linguistic practice—'empathy'. The issue has to do with the nature of the phenomenon, not its name. (See Lipps, 1903–1906.)

9. As the example of *The Hidden Face of Eve* illustrates, Mitgefühl can come about in the absence of personal connection—in this case, through literature. Enlightened education, especially an aesthetic education that offered training in mimesis and sense-memory, could markedly increase our capacities for fellow-feeling. Current battles for control of U.S. education, with an organized right wing pitted against those who favor a more multicultural curriculum, should be evaluated in this context. What is at stake in this battle is control not only of the transmission of ideas but of training in the capacity for wider sympathies.

10. I wish to thank Isaac Balbus, in particular, for his detailed critical engagement with this chapter. The following persons offered extremely helpful critical comments on earlier versions: Lorraine Code, Charles Mills, David Schweikart, Paul Gomberg, Femi Taiwo, Hollace Graff, Diana Tietjens Meyers, and Nancy Frankenberry.

References

Bulhan, Husseen Abdilahi. 1985. *Frantz Fanon and the Psychology of Oppression.* New York: Plenum Press.

Butler, Judith. 1990. *Gender Trouble: Feminism and the Subversion of Identity.* New York: Routledge.

_____. 1993. *Bodies That Matter: On the Discursive Limits of "Sex."* New York: Routledge.

Butler, Judith, and Scott, Joan W., eds. 1992. *Feminists Theorize the Political.* New York: Routledge.

Casey, Edward. 1976. *Imagining: A Phenomenological Study.* Bloomington: Indiana University Press.

Code, Lorraine. 1991. *What Can She Know? Feminist Theory and the Construction of Knowledge.* Ithaca: Cornell University Press.

Davidson, Donald. 1976. "Hume's Cognitive Theory of Pride," *Journal of Philosophy*, Vol. 70, No. 19.

El Saadawi, Nawal. 1980. *The Hidden Face of Eve.* London: Zed Books.

Frings, Manfred. 1965. *Max Scheler.* Pittsburgh: Duquesne University Press.

Gordon, R. M. 1974. "Aboutness of Emotion." *American Philosophical Quarterly*, Vol. 10, No. 1.

hooks, bell. 1981. *Ain't I a Woman: Black Women and Feminism*. Boston: South End Press.

———. 1984. *Feminist Theory: From Margin to Center*. Boston: South End Press.

Kenny, Anthony. 1963. *Action, Emotion and the Will*. London: Routledge and Kegan Paul.

Lipps, Theodor. 1885. *Psychologische Studien*. F. Vieweg u. Sohn.

———. 1903–1906. *Aesthetik*, 2 vols. B. G. Teubner Verlag.

———. 1907–1912. *Psychologische Untersuchungen*, 2 vols. B. G. Teubne Verlag.

Lugones, María, and Spelman, Elizabeth V. 1993. "Have We Got a Theory for You! Feminist Theory, Cultural Imperialism and the Demand for the 'Woman's Voice.'" In *Women and Values: Readings in Recent Feminist Philosophy*, 2nd. ed. Belmont, Calif.: Wadsworth.

Meyers, Diana Tietjens. 1994. *Subjection and Subjectivity: Psychoanalytic Feminism and Moral Philosophy*. New York: Routledge.

Noddings, Nel. 1984. *Caring: A Feminine Approach to Ethics and Moral Education*. Berkeley: University of California Press.

Passover Haggadah with Music. n.d. New York: Hebrew Publishing Co.

Random House Dictionary. 1980. New York: Ballantine Books.

Scheler, Max. 1970. *The Nature of Sympathy*, trans. Peter Heath, and with a general introduction to Scheler's work by W. Stark. Hamden, Conn.: Archon Books. [This work was first published in Germany in 1913.]

Solomon, Robert. 1976. *The Passions*. New York: Doubleday.

———. 1977. "The Logic of Emotion." *Nous*, Vol. 11, No. 1.

Spelman, Elizabeth. 1989. *Inessential Woman: Problems of Exclusion in Feminist Theory*. Boston: Beacon Press.

Taylor, Gabriele 1985. *Pride, Shame and Guilt: Emotions of Self-Assessment*. Oxford: Oxford University Press.

Thalberg, Irving. 1964. "Emotion and Thought." *American Philosophical Quarterly*, Vol. 1.

Wilson, J.R.S. 1972. *Emotion and Object*. Cambridge: Cambridge University Press.

nine

я⁄

Emotion and Heterodox
Moral Perception
An Essay in Moral Social Psychology

DIANA TIETJENS MEYERS

A number of moral philosophers not only distinguish moral perception from moral judgment and critical moral reflection but also valorize moral perception (e.g., see Sherman 1989, Nussbaum 1990, Blum 1991, and McFall 1991).[1] The importance of moral perception seems indisputable, for how one sees other people, their relations, and one's relations to them has a profound impact on choice and action. Defective moral perception throws moral deliberation and thus moral judgment off course. Moreover, it camouflages social ills and thwarts critical moral reflection.

Yet, insightful moral perception is no mean task. One sees others from one's somewhat idiosyncratic point of view, using the concepts at one's disposal, giving priority to the values one prizes, and averting one's gaze from (or possibly magnifying) the disvalues one abhors (for related discussion, see Walker 1987, 181; Kekes 1989, 143–144). One is never fully conscious of all the forces influencing one's perception. Nor are other people transparent—they reveal some of their thoughts and feelings; they keep others to themselves; they are themselves unaware of still others. A dense and complex phenomenon, moral perception depends on a vast array of dispositions, capacities, and skills. Thus, there are countless sources of distortion in moral perception, and it is very difficult to pinpoint what contributes to insightful moral perception in a wide range of situations.

Now, it seems natural to think of sensitivity as safeguarding moral perception. According to Joel Kupperman, sensitivity entails "feeling the weight of various factors (including fine gradations) as well as being perceptive enough to note their presence" (1991, 147). Sensitive people are attuned to their surroundings, and their interpretations of their experience are canny, judicious, subtle, and to the point. But the asset of sensitivity is as mysterious as the result of insightful moral perception.

To focus my inquiry, I have chosen to examine the problem of heterodox moral perception. Through heterodox moral perception, one sees social life in ways that challenge established cultural values and norms; one sees suffering or harm that others do not notice, beauty or wisdom that others regard as ugliness or folly, live options where others feel constraint, and so forth. Obviously, much heterodox moral perception is misguided. Some is delusional. Yet, heterodox moral perception is indispensable to social and political reform. Unless some people discern injustice and oppression that others deny, there will be no impetus for change.

Orthodox moral perception is not always structured in politically significant ways. But it often is, and this is so in an important class of cases. The cases I have in mind are those in which the perceived individual's group membership is salient to the perceiver and in which membership in that group has historically been viewed as undesirable and as a reason for the lower social status of members of the group. In these cases, the prejudicial structure of moral perception militates in favor of moral judgments and actions that are unfair to those individuals and that are inimical to social justice. My question is how moral perception can be configured to expose these wrongs.

I assume that every person has a moral outlook that frames that individual's moral perception, and I consider two dimensions of moral outlook. On the one hand, a moral subject commands a repertory of moral concepts— that is, a set of concepts that enables one to generate interpretations of the moral significance of situations.[2] On the other hand, perceptual receptivity is conditioned by the moral subject's emotional attitude—that is, by the affective stance (or stances) through which one meets the world and that shapes one's interpersonal encounters. It may seem artificial to separate the cognitive dimension from the emotional dimension of a moral outlook. Since repertories of moral concepts are imbued with emotion, and since emotions are inextricable from beliefs, it is clear that these two dimensions are intertwined. Nevertheless, since people's emotional attitudes and emotional responses can outstrip their cognitive capacities and thus their ability to interpret their experience, and since this possibility is crucial to understanding insightful heterodox moral perception, it would be a mistake to collapse emotional attitudes into repertories of moral concepts.

In this chapter, I argue that several emotional attitudes ordinarily considered to be epistemic vices can be feminist epistemic virtues, but that recognizing these virtues entails giving up a purely individualistic view of moral perception and moral identity. Culturally entrenched gender prejudice is encoded in unconscious schemas that shape moral perception. Counteracting these perceptual distortions requires strong medicine. I am sure that no single emotional formula or discursive protocol can account for all cases of insightful heterodox moral perception. But, in my view, philosophers tend to overestimate the efficacy of an outgoing, receptive emotional attitude and dispassionate critical reason as antidotes to these distortions. My suggestion is that a selection of generally disparaged emotional attitudes—namely, hypersensitivity, paranoia, anger, and bitterness—can be seen to facilitate moral insight into culturally and institutionally entrenched practices of domination and subordination. However, to understand cases in which hypersensitivity, paranoia, anger, and bitterness contribute to insightful heterodox moral perception, we must inquire into the moral economies of dissident political communities. In short, a tenable feminist account of the subject of moral perception must construe the individual as emotionally engaged and politically situated.

1. Prejudicial Cognitive Schemas and Moral Perception

"'Seeing as,'" observes Nancy Sherman, "is a necessary prerequisite for action" (1989, 40). A prerequisite, I would add, that presupposes mastery of a repertory of moral concepts. Barbara Herman dubs these concepts "rules of moral salience," and she contends that these rules "make up the substantive core of the agent's conception of himself as a moral agent" (1985, 428–429; also see Herman 1990, 318–319). John Kekes terms these concepts "moral idioms," and he claims that our moral idioms furnish "approving and disapproving descriptions" of people's character (1989, 135, 136, 137). Despite their differences, Herman and Kekes agree that one's repertory of moral concepts is part of one's cultural heritage and that cultures and the moral endowments they confer are not an unalloyed blessing (Herman 1985, 425; Kekes 1989, 136). On the one hand, moral traditions are salutary—they restrain many malign impulses, they elicit many kinds of decent and generous conduct, and they furnish interpretations of the meaning of human life. Yet, on the other hand, the repertory of moral concepts one's culture supplies is likely to be pernicious as well, for cultures are riddled with xenophobic and misogynist prejudice.

Even when cultures explicitly embrace the doctrines of universal personhood and equal rights, they frequently continue to purvey stories and images that implicitly perpetuate residual doctrines of group inferiority and social exclusion. The legends of heroic and noble deeds and the cautionary tales about vices through which cultures convey moral concepts often cast the society's dominant men in the admirable roles while casting the "outsiders" and women in the contemptible roles. Indeed, women and members of minority social groups are often conceptualized in ways that enforce their "difference" and that confine them to lives of moral deficiency, as judged by the standards of the dominant group. For those steeped in this lore, this moral stratification serves to naturalize and to rationalize systematic relations of domination and subordination in the family, in the economy, and in political institutions.[3]

This information coalesces in cognitive schemas that function in moral perception as mini-theories about "different" social groups (Valian n.d.). Although the subliminal cultural message and the cognitive schemas that encode it compete with the culture's declared commitment to equal justice for all, these subconscious, prejudicial mini-theories about social groups organize perception of individuals who belong to these groups. Whereas the culture's official moral beliefs stand at a remove from moral perception, for they are expressed in abstract principles or values awaiting interpretation and implementation, the cognitive schemas in which the subliminal cultural messages are encoded bear immediately on moral perception, for they specify the moral meanings attaching to membership in this or that social group. Thus, the subliminal message gains the upper hand in moral perception.

Repertories of moral concepts that are provided by traditional cultures typically pack a potent political punch. The paradigm of a moral agent that is articulated in a culture's rules of moral salience may in fact reproduce a dominant group's mode of moral agency. As Eva Kittay argues, the prevailing conception of moral personhood in contemporary social contract theory assumes that individuals are neither dependent on others for care nor encumbered by responsibilities to care for dependents (see Kittay in this volume; also see Held 1987, 116, and Baier 1987, 52–53). Yet, viewing such independence as a universal norm becomes suspect once one takes women into account, for women have traditionally borne responsibility for the care of the young, the sick, and the frail elderly. Women's traditional role reminds us not only that many adults do not fit the regnant model of personhood but also that all of us spend a lengthy childhood dependent on others and that many of us will return to a condition of dependency in old age. Insofar as a culture's rules of moral salience occlude dependency, many women's moral concerns will be denigrated, and the needs of dependents will be marginalized. Similarly, the conventions of usage for moral idioms may in fact differentiate among and disadvantage some social groups. As Ronald de Sousa observes, "An angry man is a 'manly man,' but an angry woman is a 'fury' or a 'bitch'. Or worse, she is called 'hysterical,' which denies her 'real' anger altogether" (1987, 259). To the extent, then, that a traditional repertory of moral concepts structures one's moral outlook, and to the extent that one's moral outlook structures one's moral perception, one will see people from different social groups differently. In Adrian Piper's terms, one will see the members of certain social groups through honorific stereotypes and the members of other social groups through derogatory stereotypes (1992–1993, 217–218). In either case, one's moral perception of these individuals will frequently be grievously distorted.

When a xenophobic or misogynist schema is structuring perception but is not consciously avowed (or is consciously repudiated), it subverts moral judgment. If one does not really see women as full-fledged persons, or if one cannot see a woman's anger as warranted, one is not likely to enact one's commitment to gender equality. Since relevantly different cases should be treated differently, and since one perceives gender difference as pervasively relevant, one's responses to women (and to oneself, if one is a woman) will violate one's egalitarian convictions. The "innocence" of such moral perception is particularly insidious, for the individual is not motivated to take corrective measures. Is there any way to circumnavigate a defective cultural repertory of moral concepts?

2. Emotional Attitudes and Moral Perception

According to Martha Nussbaum, "perception is not merely aided by emotion but it is also in part constituted by the appropriate [emotional] response" (1990, 79). Thus, if one is to perceive well, one's emotions must be congruent with the state of affairs one is confronting. Presumably, this does not mean that the perceiver must share the other's feelings, although sharing the other's feelings is sometimes called for (the distinction between imagining another's state of mind and sharing the other's subjective viewpoint is discussed in Piper 1991, 737, and Meyers 1994, 32–33). Rather, one must emotionally register the other's subjectivity and circumstances in a manner befitting that subjectivity and those circumstances. For example, compassion is a suitable response to another's dejection and neediness. Since the emotional component of one's moral outlook can facilitate or hinder this kind of situation-specific emotional engagement, maintaining an appropriate emotional attitude might enhance sensitivity, mitigate the effects of prejudice-infected moral concepts, and reduce distortion in moral perception.

Emotions, says Nussbaum, "can lead or guide the perceiving agent" (1990, 78; also see Sherman 1989, 45). Thus, for example, feelings of friendship may alert a person to a friend's need for help before the intellect grasps this need (Nussbaum 1990, 79). Although this observation seems correct, Nussbaum appears to be making her point by adverting to the easiest sort of case. It is obvious to most people what emotional attitude is appropriate in various kinds of intimate relationships. But what about relationships with strangers or acquaintances to whom one is not close? Nussbaum advises cultivating "emotional openness and responsiveness in approaching a new situation"— that is, readiness to experience a wide range of emotions (1990, 79). It is not obvious, however, what emotional attitude secures emotional openness and responsiveness.

Nussbaum seems to be advocating the emotional equivalent of what a consultant at the WordPerfect hotline dubbed a "vanilla boot"—a computer set up to run as few disk operating programs as possible in order to minimize interference between these programs and the word processor. A vanilla boot, though not empty, has no more content than is necessary to run your application program. Likewise, an emotional attitude, as opposed to emotional vacancy, is necessary to prime moral perception, but this emotional attitude must not be so strongly directive that it overwhelms moral perception. To clarify Nussbaum's views about which emotional attitude heightens sensitivity and reliably guides moral perception with respect to people whom one does not know or does not know well, I propose that we consider what would constitute "emotional vanilla."

Just as vanilla ice cream has flavor, so emotional vanilla must have feeling. But just as vanilla ice cream goes well with lots of other flavors, so too emotional vanilla must be plain enough to be compatible with a wide variety of superadded emotions. Presumably, the subjective states that make up emotional vanilla are not ones that are experienced as disagreeable or upsetting, for unpleasant subjective states would distract the individual from other people and interfere with moral perception. Rather, emotional vanilla is unobtrusive and agreeable. Neither agitation nor callousness promotes openness and responsiveness to others. Serenity seems better adapted to this purpose. Neither defensiveness nor defenselessness secures openness and responsiveness to others. Trust seems more appropriate. Love is too much to expect from strangers; hate is unwarranted and disruptive. Geniality seems more fitting. A temperament that is serene, trusting, and genial—a nice temperament—seems to embody a generosity of spirit and a sense of personal security that are conducive to insightful moral perception.

Before continuing, I must digress briefly to comment on a terminological question raised by the preceding remarks. Two expressions I have used—"emotional vanilla" and "emotional attitude"—may appear paradoxical. Insofar as we link emotions to passions, emotions betoken states of subjective arousal that are often associated with intense feelings. Emotions take center stage and command one's attention. They are not recessive vanilla. Emotions come and go. They are not abiding attitudes. Still, there is another familiar model of emotion. Although the ongoing love we feel for our friends, family members, and lovers may have its fervent, even tumultuous moments, such love does not throw one into a state of incessant emotional commotion. Some emotions are standing emotions, and it does not seem altogether wrong to think of them as emotional attitudes. Yet, unlike the emotional attitude I have sketched, our standing emotions are personalized. They are directed at particular individuals; they are not orientations to people in general. Nevertheless, emotional attitudes are not mere moods, for emotional attitudes are more lasting and stable.

This gap between emotional vanilla and our core conceptions of emotion may well explain why Nussbaum and others who hold that emotion guides moral perception illustrate their point with examples of moral perception in close interpersonal relationships. The attitudes that seem appropriate when approaching strangers or acquaintances who are not intimates do not seem to fit comfortably in the category of emotion. They are generalized, and they lack intense occurrent forms. No one is ever flooded with serenity, trust, or geniality. Thus, these attitudes may seem more like traits of character or personality traits. Still, they resemble emotions since they are associated with feelings. In the hope of capturing the wisdom of Nussbaum's view, I have taken the liberty of stretching our concept of emotion a bit by coining the trope of emotional vanilla and counting emotional vanilla as an emotional attitude.

There may be other recipes for emotional vanilla, but the one I have outlined seems tenable as an emotional background for moral perception of nonintimate acquaintances and strangers. Moreover, I think it is undeniable that serenity, trust, and geniality often work well together to promote emotional receptivity and thus to secure insightful moral perception. Nevertheless, I doubt that emotional vanilla always ensures insightful moral perception. In fact, I shall urge that, when coupled with a prejudicial repertory of moral concepts, this emotional attitude establishes a moral outlook that renders moral perception virtually impervious to culturally unacknowledged, yet pervasive forms of injustice and oppression. Heterodox, yet insightful moral perception is obstructed.

That this is so is most evident in the case of moral perception of injustice to oneself. People who are serene, trusting, and genial in their relations to nonintimate associates are hardly predisposed to notice that they are being exploited, discriminated against, or otherwise mistreated. For that matter, people in general are reluctant to accept that they are not in control of their lives (Taylor and Brown 1988, 196). Despite the widespread belief that the members of some social groups positively enjoy wallowing in their own oppression, most people in fact resist acknowledging that they are victims and that they are in no way responsible for their victimization (Brison n.d.). If this is so, and if emotional vanilla compounds these tendencies by making individuals kindly disposed to others, many people will find it nearly impossible to see that employers, teachers, or peers at work or at school are oppressing them.[4] It is sometimes necessary, in María Lugones's words, "to fight our own niceness because it clouds our minds and hearts" (Lugones and Spelman 1993, 21). When people are immersed in oppressive conditions, emotional vanilla renders this oppression invisible. This blindspot will be all the more difficult to dispel if their political culture and, hence, their repertory of moral concepts denies the existence of the kind (or kinds) of oppression they are suffering. A parallel argument could be developed regarding one's perception of wrongs that others are suffering, especially wrongs for which one is to some degree responsible; however, I shall not pause to pursue this point here.

Although an unsuitable moral outlook severely compromises sensitivity and can lead one to grossly misread a situation, it is sometimes difficult to gauge which moral outlook is suitable. What seems a generally serviceable emotional attitude toward nonintimate acquaintances and strangers is unlikely to overcome the strictures of a retrograde repertory of moral concepts. Emotional vanilla can secure complacency about conventional moral beliefs and unwitting complicity in maintaining a morally objectionable status quo. Unconscious prejudice may then persist with impunity, and deplorable practices may go unchallenged. Plainly, adopting the wrong moral outlook imperils moral perception.

Of course, philosophers are mindful that traditional moralities need to be critically scrutinized and occasionally modified. Kekes, for instance, notes that it may be necessary to subtract from or to augment a culture's inventory of moral idioms, and he urges that decisions about whether to alter these inventories should rest on "intelligent and sensitive discussion of contested cases" (1989, 136). Likewise, Herman holds that a culture's rules of moral salience are susceptible to criticism on the grounds that they are inconsistent or that they presuppose errors of fact (1985, 429–430). And Nussbaum stresses the role of love, including civic love and compassion, in catalyzing innovative moral reflection (1990, 83, 157, 160, 193, 210).

Although these recommendations for reshaping our moral outlook are certainly not without merit, they nonetheless strike me as somewhat naive. Kekes and Herman embrace a moral rationalism that fails to take into account just how deeply entrenched our repertories of moral concepts are and thus how immune our moral outlooks are to rational criticism and willed change.[5] In appealing to the creative and healing power of love, Nussbaum prescribes an emotional attitude that one cannot realistically expect people to adopt in a world of competing interests and historical animosities between social groups. Finally, since members of subordinated social groups often suffer from alienation from self and from self-hatred, extolling self-love seems somewhat quixotic, too. In what follows, I shall propose a politicized account of the pivotal role of emotional attitudes in shaping moral perception.

3. Rancorous Emotional Attitudes and Outlaw Emotions

A number of feminist thinkers argue that, under some circumstances, emotions generally regarded as detrimental can be moral and political achievements. Audre Lorde affirms that "anger between peers births change"; Marilyn Frye and Elizabeth Spelman show that getting angry constitutes a claim of equality and can be an act of insubordination; Naomi Scheman explicates the role of consciousness-raising in recognizing women's anger; Lynne Mc-Fall maintains that the bitterness of people who are homeless, poor, or assigned to despised social groups is justifiable (Lorde 1984, 131; Frye 1983, 90; Spelman 1989, 266–267; Scheman 1993, 24–25; McFall 1991, 153). Although superficially these authors are all pursuing the same project of reclaiming women's emotional lives, a careful examination of this literature reveals that these authors are making a number of distinct claims about the relation between emotion and moral perception.

In their discussions of women's anger, Frye and Spelman are concerned with occurrent emotional responses to particular incidents or particular states of affairs. They are concerned with what Alison Jaggar terms "outlaw emotions" (1989, 144; for related discussion, see Narayan 1988). Outlaw emotions are "inappropriate" emotions—that is, emotions that are considered disproportionate to the circumstances or that are occasioned by stimuli that do not normally elicit those responses. A woman might be humiliated, saddened, or infuriated, not flattered, by leers and whistles on the street. Her boss's or clients' bawdy jokes might prompt her to retreat into her shell or arouse indignation instead of the laughter and camaraderie that these humorists expect. The prevailing norms and values that govern interpretations of subjective experience classify these ostensibly misdirected or overblown emotions as aberrations and make it impossible for people to see them for what they are.[6]

Interpretive conventions furnish three mutually reinforcing strategies for coping with such anomalies. One strategy simply ascribes a different emotion to the woman. Anger is labeled hysterical rage; humiliation is labeled deference to male prerogatives; indignation is labeled snootiness. The second strategy explains away the emotion by ascribing a defective personality to the individual. Such a woman is insecure, nasty, charmless, humorless, and/or prudish. If all else fails, ascriptions of pathology—"She's crazy"—are sure to close the discussion.

Needless to say, some of women's anomalous emotions (like men's) are disproportionate or misdirected. Still, Frye, Spelman, and Jaggar maintain that some are in fact reasonable responses that others refuse to credit and instead mislabel or misexplain. Such failures of comprehension are not due exclusively to the perceiver's lack of empathy with the particular woman, though that may be part of the problem. Rather, such failures are dictated by, and empathy is blocked by, conventions of interpretation. According to these conventions, women's anger or other emotions are unwarranted in certain situations. So, if the women appear to be experiencing anger or some other unwarranted emotion, either they are really experiencing something else or their flawed personalities or psychological disorders are causing them to experience unwarranted emotions. In the face of such conventions, then, respecting women's emotional lives requires adopting feminist conventions of interpretation—oppositional norms and values that authorize women and men to experience the same range of emotions in the same range of circumstances and that render some of women's outlaw emotions intelligible as signs of unfair practices or oppressive conditions. Without such alternative interpretive conventions, no one will perceive women accurately.

I agree with this conclusion, but I also believe there is a dimension of the topic of women's emotions that it does not adequately address and that points to an unnoticed aspect of heterodox moral perception. So far as I can tell, Frye, Spelman, and Jaggar assume that the second and third strategies of dismissal (ascribing personality faults or psychological pathology to the individual) are variants of the first (misidentifying the individual's occurrent emotion). When accusations of the former sort are leveled, the accusers are simply wrong about the subjectivity of the accused. However, I suspect that the matter is more complicated than this analysis suggests.

When people are accused of committing a wrong that is to some extent controversial—say, sexual harassment or acquaintance rape—they often try to disarm their critics by deflecting attention from the issue and attacking the victim. Prominent among these diversionary strategies is the tactic of dismissing the complaints as products of a warped emotional attitude. "You're [they're] hypersensitive [or paranoid or angry or bitter or what have you]," spoken authoritatively and in a tone dripping with scorn, is often the first line of defense against unwelcome charges of unfair practices or oppressive conditions. It may also be the last line of defense, for this move often succeeds in shaming the victims and silencing protest.

That these rancorous emotional attitudes, as I shall call them, figure so conspicuously in the aspersions cast on defiant members of subordinated social groups is itself reason to regard such attitudes as candidates for revaluation. Now, it is obvious that charges of hypersensitivity, paranoia, anger, and bitterness are often fabricated for ulterior and nefarious purposes. Women are sometimes called hypersensitive when they are no more sensitive than anyone else. To this extent, the analysis of the systematic mislabeling of women's occurrent emotions under consideration here applies to these emotional attitudes as well. However, Audre Lorde (1984) owns up to chronic anger, and Lynne McFall (1991) argues that chronic bitterness can be justified. Although I object to the accusatory, dismissive tenor of ascriptions of hypersensitivity, paranoia, anger, and bitterness, I want to allow that such ascriptions are sometimes warranted. Despite an element of hyperbole embedded in these ascriptions, they are not always distortions arising from patriarchal conventions of interpretation.

This concession may strike some as collaboration with a culture of male dominance. Plainly, rancorous emotional attitudes are not inherently desirable. And, strictly speaking, hypersensitivity and paranoia are by definition pathologies. Hypersensitivity is abnormal or excessive sensitivity, and paranoia brings delusions of persecution. In colloquial speech, however, a hypersensitive person is someone who is characteristically bristly or querulous, and a paranoid person is someone who is characteristically wary and suspicious. Neither of these latter usages designates a clinically recognized diagnosis. Still, these colloquialisms are, in a sense, parasitic on the technical usages, for both terms retain connotations of pathology that give them their cutting rhetorical force. Anger and bitterness also carry the taint of pathology. Although anger and bitterness may be condoned as responses to specific injuries, they are considered abnormal and harmful if they come to define a person's outlook.[7] The angry or bitter person is commonly viewed as emotionally unbalanced. At the very least, these emotional attitudes are deemed unseemly, for they are thought to unleash promiscuous hostility and disgraceful self-pity.

Even if the people whom we call hypersensitive, paranoid, angry, and bitter are not victims of any true psychopathology, and even if their emotional attitudes memorialize grave and perhaps insuperable wrongs, there is ample reason to be skeptical about the desirability of these emotional attitudes. Hypersensitivity, paranoia, and chronic anger and bitterness can be emotional prisons. People who have these emotional attitudes can be obsessed with their misfortunes. They may be driven to dwell on the wrongs they have suffered, and this monomaniacal preoccupation is confining, sometimes incapacitating. Opportunities for personal fulfillment and pleasure may be overlooked and missed. Those rewards that come may not be fully appreciated and may not enhance self-esteem. Ill-at-ease with other people, rancorous individuals can have trouble forming lasting relationships. Indeed, their emotional attitudes may interfere with their ability to grasp others' needs, and this insensitivity in turn may interfere with their ability to be good friends or, for that matter, decent or bearable associates. Moreover, rancorous emotional attitudes can fuel inflated, counterproductive political analyses. They may dispose people to exaggerate lack of opportunity, discriminatory impact, constraint, hardship, and the like, to absolve themselves of responsibility for their setbacks and other misfortunes, and to harshly blame anyone who seems even remotely implicated in bringing about the perceived wrong. In sum, succumbing to hypersensitivity, paranoia, chronic anger, or bitterness may give one's tormenters the upper hand—they may take possession of one's very consciousness and gain the satisfaction of knowing that the pain they have inflicted has redoubled and reverberates throughout one's entire life. Indeed, to succumb to these emotions may be to sink to their level, for they can be morally poisonous, politically calamitous, and interpersonally ruinous.

What could possibly be said in defense of such horrible afflictions? Can a feminist in good conscience embrace charges that women, especially women who are pressing feminist demands, are beset by hypersensitivity, paranoia, anger, and bitterness? I believe that one can, and I shall argue that doing so yields provocative results regarding the question of how to theorize the subject of moral perception. Still, I take comfort from the fact that I am not the only feminist who does not repudiate rancorous emotional attitudes.

4. Rancorous Emotional Attitudes and Heterodox Moral Perception

Lynne McFall fastens on a very important point when she links bitterness to "our emotional responsibility to *feel things as they really are*" and thus to fidelity to truth (1991, 153, 156; original emphasis). In emotionally registering injustice or oppression in its full measure, bitterness bears witness to that wrong (McFall 1991, 155). McFall's point dovetails neatly with Audre Lorde's account of her anger as a black woman. Lorde tells us that her anger is her response to racism (1984, 124). But Lorde is not talking about an apt emotional response to racist incidents that occur at intervals—she is not talking about episodes of anger. Ubiquitous as racism is, Lorde figures her anger as "a molten pond at the core of me" and as "an electric thread woven into every emotional tapestry upon which I set the essentials of my life" (1984, 145). Lorde does not shirk the "emotional responsibility" that McFall delineates, for Lorde's subjectivity in no way palliates the terrible reality of unrelenting, invidious racism. Anger is a defining constituent of her moral outlook—that is, her moral identity.

Lorde certainly does not romanticize her anger: "I have lived with that anger, ignoring it, feeding upon it, learning to use it before it laid my visions to waste, for most of my life" (1984, 124). Anger like hers can be dangerous and damaging. Rancorous emotional attitudes divide women against themselves. They set women against one another (Lorde 1984, 125–126). Worst of all, they set African American women against one another (Lorde 1984, 145–147). If such emotional attitudes are desirable at all, then, they are desirable only for the dispossessed and their allies, and they are desirable only if they can be channeled in morally and politically productive ways.

"When we turn from anger," contends Lorde, "we turn from insight, saying we will accept only the designs already known, deadly and safely familiar" (1984, 131). Both Frye's and Spelman's account of why women must claim their anger and Jaggar's insistence that feminists attend to and interpret outlaw emotions rest on this very point. But again, unlike Frye, Spelman, and Jaggar, Lorde is not speaking of discrete occurrent emotions. Her anger is a global, consuming response to racism. If such anger is "loaded with information and energy," as Lorde (1984, 127) claims it is, is this information retrievable, and can the energy be harnessed for emancipatory purposes? To judge by Lorde's essays, the answer to both of these questions is a resounding YES. But it remains necessary to explore how this can be so.

My conjecture is that, when people have become hypersensitive, paranoid, angry, or bitter as a result of being subjected to a devastating injustice (or series of injustices) or to disabling systemic oppression, they become preternaturally sensitive to unjust practices and oppressive conditions. One reason for this uncommon and heightened sensitivity is that rancorous emotional attitudes provide rich mediums for outlaw emotions. Rancorous emotional attitudes lead people to be apprehensive, indignant, truculent, disappointed, incredulous, tearful, dismayed, irritated, tremulous, anxious, touchy, sullen, fretful, disenchanted, disgusted, outraged, vehement, distraught, and so forth, for no "good" reason and at the most "inopportune" moments. Moreover, individuals beset by such attitudes are highly motivated to interpret their outlaw emotions. A paranoid individual is not likely to dismiss her feelings of professional isolation and loneliness as figments of her imagination. Instead, she will try to figure out why she feels frozen out. Coupled with the disposition to experience outlaw emotions, this disposition to account for them increases the likelihood that such individuals will discern patterns of harm where nicer, milder types see only disconnected incidents or notice nothing the least untoward.

The trouble with emotional vanilla is that it insulates people from awareness of certain kinds of wrongful treatment, in part by indiscriminately quashing outlaw emotions. Likewise, a stoical, detached, or cynical person is not susceptible to experiencing and crediting outlaw emotions. In contrast, "emotional vindaloo" (to continue the flavor metaphor) nurtures outlaw emotions; and, when astutely decoded, many outlaw emotions debunk a society's self-congratulatory illusions about its own fairness and beneficence.

Here it might be objected that, however motivated they may be, hypersensitive, paranoid, angry, and bitter people are poorly equipped to interpret their anomalous emotions. They are prone to overestimate the frequency and gravity of the wrongs they suffer, and they leap at the worst possible construction that can be put on others' behavior. In short, their emotional attitudes bias them toward "discovering" injustice and oppression where none exists.

Obviously, there is something to this objection. Still, I think it is not as telling as it may initially seem. Although I am concerned with rancorous emotional attitudes that are central to a person's moral outlook, not merely with occasional attacks of rancor, the centrality of these attitudes does not render them absolutely sovereign. Except perhaps in cases of bona fide psychopathology, no one's moral outlook is composed solely of these rancorous emotional attitudes. Thus, their influence is tempered by other emotional attitudes, not to mention values, principles, interpersonal bonds, and so forth.

Rancorous emotional attitudes structure moral perception, but not in a ham-fisted, uninflected, indiscriminate way. Thus, I believe that the critique of these attitudes that I sketched at the end of Section 3 is actually something of a caricature and that the objection now under consideration is something of a red herring, for it rests on a false polarization of the vanilla-vindaloo contrast.

Still, when rancorous emotional attitudes are central to a person's moral outlook, they often overshadow its other components. These attitudes strongly influence a person's style of relating to others and markedly slant that person's moral perception. In light of the liabilities associated with emotional vindaloo, then, it might seem advisable to approach other people in emotional vanilla and to switch to emotional vindaloo only if the circumstances call for doing so.

This strategy makes a great deal of sense for purposes of what might be termed dissident moral perception. In dissident moral perception, the members of a subordinated group have identified an unjust practice or oppressive condition, and they share an understanding of what counts as a standard instance of it. However, many people have not been exposed to their analysis, have not assimilated it, or disagree with it. Sexual harassment is a case in point. For feminists and many other women, sexual harassment is part of their repertory of moral concepts. But many men either conflate sexual harassment with office romance or believe that women's definition of sexual harassment is overinclusive. With respect to sexual harassment, then, many women are members of a feminist community that validates moral perception that is at odds with the unreconstructed moral perceptions of some men. Such perception is heterodox relative to traditional patriarchal norms and values, but it is not heterodox relative to feminist norms and values that are now in wide circulation. It is dissident moral perception.

In dissident moral perception, an individual already commands the moral concepts necessary to see a particular kind of wrong. But if these concepts are to be deployed in moral perception, it is important that the individual's emotional attitude not interfere. Here, the self-protective practices of residents of major U.S. cities provide the relevant paradigm. These urban dwellers may spend a long evening at a pleasant social gathering in emotional vanilla, but far be it from them to remain in emotional vanilla when negotiating desolate city streets alone late at night. They automatically become vigilant—that is, they go into paranoia overdrive—as they leave the party. Similarly, a woman who is familiar with the concept of sexual harassment can approach her work environment in emotional vanilla but shift into vindaloo if she begins to notice objectionable behavior.

The sort of heterodox moral perception of most interest to me is different. I want to understand how people discover heretofore unacknowledged kinds of wrong. In this connection, the relevant paradigm is that of an interplanetary explorer who looks exactly like a human, has just landed on earth for the first time, has no prior intelligence about the habits of earthlings, and is taking a midnight stroll in Central Park on a balmy summer night. The visitor has no idea what to expect from the denizens of the park and, therefore, no basis for adopting one emotional attitude rather than another.

With respect to heterodox moral perception that discloses novel wrongs—wrongs that are not recognized within any moral community to which one has access—modulating one's emotional attitude to suit the different situations in which one finds oneself is not an option. Emotional suppleness and flexibility cannot solve the problem of how to *enter* situations of unknown moral character since making appropriate emotional adjustments requires that one already has a reliable impression of the sort of situation one is in. Unfortunately, taking the measure of a situation requires insightful moral perception, and insightful moral perception depends in part on having the right emotional attitude. Once one grasps a situation, one can and should modulate one's emotional attitude, but one has no basis for modulating one's emotional attitude until one has grasped the situation. Thus, in an important sense, one's initial emotional attitude is arbitrary. It depends on the sort of person one happens to be, not on the moral features of any particular situation. One can deliberately cultivate this attitude or that, but one cannot know in advance that the attitudes one has acquired will be maximally conducive to insightful moral perception.

There is no emotional attitude that is appropriate in all conceivable circumstances. Inevitably, any moral outlook—in both its cognitive and emotional dimensions—highlights some features of social experience and obscures others. For everyday purposes, moral perception, selective and somewhat skewed though it may be, suffices since it does not induce people to do anything blatantly culpable. In the ordinary course of events, many people take for granted the trustworthiness and goodwill of other people and the basic fairness of the institutions that order their lives, and they blithely proceed in vanilla mode. But as the history of feminism and other emancipatory movements has proven, these benign assumptions are often unsound: Emotional vanilla can indeed conceal self-serving conduct on the part of individuals, unjust policies and practices, and oppressive institutional structures. Just as emotional vindaloo would probably help protect the interplanetary visitors in Central Park from mishap, emotional vindaloo can help women uncover the multifarious forms that male dominance takes.[8]

I regard the idea that there is some ideal moral outlook that ensures insightful moral perception in all kinds of situations as an *ignis fatuus*. Since individuals can have only one moral outlook at a time, it follows that their moral perception will sometimes be seriously distorted and misleading. For this reason, it seems to me imperative to rethink the question of how we model the subject of moral perception. I have been speaking of individuals and their moral outlooks, and we cannot dispense with individuals. But I think we should not stop there. Heterodox moral perception obliges us to look at the moral economies of groups as well.

5. An Alternative Conception of the Subject of Moral Perception

What my discussion is leading up to is a larger project—one that I can only adumbrate here—concerning the unit of moral perception. My thought is that we must turn to group dynamics if we are to understand the contribution of hypersensitivity, paranoia, anger, and bitterness to reliable heterodox moral perception. Here I am taking a cue from Audre Lorde's plea to white women that they confront her anger. Lorde is not pretending that it is pleasant to listen to an angry person, and she is not terribly sanguine about her prospects of being heard. Lorde's prose is so eloquent that it is hard to imagine her coming across as belligerent. But we know what angry people can be like. They can be harping, carping, grim, spiteful killjoys. Far from endearing or winning, they can be tiresome, irritating, alienating—in a word, insufferable. Lousy team players, they often put other people off, and it is not unusual for them to attack their natural allies. But it seems to me that, if people with cooperative vanilla dispositions do not find ways to avail themselves of their rancorous friends' perceptions, they will miss a great deal, or they will discover it only after needless delay.

Although I am generally skeptical of analogies that liken groups to individuals, let me, with considerable reluctance and all due trepidation, offer the following analogy in the hope of making the program of inquiry I am proposing seem plausible, and also in the hope of helping readers see the contribution that hypersensitivity, paranoia, anger, and bitterness can make to the moral economy of a group. In my experience, we are all prone to psychological inertia, but nagging frustration, dissatisfaction, or anxiety sometimes grabs our attention and moves us to seek relief and change our lives. Sometimes we realize in retrospect that if we had not so resolutely confined those disagreeable feelings to the periphery of consciousness, we could have avoided a great deal of suffering—by acting much sooner and for the better.

I think that hypersensitive, paranoid, angry, and bitter people can play a role in a group moral economy similar to that of recurrent, low-intensity distress in an individual psychic economy. Most people experience some outlaw emotions, and they harbor some suspicions about the virtue of their associates and the rectitude of their society's institutions. But for the most part, they set these feelings aside and do not bother to articulate a critique. By contrast, the kvetch (sometimes too stridently) counterbalances the homeostatic tendency that favors the perpetuation of the status quo and indefinitely postpones reform. If social groups were organized to seize upon claims kindled by hypersensitivity, paranoia, anger, and bitterness and to give them a good airing and a fair hearing, insightful moral perception might be greatly increased, and emancipation might be hastened.

I am not advocating universal rancor, nor do I suggest that rancor be instilled in a few miserable souls so that they can benefit subordinated social groups. It is a fact that rancorous individuals already exist, and some of them are ahead of their vanilla peers. If they are ostracized, their prescient insights will be suppressed.

The underlying point here is indisputable, but easily forgotten: Social diversity is good; homogeneity within a group is harmful. If everyone in a subordinated social group shares the same rancorous emotional attitudes, moral perception may collapse into mass delusion. Arguably, then, there is a place for emotional vanilla in the group process of interpreting outlaw emotions. Serene, trusting, genial individuals who are sympathetic to rancorous group members may play a moderating role in this process. Their solidarity with group members who evince outlaw emotions ensures that they will take these feelings seriously, yet their niceness ensures that they will not automatically dismiss the viewpoints of unconvinced group members and outsiders. People whose moral outlook is characterized by emotional vanilla should not be regarded as arbiters of the reliability of more rancorous group members' perceptions; however, their sympathetic misgivings may provide needed perspective on the deliverances of rancorous emotional attitudes and thus help to dissuade the group from endorsing a defective repertory of moral concepts and from pursuing counterproductive political initiatives.

My attempt to reclaim hypersensitivity, paranoia, anger, and bitterness is in effect an attempt to cue a gestalt shift in thinking about moral subjectivity and agency—especially where it concerns heterodox moral perception. In this regard, the irrepressible Thomas Pynchon captured something of what I have in mind when he wrote: "Creative paranoia means developing at least as thorough a We-system as a They-system" (1973, 638). The probing of our rules of moral salience for inconsistencies or errors of fact that Barbara Herman (1985) advocates, and the careful examination of contested applications of moral idioms that John Kekes (1989) advocates, must take place in a community where the possibility that a culture's repertory of moral concepts ill serves some social groups is a prime concern. Feminist philosophers often stress the role of alternative discursive communities with respect to redefining norms and values (e.g., Frye 1983, 103, 105–107; Bartky 1990, 43; Jaggar 1989, 144; Friedman 1993, Part 3). The idea is to create enclaves in which heterodox perceptions are given their due. In advocating a group model of heterodox moral perception, I have followed their lead. To reclaim hypersensitivity, paranoia, anger, and bitterness and to understand heterodox moral perception, we must politicize moral perception.

I am not claiming that no conscientious, reflective individual could possibly discern the wrongs that hypersensitivity, paranoia, anger, and bitterness disclose. Both Kekes and Nussbaum discuss fictional characters who are so "finely aware and richly responsible" (to echo Nussbaum's appropriation of Henry James's phrase) that they are able to engage fruitfully with novel repertories of moral concepts. Indeed, I myself have argued elsewhere that an individual's moral outlook can be enriched through empathy with different others (Meyers 1994, 36–38). Although I think childrearing and educational practices should be designed to cultivate capacities that enhance individual sensitivity, I also think it is incumbent on us to realize how rare such sensitivity is and to acknowledge that our cognitive apparatus may disfavor the openness to new people and new ideas that such sensitivity requires (Goldman 1992, 35).

The solitary individual who is deeply immersed in a rich moral tradition but who is an inquisitive observer and an independent thinker should not be viewed as the sole prototype of moral sensitivity and as the only sort of person who is capable of insightful heterodox moral perception. On the contrary, we must also recognize a cluster prototype—a group of individuals some of whom have rancorous emotional attitudes that prime them to experience outlaw emotions, and whose outlaw emotions estrange them from their culture's repertory of moral concepts; a group of individuals whose solidarity provides an emotional and intellectual context conducive to developing an emancipatory repertory of moral concepts, and whose commitment to overcoming their subordination gives them the courage of their oppositional, sometimes audaciously oppositional, convictions. I would venture that the alternative I have sketched represents a more egalitarian view of moral sensitivity and, for many members of subordinated social groups, a more attainable conception of insightful heterodox moral perception.[9]

Notes

1. In the literature on these topics, there is little agreement about the distinctions among moral perception, moral judgment, and moral reflection, and inevitably there is an element of stipulation in how one demarcates these concepts. Some (e.g., Larmore 1987, 14) regard moral judgment as involving the application of principles to situations; others (e.g., Kekes 1989, 143) regard moral judgment as an interpretive process that is independent of moral principles. Larmore and Kekes seem to agree, however, that moral judgment issues in a decision about what one ought to do. My own view is that moral judgment need not appeal to principles (Meyers 1994, 128–135). But the line of thought I shall develop here does not depend on this view. Thus, I shall use the expression 'moral judgment' to refer to a process through which one reaches a conclusion about what one ought to do. Although moral perception is sometimes phenomenologically indistinguishable from moral judgment, it is always necessary to moral judgment, and it may not be sufficient for moral judgment. Also, I shall reserve the expression 'moral reflection' for those processes through which one critically examines one's moral convictions and commitments.

2. I prefer the expressions 'repertory of moral concepts' and 'emancipatory repertory of moral concepts' over 'moral theory' and 'critical social theory' because the former do not imply that moral perception and judgment must be theory-driven (for related discussion, see Walker 1992).

3. There is a rich literature examining the ways in which derogatory conceptions of gender and race are figuratively encoded in Western culture (e.g., see Lloyd 1993a and 1993b, Rooney 1991, Kittay 1988, Crenshaw 1993, and Gilman 1985; for related discussion, see Morgan 1987). That sexism and other forms of bigotry are transmitted through figurations that outlast explicit doctrines of gender and racial inferiority suggests that the scope of the project of developing an emancipatory repertory of moral concepts is broader than it is usually assumed to be. We may possess the concepts of marital rape and acquaintance rape, but if women are figured as devious, vengeful Harpies and are perceived through this figuration, these moral concepts will have little or no practical moral force. If taking a woman's word that she has been raped seems crazy, hardly anyone will ever be convicted—in conscience or in courts of law—of marital or acquaintance rape. Thus, an emancipatory repertory of moral concepts must not only provide interpretations of injustice and oppression that articulate the moral experience of subordinated social groups, but it must also furnish counterfigurations to replace prejudicial figurations of subordinated social groups (Meyers 1994, 58–61). In this spirit, Iris Young calls for social theory that functions as "social therapy" (1990, 153).

4. Critics of Carol Gilligan's ethic of care who maintain that it is an ethic that makes women complicit in their own oppression by yoking them to exploitative lovers, husbands, children, and other family members make an argument regarding the sphere of intimates that parallels the one I have given regarding the sphere of nonintimate associates. They claim that the loving, altruistic emotional attitude that shapes moral perception within the care framework often prevents women from seeing how those they love oppress and take advantage of them (Houston 1987, 253). Although I think it would be a mistake to dismiss the ethic of care on the strength of this argument, I agree that feminists must be wary of moral attitudes that shield oppressive norms and practices from view.

5. For discussion of the metaphorical structure of moral concepts and their resulting resistance to change, see Johnson (1993, 194). But also note the existence of organized social resistance to critical moral reflection and moral change. In an interview, Reverend Lou Sheldon, a leader of the evangelical right in the United States, declared, "We were here first. You don't take our shared common values and say they are biased and bigoted. . . . We are the keepers of what is right and what is wrong" (quoted in "Christian Soldiers" by Sidney Blumenthal, *New Yorker*, July 18, 1994, p. 35).

6. In my discussion, I focus on negative outlaw emotions; however, it is worth pointing out that there can be positive outlaw emotions, too. For example, in some strata of United States society, compassion for the plight of the poor is an outlaw emotion. Compassion of this kind is viewed as bleeding-heart liberalism and dismissed as sentimentality. Similarly, many men consider a man's sympathy with female rape victims or his disgust with the predatory sexual behavior of many male heterosexuals to be effeminate. Positive outlaw emotions are important to moral perception, for they can provide the basis for members of relatively privileged social

groups to identify with and stand in solidarity with members of subordinated social groups.

7. A graduate student once told me that she did not want to get involved with feminist philosophy because she did not want to be "angry all the time." Although I do not think that all feminist philosophers are angry people, her worry is perfectly understandable.

8. At this point, a reader might object that the attitude with which one enters a situation affects the way in which one will be treated. If one is combative, for example, one is more likely to be attacked. In some cases, people do bring harm upon themselves. However, in many cases, this objection amounts to nothing more than blaming the victim. Gender discrimination in hiring and promotion, sexual harassment, and sexual assault are not reserved for rancorous women. Nice women, too, are victimized by these practices.

9. I am grateful to Barbara Andrew, Alison Jaggar, Eva Feder Kittay, Elise Springer, and Margaret Urban Walker for their helpful comments on an earlier draft of this chapter.

References

Baier, Annette C. 1986. "Trust and Antitrust." *Ethics* 96: 231–260.

_____. 1987. "The Need for More Than Justice." In *Science, Morality, and Feminist Theory*. Eds. Marsha Hanen and Kai Nielsen. Calgary: University of Calgary Press.

Bartky, Sandra. 1990. *Femininity and Domination*. New York: Routledge.

Blum, Lawrence. 1991. "Moral Perception and Particularity." *Ethics* 101: 701–725.

Brison, Susan. n.d. "Self-Blame, Self-Defense, and Survival." Unpublished manuscript.

Crenshaw, Kimberlè Williams. 1993. "Beyond Racism and Misogyny: Black Feminism and 2 Live Crew." In *Words That Wound*. Eds. Mari J. Matsuda et al. Boulder, Colo.: Westview Press.

de Sousa, Ronald. 1987. *The Rationality of Emotion*. Cambridge, Mass.: MIT Press.

Friedman, Marilyn. 1993. *What Are Friends For?* Ithaca, N.Y.: Cornell University Press.

Frye, Marilyn. 1983. *The Politics of Reality*. Freedom, Calif.: Crossing Press.

Gilman, Sander L. 1985. *Difference and Pathology: Stereotypes of Sexuality, Race, and Madness*. Ithaca, N.Y.: Cornell University Press.

Goldman, Alvin I. 1992. "Empathy, Mind, and Morals." *Proceedings and Addresses of the American Philosophical Association* 66: 17–41.

Held, Virginia. 1987. "Feminism and Moral Theory." In *Women and Moral Theory*. Eds. Eva Feder Kittay and Diana T. Meyers. Totowa, N.J.: Rowman and Littlefield.

Herman, Barbara. 1985. "The Practice of Moral Judgment." *Journal of Philosophy* 82: 414–436.

_____. 1990. "Obligation and Performance: A Kantian Account of Moral Conflict." In *Identity, Character, and Morality*. Eds. Owen Flanagan and Amelie Oksenberg Rorty. Cambridge, Mass.: MIT Press.

hooks, bell. 1984. *Feminist Theory: From Margin to Center*. Boston: South End Press.

Houston, Barbara. 1987. "Rescuing Womanly Virtues: Some Dangers of Moral Reclamation." In *Science, Morality, and Feminist Theory*. Eds. Marsha Hanen and Kai Nielsen. Calgary: University of Calgary Press.

Jaggar, Alison M. 1989. "Love and Knowledge: Emotion in Feminist Epistemology." In *Women, Knowledge, and Reality*. Eds. Ann Garry and Marilyn Pearsall. Boston: Unwin Hyman.

Johnson, Mark. 1993. *Moral Imagination: Implications of Cognitive Science for Ethics*. Chicago: University of Chicago Press.

Kekes, John. 1989. *Moral Tradition and Individuality*. Princeton, N.J.: Princeton University Press.

Kittay, Eva Feder. 1988. "Woman as Metaphor." *Hypatia* 3: 63–86.

Kupperman, Joel. 1991. *Character*. New York: Oxford University Press.

Larmore, Charles. 1987. *Patterns of Moral Complexity*. Cambridge: Cambridge University Press.

Lloyd, Genevieve. 1993a. *The Man of Reason*, 2nd ed. Minneapolis: University of Minnesota Press.

_____. 1993b. "Maleness, Metaphor, and the 'Crisis' of Reason." In *A Mind of One's Own*. Eds. Louise M. Antony and Charlotte Witt. Boulder, Colo.: Westview Press.

Lorde, Audre. 1984. *Sister Outsider*. Freedom, Calif.: Crossing Press.

Lugones, María C., and Elizabeth V. Spelman. 1993. "Have We Got a Theory for You! Feminist Theory, Cultural Imperialism and the Demand for 'The Woman's Voice.'" In *Women and Values*. Ed. Marilyn Pearsall. Belmont, Calif.: Wadsworth.

McFall, Lynne. 1991. "What's Wrong with Bitterness?" In *Feminist Ethics*. Ed. Claudia Card. Lawrence: University Press of Kansas.

Meyers, Diana Tietjens. 1994. *Subjection and Subjectivity: Psychoanalytic Feminism and Moral Philosophy*. New York: Routledge.

Morgan, Kathryn. 1987. "Women and Moral Madness." In *Science, Morality, and Feminist Theory*. Eds. Marsha Hanen and Kai Nielsen. Calgary: University of Calgary Press.

Narayan, Uma. 1988. "Working Across Difference: Some Considerations on Emotions and Political Practice." *Hypatia* 3: 31–47.

Nussbaum, Martha C. 1990. *Love's Knowledge*. New York: Oxford University Press.

Piper, Adrian M. S. 1990. "Higher Order Discrimination." In *Identity, Character, and Morality*. Eds. Owen Flanagan and Amelie Oksenberg Rorty. Cambridge, Mass.: MIT Press.

_____. 1991. "Impartiality, Compassion, and Modal Imagination." *Ethics* 101: 726–757.

_____. 1992–1993. "Xenophobia and Kantian Rationalism." *The Philosophical Forum* 24: 188–232.

Pynchon, Thomas. 1973. *Gravity's Rainbow*. New York: Viking Press.

Rooney, Phyllis. 1991. "Gendered Reason: Sex Metaphor and Conceptions of Reason." *Hypatia* 6(2): 77–103.

Scheman, Naomi. 1993. *Engenderings: Constructions of Knowledge, Authority, and Privilege*. New York: Routledge.

Sherman, Nancy. 1989. *The Fabric of Character*. Oxford: Clarendon Press.

Spelman, Elizabeth V. 1989. "Anger and Insubordination." In *Women, Knowledge, and Reality*. Eds. Ann Garry and Marilyn Pearsall. Boston: Unwin Hyman.

Taylor, Shelley E., and Jonathan D. Brown. 1988. "Illusion and Well-Being: A Social Psychological Perspective on Mental Health." *Psychological Bulletin* 103(2): 193–210.

Valian, Virginia. n.d. *Why So Slow? The Advancement of Women*. Unpublished manuscript.

Walker, Margaret Urban. 1987. "Moral Particularity." *Metaphilosophy* 18: 171–185.

———. 1992. "Feminism, Ethics, and the Question of Theory." *Hypatia* 7: 23–38.

Young, Iris Marion. 1990. *Justice and the Politics of Difference*. Princeton, N.J.: Princeton University Press.

ten

❧

Human Dependency and Rawlsian Equality

EVA FEDER KITTAY

> *"That all men are created free and equal."* . . .
> *That's a hard mystery of Jefferson's.*
> *What did he mean? Of course the easy way*
> *Is to decide it simply isn't true.*
> *It may not be. I heard a fellow say so.*
> *But never mind, the Welshman got it planted*
> *Where it will trouble us a thousand years.*
> *Each age will have to reconsider it.*
> —Robert Frost, from "The Black Cottage"

1. Introduction

1.1. Defining the Problem

The liberal tradition in ethics and political theory is based upon the view that within a just society all persons should be treated as free and equal. 'All persons' would include the formerly disenfranchised—for example, women and black men. It would also include persons with special needs who are dependent upon others in basic ways—that is to say, children, the disabled, and the frail elderly. In order for persons with the special needs of dependents to be included in the community of equal citizens, however, these persons' needs require special consideration. There is, furthermore, a class of persons upon whom the dependent persons depend. These persons I call *dependency workers*. They are individuals who devote a major part of their lives (whether full or part time and through paid or unpaid labor) to attending to the dependency needs of others. As long as any of us are dependent, and as long as dependency care is a primary responsibility, our capacity to participate as equals in a community of free and equal persons is restricted by natural and social circumstance. Although the bounds of justice are drawn within reciprocal relations among free and equal persons, dependents will continue to remain disenfranchised, and dependency workers who are otherwise fully capable and cooperating members of society will continue to share varying degrees of the dependents' disfranchisement.

John Rawls, the most distinguished contemporary representative of the liberal view, defines the political in terms articulated by traditional Western political philosophies; he joins those who have omitted responsibility for dependents from, or relegated it to the periphery of, the political.[1] The presumption has been that these responsibilities belong to citizens' *private* rather than *public* concerns—a dichotomy that appears reasonable only by virtue of the neglect of dependency in delineating the political. The particular situation of those who care for dependents becomes invisible in the *political* associations of equals. Enlightenment's progeny, equality for all, fails to illuminate the nether world of dependency or shine its beneficent light on the inhabitants, the dependent and the dependency worker.

The dependency care I want to spotlight centers on the most acute moments of human dependency: helpless infancy and early childhood, frail old age, and incapacitating illness and disability. I focus on utter dependency because the inequities in the organization and distribution of dependency work, and the impact of these inequities on the possibility of equality for all, are most evident when dependency is a feature of our human condition rather than a consequence of socially prescribed roles, privileges, or distribution policies.[2] As such, dependency has a number of features that are separable in its lesser forms but inexorably linked in utter dependency, the form that concerns us here. First, the dependent requires care and caring persons to meet fundamental needs for survival and basic thriving. Second, while in the condition of dependency, the dependent is unable to reciprocate the benefits received.[3] And, third, the intervention of another is crucial to ensure that the needs of the dependent are met and that the interests of the dependent are recognized in a social context.[4] Dependency so understood underscores not only the limitations of an individual's capability but also the necessary labor of a dependency worker. The dependency worker, clearly, is not dependent in the sense outlined above. Nonetheless, the dependency worker, by virtue of her attention to her charge, becomes vulnerable to a *derived*[5] dependence: a dependence upon others to secure her own interests, which is derived from her responsibilities to turn her efforts to the individual who is dependent because she is too young, too feeble, too ill, or too disabled to fend for herself.[6]

Rawls may be said to address these concerns indirectly, in terms of either his presupposition that the needs of dependents are met in the nonpolitical domestic domain or his concern for "the least well-off"; but he does not deal with them directly. Most important, Rawls does not consider these concerns as central to the political aim of his theory. Especially as he refines the political focus of his work in *Political Liberalism* (1992), concerns of this sort are excluded. The exclusion is not trivial, nor is it Rawls's alone.

It is my view that liberal political theory and Rawls's theory, in particular, are flawed in that they do not take this issue of dependency to be central. All of us are dependent in childhood; most of us are dependent in old age; and many of us are dependent for long periods of time (sometimes throughout a life) because of ill health. Dependency is thus a matter for us all in our lives as social beings. Most women—by virtue of their traditional roles and the ineluctable demands of dependency—and some men, primarily those from marginalized classes, find themselves with the responsibility to care for dependents. In assuming these duties, they have too often found themselves stigmatized as dependents. As such, they have not been able to function as equals in a society of equals.

Because dependency strongly affects our status as equal citizens (i.e., as persons who, as equals, share the benefits and burdens of social cooperation), and because it affects all of us at one time or another, it is not an issue that can be set aside, much less avoided. Its consequences for social organization cannot be deferred until other traditional questions about the structure of society have been settled, without distorting the character of a just social order. Dependency must be faced from the beginning of any project in egalitarian theory that hopes to include *all* persons within its scope.

1.2. The Dependency Critique of Liberal Equality

Collecting and refashioning the work of the years since his singularly influential *A Theory of Justice* (1971), Rawls, in his most recent book, *Political Liberalism* (1992), pares down the concept of "justice as fairness" to what he considers its political heart. The task is to refine the argument and answer his critics. Rawls, who has insisted throughout his work that gender, along with race, is irrelevant in considering persons as equal, briefly addresses feminist commentators (see Kittay 1994). He acknowledges the theory's dependence on a "few main and enduring classical problems" of political philosophy (Rawls 1992, xxix). These underlie much of the criticisms from feminist quarters, criticisms aimed at the masculine bias of the tradition's conception of the person. Defending the theory's conception of the person as merely a "device of representation," as opposed to a characterization of persons in a full sense, he opines optimistically that "alleged difficulties in discussing problems of gender and the family can be overcome" (1992, xxix).

With the publication of *Political Liberalism*, it is fitting to reexamine the
Rawlsian construction with respect to the equality of women—a population
too often excluded even in the most egalitarian liberal theories. Rawls intends to include women within the scope of his theory. But given the starting
points of the work, can he succeed?

Rawls's theory begins, as do all contractarian theories, by construing society as an association of equals, conceived as individuals who are more or less
equal in their ability to compete for the benefits of social cooperation.
Equality forms one of the two pillars (the other being liberty) on which liberal political theory is erected; and, appropriately, equality is at the core of
Rawls's theory. Indeed, equal divisions of the benefits and burdens of social
cooperation serve as a benchmark for "justice as fairness" (Rawls 1992, 282).
Equality plays its role both foundationally and normatively. The theory is
based on the conception of all persons as moral equals; and it develops a concept of justice that issues in a relatively egalitarian society—a society in
which basic political liberties are enjoyed equally by all and in which a fair
economic distribution, in combination with equal opportunity, advantages
the least well-off.[7]

Historical formulations of this fundamental level of equality betray an androcentric view of society. The historical development of this ideal since its
emergence as a challenge to feudalism has been an ideal for male heads of
households only.[8] The equality of heads of households banishes feudalistic
dependencies that were the product of hierarchical political organization.
The dependencies and resultant hierarchies that attend human development,
disease, and decline remain within the household. Yet accompanying the
egalitarian challenge to patriarchal, feudalistic hierarchies was a stress on individuals—that is, on the individualism championed in the theory of rights
and political liberties. This overlay of individualism creates a conceptual illusion that dependencies do not exist—or at least are not a political matter. The
illusion makes it appear that the extension of equality to all, not only to
heads of households, is an easy matter.

From interdependencies that grow out of our dependencies emerge the
central bonds of human life—bonds based on the vulnerabilities of the dependent person, on the one hand, and on the trust invested in the dependency worker, on the other. Those vulnerable in the sense that they require
care are also vulnerable in that they often have no voice—at least no public
voice—save that of their caretaker, the dependency worker, who is charged
with articulating and meeting their needs.

But the voice of the dependency worker is not the independent voice of
the equal autonomous agent of liberal political theory; it is a voice sometimes blending the interests of the caregiver and care-recipient, sometimes
torn between conflicting interests. Either because the obligation devolves on
the dependency worker, or because it is one of a very few options available,

or because she freely chooses it from a wide variety of possibilities, she enters the "fair and equal" competitive arena with a handicapping condition: Along with the same responsibilities other citizens have to each other and to themselves, the dependency worker has the added responsibility of meeting the needs of another who is unable to care for himself. Given the cycle of human life, and given the pivotal place of *dependency work* in social life, its just organization is as central to the formation of a just society as is development of the principles of distribution under conditions of moderate scarcity.

Calling attention to the neglect of dependency, and to the consequences of that omission in theories of equality and social justice, constitutes what I call the *dependency critique.*[9] To the extent that the responsibility for providing the care required by dependents has traditionally fallen to women, this critique of liberal theories of equality is inspired by feminist concerns. As such, it provides a framework for rethinking the distribution of goods and responsibilities across gender lines, without staking the interests of some women against the interests of others.[10]

1.3. Dependency as a Criterion of Adequacy Applied to Rawls's Theory of Justice

The principles of justice proposed by Rawls are intended to govern the basic structures of a well-ordered society; these principles, he argues, would be chosen by reasonable and rational persons under certain specified conditions—conditions simulated in the *original position*. In the context of Rawls's constructivism,[11] the *original position* (henceforth OP) is a hypothetical position from which representatives of citizens in a well-ordered society choose the principles of justice that they want their basic social structures (i.e., their laws and institutions) to embody. The participants in the OP are all modeled on equal and free moral persons, who are rational and mutually disinterested. They know general facts about human nature and society but are ignorant of their own station in life, their "conceptions of the good," and "their special psychological propensities" (Rawls 1971, 11). This *veil of ignorance* over participants in the OP should ensure that the choice of principles is unaffected by knowledge of one's own place in society, one's own vision of the good, or one's particular psychological proclivities; it should guarantee that parties choose principles impartially and, therefore, fairly. Parties in the OP are representatives of mutually disinterested *rational* agents concerned primarily with their own well-being. The constraints of the OP reflect fair terms of social cooperation to which rational persons could agree.

In "Kantian Constructivism in Moral Theory: The Dewey Lectures 1980" (1980, 520), Rawls exhibits the methodology and foundational concepts of *A Theory of Justice* (1971) in what he later calls "model-conceptions." (Rawls

1980, 520). The OP mediates between the "model-conceptions" of a *well-ordered society* and of a *moral person*, modeling the "way in which the citizens in a well-ordered society, viewed as moral persons, would ideally select first principles of justice for their society" (Rawls 1980, 520). Answering criticisms addressed to his model-conceptions, Rawls asserts, in one of his later works,[12] that thinking of ourselves as participants in the OP is analogous to "role-playing" (1992, 27).[13] Thus the OP and the model-conceptions are meant "to show how the idea of society as a fair system of social cooperation can be unfolded so as to find principles specifying the basic rights and liberties and the forms of equality most appropriate to those cooperating, once they are regarded as citizens, as free and equal persons" (Rawls 1992, 27).

My claim is that those within relations of dependency fall outside the conceptual perimeters of Rawls's egalitarianism. I shall trace the conceptual shape of this exclusion in Rawls through an analysis of the five presuppositions standing behind the concept of equality as we find it in Rawls's constructivism. In the concluding section, I return to the principles selected in the OP. I argue that they cannot accommodate the objections of the dependency critique if the foundational assumptions are not altered. In pointing to omissions in the theory, I contemplate ways in which the Rawlsian position could be amended. Whether the suggestions put forward suffice to make the theory amenable to dependency concerns without introducing new incoherencies for the theory is a question I leave for Rawlsians. My aim is neither to reform Rawls's political theory nor to say that it cannot be reformed. Rather, I offer the arguments of the dependency critique as a criterion of adequacy, one applicable to *any* political theory claiming to be egalitarian.

1.4. *The Arguments in Outline*

"Equal justice," writes Rawls, "is owed to those who have the capacity to take part in and to act in accordance with the public understanding of the initial situation" (1971, 505). The moral equality of all members of a well-ordered society is represented in the model-conception of the person. In the "Dewey Lectures," he writes, "The representation for equality is an easy matter: we simply describe all the parties in the same way and situate them equally, that is, symmetrically with respect to one another. Everyone has the same rights and powers in the procedure for reaching agreement" (1980, 550). 'Equality' in this passage refers to the identity of members with respect to certain salient features: their rights and their powers in the procedure for reaching agreement. It also means that the parties are equally situated with respect to one another.[14] Representing equality here seems unproblematic. But, I wish to argue, what makes it an "easy matter" is that so much has been presumed already. Let us see if we can make the presumptions evident.

First, note that this representation of moral equality begins with an "idealization" of citizens in a well-ordered society, initially introduced when Rawls attempts to state the sense in which citizens in a well-ordered society are equal moral persons, that "all citizens are fully cooperating members of society *over the course of a complete life*" (1980, 546; emphasis added).

For Rawls this means that no one has particularly taxing or costly needs to fulfill, such as unusual medical requirements. In *Political Liberalism*, he writes, "The normal range [of functioning] is specified as follows: since the fundamental problem of justice concerns the relations among those who are full and active participants in society, and directly or indirectly associated together over the course of a whole life, it is reasonable to *assume that everyone has physical needs and psychological capacities within some normal range. Thus the problem of special health care and how to treat the mentally defective are set.* If we can work out a viable theory for the normal range, we can attempt to handle these other cases later" (1992, 272: note 10). That is, the case must initially be made for the "normal" situation and then be modified to include important but unusual considerations such as special medical requirements.[15]

Second, as everyone is equally capable of understanding and complying with the principles of justice (to a certain minimal degree), and is equally capable of honoring them, and insofar as each person is free (i.e., is a "self-originating" or "self-authenticating source of valid claims"),[16] each views her- or himself as worthy of being represented in a procedure by which the principles of justice are determined. An equality with respect, first, to a sense of justice and, second, to freedom as being a self-authenticating source of valid claims establishes the grounds for the claim to equal worth.

Third, the realization of equality assumes a common measure. But insofar as each person forms his or her own conception of the good, Rawls proposes an index composed of those goods all persons require given the two moral powers of a person: an ability to form and revise one's conception of one's own good and a sense of justice. The possession of these two moral powers is itself a feature of the modeling of the parties as equals.[17]

Fourth, the representation of the parties as equals turns on a conception of social cooperation. The equality of those representing citizens requires that persons possess the two moral powers and have normal capacities because these are the only requirements for establishing fair terms of social cooperation.[18]

And, finally, the entire edifice rests on what are identified as the "circumstances of justice." These are the circumstances under which a society of free and equal persons who share the benefits and the burdens of social organization is constituted.

Rawls's account, by his own insistence, is an idealization. Still, he acknowledges that it must take into account "an appropriate conception of the person that general facts about human nature and society allow" (1980, 534). Unfortunately, however, Rawls's idealization neglects certain scarcely acknowledged facts bearing on "an appropriate conception of the person" that are of the utmost importance in social organization—namely, facts of human dependency. The question then arises as to whether, given the Rawlsian idealization, the equality of citizens applies to those individuals who are dependent either in the primary sense or in the derived sense, even in a fully compliant well-ordered society.

The succession of the above considerations follows the reliance of each idea upon its successor. To bring us closer to the logic of theory construction, I invert the order. I argue that the fact of human dependency is excluded from each of the following considerations, and that we must not exclude such concerns if we are to develop a just social organization capable of meeting dependency needs:

1. The *circumstances of justice* that determine a well-ordered society's conceptual perimeters.
2. The *conception of social cooperation* that supposes equality between those in cooperative arrangements.
3. The *moral powers of a person* relevant to justice as (a) a sense of justice and (b) a conception of one's own good; and list of *primary goods* based on these moral powers that serves as index for interpersonal comparisons of well-being.
4. The *conception of free persons* as those who think of themselves as "self-originating sources of valid claims."
5. The *norm* appealed to and projected into the *idealization* that *"all citizens are fully cooperating members of society over the course of a complete life."*

These points are addressed in the five major sections that follow.

2. The Circumstances of Justice for a Well-Ordered Society

2.1. Dependency as Both an Objective and a Subjective Circumstance of Justice

The general facts about human nature and society that constrain the conception of the person and of the well-ordered society constitute the most fundamental presuppositions for the conception of equality and justice evoked in Rawls's scheme. The most general of these facts are encapsulated in what Rawls, invoking Hume, calls the *circumstances of justice*. These are either objective or subjective (see Rawls 1971, 126–127; 1980, 536). Because each is so fundamental, the effect of overlooking an important circumstance has serious consequences for the whole theory.

According to current estimates, as many as one-third of the people in the United States are dependent. In complex societies nearly two decades are required to train people to be "fully cooperating members of society," and in all societies approximately ten childhood years are spent in nearly total dependence on an adult. As we live longer and longer, a greater portion of our lives is led in a state of frail old age when, once again, we cannot be fully cooperating members of society.[19] Indeed, despite advanced medical care, serious disabling conditions strike as much as 10 percent of the U.S. population. Surely, one would think, such a fundamental feature of our lives would be included among the circumstances of justice.

At the same time, we have to recognize dependency in its subjective forms—that is, as it affects our needs and desires. We have the need and desire both to be cared for and to care (or have someone care for) those who are important to us. Having these desires satisfied and these needs met are part of any conception of the good (see Section 4 below). By contrast, not everyone's conception of the good will include doing what is necessary to take care of these needs and desires. A just distribution of the burdens and responsibilities attached to meeting these needs is required in the same way that adjudicating between differing conceptions of the good is required of a just form of social cooperation. Furthermore, the subjective conditions resulting from inevitable human dependencies, such as the fact of differing conceptions of the good, are at the heart of considerations that propel us into social and political associations.

2.2. The Absence of Dependency Considerations

From the "Dewey Lectures" onward, Rawls speaks only of the objective circumstance of moderate scarcity—that is, of the condition in which natural resources are neither so abundant that distributive problems do not arise nor so scarce that cooperative arrangements cannot be realized. With respect to the subjective circumstances of justice, Rawls speaks primarily of the condition that "persons and associations have contrary conceptions of the good as well as of how to realize them" (1980, 536).

But even under conditions of affluence, there are important questions to raise with respect to both the distribution of resources devoted to meeting dependency needs and the distribution of the burdens and responsibilities of dependency work. Distributive questions with respect to dependency needs are not traceable to circumstances of justice concerning moderate scarcity. Yet nowhere in Rawls's work is human dependency explicitly cited among the circumstances of justice.

In the earlier works, we can find allusions to dependency concerns in two passages. First, Rawls (1971, 127) includes the equal vulnerability of all to attack and to being hindered by the united force of the others in the more complete enumeration of objective circumstances. This vulnerability, however, should not be confused with the vulnerability of dependency. Rawls speaks of an *equal* vulnerability (consider, for example, our equal vulnerability to being attacked). Vulnerability originating in dependency is not a condition in which all are *equally* vulnerable but, rather, one in which some are *especially* vulnerable.[20] The unequal vulnerability of the dependent and, secondarily, of the dependent's caretaker is an inequality in starting positions that, if left unaddressed, will be injected into the political situation.

Second, and more promising, is a passage in which Rawls says it is "essential . . . that each person in the original position should care about the well-being of some of those in the next generation . . . [and that] for anyone in the next generation, there is someone who cares about him in the present generation" (1971, 129). These remarks are provoked by Rawls's worry that if the generations are mutually disinterested, then there is no impetus to prevent the depletion of resources for future generations. Thus Rawls is led to propose a "motivational assumption" that will generate a "just savings principle"(1971, 285). Specifically, he proposes that the parties to the OP represent generational lines and that they be heads of households, thereby securing the interests of subsequent generations.

Although Rawls speaks of each person in the OP caring about the welfare of some in the next generation, the concern is with a scarcity of resources across generations, not the care of dependents. Even as he talks about a member of each generation "caring about" one in the next, he urges us not to presuppose extensive ties of natural sentiment.[21]

2.3. Can Dependency Concerns Be Introduced Through the Device of Representation?

Rawls does not introduce representation by heads of households to solve problems arising from dependency; in *Political Liberalism*, in fact, he abandons the idea altogether. Might this device, nonetheless, be helpful in considering the circumstance of dependency, by having household heads represent the interests of dependents and familial caretakers?

In real politics, having one's own interests represented by someone who is differently situated is always a risky matter. Abigail Adams thought herself *represented* by her husband, but in the constitutional assembly, composed only of male heads of households, no one seemed to have heeded her call to "remember the Ladies."[22] But the OP posits a hypothetical representation: Why not just stipulate that those represented are represented faithfully?

The difficulty with such hypothetical representation in the Rawlsian framework was pointed to first by Jane English (1977) and later by Susan Okin. Using heads of households as representatives means that, although the family is one of the basic structures of society, justice cannot be said to pertain *within* it—a difficulty for gender equality among those who share a household.[23] If parties to the OP already have a determined social position relative to the family, they will not choose the principles of justice in ignorance of their social position. And in the framework of Rawlsian constructivism, only principles that we choose in ignorance of our social position will issue in fair principles with respect to the basic institutions. Since Rawls does want to say that the family is a basic institution, and since justice should then pertain to the family, the parties cannot be heads of households.

Okin's suggestion is that individuals, not heads of households, should be representatives. My question, then, is whether the parties representing individuals will represent the interests of both dependents and caretakers. If human dependency counts among the general facts to which representatives in the OP have epistemic access, they know that when the veil is lifted they may find themselves dependent or having to care for dependents. And if the representatives are individuals instead of household heads, they should be considering such contingencies in choosing their principles.

Although the theory allows an individual in the OP to imagine her- or himself to be a dependent or a dependency worker, the construction of the OP does not guarantee that the principles of justice chosen will reflect the concerns of either. Whereas the Rawlsian construct allows for the possibility that a representative *may* imagine her- or himself as a dependent or as having responsibility for a dependent's care, it does not necessitate that a representative *will* do so when choosing the principles for a well-ordered society. Indeed, dependents do not form an obvious constituency within the Rawlsian construct.[24] Surely, some persons, envisioning themselves as having dependency responsibilities, may choose to adopt other-directed interests as their own. But in this case, the representation of these dependents is a contingent matter and not one integral to the procedure of determining the principles of justice. (For a related discussion, see Subsection 6.2 below.)

If we insist, instead, that the parties represent generational lines,[25] we face still another predicament. If the rational choices of individual parties modeled in the OP (along with the other conditions stipulated of the OP) sufficed, there would be no need for any additional motivational assumptions, such as the one securing resources for future generations. The motivational assumption is necessary just because we may find too few in any one generation willing take responsibility for those in the next, if we must rely on individual voluntary decisions to ensure that everyone in a future generation will have someone who cares about his or her interest.[26] The choice not to take on such responsibility is neither irrational nor unreasonable, and it accords with our reflective judgments, as the social acceptance of remaining childless shows.[27] The mandating of such a responsibility could be seen as a serious constraint on individual conceptions of the good. The "just savings principle" stands in lieu of a mandate that each person in a society care about another in the next generation. But if the mandate itself is an undue constraint on each person's conception of the good, why is the substitute more acceptable, since it requires that we refrain from the enjoyment of at least some of our resources for the sake of a future generation whose well-being may play no role in our own conception of the good? Either Rawls's motivational assumption fails or it allows into his scheme principles that constitute an unpalatable constraint on each person's choice of the good.

Now, if the presumption that each party in the OP is a head of household—which still precludes supposing extensive ties of natural sentiment—and if this presumption is too strong to accommodate certain rational and reasonable conceptions of the good, then it surely cannot be helpful in addressing the needs of dependents whose care requires a commitment stronger still than the preservation of resources for the future. Therefore, we are confronted with the problem that however we conceive of the parties in the OP, as representatives of individuals or as representatives of households (or generational lines), the representation of dependents and those caring for dependents is not ensured by the construction of the OP. And this is so even if we include facts concerning dependency among those that parties in the OP would know while under the veil of ignorance.

2.4. Chronological Unfairness and Intergenerational Justice

Rawls (1992) revised his strategy to ensure the just savings principle. Acknowledging a proposal previously suggested by English (1977), he now maintains that "the parties can be required to agree to a savings principle subject to the further condition that they must want all *previous* generations to have followed it" (Rawls 1992, 274). Thus the motivational assumption that "constrains the parties from refusing to make any savings at all" remains (Rawls 1992, 274: note 12) and is captured by a form of reciprocity peculiar to the savings principle. Rawls had earlier noted:

> Normally this [reciprocity] principle applies when there is an exchange of advantages and each party gives something as a fair return to the other. But in the course of history no generation gives to the preceding generations, the benefits of whose saving it has received. In following the savings principle, each generation makes a contribution to later generations and receives from its predecessors. (1971, 290)

It is a natural fact that "[w]e can do something for posterity but it can do nothing for us" (Rawls 1971, 291). This fact involves "a kind of chronological unfairness since those who live later profit from the labor of their predecessors without paying the same price" (Alexander Herzen, cited in Rawls 1971, 291); being unalterable, however, this condition is itself not a question of justice but a consideration that we have to acknowledge in fashioning the just society.

Similarly, there are unalterable conditions proceeding from the facts of human development, disease, and decline. First, the dependent needs care and is not equal in situation or power to those who are relatively independent. Second, the dependency worker has a particular interest in the welfare of others, and her independence as a self-originator of desires and claims is constrained in a way not characteristic of the unemcumbered independent agent (see Subsection 5.1 below). What is not unalterable is the level of support extended to the dependent and the dependency worker. If we need a just savings principle (however formulated) to ensure that the well-being of future generations is not jeopardized, we need a similar principle to ensure that the well-being of dependents and their caretakers is not jeopardized, since the natural developmental process to which the first is addressed is mirrored within the life history of each individual as well—and if the first needs to be addressed by a theory of justice, so does the second.

The essential point is this: To capture these circumstances of justice in the OP, we need to provide additional motivational assumptions that constrain the parties from choosing principles that fail to address dependency concerns. If dependency concerns are among the circumstances of justice, then our conceptions of social goods and social cooperation need to be reexamined in light of the consequences of human dependency—that is, with attention to the ties between persons, and to the costs in human and material terms effected by human dependency.

3. The Public Conception of Social Cooperation

3.1. Dependency Concerns in Rawls's Conception of Social Cooperation

For Rawls, social cooperation is more than "simply . . . coordinated social activity efficiently organized and guided by publicly recognized rules to achieve some overall end" (1992, 300). Indeed, it also demands "fair terms of cooperation" among citizens—namely, terms that citizens can accept not only because they are *rational* (in that they satisfy each person's view of their rational advantage) but also because they are *reasonable* (in that they recognize and accept that not all people have the same ends when engaging in social interaction).

In another work (Kittay 1995a), I claim that the Rawlsian position should, but does not, include dependency concerns as part of an adequate conception of social cooperation.[28] Dependency concerns fall within the purview of a notion of social cooperation pertinent to political justice for at least three reasons: first, because they are rational and reasonable considerations in choosing a conception of justice; second, because a society that does not care for its dependents or that cares for them only by unfairly exploiting the labor of those who do the caring cannot be said to be well-ordered (see Subsection 3.3); and, third, because when we reorient our political insights to see the centrality of human relationships to our happiness and well-being, we recognize dependency needs as basic motivations for creating a social order. In short, the reorientation of our political insights focuses our attention on the justice of providing *both* for dependents—who, even in their neediness, contribute to the ongoing nature of human relationships—*and* for those who care for dependents—whose social contribution is obscured when we are looking only at the social cooperation between independent and fully functioning persons.

3.2. Fair Terms of Agreement and Reciprocity

One way to construe the arguments summarized here is to say that dependency concerns fall within political justice but outside of justice as fairness. Rawls, who notes that justice as fairness may not be entirely coincident with political justice, remarks, "How deep a fault this is must wait until the case itself can be examined" (1992, 21). He reminds us that political justice needs to be complemented by additional virtues (1992, 21). I suggest another possibility. We can reconceive fairness. By enlarging the concept of reciprocity, we return to some of the ideas expressed in Subsection 2.4, but now applied to relations in which not all are independent and fully functioning.

The reciprocity and mutuality articulated in fair terms of cooperation apply to "all who cooperate." Each, then, must "benefit, or share in common burdens, in some appropriate fashion judged by a suitable benchmark of comparison" (Rawls 1992, 300). Because the relations of dependents and dependency workers to one another and to the larger society do not fit standard models of reciprocity, it is difficult to include dependency concerns within a conception of justice as fairness. This conception implicitly excludes severely disabled, permanently dependent people, especially those who are mentally incapacitated, from social cooperation and therefore citizenship.[29] They can neither reciprocate the care they receive nor, in relevant senses, "restrict their liberty in ways necessary to yield advantages to all."[30] Temporarily dependent persons may be able to collect on benefits they had bestowed on others when they were fully functioning, or they may be able to defer reciprocation. But the opportunity to reciprocate may never come:

A child may not reach maturity; an ill person may die or become permanently incapacitated; a now needy and elderly parent may never have been an adequate provider or nurturer. How then is the caretaker's contribution to be reciprocated? Unless the needs of the caretaker are to be met through or by means of some other form of reciprocity, the only available moral characterization of the caretaker's function is that it constitutes exploitation or supererogation.

3.3. Doulia

The need, then, is to expand the notion of reciprocity and, in so doing, to open a conceptual space for dependency concerns within social cooperation in a just society. To fix our ideas, we consider the situation of the postpartum mother caring for her infant. The extreme neediness of the infant and the physiological trauma of having given birth create a special vulnerability for the mother. Some traditional cultures and religions mark this period of maternity: The mother is enjoined to care for her child while others attend to her needs and household and familial duties. Some assign a "doula," a postpartum caregiver who assists the mother and, at times, relieves her. Today, in the United States, where families are geographically dispersed and lack community support as well as adequate workers' leave policies, a fledgling effort is being made to adopt the idea of the doula. By contrast to the time-worn paid help known as the "baby nurse," who displaces the mother by taking over care of the infant, the doula assists by caring for the mother as the mother attends to the child.[31]

The word 'Doula' originally meant slave or servant in Greek. So it is rather intriguing to redirect the concept and signify instead a caretaker who cares for those who care for others. In place of the notion of a servant fulfilling the function of a doula, then, we need a concept of interdependence that recognizes a relation not so much of reciprocity as of nested dependencies, linking those who help and those who require help in order to give aid to those who cannot help themselves. Extending the notion of the service performed by the doula, let us use the term 'doulia' to refer to an arrangement by which service is passed on so that those who become needy by virtue of tending to those in need can be cared for as well.[32] Doulia is part of an ethic that is captured in the colloquial phrase "What goes around comes around."[33] If someone helps another in her need, someone in turn will help the helper when she is needy—regardless of whether the neediness derives from her position as caretaker or from circumstances that pertain to her health or age. We can state a principle of doulia: *Just as we have required care to survive and thrive, so we need to provide conditions that allow others—including those who do the work of caring—to receive the care they need to survive and thrive.*

Since society is an association that persists through generations, an extended notion of "reciprocity," a transitive (if you will) responsiveness to our dependence on others, is needed for justice between generations. As Rawls recognizes, the care we take to hand over a world that is not depleted is never reciprocated to us by those whom we benefit. Rather, the benefit we bestow on the next generation ought to be the benefit we would have wanted the previous generation to bestow on us. The resemblance between this extended notion of reciprocity and doulia is not accidental.[34] In both contexts, we deal with human development and with its "chronological unfairness." Moreover, just as the gains and savings from a previous generation pass from us to the next generation, the care a mother bestows on her child calls for reciprocation from the adult child not only back to the parents but also forward to a future generation.[35]

The doula, who serves as our paradigm, is engaged in private interactions. Rawls's concerns are limited to the public—to the basic structure of society. Although the paradigm concerns domestic interactions, I am arguing for an analogical extension of the idea of doulia to the public domain. The caretaker has a responsibility to care for the dependent, and the larger society seeks ways to attend to the well-being of the caretaker, thereby allowing the caretaker to fulfill responsibilities to the dependent without exploiting the labor and concern of the caretaker. This is a *public* conception of doulia. As human dependency is inevitably a circumstance of justice that marks our most profound attachments, and as care of a dependent morally obliges the dependency worker to give a certain priority to the welfare of her charge (see Subsection 5.2), a public conception of doulia is needed to accomplish the tripartite goal of treating the dependency worker equitably, providing care for dependents, and respecting the dependency relations in which fundamental human attachments grow and thrive.

"Although a well-ordered society is divided and pluralistic . . . the public agreement on questions of political and social justice supports ties of civic friendship and secures the bonds of association," writes Rawls (1980, 540). But as potent as the bonds of association created by public agreement may be, they are not as powerful as those created by caring relationships. The latter are bonds that tie individuals together into families, kin, and other intimate relations, bonds that allow individuals at different stages of life to withstand the forces that act upon them. Indeed, these intimate bonds make civic order and civic friendship possible (see Held 1987a). A political theory must therefore attend not only to the well-being of dependents *and* of their caretakers but also to the *relation* of caretaker and dependent upon which all other civic unions depend.[36] Without practices based on an implicit principle of care, human beings would either not survive or survive very poorly—and surely would not thrive.[37] Principles of right and traditional notions of justice depend upon a prior and more fundamental principle and practice of care. Roughly stated, such a principle holds that, in order to grow, flourish, and survive or endure illness, disability, and frailty, each individual requires caring relationship with significant others who hold that individual's well-being as a primary responsibility and a primary good.

In constructing a just social order, then, we need a theory that acknowledges the fact that humans are dependent for periods of their lives—rather than ignoring that fact through idealizations in which men (to use Hobbes's term) spring from the earth "like mushrooms," or ones in which citizens are fully functioning throughout a life span, or ones that merely presuppose that caring is done, somehow, by someone. Such theories and the societies they envision occlude any principle of care and the fundamental associations it would create. But for a society to attend to the need for care and do so justly, it is not sufficient for the dependency worker alone to be caring. Indeed, this objective requires the establishment of a social principle that provides the basis for social institutions that aid and support dependency workers in their caring responsibilities. But then such a principle, in turn, requires the broadened conception of reciprocity (and a suitably modified sense of fairness *within* each generation) expressed in the concept of doulia. Such a principle would be instantiated when the value of receiving care and giving care is publicly acknowledged; when the burdens and cost incurred by doing the work of caring for dependent do not fall to the dependency worker alone (even when that dependency work is freely assumed); and when the commitment to preserving caring *relations* is assumed by the society. Such a principle would mandate, first, a *social responsibility* (derived from political justice realized in social cooperation) for enabling dependency relations satisfactory to dependency worker and dependent alike; and, second, social institutions that foster an attitude of caring and a respect for care by enabling caretakers to do the job of caretaking without becoming disadvantaged in the competition for the benefits of social cooperation—a competition that now favors those situated as equal and independent persons unencumbered by dependency demands.

The Rawlsian (and the liberal) account of a well-ordered society as characterized by the narrower notions of justice and of right, then, is either incomplete or inadequate. And this is so not for the reason communitarians have stressed—namely, that, on the one hand, it purports more of a conception of the good life than it admits to, and that, on the other hand, it fails to provide enough of a guide to the good life to be fully satisfying. Rather, a society cannot be well-ordered—that is, it cannot sustain its members and provide them with a basis for self-respect (see Subsection 4.4)—if it fails to be a society in which care is publicly acknowledged as a good for which the society as a whole bears a responsibility to provide in a manner that is just to all.

Rawls, speaking of the need to give priority to the basic liberties, points out that even when the political will does not yet exist to do what is required (as it might not in a society that is less than well ordered), "part of the political task is to help fashion it" (1992, 297). Likewise, if the political will to imbue citizens with sensitivity and a sense of priority for care does not yet exist, it is "part of the political task . . . to help fashion it" (1992, 297).

4. The Two Powers of a Moral Person and the Index of Primary Goods

4.1. The Omission of Care as a Primary Good

Social cooperation, as Rawls understands it, is achievable among persons conceived as having certain moral capacities, a sense of justice, and a conception of their own good. Presupposing "various general facts about human wants and abilities, their characteristic phases and requirements of nurture, relations of social interdependence, and much else" (1992, 307), Rawls generates an index of *primary goods*, goods that presume the possession of the two moral powers and that serve as a basis for making comparative assessments of interpersonal well-being.

The list of primary goods has remained unaltered since *A Theory of Justice*:

1. The basic liberties (freedom of thought and liberty of conscience)
   . . . .
2. Freedom of movement and free choice of occupation against a background of diverse opportunities . . . as well as [the ability] to give effect to a decision to revise and change them. . . .
3. Powers and prerogatives of offices and positions of responsibility
   . . . .
4. Income and wealth. . . .
5. The social bases of self-respect. . . . (Rawls 1980, 526)[38]

Without questioning the merit of such a gauge as a measure for interpersonal well-being,[39] I want to ask: Does this list adequately address needs of dependents[40] and those who care for them?

The question presumes that the two moral powers Rawls attributes to citizens are the only ones relevant to persons as citizens. Indeed, the list of goods is supposed to have been motivated by a conception of moral persons as those possessing a sense of justice and the capacity to form and revise a rational life-plan. Assuming, then, that individuals in dependency relations count as citizens, assessing the adequacy of the list requires asking whether these moral powers suffice as the moral powers of citizens in a society that takes dependency needs seriously.

An ethic reflecting concern for dependents and those who care for them demands, first, a sense of attachment to others; second, an empathetic attention to their needs;[41] and, third, a responsiveness to the needs of another. Such an ethic goes well beyond duties traditionally assigned to justice, but in the context of caring relations they are not supererogatory. Fulfillment of these duties requires the cultivation of capacities that, although they are not required by justice as traditionally conceived, *are* required by a state which recognizes that taking dependency seriously is a requirement of justice.

Neither of Rawls's two moral powers requires such concern nor yields such an ethic. First, for some the good will include attachments of sentiment, leading them to cultivate capacities to care for others; still, this remains a private matter requiring no responsibility on the part of the society at large and no assurance that dependents can be cared for without extracting undue sacrifices from those upon whom the responsibilities fall. (See Subsections 2.3 and 6.2.) Second, unlike the ability to form and revise a conception of one's own good, a sense of justice is necessarily an other-directed moral power. Though one that involves reciprocity, it does not necessarily entail an empathetic attention to the needs of another who may be incapable of reciprocating. Thus, the moral capacities for care are never invoked in the moral capacity of justice as construed in Rawlsian constructivism.[42]

A construction adequate to meeting dependency needs justly would expand the list of moral powers and amend the list of primary goods.[43] The moral powers of the person should include not only (a) a sense of justice (construed in the more narrow sense that Rawls suggests) and (b) a capacity to pursue a conception of the good but also (c) a capacity to respond to vulnerability with care.[44] Neither (a) nor (b) addresses citizens who are vulnerable to the dependencies of age, illness, or disability, or who have to care for others in that state of dependency. Although justice and caring have often been seen as distinct, even opposing, virtues, the arguments put forward in this chapter press for a different view. In short, a justice that does not incorporate the need to respond to vulnerability with care is incomplete, and a social order that ignores care will itself fail to be just.

4.2. Care as a Primary Good Issuing from the Moral Power to Care

Rawls's list of primary goods neglects the goods that issue from a commitment to care: (a) the understanding that we will be cared for if we become dependent, (b) the support we require if we have to take on the work of caring for a dependent, and (c) the assurance that if we become dependent, someone will take on the job of caring for those who are dependent upon us. We can possess basic liberties, freedom of movement and choice of occupation, the powers and prerogatives of public office, even income and wealth, without the assurance that we will be cared for if we become dependent; that when we are called upon to do the work of caring for a dependent, we will be adequately supported in our undertaking; and that, as we focus our energies and attention on another, we do not thereby lose the ability to care for ourselves.

Must these concerns be reflected in a list of *primary goods*? That is, are they goods basic for any individual who is capable of fashioning a conception of the good for herself and needed whatever her life-plan happens to be? And, if this is so, are they also among those needs "relevant in questions of justice?"(Rawls 1982, 172).[45]

The answer to both queries is "yes." Regardless of how we fashion our conception of the good, we would want to be cared for when we are dependent and would want to be adequately supported if we find ourselves having to be responsible for the care of a dependent. Moreover, if, as I shall demonstrate in the next section, the failure to secure these conditions impairs the capability of those most vulnerable to dependency and dependency work to participate as equals in an otherwise well-ordered society,[46] then these conditions are indeed relevant to questions of justice. Therefore, the good *to be cared for in a responsive dependency relation if and when one is unable to care for oneself, as well as to meet dependency needs of others without incurring undue sacrifices oneself*, is a primary good in the Rawlsian sense because it is a good of citizens as they pursue their own conception of the good and exercise their moral faculties of justice and care.

Furthermore, like all the other primary goods, such a good has a bearing on the social bases of self-respect for the members of the well-ordered society. In this connection, consider Patricia Williams's (1991, 55) citation of the following passage from Marguerite Duras's *The Lover* (1985): "We're united in a fundamental shame at having to live. It's here we are at the heart of our common fate, the fate that [we] are our mother's children, the children of a candid creature murdered by society. We're on the side of society which has reduced her to despair. Because of what's been done to our mother, so amiable, so trusting, we hate life, we hate ourselves."

To the extent that we grow into a relatively safe and secure adulthood in consequence of care secured through the sacrifice of another, a sacrifice that can never be adequately restored, we carry with us a shame that diminishes self-respect. We are diminished in this way as long as we live in a society where care can be had only through such a sacrifice.

If women, through their maternal roles, have been sacrificial lambs, they have also been the ones who have recognized care as a primary good and have engaged in political struggle when their ability to care has been undermined. Indeed, as historian Temma Kaplan (1982, 1992) has documented, the political participation of women in diverse nations, cultures, and historical periods is tied to circumstances rendering women unable to give care to their families. Through their willingness to engage in political struggles to ensure their ability to care for their families, women, at least, have contended that being able to care for others is a primary social good. The political nature of these struggles is consistent with Rawls's conception of self-respect, which is contingent not only on the way the individual conducts herself privately but also on "the public features of basic social institutions" and "publicly expected (and normally honored) ways of conduct" (Kaplan 1992, 319).

5. Free Persons Are "Self-Originating Sources of Valid Claims"

Equal persons in a well-ordered society must also be regarded as free. In fact, our contemporary sensibility refuses to tolerate slavery, serfdom, or any similar bondage within a well-ordered society. Rawls contrasts the free citizen to the slave or bondsman. In the "Dewey Lectures" he depicts citizens in the well-ordered society as "self-*originating* sources of valid claims" (1980, 543; emphasis added), and in *Political Liberalism* he depicts them as "self-*authenticating* sources of valid claims" (1992, 33; emphasis added).[47] Rawls also contrasts claims originating from ourselves with those derived from our social role, wherein we act for others upon whose rights and powers our own depend. In the next two subsections, I will argue that being a "self-*authenticating* source of valid claims" is an inapt characterization of freedom for the dependency worker. But because it is an important feature of the freedom that Rawls attributes to the "free and equal citizen," parties to the OP who are modeled on free persons (in this sense) do not represent the dependency worker.

5.1. Is the Dependency Worker a Self-Originator of Claims?

What should we say of the mother and her claim to, say, the right to education—not for herself, but for her child? Is hers a self-originating claim, or is it a claim derived from prior duties or obligations owed to society or to other persons—that is, one derived from or assigned to her particular social role? The parent who presses the claim on behalf of the child also sees it—appropriately, I believe—as her own interest.[48] A caring and responsible parent is one whose self-respect is bound up with the care she attempts to provide and the opportunities she attempts to make available to her children. Therefore, the claims she makes on their behalf are reasonably experienced as self-originating claims, although they are claims made on behalf of another within the context of a social role.

The dependency worker whose relation to the charge is more distant, and so whose own well-being is less intimately tied to her charge, may nonetheless make claims on the other's behalf—claims that exceed the dependency worker's prescribed duties. When her claims (in contrast to the mother's) go beyond prescribed duties, the *specific* claims cannot be said to originate in her social role, even if, in general, her claims on behalf of her charge derive from her social role. Thus, *both* for the mother (who, in making claims for her child, remains within her socially defined role but experiences those claims as her own) *and* for the other dependency worker who does not so closely identify her good with that of her charge (yet whose claims on behalf of her charge will exceed her specified responsibility), freedom is as bound up with claims that originate from others (i.e., the cared-for) as with those that originate independently.[49]

It is important to stress here that a thick involvement of the dependency worker in the welfare of her charge is generally not, as so often portrayed, a neurotic, compensatory action on the part of an individual who has no hope of being a person in her own right. Because dependency work is frequently accomplished under oppressive conditions, it is easy to miss the fact that deep involvement is a normal and necessary part of good dependency work—whereas overinvolvement and self-abnegation may not constitute good care-taking. A feverish child who wakes in the middle of the night has a claim on her caretaker's attention, even if the caretaker is very tired or even ill.[50] Whether a dependency worker presses for a child's educational opportunities or ignores her own fatigue to care for the ill child, her actions are good car-ing—not, generally speaking, neurotic overidentification or self-abnegating self-sacrifice. Caring about the welfare of persons for whom we are responsi-ble and care for is entailed in normal and *effective* caring. In fact, the failure of much institutionalized caretaking is traceable to the difficulty of evoking this thick involvement on the part of the caretakers—who, so often, *don't care*.

The dependency worker cannot be said to be a self-originating source of claims, at least not in the terms suggested in the "Dewey Lectures." Any re-tort that it is only the dependency worker, *qua* dependency worker, who fails to be a self-originating source of claims (since these claims issue from her as she fills a particular social role) fails to recognize an important differ-ence between dependency work and most other forms of labor. Because of the moral demands of the work (see Subsection 4.2), dependency worker's moral self cannot easily be peeled from her social role.[51] Therefore, freedom that demands a view of oneself as a self-originator of valid claims is not a freedom applicable to the situation of the dependency worker.

Of course, Rawls's theory is normative, not descriptive. Slaves, for exam-ple, would not count among the free individuals who have an equal claim to the fruits of social cooperation, since they, too, are not self-originating sources of valid claims. But in a well-ordered society all should be treated as free and equal, and so slavery would be impermissible. We cannot similarly interdict dependency work, nor would we want to.[52] If, as Rawls writes, the members of a well-ordered society are to "view their common polity as ex-tending backward and forward in time over generations" (1980, 536), and given that the course of human development inevitably requires that some care for dependents, we cannot tell the dependency worker to abandon her concern for the well-being of her charge, even though this concern renders her freedom—construed as the self-origination of valid claims—an empty abstraction.

The etymology of doulia as slavery is instructive here. Whereas slavery is a morally impermissible form of service, dependency work is an inescapable one. Whereas slavery, under even the most favorable conditions, is demeaning and dehumanizing, dependency work, under the right conditions, reaches into the core of our humanity. And whereas slavery is the most debased of human relations, dependency work forms the most fundamental of social relations. Nonetheless, the restraint on freedom that dependency work shares with slavery has tainted this form of labor—especially now, at a time when freedom as the self-origination of valid claims is so highly prized. Only by naturalizing dependency work (consider, for example, the assumption that women are *naturally* better with children, the sick, the elderly) have ideologues made its constraints on freedom palatable to a modern sensibility.[53] Indeed, as a result of the naturalization of this labor, the coercion required for the *modern* woman to engage in dependency work has been overlaid with sentimentality (see Badinger 1980). This is not to say that dependency work cannot be intensely rewarding. Not only *can* it be, but, under favorable conditions, it *is*. When we highlight this sense of freedom, however, we are less likely to see dependency work as the vital, fulfilling, humanizing work it is.

5.2. Is the Dependency Worker a Self-Authenticator of Claims?

The criticism launched here is against an individualistic view of citizens and their representatives in the OP. And the formulation in the "Dewey Lectures" may be most susceptible to such a reading.[54] Earlier, Rawls had explicitly warned against construing the self-interestedness of the participants of the OP as reflecting interest only in their selfish pursuits: "There is no inconsistency, then, in supposing that once the veil of ignorance is removed, the parties find that they have ties of sentiment and affection, and want to advance the interests of others and to see their ends attained" (1971, 129). Thus the parties in the OP may represent the wants and interests of others (and when the parties are heads of families they presumably do), and self-originating claims need not be self-interested. For example, if I want whatever *J* wants, then although the content of my wants is determined not by me but by *J*, the claim is self-originating if *my* want is to want what *J* wants. This is a noncoerced, other-linked, second-order wanting. One who voices such a want is less like the slave, and more like the churches, voluntary agencies, and so on, that press claims on behalf of others.[55]

This wanting can be assumed in a variety of ways, not all of which have the same moral standing or the same moral consequences. We need to distinguish between two kinds of relations based on noncoerced, other-linked wanting. In the first instance, if we exit we do so without jeopardizing the vital interests of those in the relationship. In the second, we do not have such an exit option. Labor regulations prohibiting certain workers from striking because others are vitally dependent upon them recognize this distinction.

The dependency worker—especially one who is unpaid and whose responsibilities are familial—rarely has a morally acceptable option of exiting from her relation to the dependent. Even when she no longer wants to want what her charge wants, she feels morally obliged to continue assuming the other's interests. At best, the daily hour-to-hour responsibilities can be given over to a paid dependency worker. But this substitute's obligation is as morally (even legally) compelling as that of the original dependency worker until the substitute is herself relieved. For example, in group homes for the retarded, as in many other facilities that provide twenty-four-hour care, workers are mandated to work overtime if their replacements fail to show up, and they must remain on duty until they are relieved. Clearly, the interests of a paid dependency worker in such a situation *must* be subservient to those of her charges, whether or not she wants them to be.

Well, one can respond, to some extent all workers must subordinate their own wants in a work situation. Yet they would ordinarily be held to that obligation only for a contracted period of time or amount of work. For the dependency worker, however, mandated overtime, unlike the hours for which she contracted, is work-time controlled—both legally and morally—by the needs of a dependent. The dependency worker does not have the option to leave because she has a better-paying job awaiting her after-hours, or because she doesn't need the extra pay, or because she just doesn't want to work anymore. Although the dependency worker either need not or does not distinguish between self-interested preferences and non-self-interested preferences, when there is a conflict she may be so situated that the moral, and sometimes legal, obligation falls upon her to favor the latter.[56]

Perhaps the disparity between the demands of dependency work and the status of the individual as a self-originator of valid claims is not irreconcilable. In Rawls's (1971) portrayal of the party in the OP as the head of a generational line, that party—like the dependency worker—would, in a less-than-voluntary-yet-not-coerced manner, assume the responsibility of representing the claims of third parties and be morally compelled to protect the interests of the members of the household under the same constraints-of-exit options as the dependency worker. And the representatives of generational lines or heads of households would similarly be morally obliged to balance their self-interest against the interests of those they represent, and may even have to prefer the interests of third parties over and above their own. The Rawlsian would thus remind us that only the mutual disinterestedness of the parties—not the mutual disinterestedness between the individuals of the society—is important for the OP.

Although Rawls has dropped the notion of generational lines, he has replaced the idea of parties being self-originators of valid claims, as used in the "Dewey Lectures," with the idea that parties are "self-authenticating" sources of valid claims. The revision seems to address some communitarian and feminist objections to a metaphysical conception of a person that is highly individualist—a problem aggravated when we relinquish the idea of parties as representing generational lines or heads of households. By shifting to the "self-authenticating" formulation, Rawls allows himself to state: "Claims that citizens regard as founded on duties and obligations based on their conception of the good and the moral doctrine they affirm in their own life are also, for our purposes here, to be counted as self-authenticating" (1992, 32).

This new formulation opens a space for an expanded notion of "self"-interest, compatible with the interest of the dependency worker. The mother who insists on a child's right to an education may not be acting on a self-originating claim, but she surely is acting on a self-authenticating one. The particular claims she makes as a dependency worker may be self-authenticating in this sense. But the solution is only partial, for it returns us to the vagaries of the relatively arbitrary choices that individuals make about their work and their conception of the good, and to the uncertainty of whether or not their representatives in the OP will choose principles that will take care of dependency needs in a just and equitable fashion, as judged by our considered reflections (see Subsection 2.3 above). Indeed, without the assurance that dependency concerns will be handled equitably, we still have to question the self-authenticating nature of the choice to be a dependency worker.

If dependency work were well paid, had a high status, or received some other social recognition, we could conclude that the constraint of freedom and its other demands explain the sufficient supply of dependency workers. The disparity, however, between the rewards offered in the labor market and the vital interest to have good dependency care makes it clear that market forces have not been relied upon to supply adequate dependency work. Indeed, a clear-eyed look at the nearly universal twin features of female caregiving and female subordination reveals (a) that a certain class of persons has been subjected to and socialized to develop the character traits and the volitional structure needed for dependency work;[57] (b) that certain sexual behaviors commensurate with forming attachments, being submissive to another's will, and so forth, have been made compulsory for women (see Rich 1978); and (c) that poor women and women of color have been forced into paid employment as dependency workers by the scanty financial resources and limited employment opportunities available to them, and middle-class women have been forced out of paid employment not commensurate with their (largely unpaid) duties as dependency workers. It has not merely "happened" that women have consistently "chosen" to make dependency relations and dependency work central to their vision of the good life, whereas men have chosen a wider variety of options.[58] Because care of dependents is nonoptional in any society, some societal measures are inescapably taken to meet the inevitable need for care. If the means by which a society distributes responsibility for dependency work is not guided by principles of justice, then coercive measures—often in the guise of tradition and custom, sometimes in the guise of merely apparent voluntary life choices—are the predictable response.

The contention that dependency work is freely chosen and results in self-authenticating, if not self-originating, claims pushes the problem of distributing dependency work back into the realm of the private—into private choice and so outside the purview of public demands of justice. The consequence is that many claims are presumed to be "self-authenticated" when they are really heteronomous. The dependency worker who fits this description will be no more a self-authenticated source of valid claims than a self-originating source of such claims.[59]

The self-origination of claims may be an inapt characterization of the dependency worker's freedom in any society; but a "well-ordered society" that is not yet a society in which the principles of care and doulia are operative is also not one in which dependency workers can be said to be self-authenticating sources of valid claims. The dependency worker would not yet be among the free citizens of such a putatively well-ordered state. If only those who are equals and free in the Rawlsian sense are eligible to participate in social cooperation, then dependency workers cannot be included among the "free" individuals who have an equal claim to the fruits of social cooperation.

6. The Idealization That "All Citizens Are Fully Cooperating Members of Society"

6.1. Fully Cooperating Throughout a Life— The Strong Interpretation

Representing the equality of citizens in a well-ordered society, claims Rawls, requires the idealization that "all are capable of honoring the principles of justice and of being full participants in social cooperation *throughout* their lives" (1980, 546; emphasis added). Rawls presumes this to be an innocent idealization, thereby greasing the wheels of the theoretical apparatus that allows us to pass over the few difficult cases—for example, persons with "unusual and costly medical requirements." He justifies his exclusion of "hard" cases" such as disabilities and special health needs by claiming that they are "morally irrelevant" and can "distract our moral perception by leading us to think of people distant from us whose fate arouses pity and anxiety" (Rawls 1975a, 96).

But this idealization is seriously misleading. Amartya Sen remarks that leaving out disabilities, special health needs, or physical or mental defects, "for fear of making a mistake, may guarantee that the *opposite* mistake will be made" (1987, 157).[60] The opposite mistake, I contend, is to put too much distance between the "normal functioning individual" and the person with special needs and disabilities. Not a single citizen approaches the ideal of full functioning *throughout* a lifetime. The idealization, in contrast, suggests that those who are not fully functioning are relatively few, and that the consequences of special needs are brokered only in monetary terms.

Perhaps by pressing the phrase "*throughout* their lives" I have interpreted Rawls too strongly, inasmuch as this phrase suggests that full functioning at *every point* in a complete life is the requirement for equal citizenship. Rawls also uses the phrase "over the course of a complete life" (which survives the revision of the "Dewey Lectures" in *Political Liberalism*). A weaker requirement is to be a fully cooperating member of society at just those points when it would be reasonable to expect an individual to be fully functioning. The fact, for example, that one-third of the population is dependent at any given time doesn't necessarily imply that those within that one-third are not "equal," since they may well be equal *over* the course of a complete life.[61] Even though individuals who are underage, or disabled, are equal citizens only *in potentia*, their representatives in the OP are modeled as rational, symmetrically situated, fully functioning parties, with equal powers.

6.2. Fully Cooperating over a Lifetime— The Weak Interpretation

If we accept the weaker reading of the idealization of full functioning, then parties all come to the "bargaining table" of the OP with a knowledge that they are dependent at some time in their lives (and may have to take on dependency responsibilities), even though as rational autonomous representatives (Rawls 1992, 316), they come to the bargaining table of the OP in full possession of their power. Since those whom the parties represent are dependent *in potentia* (and possibly dependency workers *in potentia*), it seems as if the situation of the dependent (at least) should be robustly represented in the party to the OP. Behind the veil of ignorance we do not know if we are dependent or independent, dependency workers or unencumbered persons. It should be the case that either the nature of the representative or the construction of the situation in which the representative deliberates will allow the interests of the dependent and the dependency worker to be taken into account in choosing the principles of justice. Indeed, as I argued in Subsection 2.3, although nothing in the construction of the OP prevents a representative in the hypothetical situation of the OP from thinking about her- or himself as a dependent or a dependency worker, nothing ensures it either, so these concerns will not necessarily be represented. Since only the least well-off is guaranteed representation, I will argue in Subsection 7.1 that assimilating either dependent or dependency worker to the position of the least well-off is warranted neither by Rawls's theory nor by our considered reflections.

However, *if* dependency is recognized as one of the circumstances of justice, then the dependent, at least, *is* represented—as a fully functioning citizen in a period of dependency, such as early childhood. If I imagine myself as a party to the original position, I consider that I will have such periods of dependency and will want to choose my principles of justice in such a way that, while I am in this state, my interests are protected. Since I will also think that, in all likelihood, I will not always be dependent, I will want to choose principles capable of generating policies that balance my concerns during periods of dependency with those during periods of full functioning. In this way, the weak interpretation does allow for the concerns of the dependent to be included.

However, as long as nothing in the construction of the OP ensures that any parties to the OP will imagine that their own conception of the good, or their own rational self-interest, necessitates that they be the ones who will meet the needs of the dependent, the problem of representing the dependency worker has not yet been solved. If we think of citizens as fully functioning and ignore periods of dependency, there is no internal incoherence in a theory that does not ensure that parties to the OP represent dependency workers, since the theory simply is not concerned with such needs nor with the justice or injustice of how these needs come to be met. But because such a theory has completely neglected dependency concerns, it is not true to the realities of human life that move us to seek social alliances. Once we stop ignoring dependency, we are obliged to think of how dependency needs are met in a manner that is equitable to all.

Yet as a representative in the OP who knows that we all have periods of dependency, I *do* consider that I may choose (or may be called upon to take on) dependency work. What kind of bargaining position would I need, then, with respect to the other parties? I would be situated symmetrically to the other parties only if they too envision the possibility of becoming dependency workers themselves. They may do so; but because nothing in the moral psychology that Rawls sketches for us ensures that they will,[62] they may not.

Why is being situated symmetrically to the other parties a problem for the representative of the dependency worker? The reason is that, if I am a dependency worker, I cannot think only about my own interests but must also consider those of the dependent (see Section 5). The egalitarian benchmark that constrains the OP is that each participant counts for one when choosing the principles of justice. The idealization of citizens as fully functioning over the course of their lives is needed for this modeling of the parties because only then are we *able* to think of each citizen as counting for one in the distribution of both the benefits and the burdens of social cooperation. All representatives of such citizens in the OP go to the bargaining table knowing that, whatever position they hold in society, whether successful at a lucrative profession or employed as street sweepers, they have an equal voice in the choice of the fundamental principles governing the basic structure because they are each fully capable of participating according to the terms of fair social cooperation.

Reflect on what happens during those periods when we are not fully functioning and are dependent. The question of whether we are (temporarily) too disabled or too young to cooperate fully in benefits and burdens is morally irrelevant. Those so incapacitated still must have rights. But these rights would thus be in need of protection by others whose powers are intact. The dependent, however, cannot assume the burdens and responsibilities of social cooperation while in a state of dependency, even though as a citizen she or he should be able to enjoy the benefits of social cooperation. A dependent can define the terms of political participation *only* to the extent that she can speak on her own behalf, can be heard as an independent voice (neither is generally true of "underage" individuals), and can act on her own behalf (an option that is circumscribed by virtue of the dependency). For the rest, she must depend on those responsible for her well-being. Another must hold the rights of the dependent in trust,[63] just as another must take on the care for the physical well-being of the dependent. In this connection, recall Section 5, where I argue that the dependent's neediness not only poses burdens of maintaining the dependent but also compromises the dependency worker's status as a "self-originating source of claims."

If we all took turns being dependent and dependency workers, we would repay the debt, incurred during periods of dependency, of benefits-received-without-burdens-assumed. But there is no reason to suppose such a state of affairs exists—that is not what is implied in the norm of all citizens being fully functioning over the course of a life. Therefore, the burdens and responsibilities of the dependent, which are assumed by the dependency worker, make the interests of the dependency worker importantly different from those of the unencumbered and fully functioning citizen. In the economy of social cooperation, the dependency worker assumes the burdens and responsibilities of more than one, and the dependent those of less than one, whereas the independent, full-functioning citizen counts for one. In terms of benefits, however, the dependent, like the full-functioning citizen, counts as one. In contrast, if the dependency worker must also secure rights and benefits for her charge, even at the expense of her own rights and benefits, her own welfare comes to count for *less* than one.

If parties representing citizens who take on dependency work can be said to do so simply as one among many possible conceptions of the good, then they should accept the disadvantage along with the advantage of that individual's autonomous choice, as must all citizens who form a conception of the good. But taking on dependency work is not one choice of the good life among others. For (a) if none made such a choice, society could not continue beyond a single generation (see Subsection 2.1), so this conception of the good would be one that occupies a special place with respect to the welfare of society. And (b) when one takes on dependency responsibilities, one becomes poorly situated in a system of social cooperation in which each counts as one (see Subsection 3.1).

Unless some device acknowledges the fact that some citizens will be disadvantaged even as they provide the labor needed to care for and reproduce other citizens, and provides a mechanism for equalizing the prospects of all, situating their representatives symmetrically to those of unencumbered citizens cannot do the job of fairly representing all. The veil of ignorance won't suffice as such a device, because it gets us only the reasonableness needed for social cooperation when all the rational agents represent free and equal citizens—but we must remember, first, that dependency workers are not free in the requisite sense and, second, that the social cooperation in which dependents and dependency workers engage is not social cooperation among equals. That is why, at the very least, we need a motivational assumption akin to the just savings principle (see Subsection 2.4), but one that recognizes the role of dependency and care in the lives of each of us.

The symmetries that allow the rational party to simulate the commitments of a rational and reasonable person do not hold for conditions pertinent to the dependency relation; moreover, they arise even on the weaker interpretation of the norm of full functioning. So whether we say that we are fully cooperating members of society throughout our lives, or over the course of our lives, the idealization is questionable at best, pernicious at worst. Its virtue springs from the Kantian position that autonomy is that feature of human existence which gives us our dignity. But it fosters a fiction that the incapacity to function as a fully cooperating societal member is an exception in human life, not a normal variation; and that the dependency is a phase normally too brief and episodic to concern political life, rather than a periodic, and often prolonged, phase of our lives whose costs and burdens ought to be justly shared.

Autonomy in the sense of self-governance is surely of special importance. But this Kantian consideration must find its way into a more adequate representation of persons, one capable of acknowledging dependency as an obligatory limitation to self-governance. Neither the condition of the self-governing adult (the liberal Kantian model) nor the condition of a minor (the secular and religious authoritarian model) ought to serve as the "normal" condition of persons when choosing the design of a social order. I am proposing instead that the full range of human functioning[64] is the "normal" condition. Otherwise, representing dependents and their caretakers within the OP and within the well-ordered society becomes *a problem;* and the demands on those who care for them, a personal issue standing outside considerations of equality and justice.

The adoption of the norm that all are fully cooperating members over the course of a lifetime makes plausible the modeling of citizens in the well-ordered society as parties in the OP who are symmetrically situated. But between the idealization (of equal situation and equal powers) and the reality (of asymmetries of situation and inequalities of capability) lies the danger that dependents and dependency caretakers will fall into a worst-off position. The procedure of construction modeled by the OP "shows how the principles of justice follow from the principles of practical reason in union with conceptions of society and person" (Rawls 1992, 90). Although Rawls believes that the conception of the person he employs is itself an idea of practical reason (1992, 90), it is an idea inadequate to the fact of humans vulnerable to dependency. To model the representative party on a norm of a fully functioning person, then, is to skew the choice of principles in favor of those who can function independently and who are not responsible for assuming the care of those who cannot.

7. Conclusion: The Principles of Justice and Dependency Concerns

Sections 2 through 6 have shown that Rawls's model-conceptions omit dependency concerns and, hence, are inadequate for a truly egalitarian theory of justice. Can we now conclude that the presumably egalitarian suppositions do not yield sufficiently egalitarian outcomes? Ultimately, a definite answer rests on the capacity of the chosen principles to accommodate dependency concerns. The principles of justice chosen by the parties to the OP are selected from a "short list" of principles drawn from traditional Western political thought—none of which consider the justice of dependency arrangements for dependency worker and dependent alike. Therefore, no principle on the short list is more likely than any other to accommodate such concerns. For example, some of the argument in Subsection 6.2 not only runs counter to contractarian assumptions but also points to a difficulty with at least one form of utilitarianism: preference-satisfaction utilitarianism. Do the preferences of a mother for the goods pertaining to the well-being of a child count as the preferences of one individual, the concerned mother, or of two, mother and child? If they count for one only, then how are we to tally the preferences of the child? If they count for two, we violate the egalitarian principle that each counts for just one. Few, if any, political theories have focused on the consequences of dependency and dependency work, because few, if any, have seriously concerned themselves with the lives led by those persons (e.g., women) who have had to deal with inevitable dependencies.

Now that these concerns have been raised, however, we can use the notion of reflective equilibrium to "test" the adequacy of the principles that emerge. If those principles yield an egalitarian outcome for dependents and dependency workers, the arguments in Subsections 2 through 6 could be rendered superfluous. The first principle, the principle of equal liberties, is irrelevant to our concerns, although dependency concerns introduce a worry that those who do dependency work will not be guaranteed the fair value of the political liberties. But I shall not take up this matter here. I proceed to demonstrate that the second principle, the difference principle, fails in the relevant respects.

7.1. Dependents and Dependency Workers as the Least Well-Off

The latest formulation of the difference principle states, "Social and economic inequalities are to satisfy two conditions: first, they are to be attached to positions and offices open to all under conditions of fair equality of opportunity; and second, they are to be to the greatest benefit of the least advantaged members of the society" (Rawls 1992, 6).

Dependency work, when done for pay, is poorly paid. Furthermore, it is largely gender-determined. If the second principle is to ensure a fair distribution of goods to those in dependency relations, it must be interpreted in such a way that (a) the group that is least advantaged includes paid dependency workers and that (b) fair equality of opportunity precludes all forms of sex discrimination that restrict women to poorly paid or unpaid work. If fair equality of opportunity is realized, then the question is: Will distributive policies favoring the least well-off ensure adequate fulfillment of the needs of dependents and caretakers?

I do not believe they will. Fair equality of opportunity would mean that a woman who chooses dependency work as paid labor, even when the work is poorly paid, makes her choice unconstrained by gender discrimination. And if that choice puts her among the ranks of the least advantaged, she would know that justice required distributive policies that would not favor any other group unless they ameliorated her condition—an outcome that would doubtless be an improvement over today's situation.

But would such an outcome be good enough? Paying workers so poorly that this indispensable contribution to the well-being and sociality of any society places the paid dependency worker in the least-favored situation seems not to cohere with our reflective judgments of what is fair. The least-favored situation, we would think, is the condition inhabited by those so poorly endowed that they simply cannot take advantage of fair equality of opportunity to better their condition. Moreover, is it reasonable to expect the dependency worker to continue to be sufficiently motivated to give the *caring* care critical to good dependency work, all the while assuming the status of the least well-off, when truly fair equality of opportunity is in the offing? Normally, some degree of coercion is present when dependency labor is had "on the cheap."

Perhaps, then, market forces will push up the monetary value of dependency work: If we want good day care for our children, then we will have to pay good money for it—and both children and their caretakers will be well situated. So it may seem if we look only at paid dependency work. But much dependency work has been done as unpaid labor, and because such work involves affective bonds and is infused with social meaning, it is likely to remain so. Due to the importance of these bonds to the quality of care—*who* does the caring is frequently as important as the care itself—the dependency worker is nonfungible. (Though especially true of dependency workers who are familial and unpaid, this conclusion also applies to paid dependency workers.) I would venture to say that, as long as dependency work continues to be unpaid and filled with social and affective significance, even fair equality of opportunity for all is unlikely to alter wages significantly because the value of such work will not be assessed in market terms. Under the best scenario, assimilating the dependency worker to the level of the least well-paid worker will make the dependency worker better off than she is now. But this solution does not reach into the situation of the unpaid dependency worker, nor does it touch the individual whose dependency caregiving is a major responsibility along with waged work. The nonfungible nature of much dependency work not only vitiates much of the *freedom* assumed to be available to the caretaker under equality of opportunity; indeed, it also constrains her, by ties of affection and sentiments of duty to her charge.[65]

7.2. The Dependency Relation as a Social Position

A less Rawlsian option would be to count the position of the dependency worker, along with that of the citizen and the least advantaged, as a distinct social position (see Rawls 1971, 95ff.) Although Rawls does not encourage us to multiply social positions, this strategy would ensure that no advantage in the distribution of goods could accrue to those better off than the dependency worker unless the inequality benefited the dependency worker. However, given Rawls's two moral powers and his list of primary goods, there is no basis within his theory upon which to construct such a new social position. To create a special social position for the dependency worker would seem arbitrarily to favor one form of socially useful labor over others—a form of labor, moreover, that a person would choose because it somehow fits with his own conception of the good life.

If, however, we add to the other moral powers the capacity to give care, and if we include goods related to our interdependence in states of vulnerability in the index of primary goods, we can make a case for adding the dependency worker and the dependent to the short list of social positions from which to consider issues of fairness and just distributions. For example, we can make a case for a paid employee who is in a dependency relation, and so has dependency responsibilities, to receive additional pay, benefits, time off, or services, which would enable her to support the dependency relation in a manner suitable to the situation. She could then opt to pay another *adequately* to do all or some of the dependency work or do the dependency work herself by virtue of the freed-up time and added support. This outcome would be seen not as a privilege but, rather, as what is properly due citizens of a just and caring society—enabling us each to be cared for without extracting an undue burden from those charged with our care. But if being cared for by one upon whom you depend and being able to give care to one who depends on you are not seen as primary goods, then there would be no reason for principles of justice to be chosen that would facilitate such policymaking. Inasmuch as the difference principle is based on a list of primary goods blind to dependency, it fails to accomplish this task.[66]

7.3. A Third Principle of Justice?

The social position of the citizen gives rise to the first principle of justice. The social position of the least advantaged gives rise to the difference principle with fair equality of opportunity. If we were to amend the theory of justice as fairness to include the social position of the participants in a dependency relation, it would most likely give rise to a third principle of justice, one based not on our equal vulnerability or on our having some minimal powers of rationality, a sense of justice, and a vision of our own good, but, rather, on our unequal vulnerability in dependency, on the moral power to respond to others in need, and on the primacy of human relations to happiness and well-being. The principle of the social responsibility for care would read something like this: *To each according to his or her need for care, from each according to his or her capacity for care, and such support from social institutions as to make available resources and opportunities to those providing care, so that all will be adequately attended in relations that are sustaining.*

I see no natural way of converting such a principle to either of Rawls's two principles of justice. Therefore, it remains the claim of this chapter that the theory of justice as fairness, relying as it does on the suppositions outlined and contested above, falls short of meeting dependency concerns and so fails to sustain the egalitarian vision that purports to inform it.

Once we understand that we cannot neglect the circumstance of human dependency within the sphere of the political, that it is a fact that pervades social structures, that it extends throughout our lives, and that it connects us with one another and spans the generations, the significance of care and the centrality of those who give care recast and refocus the political considerations of equality and of freedom as well as the moral understanding of the person and the nature of moral and political obligation and responsibility.[67]

Notes

1. See, for example, Rawls (1992, xxviii–xxix) for the characterization of his project. Rawls acknowledges that a conception of justice "so arrived at may prove defective" (1992, xxix). My claim is that it is defective because it is so arrived at.

2. I am not assuming that any features of human life are untouched by social factors, nor that these social factors can be neatly bracketed. Nonetheless, development, decline, and disease are inescapable conditions for natural beings, and these set the parameters for the dependency that is equally inescapable.

3. In one sense, the inability to reciprocate is a function of dependency only in the context of certain socially based distribution policies. Such policies also make those who are or become dependent especially vulnerable to impoverishment and, hence, unable to reciprocate benefits they have received. In an other sense, however, during the time people are very ill or very young, they are at the mercy of others to dispense whatever resources those people have. In *this* sense, the infant heir and the beggar's child both require a third-party intervention to repay their caretakers. I focus on the second sense inasmuch as I am looking at dependency through dual lenses, that of the dependent and that of the dependency worker. In this connection, it may be helpful to see the difficulties raised by dependency in terms of capability rather than resources (see Sen 1992). Thus, although the child of the poor and the child of the wealthy have differing resources, by virtue of their dependency their inability to convert those resources into functionings and capabilities is more similar than their resources are different.

4. The person who intervenes may or may not be the same person who provides hands-on care. But the person who provides hands-on care is virtually always in a position of having to interpret the needs and desires of her charge. This person is not always, however, the one empowered to translate those needs into socially understood interests.

5. The terms 'inevitable dependency' and 'derived dependency' were independently arrived at by Martha Albertson Fineman (1995) and myself (Kittay 1991)

6. Henceforth, all references to a "dependent" will be to the primary dependent.

7. Rawls says that equality operates on three levels: (a) the administrative and procedural (i.e., the impartial and consistent application of rules, constituted by the precept to treat likes alike); (b) "the substantive structure of institutions" (Rawls 1971, 505), requiring that all persons be assigned equal basic rights; and (c) the situation of the original position addressing the basis of equality, those "features of human beings in virtue of which they are to be treated in accordance with the principles of justice"

(Rawls 1971, 504). At the first of these levels there are inequalities for dependency workers and dependents that could be defended. One can argue, for example, that persons unable to fill a job because of a disability, or because they have dependency responsibilities, cannot be eligible for equal opportunity considerations. We can justify some inequalities at the second level as well. Minors do not have the right to vote. And severely retarded individuals cannot be assigned rights and freedoms requiring higher mental abilities. Rights, after all, can be granted only to those capable of understanding and acting on them. Responsibilities of dependency work, in contrast, should not affect the equal assignment of basic rights. (Note that, formerly, women's responsibilities as dependency workers were deemed sufficient to exclude them from many economic and political rights. If we count pregnancy as "dependency work"—insofar as it involves the care and nurture of a completely dependent being—then, as shown by the abortion debate, along with controversies concerning surrogate mothering, suitable work environments of pregnant women, and the prosecution of pregnant women abusing drugs, the assignment of equal basic rights to these dependency workers is still not a resolved issue.) Accordingly, the objective of this chapter is to show that even though we can grant that some inequalities are justified, there is a more fundamental problem for the achievement of full moral equality at the third, and most fundamental, level.

8. See Okin (1979) for a deft interpretation of canonical texts. See also Pateman (1989) and Benhabib (1987) for further discussion of this issue.

9. A number of feminist theorists have regarded the work of Rawls and other liberal philosophers with an eye toward issues of dependency, but without articulating the dependency critique. Overall, there are too many feminist criticisms of liberal political philosophy to list in a single chapter such as this one; suffice to say that some of them are more closely tied to dependency than others. These writers have spoken of "the need for more than justice," as Annette Baier entitles one work (1987) expounding this theme. Baier expands on this theme in a number of other works as well (1985, 1986, 1987, 1994). Other writers—for example, Minow (1990), Pateman (1989), and Held (1978, 1987a, 1987b)—have shed light on the unacknowledged gender considerations that undergird legal theory and a social contract engaged in by men. In this connection, also see the essays in Phillips (1987). Fineman (1991, 1995) comes very close to articulating the dependency critique as I conceive it. And Susan Okin (1979, 1989a, 1989b) brings both the historical and the contemporary neglect of women's involvement in dependency to the forefront of her political considerations. I owe much to her systematic analysis and feminist, but sympathetic, critique of Rawls. My examination of Rawls is deeply indebted to these writers and others too numerous to mention, and intends to carry these discussions further.

10. I take this framework to be a central thrust of the dependency critique, an issue that I discuss further in Kittay (1995b). The objective underlying my adoption of the dependency critique is precisely to understand how a more equitable arrangement of dependency can be established not only between men and women but among women themselves. As bell hooks (1987) asks: "Since men are not equals in white supremacist, capitalist, patriarchal class structure, which men do women want to be equal to?" The point captured by bell hooks and stressed by a number of feminists is that the striving for equality on the part of the largely white and middle-class women's movement presumes an egalitarianism into which women can integrate themselves.

The force of this critique emerges with special poignancy when one looks at the complexion of dependency workers in countries blighted by racial and social inequities. The figures concerning, for example, the employment of immigrant women tell much of the story. Consider the findings reported by the National Council for Research on Women: "The International Labor Office estimates that more than 350,000 illegal immigrant women work as domestics in the current U.S. market (Stalker 1994, 149). Although these women are ultimately statistically invisible, the effects of their labor are more than apparent in the lives of professional families throughout the U.S." (Capek and Kenny, 1995).

11. This method is characterized by Rawls, first, as a procedural interpretation of Kantian moral conceptions (particularly those principles regulative of the kingdom of ends (1971, 256)); then, as *Kantian constructivism* (1980); and, later, as *political constructivism* (1992). These alterations do not affect the argument presented here, however. The method is supposed to be constructivist in that "it does not accept any intuitions as indubitable and does not begin with the assumption that there are first principles in moral theory" (Baynes 1992, 55).

12. These later writings are intended to answer criticisms that the conception of the person is a metaphysical one specific to certain liberal theories and that the principles of justice chosen are not as purely constructivist as Rawls claims. See especially Nagel (1973), Hart (1975), and Sandel (1982). Rawls's (1992) response is to distinguish "political liberalism" from liberalism as a "comprehensive moral doctrine" (also see Rawls 1985). In addition, he clarifies the basis on which parties in the OP adopt the basic liberties and their priority, avoiding both metaphysical conceptions of the person and particular psychological propensities (see Rawls 1982, 1992). The argument in this chapter is, nonetheless, that the individualism at the core of the theory—which Nagel (1973, 228) notes is augmented by the motivational assumption of mutual disinterestedness—does predispose the parties in the OP to ignore the concerns of both dependents and dependency workers.

13. Also see Rawls (1975b, 542ff.).

14. In *Political Liberalism*, Rawls writes, "To model this equality in the OP we say that the parties, as representatives of those who meet the condition, are symmetrically situated. This requirement is fair because in establishing fair terms of social cooperation (in the case of the basic structure) the only relevant feature of persons is their possessing the moral powers . . . and their having the normal capacities to be . . . cooperating member[s] of society over the course of a lifetime" (1992, 79). The OP is regarded as fair because it presumably models this equality. Rawls further writes that "citizens are equal in virtue of possessing, to the requisite minimum degree, the two moral powers and other capacities that enable us to be normal and fully cooperating members of society. All those who meet this condition have the same basic rights, liberties and opportunities and the same protections of the principles of justice" (1992, 79). He then continues, "To model this equality in the OP we say that the parties, as representatives of those who meet this condition, are symmetrically situated" (1992, 79).

15. In the "Dewey Lectures," Rawls writes simply: "[T]he idealization means that everyone has sufficient intellectual powers to play a *normal* part in society, and no one suffers from *unusual* needs that are *especially difficult* to fulfill, for example, *unusual and costly medical requirements*" (1980, 546; emphasis added). Thus the idealization requires the condition not only of adulthood but also of health. Since both children

and the temporarily disabled merely temporarily and contingently fail to meet the requirements for equal moral worth, they are included in the category of equal citizen (see Rawls 1971, 509). The appropriate treatment of those who are permanently disabled seems to be another matter, one that is further explicated in Note 29.

16. In *Political Liberalism* Rawls drops 'self-originating source of claims' (1980, 544) and substitutes 'self-authenticating source of valid claims' (1992, 32). See Section 5.2 for a discussion of the difference between these two phrases.

17. Rawls acknowledges that some will have a more developed sense of justice than others. Equality with respect to a sense of justice demands only that persons have a sense of justice "equally sufficient relative to what is asked of them" (1980, 546), insofar as they are "fully cooperating members of society over a complete life" (1980, 546).

18. See Note 17. Rawls also writes of "the equally sufficient capacity (which I assume to be realized) to understand and to act from *the public conception of social cooperation*" (1980, 546; emphasis added).

19. According to the *New York Times* (November 14, 1989, pp. A1, B12), a 1985 survey found that "about one in five employees over the age of 30 was providing some care to an elderly parent." The same article reported that almost one-third of part-time workers in the United States spent more than twenty hours a week helping older relatives and, of those not employed who had previously held jobs, 27 percent had taken early retirement or resigned to meet their responsibilities.

20. See Goodin (1985) for a very useful discussion of the obligation to protect those who are vulnerable.

21. Rawls is not concerned here with the dependencies at issue in this chapter, at least not insofar as these are the ones to which *women* usually attend. This is evident in his language: "Nevertheless, since it is assumed that a generation cares for its immediate descendants, as *fathers, say, care for their sons*, a just savings principle . . . would be acknowledged" (1971, 288; emphasis added). And on the following page he writes, "Thus imaging themselves to be *fathers*, say, they are to ascertain how much they should set aside for their *sons* by noting what they would believe *themselves* entitled to claim of their *fathers*" (1971, 289; emphasis added). No mothers or daughters appear on these pages. During a discussion in April 1993, Professor Rawls indicated to me that he meant to include both parents—the mother as well as the father—among the representative heads of households. How different would the theory look if fathers *and mothers* had been included among the parties in the OP? That would depend, I think, on whether the dependency concerns for which mothers have traditionally been responsible are included as well.

22. So she admonished her husband. Still, the representation granted the paterfamilias is different from the one necessitated by dependency work, when the heads of households represent those who are capable of speaking for themselves. The dependency worker must represent the needs of those too young, frail, weak, or ill to come before a public forum and speak for themselves.

23. Okin (1989b) makes the additional point that the phrase 'head of household' is gendered masculine. If we want to speak of a woman who heads a household, we say 'female head of household'. The latter phrase invariably denotes a household in which there is no healthy adult male.

24. Contrast the case of dependents to what Rawls calls the "relevant positions" of "equal citizenship and that defined by [an individual's] place in the distribution of income and wealth" (1971, 96).

25. The representatives in the OP are envisioned by Rawls to be of the same generation. One who adopts the standpoint of the OP thus assumes a "present time of entry" into the OP and that the representatives can communicate with other parties in the OP (see Rawls 1971, 136–142) If parties represent generational lines, there is little point in asking what temporal position they occupy relative to one another with respect to the issue of mutual disinterestedness. But if the representatives represent individuals, the question is pertinent. Now, however, the requirement of mutual disinterestedness is questionable. If one representative is representing an individual living today and another is representing the other's ancestor, we cannot say with assurance that the parties are mutually disinterested.

26. It may seem possible to construe an ambiguity in Rawls's notion that each individual in a future generation should have someone who cares about her or him—that is, an ambiguity between (a) each assuming a special responsibility for someone in the next generation, as in the case of a parent to a child, and (b) each acting responsibly to the next generation. Yet Rawls himself seems to see not an ambiguity but a relation between these seeming alternatives. He writes: "Those in the OP know, then, that they are contemporaries, so unless they care for at least their immediate successors, there is no reason for them to agree to undertake any savings whatever" (1971, 292).

27. This acceptance, however, is culturally relative. Even within liberal societies where no moral stigma attaches to remaining childless, the choice is better tolerated in the case of men than of women. (see Meyers 1993). For a different cultural view, see the powerful drama of Frederico Garcia Lorca entitled *Yerma.*

28. One plausible exception is health care, which, arguably, *is* a dependency concern. And Rawls wants an extension of his theory to cover "*normal* health care" (1992, 21; emphasis added). But excluded from this category are the daily care of infants and children—which is not *health* care as such—and the care of persons with long-term medical or disabling conditions—which is generally not included within *normal* health care. (In this connection, see also Note 43.)

29. Rawls writes that "we take the two moral powers as the necessary and sufficient condition for being counted a full and equal member of society in questions of political justice. Those who can take part in social cooperation over a complete life, and who are willing to honor the appropriate fair terms of agreement, are regarded as equal citizens" (1992, 302). This is a very strong claim, and a puzzling one. For why should the contingent fact that some people are born, let us say, "sufficiently" mentally disabled necessitate their exclusion from citizenship? There are some political activities they may not be able to engage in—for example, they may lack the political understanding required to vote—but surely they need to receive the protections of political justice all the same. (I thank Susan Okin for her discussions with me on this point.) The only rationale consistent with the aforementioned theory is that although their condition is no less due to contingent factors, they will never be able to participate in the social cooperative situation as understood by Rawls.

30. The full passage reads as follows: "The main idea is that when a number of persons engage in a mutually advantageous cooperative venture according to rules, and

thus restrict their liberty in ways necessary to yield advantages for all, those who have submitted to the restrictions have a right to a similar acquiescence on the part of those who have benefitted from their submission" (Rawls 1971, 112).

31. See Aronow (1993). One of the doulas "recalls arriving at homes late morning to find mothers who haven't eaten or dressed. 'They are so concerned that the baby is O.K., they forget to take care of themselves'" (Aronow, 8).

32. I wish to thank Elfie Raymond for helping me search for a term with the resonance necessary to capture the concept articulated here.

33. The importance of this ethic within the African American community is documented in Stacks (1974).

34. It may be unclear whether Rawls's new principle of intergenerational justice and my principle of doulia are truly instances of reciprocity, inasmuch as we are enjoined to give back to a party other than the one from whom we have received, but also inasmuch as both principles enjoin us to give what we would have *wanted* to receive, not necessarily what we have *in fact* received. Nonetheless, the survival of a generation depends on its having received a world not entirely depleted of resources, and the survival of an individual depends on care sufficient to bring her or him to adulthood. So there is a minimal sense in which both are principles of reciprocity, for we are enjoined not only to give but also to give *back*. That is, we would not be in a position to consider what we would want others to provide us if we were not already recipients, even to a minimal degree, of those goods. But it is not reciprocity in the sense of returning *either* to the *same party* or in the *same measure* that which we have received.

35. This is not to say that we have a duty to *have* children because we have been cared for, but I do suggest that, to any children we have, we owe the care we would have wanted to receive (and, at the very least, the care that was necessary to allow us to survive and thrive). I further suggest that the care bestowed on us—and some care must have been bestowed on us if we survived—should in fact be *reciprocated* through care to the next generation.

36. For a concrete public-policy example of the difference effected by this understanding of social cooperation, see Kittay (1995a).

37. Even a Hobbesian state of nature is barely conceivable without some principle of care (however attenuated). *Contra* Hobbes, we mischaracterize social organizations if we conceive of men springing from the earth "like mushrooms," already fully grown. (See Hobbes 1966, 109; also see Benhabib 1987 for a discussion of this passage.)

38. Rawls later (1992, 308–309) gives essentially the same list but accompanies it with explanations of why each element is included. Conspicuously absent from the considerations adduced in these explanations, however, are the elements of "nurture," "interdependence," and "phases of life," all of which are mentioned as general facts about human life on the preceding page (1992, 307). Effectively, these elements are still omitted in the hard-core center of Rawls's theory.

39. See Nagel (1973, 228) for the criticism that the ignorance concerning one's own conception of the good does not necessarily result in an index of primary goods that is equally fair to all parties, "because the primary goods are not equally valuable in pursuit of all conceptions of the good." One may claim that my argument is already

implicit in Nagel's if one supposes that dependency concerns are important to some conceptions of the good—more important, perhaps, than many of the other goods currently in Rawls's index. But the criticism that I put forward differs from Nagel's. I am arguing that, regardless of one's conception of one's own good, the dependency concerns would belong on a list of primary goods. For an excellent discussion of the controversy surrounding the claim that such an index is the best way to make inter-personal comparative assessments of well-being, see Daniels (1990).

40. See Arrow (1973) and especially Sen (1987, 1989, 1990) for arguments that the variations in capabilities between persons may be so significant that one index cannot be adequate to meet the needs of all citizens. Also see Rawls (1992, 182 ff.) for his an-swer to this objection.

41. Meyers (1993, 1994) speaks of the necessity of empathetic thought as a feature of a moral person. What I am considering is precisely such a moral capacity.

42. As I remarked above, a number of writers have urged the need for "more than justice." See especially Baier (1987), Held (1993), Tronto (1993), and Ruddick (1995).

43. Norman Daniels argues that the Rawlsian primary good of opportunity can be extended to cover health-care needs. First the health-care needs of "normally active and fully functioning" persons are calculated at the legislative stage; then "special needs" can be considered. Health care demands "those things we need in order to maintain, restore, or provide functional equivalents (where possible) to normal species function" (1990, 280). Daniels not only emphasizes the relevance of normal functioning to equality of opportunity but also proposes the concept of "normal op-portunity range." Appropriate health care, as determined partially by culture and partially by individual talents and skills, can allow a person to "enjoy that portion of the range to which his full array of talents and skills would give him access, assuming that these too are not impaired by special social disadvantages (e.g., racism and sex-ism)" (1990, 281). The handicap with respect to normal functioning refers to one of Rawls's two moral powers, the power to form and revise our own vision of the good. Rawls takes up this suggestion: "The aim is to restore people by health care so that once again they are fully cooperating members of society" (1992, 184ff.). However, though health care is an integral part of dependency care, Daniels's solution will not be adequate for three reasons. First, "normal opportunity range" is ill-defined for many sorts of disabilities and illnesses—for example, Down's syndrome and, espe-cially, severe mental retardation. Second, providing the "functional equivalents" to "normal species functioning," even when doing so falls far short of a complete restoration, can require resources extensive enough that an explicit commitment in the founding principles themselves may be needed for its realization. And, third, we need to consider whether a social commitment to restore, when possible, the depen-dent to full functioning will also compensate dependency workers without exploiting them. This final point is not Daniels's concern, but it is integral to any adequate reck-oning of justice that includes dependency. Since no dependent can be restored to any degree of functioning without a significant infusion of caring labor, we have to ask about the cost to the dependency worker and the level of compensation. In this con-nection, see Kittay (forthcoming).

44. I emphasize that (c) calls for the *capacity* to respond, not for the response itself. We must understand such a capacity (along with a sense of fairness) as fundamental to moral persons, if we want basic institutions to incorporate principles ensuring

support for relations in which dependents are cared for without sacrificing the interests of caretakers. *Response* to the needs of another is itself a normal moral behavior, but one that may not always be required for justice.

45. As Rawls (1982) stresses, we assess needs in many different contexts and for many different reasons, but the index of primary goods includes only those needs relevant to justice.

46. In criticizing Rawls's use of primary goods, Sen (1990) argues that guarantees of primary goods do not serve justice for those so handicapped that they cannot make use of the goods. Sen's important argument is orthogonal to my own. The demands of care are primary goods that reflect a relation between persons and the resources for their well-being. (See also Note 59.)

47. In the "Dewey Lectures" Rawls also writes: "[S]laves are human beings who are not counted as self-originating sources of claims at all; any such claims originate with their owners or in the rights of a certain class in society" (1980, 544). And in an analogous passage in *Political Liberalism* he writes: "[S]laves are human beings who are not counted as sources of claims, not even claims based on social duties or obligations. . . . Laws that prohibit the maltreatment of slaves are not based on claims made by slaves, but on claims originating from slaveholders, or from the general interests of society (which do not include the interests of slaves). Slaves are, so to speak, socially dead: they are not recognized as persons at all." (1992, 33).

48. One might reply, as did a reviewer, that the valid claim is the *child's*. The mother may have a valid claim to her own education, but the claim to her child's education should not be expressed as *her* claim. To this I say that the child's is *one* relevant valid claim, and usually, at least when the child is very young, not a self-originating one. The child's claim originates with an adult responsible for the child's well-being. In fact, that claim lacks efficacy as long as the child's status as a minor excludes her from political participation. The claim not only originates with, but must also be pressed by, an adult whose voice can be heard in the relevant arena.

49. The communitarian critique expounded by Sandel (1982) raises some similar points about a self-definition that includes centrally the well-being of others. But whereas Sandel's account locates the difficulty in Rawls's prioritization of the self over its ends (1982, 19), I locate it in a conception of self so individuated that dependency concerns are not normally comprehended as intrinsic to it.

50. Perhaps we should interdict dependency work if it demands a psychology in which the dependency worker's self-worth is more a function of another's accomplishments and welfare than of her own. Some jobs do seem inherently oppressive— say, coal-mining. One may argue that no wage can compensate for the diminution in well-being that a coal-miner must suffer, and that justice demands abolishing coal-mining. But dependency work has another character, and justice could never demand that we abolish it. A tension between maintaining that dependency work be more highly valued and that dependency work is too oppressive and ought not to be foisted on anyone is not inevitable. If dependency work appears oppressive it is because the norm of freedom is shaped without attention to the role of dependency in our lives. If it is oppressive, it is so within a social setting that fails to foster the well-being of dependency workers and their charges.

51. Chodorow (1978) and Gilligan (1982) are only two of the most prominent thinkers who argue that for many women the self is experienced as a relational self

and that such a relational self is importantly tied to women's functions as caretakers. In this chapter, I have relied on the persuasiveness of these and other feminist discussions of the self-conception of many women as relational.

52. See Note 50.

53. Rousseau's writings not only embody this image, linking it to an Enlightenment ideal of freedom for male citizens, but have also exerted much influence on women's actual behavior. See Rousseau (1762), Wollstonecraft (1792), Badinger (1980), and Held (1993, esp. ch. 6).

54. Yet even in the "Dewey Lectures," Rawls writes, "These remarks . . . [are] to indicate the conception of the person connected with . . . the principles of justice that apply to its basic institutions. By contrast, citizens in their personal affairs, or within the internal life of associations, may . . . have attachments and loves that they believe they would not, or could not, stand apart from" (1980, 545).

55. This way of putting the criticism is taken nearly verbatim from some very interesting and useful comments provided by John Baker.

56. Consider the horror that yielded the *New York Times* story about the physically and mentally handicapped children who were abandoned in a besieged Bosnian hospital. The reporter, John Burns, wrote about Edin, one of the children who died: "Unlike 200,000 others whom the Bosnian Government estimates to have died in the war, Edin was not blown apart by heavy artillery, cut down by snipers, tortured or burned alive. He was simply left to fend for himself, an infant in a cot who was so severely handicapped that he had spent most of his life at the hospital" (July 20, 1993, p. 1). The sentiment expressed is one of moral horror at the abandonment such helpless individuals. "It's monstrous," said Brigadier General Vere Hayes, chief of staff for the United Nations protection force in Bosnia. There is, at least *prima facie,* a special obligation not to abandon such helpless persons—regardless of the cost to the staff.

57. See, for example, Beauvoir (1952), Chodorow (1978), Dinnerstein (1977), Gilligan (1982), and Bartky (1990).

58. In this connection, see the essays in Trebilcot (1987).

59. The relation between dependency worker and dependent seems to hover between servitude and paternalism. On the one hand, the dependency worker's self-respect is partially a function of how well she meets the needs of another; on the other, she has the awesome power to respond to and interpret the needs of a helpless other. In short, she has too little power with respect to those who stand outside the dependency relation and potentially too much power with respect to her charge. In arguing against the powerlessness of the dependency worker vis-à-vis the world outside the dependency relation, we must be sensitive as well to the dependent's vulnerability to her caretaker's power within this relation. But though paternalism in dependency relations is always a danger, it is not one augmented by any of the proposals made here. On the contrary, the dependency worker who has her interests taken care of in an appropriate and just manner will be less, not more, likely to live her life through her charge, and less, not more, likely to find other ways to discharge ambition and power than through paternalistic behavior. But a system that pays adequate attention to the dependency relation will be one seeking not only to empower the dependency worker with respect to her own interests but also, whenever possible, to decrease the dependency of the dependent as well. When dependency is relegated to the status of an afterthought, neither caretaker nor charge is well served.

60. Sen argues that because people have very different needs, an index of primary goods is not a sufficiently sensitive measure of interpersonal comparison of well-being. Primary goods are the "embodiment of advantage," whereas advantage itself ought to be understood as "a *relationship between persons and goods*" (Sen 1987, 158; original emphasis). Rawls replies that he assumes that citizens do have, "at least to the essential minimum degree, the moral, intellectual, and physical capacities that enable them to be fully cooperating members of society over a complete life" (1992, 183). "The aim," he continues, "is to restore people by health care so that once again they are fully cooperating members of society" (1992, 184). Variations in physical capacities due to disability or disease can be dealt with at the legislative stage.

61. I thank Annette Baier for calling this alternative interpretation to my attention. The reading consistent with the weaker claim gains support, first, in Rawls (1971, part 3, especially section 77), where he is careful to insist that the mere potentiality to have the features of a moral person is sufficient to bring into play the claims of justice; second, in Rawls (1982, 15); and, third, in Rawls (1992, 301), where he identifies the points of entry and exit into society as birth and death.

62. See, for example, the moral psychology that Rawls outlines in section 7 of *Political Liberalism* (1992), especially the enumerations on page 86. If these included dependency concerns and relational capacities, then perhaps there would be motivation sufficient for all parties to consider that they may be taking on responsibilities for dependents.

63. See Schwarzenbach (1986) regarding the notion that parents are "stewards" to their children.

64. I use the term in a manner similar to that in Sen (1992) and Nussbaum (1988a, 1988b).

65. Recently, the U.S. Congress seriously entertained the notion of orphanages in which to place children whose parents were deprived of the public assistance they depended upon to care for their children. This policy recommendation epitomizes a disregard for the value and integrity of the relation of dependency worker and dependent. The recommendation was dropped because it was reckoned to be too costly, not because its severing of the bonds of the dependency relation was considered immoral or unjust.

66. The difference principle is the distributive principle applicable to certain goods on the list of primary goods (especially income and wealth) and not others (e.g., the basic liberties). To determine if it would be applicable to the added primary good(s) concerning care, we would have to consider whether and how the Rawlsian project could coherently be reworked to include dependency concerns. This is too large a project for the present chapter, which aims to be a critique rather than a reconstruction. Suffice to say that I do not mean to suggest that a difference principle that applies to distributive problems concerning dependency care and dependency work is, in principle, not possible.

67. This chapter is the result of an effort in which many have participated. I would like to thank Annette Baier, Susan Brison, Ellen Feder, Susan Okin, William Kymlicka, and Michael Simon for their helpful comments on the initial shorter version of the paper. And I would especially like to thank the many friends and colleagues who have read and supplied extensive comments on later drafts of the present long version: Jonathan Adler, John Baker, Kenneth Baynes, Robert Goodin, Alistair

MacLeod, Diana Tietjens Meyers, Elfie Raymond, George Sher, and Anthony Weston, as well as a number of anonymous reviewers. I have benefited from these comments, even if the current version does not reflect all the sage advice I received. A special thanks is reserved for Leigh Cauman, Neil Tennant, and Jeffrey Kittay for the painstaking care they took in both philosophical content and stylistic matters. I also wish to thank Barbara Andrew, Barbara LeClere, and Eric Steinhart, my research assistants. This chapter emerges in part out of research made possible by a Founders Fellow grant from the American Association of University Women (AAUW).

References

Aronow, Ina. 1993. Doulas step in when mothers need a hand. *New York Times (Westchester Weekly*, Sunday), August 1, 1993, pp. 1, 8.

Arrow, Kenneth J. 1973. Some ordinalist utilitarian notes on Rawls's *Theory of justice. Journal of Philosophy* 70: 245–263.

Badinger, Elisabeth. 1980. *Mother love: Myth and reality.* New York: MacMillan.

Baier, Annette. 1985. Caring about caring: A reply to Frankfurt. In *Postures of the mind: Essays on mind and morals* (pp. 93–108), ed. Annette Baier. Minneapolis: University of Minnesota Press.

_____. 1986. Trust and antitrust. *Ethics* 96: 231–260.

_____. 1987. The need for more than justice. In *Science, morality and feminist theory* (pp. 41–56), ed. Marsha Hanen and Kai Nielsen. Minneapolis: University of Minnesota Press.

_____. 1994. *Moral prejudices: Essays on ethics.* Cambridge, Mass.: Harvard University Press.

Bartky, Sandra. 1990. *Femininity and oppression.* New York: Routledge.

Baynes, Kenneth. 1992. *The normative grounds of social criticism: Kant, Rawls, and Habermas.* Albany: State University of New York Press.

Beauvoir, Simone de. 1952. *The second sex,* trans. H. M. Parsley. New York: Alfred Knopf.

Benhabib, Seyla. 1987. The generalized and the concrete other. In *Women and moral theory* (pp. 154–177), ed. Eva F. Kittay and Diana T. Meyers. Totowa, N.J.: Rowman and Littlefield.

Capek, Mary Ellen, and Lorraine Delia Kenny. 1995. *Issues Quarterly,* Vol. 1, No. 3 (a publication of the National Council for Research on Women, New York).

Chodorow, Nancy. 1978. *The reproduction of mothering: Psychoanalysis and the sociology of gender.* Berkeley: University of California Press.

Daniels, Norman. 1988. *Am I my parents' keeper? An essay on justice between the younger and the older.* New York: Oxford University Press.

_____. 1990. Equality of what: Welfare, resources, or capabilities? *Philosophy and Phenomenological Research* 50 (suppl. vol.): 273–296.

Dinnerstein, Dorothy. 1977. *The mermaid and the minotaur: Sexual arrangements and human malaise.* New York: Harper and Row.

English, Jane. 1977. Justice between generations. *Philosophical Studies* 31(2): 91–104.

Fineman, Martha Albertson. 1991. *The illusion of equality.* Chicago: University of Chicago Press.

_____. 1995. *The neutered mother, the sexual family and other twentieth century tragedies*. New York: Routledge.

Gilligan, Carol. 1982. *In a different voice*. Cambridge, Mass: Harvard University Press.

Goodin, Robert. 1985. *Protecting the vulnerable*. Chicago: University of Chicago Press.

Hart, H.L.A. 1975. Rawls on liberty and its priority. In *Reading Rawls: Critical studies of* A Theory of Justice (pp. 230–252), ed. Norman Daniels. New York: Basic Books.

Held, Virginia. 1978. Men, women, and equal liberty. In *Equality and Social Policy* (pp. 66–81), ed. Walter Feinberg. Urbana: University of Illinois Press.

_____. 1987a. Feminism and moral theory. In *Women and moral theory* (pp. 111–128), ed. Eva F. Kittay and Diana T. Meyers. Totowa, N.J.: Rowman and Littlefield.

_____. 1987b. Non-contractual society: A feminist view. *Canadian Journal of Philosophy* 13: 111–137.

_____. 1993. *Feminist morality: Transforming culture, society, and politics*. Chicago: University of Chicago Press.

Hobbes, Thomas. 1966. Philosophical rudiments concerning government and society. In *The English works of Thomas Hobbes*, Vol. 2, ed. Sir W. Molesworth. Darmstadt.

hooks, bell. 1987. Feminism: A movement to end sexist oppression. In *Equality and Feminism* (pp. 62–76), ed. Anne Phillips. New York: New York University Press.

Kaplan, Temma. 1982. Female consciousness and collective action. *Signs* 7(3): 545–566.

_____. 1992. *Red city blue period: Social movements in Picasso's Barcelona*. Berkeley: University of California Press.

Kittay, Eva Feder. 1991. Dependency, vulnerability and equality. Paper delivered at the Department of Philosophy Colloquium, SUNY/Purchase, November.

_____. 1994. A Review of John Rawls's *Political Liberalism. APA Newsletter of Feminism and Philosophy* (Fall).

_____. 1995a. Taking dependency seriously: The Family and Medical Leave Act considered in light of the social organization of dependency work and gender equality. *Hypatia* 10(1, Winter): 8–29.

_____. 1995b. Dependency work, political discourse and a new basis for a coalition amongst women. Paper delivered at the Women, Children, and Poverty: Feminism and Legal Theory Workshop, Columbia Law School and Barnard College Institute for Research on Women, June.

_____. forthcoming. *Some mother's child: Equality, dependency and women*. New York: Routledge.

Kittay, Eva F., and Diana T. Meyers, eds. 1987. *Women and moral theory*, ed. Eva F. Kittay and Diana T. Meyers. Totowa, N.J.: Rowman and Littlefield.

Meyers, Diana T. 1993. Moral reflection: Beyond impartial reason. *Hypatia* 8: 21–47.

_____. 1994. *Subjection and subjectivity*. New York: Routledge.

Minow, Martha. 1990. *Making all the difference*. Cambridge, Mass: Harvard University Press.

Nagel, Thomas. 1973. Rawls on justice. *Philosophical Review* 82: 220–234.

Nussbaum, Martha. 1988a. Nature, function, capability: Aristotle on political distribution. *Oxford Studies in Ancient Philosophy* 1 (suppl. vol.): 145–184.

_____. 1988b. Non-relative virtues: An Aristotelian approach. *Midwest Studies in Philosophy* 13: 32–53.

Okin, Susan. 1979. *Women in western political philosophy*. Princeton: Princeton University Press.

_____. 1989a. Humanist liberalism. In *Liberalism and the moral life*, ed. Nancy Rosenbaum. Cambridge: Harvard University Press.

_____. 1989b. *Justice, gender and the family*. New York: Basic Books.

Pateman, Carole. 1989. *The sexual contract*. Stanford: Stanford University Press.

Phillips, Anne, ed. 1987. *Feminism and equality*. New York: New York University Press.

Rawls, John. 1971. *A theory of justice*. Cambridge, Mass.: Harvard University Press.

_____. 1975a. A Kantian concept of equality. *Cambridge Review* (February).

_____. 1975b. Fairness to goodness. *Philosophical Review* 84.

_____. 1982. Social unity and primary choice. In *Utilitarianism and beyond*, ed. Amartya Sen and Bernard Williams. New York: Cambridge University Press.

_____. 1980. Kantian constructivism in moral theory: The Dewey lectures 1980. *Journal of Philosophy* 77(9): 515–572.

_____. 1985. Justice as fairness. *Philosophy and Public Affairs* 14: 227–251.

_____. 1992. *Political liberalism*. New York: Columbia University Press.

Rich, Adrienne. 1978. Compulsory heterosexuality and lesbian existence. *Signs* 5(4): 632–660.

Rousseau, Jean-Jacques. 1762. *Emile, or On education*, trans. Allan Bloom. New York: Basic Books. (Reprinted in 1979.)

Ruddick, Sara. 1995. Injustice in families: Assault and domination. In *Justice and care: Essential readings in feminist ethics*, ed. Virginia Held. Boulder, Colo.: Westview Press.

Sandel, Michael J. 1982. *Liberalism and the limits of justice*. Cambridge: Cambridge University Press.

Schwarzenbach, Sybil. 1986. Rawls and ownership: The forgotten category of reproductive labor. In *Science, morality and feminist theory*, ed. Marsha Hanen and Kai Nielsen. Minneapolis: University of Minnesota Press.

Sen, Amartya. 1987. Equality of what? The Tanner lecture on human values. (Delivered in 1979.) In *Liberty, equality and law: Selected Tanner lectures* (pp. 137–162), ed. Sterling M. McMurrin, Cambridge: Cambridge University Press.

_____. 1989. Gender and cooperative conflict. In *Persistent inequalities* (pp. 123–149), ed. Irene Trinker. New York: New York: Oxford University Press.

_____. 1990. Justice: Means v. freedom. *Philosophy and Public Affairs* 19(2): 111–121.

_____. 1992. *Inequality reexamined*. Cambridge, Mass: Harvard University Press.

Stacks, Carol B. 1974. *All our kin: Strategies for survival in a black community*. New York: Harper and Row.

Stalker, Peter. 1994. *The work of strangers: A survey of international labor migration*. Geneva, Switzerland: International Labor Office.

Trebilcot, Joyce, ed. 1987. *Mothering: New essays in feminist theory*. Totowa, N.J.: Rowman and Littlefield.

Tronto, Joan. 1993. *Moral boundaries: A political argument for an ethic of care*. New York: Routledge.

Williams, Patricia. 1991. On being the object of property. In *At the boundaries of the law*, ed. Martha Albertson Fineman and Nancy Thomadson. New York: Routledge.

Wollstonecraft, Mary. 1792, 1988. *A vindication of the rights of woman* (2nd ed.), trans. and ed. Carol Poston. New York: W. W. Norton.

About the Book and Editor

How is women's conception of self affected by the caregiving responsibilities traditionally assigned to them and by the personal vulnerabilities imposed on them? If institutions of male dominance profoundly influence women's lives and minds, how can women form judgments about their own best interests and overcome oppression? Can feminist politics survive in the face of the diversity of women's experience, which is shaped by race, class, ethnicity, and sexual orientation, as well as by gender? Exploring such questions, leading feminist thinkers have reinvigorated work on the concept of self and personal identity, as demonstrated by the discussions in this insightful volume.

The concerns that animate feminist scholarship have prompted feminist philosophers to sideline the theme of individualism and to focus on the theme of intersubjectivity. In conceptualizing the self, the contributors to this volume highlight emotional bonds among people, the stories people tell one another, and the systems of categories and behavioral norms that unite and divide groups of people. Topics addressed include sexual violence and the self, the social self and autonomy, the narrative self and integrity, self-ownership and the body, forgetting yourself and your race, group membership and personal identity, grief and gender, sympathy and women's diversity, emotion and emancipatory epistemology, and dependency and justice. This volume will be important reading for students of feminist theory, ethics, and social and political philosophy.

Diana Tietjens Meyers is professor of philosophy at the University of Connecticut, Storrs. She is the author of *Subjection and Subjectivity: Psychoanalytic Feminism and Moral Philosophy; Inalienable Rights: A Defense;* and *Self, Society, and Personal Choice.* She is the editor of *Feminist Ethics and Social Theory: A Sourcebook* and co-editor of numerous books, including *Women and Moral Theory.*

About the Contributors

Anita L. Allen is associate dean for research and a professor at Georgetown University Law Center. She earned her law degree from Harvard University and her Ph.D. in philosophy from the University of Michigan. She has published many scholarly articles in academic journals, including several relating to women's reproductive rights, the right to privacy, law in literature, and race policy. She is the author of *Uneasy Access: Privacy for Women in a Free Society* and co-author of a casebook, *Privacy: Cases and Materials*.

Sandra Lee Bartky is a professor of philosophy and women's studies at the University of Illinois, Chicago. She teaches feminist theory, phenomenology, post-structuralism, and critical theory. She is the author of *Femininity and Domination: Essays in the Phenomenology of Oppression*, which deals with such topics as female embodiment, beauty norms, sexual objectification, internalized oppression, and the exploitation of women's emotional labor.

Susan J. Brison is an assistant professor of philosophy and women's studies at Dartmouth College. She co-edited *Contemporary Perspectives on Constitutional Interpretation* and has published articles in the areas of social and political philosophy and philosophy of law. She is currently working on two books, one on speech, harm, and conflicts of rights and the other on the aftermath of sexual violence.

Jennifer Church is an associate professor of philosophy at Vassar College, where she is active in the Women's Studies Program. She has published articles on the nature of consciousness, emotion, irrationality, and psychoanalysis. A forthcoming book is tentatively entitled *The Difference That Consciousness Makes*.

Marilyn Friedman is an associate professor of philosophy at Washington University in St. Louis. She has published numerous articles in the areas of ethics, social philosophy, and feminist theory. Her books are entitled *What Are Friends For? Feminist Perspectives on Personal Relationships and Moral Theory; Political Correctness: For and Against* (co-authored); *Feminism and Community* (co-edited); and *Mind and Morals: Essays on Ethics and Cognitive Science* (co-edited).

Eva Feder Kittay is a professor of philosophy at SUNY, Stony Brook. She has published numerous articles in philosophy of language and feminist philosophy; she is the author of *Metaphor: Its Cognitive Force and Linguistic Structure;* and she is the co-editor of *Frames, Fields, and Contrasts: New Essays on Lexical and Semantic Structure* and *Women and Moral Theory*. Currently, she is writing a book on equality and dependency, entitled *Some Mother's Child: Equality, Dependency, and Women*.

Naomi Scheman is a professor of philosophy and women's studies at the University of Minnesota. Her collected papers in feminist epistemology were published in *Engenderings: Constructions of Knowledge, Authority, and Privilege*. She is editing a volume on Wittgenstein in the *Rereading the Canon* series, and she is writing a book with the working title *Shifting Ground: Closets, Margins, Diasporas, and the Reading of Wittgenstein.*

Elizabeth V. Spelman is a professor of philosophy at Smith College. She is the author of *Inessential Woman: Problems of Exclusion in Feminist Thought,* and she is at work on *Fruits of Sorrow: Use and Abuse of Suffering.*

Margaret Urban Walker is an associate professor of philosophy at Fordham University. She has published articles on moral agency, judgment, responsibility, and feminist critique of ethics. Her book *Moral Understandings* will be published in 1997.

Index

Breinigsville, PA USA
18 October 2009
226007BV00001B/94/A